To John Burland

With best wishes

Alcon Copisarow

UNPLANNED JOURNEY

FROM MOSS SIDE TO EDEN

MEMOIRS OF
ALCON CHARLES COPISAROW

Published by Jeremy Mills Publishing Limited

113 Lidget Street
Lindley
Huddersfield
West Yorkshire HD3 3JR

www.jeremymillspublishing.co.uk

First published 2014
Text © Alcon Copisarow
Images © Diana Copisarow, unless credited otherwise

ISBN: 978-1-909837-21-8

Contents

Foreword
by The Rt Hon the Lord Woolf

Just before Sir Alcon's ninety-fourth birthday I received a draft of his memoirs to enable me to write this Foreword. Having read them, I am confident that everybody who does so will agree that we are extremely fortunate that Alcon's family persuaded him that now was the time for him to publish. If he had not done so, we would be deprived of a very personal and contemporary insight into many of the events that have influenced the character of this country today. Furthermore, the more time that passes the greater will be the interest in their contents.

For me their attractiveness is due to the fact that they are a remarkable record of Alcon's unique, multifaceted career. They are easy to enjoy because each different facet or phase of Alcon's life is set out in a pithily entitled separate chapter. They end with an appendix which contains the text of a lecture which he gave to the Athenaeum (of which he has been the Chairman and longstanding Trustee) on the 4th October 1999, entitled '175 Years of The Athenaeum'. The lecture demonstrates his great powers of description, charm, wit and erudition. They provide a model of what a commemorative lecture should be. If no other record remained of his career, the preservation of this lecture would have justified this publication. But as it is, we receive so much more from the account it contains of Alcon's life.

A life that stretches in these memoirs from his first day at a school in Moss Side in 1925 to his becoming the very energetic first Chairman of the Trustees of the hugely successful and innovative Eden Project, which in 2000 was part of the Millennium Celebrations. This was a remarkable appointment for a person of Alcon's then already advanced age. It was testimony to the high reputation he had earned and confirmation that the passage of time had not diminished his abilities.

The years that intervened were for this country a period of extraordinarily eventful challenges and political and social change. In the case of many of the challenges and the changes that took place Alcon played a significant role. In each activity in which he was involved, Alcon became totally immersed both in the activity and in all those who were involved with him. They differed in their significance but not in their collective importance. When they are looked at collectively what is striking, irrespective of whether Alcon was in his twenties or in his nineties, is that he exercised a remarkable influence over those with whom he was involved, regardless of his or their seniority.

Alcon, when acknowledging that he has had a good life, modestly attributes what he has achieved primarily to good fortune. Here I have to differ. My explanation for what was a phenomenal career lies in Alcon's personality, his intelligence, enthusiasm and drive which results in a broad range of people with whom he has been involved concluding that difficult assignments could with confidence be safely entrusted to him. They were obviously also attracted to him. Likewise, this attraction would be matched by his interest in them.

For me and I suspect for many others, a word I would associate with Alcon is 'formidable'. He looks and is distinguished. He is tall with striking, sharply defined features. They are far more exotic than the conventional English good looks and I suspect that, at least in part, they must be attributable to his Jewish multinational Russian/north-eastern European heritage; possibly leavened by a touch of Greek, reflecting his unusual surname. In his company you are rapidly aware of his intelligence and energy accompanied by a wide-ranging enthusiasm.

Despite his advanced years Alcon has a remarkable memory and highly developed powers of recall so that he can bring to life his activities, irrespective as to whether they were as a young sailor or the first non-American senior partner of a large organisation of international importance, such as McKinsey. It seems that in any organisation with which he became involved, he was inevitably going to progress rapidly to a higher echelon. Even in the war as a lieutenant in the Navy, his qualities resulted in his being transferred to our Embassy in Washington to make a contribution to Anglo-American relations. It did not matter whether the organisation was the Civil Service, the Foreign Office, McKinsey, or one of many charitable endeavours. In all these activities, he is a remarkable observer. At the Paris Embassy he deployed his people talents as one distinguished ambassador followed another – Gladwyn Jebb, Pierson Dixon and then Ashley Clarke in Rome and George Labouchère in Brussels – each was carefully observed and his impressions precisely memorised so that they could be reproduced in these memoirs, usually accompanied by an amusing anecdote.

The same was true in British industry where, as in the Navy and the Civil Service, the fact he was both innovative as a scientist and engineer and also highly articulate may have contributed to his influence.

However, the McKinsey man was also totally committed to his family. He was fortunate, that, as he reveals, although he was previously engaged, that engagement came to an end just before it was too late and it was Diana who he married, and it is Diana who continues to share to the full his many enthusiasms and becomes his lifetime companion. She has been the ideal person to do so because she must be one of the few, if not the only person, who is endowed with the energy and drive to match Alcon's.

I end this foreword with the warning that it would be a mistake to regard these memoirs as the last chapter in the story of Alcon's life. In January 2000 he resigned from the Eden Project after a health warning, notwithstanding the great satisfaction it gave him because of 'the difference it made to the economy of Cornwall, in educating the public and in meeting the ideals of the first Earth Summit'. Within a short time, if my memory is correct, he was alerting me and no doubt others that he was free to take on new assignments. The inquiry should be taken seriously since, as the memoirs make clear, he has only recently been engaged by a cruise line to join with Diana on more than one cruise, as a lecturer.

I await developments!

HARRY WOOLF
18th July 2014

Acknowledgements

In beginning to express my thanks to all those who have contributed to the preparation of this book, Lord Woolf comes first. At a time when he was especially busy otherwise, he found time to read the draft and write the Foreword. With his typical generosity and, in this case, an element of flattery which does not escape notice when objective appraisals are to be expected from a Lord Chief Justice, he sets the tone and enhances the value these memoirs may offer. I am deeply indebted to him.

I am grateful to all those who gave their permission to quote from letters and reproduce photographs: to James Harding, Editor of *The Times* until last year, to the late Roald Dahl for the correspondence he provided, for the gift from Trog of his original cartoon, to the Athenaeum Club and to Churchill College.

I thank all those who read relevant chapters and made pertinent suggestions and corrections – notably HRH The Duke of Edinburgh and HRH The Prince of Wales. Of particular help were Sir Martin Gilbert on *Early Life* and *Anglo-American Relations*, Sir Richard Dearlove and Lord Hennessy on *Defence of the Realm*, the late Sir Michael Palliser, Sir Terence Heiser and Sir Ronald Arculus on *Public Service*, Sir David Cannadine on *The McKinsey Experience* and the late Guy Whalley, Trustee of The Eden Project.

Both Professor Felipe Fernandez-Armesto and Christopher Lee read more, made valuable suggestions and encouraged me to complete the book 'before my memory failed me'. Bruce Hunter, the leading literary agent now in retirement, a source of encouragement throughout, read it all with great care and to my surprise gave it his wholehearted approval.

I am indebted to them all. The best things in the book come directly or indirectly from others. The deficiencies, speculations, inferences, exaggerations and mistakes are all mine.

I would like to thank McKinsey's London office for the facilities they provided; Kate Roberton, who spent many months there in transcribing and rearranging my degenerate copperplate handwriting into decipherable text until she left to marry her fiancé George Sale. Special thanks go to Dominic Barton, now global managing director of the firm who, without having read the text, gave the book a plug to former directors of the firm, when addressing them at a conference in Berlin in June.

My publisher's efforts speak for themselves: Jeremy Mills, his production manager Hazel Goodes and her team have gone out of their way to meet my wishes with exemplary efficiency. I would commend their services to any author or institution seeking the utmost co-operation and professionalism.

Every member of my family in addition to their encouragement to 'finish it before it's too late' has played some part in preparing the finished work for publication – from the retrieval and selection of old photographs, to recalling the minutiae of incidents I only dimly remember. Rosalind teemed with ideas and suggestions, which I took on board. Katharine played the key role in critically reviewing and making perceptive comments on the structure and undertaking the painstaking copy-editing of the entire draft. She did this and discussed it with me with endless patience, to make further invaluable improvements. When Jeremy Mills, with his wide experience and eagle eye, had read every word he wrote, '99.9% correct. I suspect that someone with quite advanced editorial training and proofreading skills has already looked at this manuscript in some depth!'

These memoirs would never have been completed without her.

Dedication

At the very outset I wish to mention Diana. She has been my constant and only companion since she was in her teens, for four fifths of her life – my greatest good fortune. My story is really our story, for she has so enhanced my own. I hope she will find the time, apart from continuing to look after me that is, of setting out her own version of our times together. In her own right, her contribution to the welfare of others dwarfs mine. To Diana I dedicate these memoirs.

Alcon Copisarow

October 2014

Preface

It was a summer's evening, the end of a warm day with a soft breeze eddying around Montmartre. It was the kind of evening when Paris is at its best, and dinner promised a few hours' rich enjoyment. The man on my right had spoken little, but I hoped, as the vodka flowed, that he would have a story to tell, for he was the man who murdered Rasputin.

It is almost sixty years since that dinner party took place and I marvel to this day at how a young British scientist could have found himself in such curious company. But when I was young nothing surprised me. Even now, relaxing in the garden, it takes little for images, voices and events from a life of unforeseen variety to flood back.

Yet, writing about them calls for more effort than simply remembering them. Friends suggested that I write my memoirs. A publisher pointed out that it was no longer worth their while, except in the case of the famous, particularly young celebrities. In any event I was busy otherwise, and this was my excuse, at least for delay.

It was members of my family in the main who persuaded me to make a start. Initially, perhaps out of curiosity, then a real interest in earlier generations and their own heritage, and eventually persuasive arguments – that I had first-hand experiences spanning most of the twentieth century, had participated in key events where living witnesses were now few, and had met and discussed them with personalities of world fame. I was still somewhat reluctant.

I showed one or two draft chapters to others with professional interests, and was positively encouraged to expand my memoirs as comprehensively as I could. Three friends in particular, whose work and judgement I admired, were most persuasive – the late Erich Segal (*Love Story*), Christopher Lee (*This Sceptred Isle*) and Roger Scruton, the distinguished philosopher. And so, it is in my tenth decade that I have ventured on writing this, my first book, completing it all with a fountain pen, as I begin my ninety-fifth year.

But where could I begin? I came across an old manuscript by my father about his family and upbringing. It was illuminating. As I read I realised how many more questions I would have liked to put to him. Perhaps our children and grandchildren might one day feel the same.

I have not kept regular diaries, nor the documents to write a comprehensive autobiography, but I have retained correspondence, appointment books and occasional speeches in which I recorded some conversations and noteworthy events and meetings the source material for these memoirs.

My scientific education had taught me to be accurate, analytical and objective in drawing conclusions. I realised that my memoirs inevitably would be subjective. It would be for others, if they wished, to make their own appraisals.

Any lack of objectivity, however, did not put me off. I thought of the historical biographies I had read. I was amazed by the difference in judgements of authors of repute. Marlborough, a hero to many, lived according to Chesterton on the margins of treason, and deemed a traitor by Macaulay. When I dipped into the biographies of Northcliffe, I found he was elevated to sainthood by some, but branded a devil by others – perhaps by the enemies of those who survived him. I hope I might avoid both these extremes in these memoirs.

First-hand experiences and personal views are set against the backdrop of rapidly changing times. As a child throughout the twenties, serving in World War II and the Cold War, and in all that has followed, the changes I experienced were profound. In my approach, I have attempted to reflect my mindset at the time, particularly in regard to the decisions I made and the risks I took. Only in the final chapter have I aimed to address some afterthoughts. Have my views changed? Have my values remained constant? For these, hindsight is necessary.

What emerges as a consequence is my life story – a life of good fortune, time and again finding myself in the right place at the right time, in the right company. To those who made it possible I express my heartfelt gratitude.

THE
EARLY YEARS

CHAPTER I

What's in a Name?

My parents and I arrived at St Margaret's, just five minutes' walk from home in Moss Side. We crossed the asphalt playground where, in spite of the rain, boys were playing conkers and marbles, girls competing with skipping ropes. It was the summer of 1925, my first day at school. I was put into a class of forty children, all five years old. The teacher began entering my name on the school register, but had difficulty with the spelling. 'Perhaps it would be easier if we called you Alcon Cope?' 'No,' I insisted. 'My name is Copisarow.' I thought I was being deprived of something quite special. My father seemed to understand – the loss of identity, merely for convenience. He smiled.

Years later I was to speak of this to Lord Hailsham, after he had sent me a copy of his autobiography, *The Door Wherein I Went*. I did ask my father, of course, where our name came from. There was no written record. A legend grew up, that our ancestors had travelled over a thousand years earlier from Greece to live in Khazaria. They were attracted as immigrants by the Khazar king himself who had converted to Judaism around 700 AD It was suggested that the name Copisarow derived from the Greek. More probably it was a composite place name of where the family lived. After the territorial partition of 1772 many surnames were constructed with Russian endings. Kopys was a town on the River Dnieper, north of Mohilev, where we had a family link.

Today, before me, I have a Russian manuscript, over a hundred years old. It is heavily sealed with wax and signed personally by Inspector Sokolovsky, Archpriest Boujunoff and each of the nine examiners. It is my father's school leaving certificate.

Presented to Maurice Copisarow, of the Jewish faith, son of a commoner of the town of Biruch in the government of Voronez; born 4th August 1889 in the same town; passed his four years of elementary education in the municipal school of Novo-Oskol, government of Kursk; passed the final examination, from 28th April to 4th June 1908, in the gymnasium grammar school of Orenburg, in all subjects taken:

Russian (language, literature and Slavonic church); Philosophy, Logic and Psychology; Law and Jurisprudence; History; Latin; German; Mathematics; Physics; Mathematical Geography; Geography and Natural Sciences.

By virtue of which he is awarded this Certificate, granting him the rights contained in paragraphs 130–132 of the Emperor's Act of 30th July 1871. Orenburg 6th June 1908.

It was only after he died in 1959 that I realised how little I knew of his family and life in Russia, until the age of nineteen. My father gave me the name Alcon, after his father Elkanah and it has been given to our grandson, in turn. I never knew my paternal grandfather and was keen to learn all I could about him from my father. He was conscripted into the army of Tsar Alexander II. As a Jew he was ineligible to hold a commission, but he completed his long military service as a Warrant Officer and was thereby permitted to reside outside the Pale of Settlement – the home of almost all the five million Russian Jews from the 1860s to the 1880s. The privilege was granted to just a few professionals and merchants of the first guild, who paid the highest taxes. Before the army, his education had been almost wholly a study of the Talmud. His family, who were Cohens, recited their prayers at home twice a day. As a soldier he struggled valiantly in an attempt to keep this up. On his release, however, he saw how much had changed in just two decades for the few Jewish ex-servicemen he had known. They continued to recite prayers as they had in childhood, but their Jewish spirit had gone. They barked like drill-sergeants, their religious inheritance all but disappeared, and were no longer able to teach their children.

My grandfather strove hard in Biruch's small community to recapture the spirit and build on his own study of the Talmud. He married Deborah Rachel Ben Schneur Zalman. My grandmother was from the family of Schneur Zalman of Lyady, who died in 1813, and whose great-grandson Solomon Zalman lived until 1900. Schneur was founder of the Chabad Chasidim. Standing for knowledge, wisdom, and understanding, this movement, which my family lost touch with, continues worldwide to this day. It stresses the intellectual rather than the spiritual approach to the study of the Torah. After 1866 the family settled in the town of Kopys where my grandparents met. They had three children – my aunt Sonya, my uncle Joseph and eleven years later, Maurice, my father. My grandfather took on all the duties of a communal rabbi, acting as Minister, teacher and judge of dietary, hygiene and sex laws. Home served as synagogue, school and community centre. One of his saddest duties was to console the parents of a few boys aged twelve to fifteen who had been kidnapped by gangs and forced into the army to serve for up to twenty-five years.

Though Biruch was spared many of the deprivations of the Pale of Settlement the younger members of the small Jewish community were still ostracised and insulted. The pogroms took place some distance away, but news of them brought fear. Unloved by the Russian orthodox clergy, educationally hampered and dispirited, they faced the long-term prospect of exclusion from public employment. Many, not content to be labourers or petty traders, sought ways of developing what talents they had in the hope of gaining their freedom. For those without a higher education it was particularly difficult. Many of the young left, breaking close family bonds and leaving parents distraught.

Sometimes, in my childhood years in the twenties, my father would recount stories to my sister and me about his own childhood in Biruch, a sleepy town on the slope of a hill. He told us how, just below it, on the vast black soil region, the river Teekhoia Sosna threaded its way down to the Don. Life was primitive in Biruch – no roads, water pipes, sewers or fuel other than wood. In the rainy season he was called out to rescue horse-drawn carriages whose wheels had sunk into the mud. Those on foot sometimes lost their boots and were found clinging to fences and trees. His face would light up when he described how in summer the place was transformed. Orchards of cherries, plums, apples and pears surrounded the cottages, and beyond them woods of pine, lime, poplar and the mighty oaks. In winter, snow-clad treetops dazzled in the sun. The bells of the lively troikas jingled and when the blizzards came all landmarks were obliterated – and across the desolate scene, on the prowl, were howling packs of hungry wolves. He painted a vivid picture.

He told us about the oaks that were planted long before the reign of Peter the Great. They were felled to build naval vessels, some to sail down the Donetz and Don into the Sea of Azov, others west to the Baltic. There was a royal carpenter, whose black felt hat, chair, mug and axe were still on display in Valujki nearby. And then there was market day. Going into town was a spectacular sight as the Ukrainian Cossacks came riding in. They mingled in the crowd with the fairer, plainer Muscovites. The southerners were quite different in their dress and dialect from those who came in from the north, but over tankards of the local kaba they chatted noisily together about their work and their crops: rye and wheat in the north, sunflowers and clover in the south. The principal industry was sunflower oil, cattle fodder, fuel and its by-products, made in Alexejevski, south of Voronez.

My grandparents moved the family east to Orenburg, where higher education was more freely available. Even there, however, from all the high schools across the entire Government of Voronez – including Ostrogozhsk, Slaviansk, Kharkov and Voronez – only one boy in 500 admitted to the University of Orenburg could be Jewish. For the rest, my father among them, some tried to find a university place abroad.

After my father died I came across some notes he had typed years earlier, on an antiquated Yost machine, about a few families he had known during his schooldays. The Kotunskis were one of the very few Jewish families with property. They were cigarette manufacturers. Of their three sons Ekusielj gained a distinction in medicine in Kharkov, took a higher doctorate in Vienna where he married an Austrian girl, and returned home to become head of a sanatorium in Saratov. Aaron, his mischievous brother, went off to the Crimea as a sailor, returning ten years later and almost unrecognisable as a fit and bronzed Captain in the Dubrovolnah premier merchant fleet. Michael became an engineer in Zurich and never returned. There were others too: Uralski, a professional boxer and Azeffski, an unscrupulous adventurer. According to my father's notes he went to Switzerland, published an underground revolutionary newspaper, became an agent of the Russian secret police, betrayed many of his comrades and was eventually tracked down and shot. Schwartzman, only a few years older than my father, was one of those who dreamed of a new exodus to Palestine. He went there as a pioneer, draining the swamps in 1909 and laying the foundations of Tel Aviv, only to succumb to malaria.

My father often received letters from his brother Joseph in Orenburg, which we read to him as his eyesight began to fail. They were either in Hebrew or Russian, needing translation too. The names of acquaintances were occasionally disguised in case letters were opened. News of the family was sometimes a light relief, sometimes worrying with reports of ill health and financial hardship. I remember one such letter arrived in which Joseph told his brother that their mother had died. He wrote, 'We bless you for paying for the funeral, a headstone and acacia and lilac we have planted around mother's grave.' My father, who had promised to see her again, broke down and went to bed.

My mother had arrived in England in 1902 without any knowledge of the language. Until then her father Eli Cohen had lived in Gomel, now in Byelorussia, as a small trader in furs and tailoring and only just managed to escape from the pogroms. Like so many others in the Pale of Settlement he aspired to get away to Palestine when Theodore Herzl had been advocating the establishment of a Jewish State. In 1897 a few delegates from Gomel were able to attend the first Zionist Congress in Basle and give him their support. But then disaster struck. In the mob violence of 1902 and 1903 hundreds were killed and injured in Kishinev, homes and synagogues were destroyed elsewhere, and looting and rape were widespread. Some of Eli's neighbours survived by deception, disguising their flats with a cross or other religious icons in their windows. The mob broke into his home whilst he was out and set fire to it. His beautiful wife Sarah nursing their baby was left to die in the fire.

Their village in Gomel was by the River Sozh, a tributary of the Dnieper, which was frozen for five months of the year. But my mother's early memories were of taking the river steamer to Mohilev during the summer months. Her father rescued his children and finally they found their way to England. Arriving in Manchester, he opened a furriers shop in the heart of the well-established Jewish community in Cheetham Hill Road. His daughter Eda, my mother, was then seven years old. After leaving school she trained to become a skilled tailoress and joined a ladies' fashion house where she worked until she married.

For his part, my father could not get into a Russian university. Bribery was rife. In any event there was no money. With ambition, but without opportunity in Russia, and a need to support his parents, he felt he had to go abroad. After much soul-searching he decided to leave his small, close-knit family, the culture of generations, and come to England. England had a reputation for decency, incorruptibility and civilised people. And to Manchester University in particular, because of its international standing in physics, chemistry and philosophy and where fellow Russian Chaim Weizmann was Senior Lecturer in the Chemical Department. No less important, he could join his uncle, Eli Cohen.

To become an undergraduate he had to learn English and also find work to pay his fees. A clothing factory gave him a penny for each cap he pressed. By putting in very long hours, within a year he was able to enrol. The Laski family went out of their way to help him. Nathan Laski was a successful cotton exporter, a Liberal and the most prominent member of the Manchester Jewish community. He and his wife Sarah were generous with their hospitality, welcoming the young to Smedley House, their home. Their three children were my father's contemporaries.

Harold was the controversially famous political theorist; his elder brother Neville was a judge and father of Marghanita, the writer, and Mabel, his sister. On arriving at the University, then Owen's College, it was Sarah who introduced my father to Weizmann. It was a meeting that was to set the direction of his life thereafter.

Weizmann himself had a few years earlier escaped from the pogroms of Russia. Like many others his childhood dream inspired by Ahad Ha'am was of liberation, emancipation and a return to Zion. His heart lay there, but culturally and intellectually he moved more easily through Western Europe. And so he came to Manchester in 1905 to pursue research in organic chemistry.

My father wanted to study philosophy, the subject which interested him most, and went to discuss this with Weizmann, who advised him not to. It was a luxury and he told my father that he had to be practical and make himself useful and self-sufficient as soon as possible. He should read chemistry. And this he proceeded to do, though it was a struggle. In his first year examination he had to discuss a quotation from Lavoisier. He said to the invigilator he could not understand the French, only to be told, 'Surely all foreigners understand foreign languages.'

He quickly discovered how great the university was. He attended Rutherford's physics lectures. Rutherford had just shown in 1908 that solid mater was not solid and atoms were not like billiard balls, as was then believed. When he shot a stream of helium atoms at a sheet of gold foil most of the particles went through the spaces, and electrons were spinning in orbit around it. My father also crept into philosophy classes where Alexander was holding forth on space, time and deity, and heard with amusement that at the very moment Weizmann was speaking of the return of Jewry to the Promised Land, Elliot-Smith a few rooms away was lecturing nostalgically on the Ancient Egypt from which they had escaped. Working at night and studying by day he graduated in 1913.

Weizmann told him that if ever England were to go to war with Germany, they could make a vital contribution with research on the manufacture of munitions. He went on to explain to C.P. Scott, editor of the *Manchester Guardian*, how important this could be and was immediately introduced to Lloyd George. Weizmann told him he would be wrong to assume that a British embargo and blockade would deprive Germany of the all-important Chilean nitrates for explosives. Haber's work in Switzerland synthesising ammonia would now enable Germany to manufacture both fertilisers for food and munitions for war. He told him of a new method of making acetone, which he had developed, and of its potential significance.

It was 1914 and my father was flattered to be the one told of this meeting, but he did not realise he was being recruited to assist Weizmann in the work. In the months that followed, Weizmann proposed an organic synthesis and asked my father to help develop it. He was quite inexperienced, but he thought the method was impracticable. He eventually summoned the courage to say so and to propose an alternative process. I realised what a nerve-racking experience it must have been as he told me how he had arrived early at the Schorlemmer laboratory and spent a long time giving his bench a gleaming polish with a wax turpentine mixture, to pluck up courage before finally taking the plunge. Weizmann had listened carefully, patted him on the shoulder, withdrew his own proposal and told him to carry on. The joint paper with Weizmann was published in 1915 and not only won him the two-year Dalton Research Fellowship, but also resulted in his immediate naturalisation. My father had become a British subject.

As the war developed, many earlier plans had to be scrapped. German pre-eminence or monopoly in synthesising chemicals, drugs and dyes, the introduction of TNT as the standard high explosive and the initiation of trench warfare all made Britain's unpreparedness alarming. As Minister of Munitions, Lloyd George appealed for scientists. An Army Chemical Corps was set up, where my father's two professors Dixon and Lapworth were engaged in analysing coal tar taken from the gas works. Weizmann concentrated on adapting his fermentation process to produce from maize the acetone urgently needed for cordite. My father set to work to synthesise phenol.

Within a few months Weizmann was appointed Director of the Admiralty Chemical Laboratories and left for London. He asked my father to join him. It was a difficult decision, not so much because of his family connections in Manchester, but because Weizmann's head of Department, Professor Lapworth, had just asked my father to take over his own well-equipped Perkin Laboratory and work with him. He chose to remain in Manchester with Lapworth. Little did he know that it was a decision that was to cost him his eyesight.

Now, with a three-year appointment and assisted by a few of the ablest students keen to work with him, he volunteered to take part in the national programme for TNT production. Armed with a Royal Society Certificate signed by Lloyd George, he established a TNT analytical laboratory at Morris's in Gorton. He wanted to ensure that the Woolwich Arsenal specifications were strictly adhered to. The engineer sub-manager there had insisted that washing of the plant with alkalis was safe. My father disagreed and warned them of the dangers. As he had no authority to interfere with plant operations his advice, that working with water was imperative, was over-ruled. It was a fatal mistake. There was an explosion at Silverton, killing 150. More died in further explosions at Ashton and Gretna. The women working there, in the shell-filling factories, and the wives and daughters of those serving at the front, went on strike. Only then was his water-washing process accepted and purification for shell-filling made compulsory. Then, gradually, the shell-fillers returned to work.

By the time my father had left Gorton his appearance had changed remarkably. Picric acid and phosgene had discoloured his flesh – even to the bones of his hands – and his eyesight slowly began to fail. Confirmation of the cause became fairly conclusive soon after, from an unexpected source. In America, a number of young women who had suffered in the same way were all found to have been prescribed slimming drugs containing similarly harmful ingredients.

Until the end of the war, however, he was still highly effective. Holding an Honorary Fellowship of the University, he set to work to find new uses for the enormous quantities of hazardous waste products of the munitions factories. Publication of much of his research was held back for security reasons, but after the armistice he was allowed to take out a number of patents. And at last his financial concerns were over, or so he thought.

Marrying in 1919 in Manchester, my parents had a holiday house at St Anne's-on-Sea, where I was born in June 1920. It was only eighteen months later that my father's failing eyesight deteriorated rapidly. He had been seen by one consultant after another, including Sir Stewart Duke Elder, the King's eye surgeon, and was advised that his sight might be partially saved by special treatment. In November 1921 C.P. Scott of the *Manchester Guardian* wrote to my father saying he had been treated successfully before the war by a Dr Stock in Germany and recommended he saw him. Scott was just leaving for America, but with the help of Israel Sieff he located Stock, now heading the Augenklinik in Tübingen, and made the introduction and arrangements. I went there with my parents for what was intended to be a short visit. But we stayed for my father to undergo eight operations over a period of six months – all unsuccessful. There was, however, one happy event, the birth of my sister Amelia, just as I was beginning to speak my first words which, to my parents' surprise, were German. When I see a photograph of three nurses taken on my second birthday in the Augenklinik, this may have been my very first memory.

Although I did not remember it at the time, my father told me of the sabre fencing between medical students at the university. When they drew blood they shouted, 'Yes, that's what we'll do to England.' Hitler at that very time was launching his ominous campaign of National Socialism. Back in Manchester my father, most concerned about the outlook, wrote to the *Manchester Guardian*. I have just found the copy I made of his letter in my schoolboy handwriting, dated 18th January 1923. He put much of the blame on reparations and on France for a blockade of Germany: 'It is leaving her schools and hospitals without coal. Why cause her unnecessary suffering? Why drive the German people to ruin and despair? It fosters

European militarism and keeps the munitions factories of Petrograd and Moscow very busy – a sure omen for a new world conflagration.'

I remember one incident, when my parents had left a deposit of 20,000 marks in Germany, asking the bank manager to buy some cigars and chocolates for the hospital staff for Christmas. Receiving no word of thanks he asked whether this had been done. The envelope with the reply did not need to be opened. As a result of unprecedented inflation the stamp was overprinted '2,000 million marks.'

Three years later, leaving St Margaret's School one day I accidentally dropped my new cap in the rain. Picking it up I blurted out, 'Meine hutte ist schmutzig.' The teacher was horrified. It was a Church school where the Rector not only took prayers, but also played almost as prominent a part as the headmaster. When my parents explained that I was a Jew, the Rector immediately replied, 'Right! When the school is in Assembly reciting the Lord's Prayer, you go into the corner classroom with the two other Jewish boys and read a piece from the Old Testament, chosen by your parents.' This was four years before my first synagogue classes in Hebrew. I think my parents had sent me to a Church school in the belief that my religious upbringing at home would be more influential than that at school.

At the start of each day the whole school, perhaps 200 boys and girls, came together for a session with Mr Hughes, the headmaster. He had a huge white moustache. We invariably began in unison reciting the multiplication tables up to twelve. Then followed General Knowledge, the world's capitals and current affairs. 'Who is the Prime Minister? Who is the President of the Board of Trade?' And the whole school replied. When I reported this at home, my father taught me the names of every member of the Cabinet. Then once, when the headmaster asked, 'Who is the Secretary of State for Foreign Affairs?' I was the only voice to call out, 'The Marquis Curzon of Kedleston.' The headmaster, surprised to hear a lone voice from the bottom of the school, said softly, 'Lord Curzon.' He kept us in touch with current affairs and proudly announced one day, for reasons best known to himself, that a Mr and Mrs Simon, who lived in Wythenshawe, had given their house and park to Manchester. The news he omitted to inform the school that day was that the Duchess of York had just given birth to a baby girl – our future Queen.

Boys who misbehaved had to stand on a chair throughout the lesson. The girls were well-behaved. Showing disrespect to a teacher was an offence punished with a tawse on the hand. The occasional school bully was sent to the headmaster who took him to the cloakroom. There he was strapped on his behind, came out crying, and with a letter from the headmaster requiring an acknowledgement from the parents. Everyone called Mr Hughes 'Pecker' because of his long nose, but there was consternation when a mother arrived asking for Mr Pecker!

The schoolyard was too small for sports or games. All I could boast was a prize-winning conker, which I carefully steeped in vinegar each night, and a prize for drill in our annual drill-hall presentation to parents. We were taken to the Free Trade Hall where Hamilton Harty was conducting the Hallé Orchestra in a performance of the *Flying Dutchman*. I remember being told off for getting up too soon to put my raincoat on, thinking the performance had finished.

I found something interesting in all the subjects we took, doing well in no small measure thanks to Arthur Mee's *Children's Encyclopaedia*, which we read at home. I must have learned as much from that as I did from school lessons. But there was one regret. Coming near the top of the class each year, I was moved from Standard 2 to 4, and 4 to 6 in three years, so I missed out on the history of the Middle Ages, the 18th century, and more.

My memories of the world beyond home and school during those early years are few. But I particularly remember the sight of Uncle Jack, my mother's brother, on long-delayed demobilisation from the army. He arrived one day from Siam, in puttees, and brought me a box of coloured plasticine.

Near to us over a bridge I remember seeing a never-ending line of tired and dejected marchers. It was the 1926 Miners' Strike. Then there was my visit to hospital with my parents for a tonsil operation. I smelt the chloroform they were about to give me, it was horrid and I pushed it away. My father, on hand, whispered in my ear, 'When they say breathe in and count, take no notice. Breathe out instead and that will fool them.' I gather I only counted up to two.

The outlook was bleak for my father. The worrying prospect of permanent unemployment for a talented and ambitious young scientist with a family made him ill. He had to undergo four operations for gastric and duodenal ulceration, was unable to take food by mouth and for many months my mother was feeding him artificially through a tube in his side. His weight fell from fourteen stone to eight. My mother came to the rescue in becoming the sole breadwinner whilst caring for two small children. With the remaining proceeds from the chemical processes my father had patented, they bought the small house and a shop close to Alexandra Park, in Moss Side, at the edge of what was then an attractive suburb.

I well remember the early days of the Alexandra Fur Stores, the grandiose name we gave 145 Alexandra Road. It faced a tramway and behind us ran rows of smaller houses built back-to-back. My mother had established a furrier's business, having learned about sables, mink, foxes and chinchilla from her father, and furs were highly fashionable at the time. Beneath the shop there was a large cellar into which lorry loads of coal were tipped. Each morning a horse-drawn float would deliver the milk and this went, long before refrigerators, straight into a jug on a slate shelf in the scullery. In the attic my father set up a small laboratory with the most basic apparatus to experiment.

I remember we had an unusual range of visitors. Some were customers for the shop, usually the wives of university professors, and others were research students who called to talk to my father. For a few years we employed a live-in maid called Lavinia, an Irish girl, totally content with her weekly wage of eight shillings. When she left to marry, it was with a present of a wedding dress, made by my mother. Luckily this was just as we found we could no longer afford to keep her. I volunteered eagerly for the jobs of beating the rugs on the clothes-line with a bamboo racquet, helping with the laundry by dunking the blankets with a dolly-peg in a galvanised iron tub, and trying to turn the handle of a heavy wooden mangle. I actually enjoyed these chores – I could see the results and it pleased my parents.

Every day I walked into Alexandra Park with my father and sister, along the half-mile avenue of limes, through the cactus house and around the serpentine lake. There was an island in the middle with a clock tower, but this had been taken to Belle Vue. We fed the ducks and played hide-and-seek among the rhododendrons. Sometimes my father would emerge from behind them carrying an apple and a banana, pretending he had found them both on the same tree. On Sunday afternoons on the bandstand, a brass band would play excerpts from Gilbert & Sullivan, Offenbach and Strauss.

Whilst we were out walking my mother looked after the shop and was kept busy at home, when she wasn't interrupted by a customer. Then one day, just after my fifth birthday, she announced she now had a new responsibility. Having reached the age of thirty she was entitled to vote in a General Election and she was going to do so. Even though her vote was not critical in our Moss Side constituency, then staunchly conservative, led by Sir Joseph Nall, she valued her right to vote.

A happy day for us all was when my mother had sold a sable or other expensive coat. We celebrated with a matinée performance, a pantomime at the Palace Theatre, with Evelyn Laye in *Lilac Time* or seeing Anna Neagle and Marie Burke at the Paramount, and then on to the State Café in Piccadilly for tea. There we were served preserved ginger on large nickel silver plates. When my sister and I were a little older we went to the Midland Hotel for supper. I was intrigued when my mother with a single word could order two dozen different dishes. It was much later I discovered that the magic word was 'hors d'oeuvres'.

My father would talk about his student days before 1914, when there was a Winter Garden and German restaurant in the hotel and they were served Lowenbrau from barrels on ice, together with schnitzels. But all that had vanished overnight thanks to the Kaiser. One evening my father went with some fellow students to the Gaiety Theatre, where Sybil Thorndike was performing in a Bernard Shaw play, and they came back to the hotel with Annie Horniman. There they discussed Shaw, enthusiasm for his plays soon turning to criticism of his Fabian politics. Then Annie Horniman spoke up for him. 'He's kind and generous and is the only dramatist who doesn't leave my bathroom looking like a pigsty!'

The Hallé's Thursday Night Concerts were another fixture so popular that the railways ran a special Hallé train for the more affluent residents of Bowden and Alderley Edge. Even when there was nothing to celebrate at home we were not deprived of entertainment. Armed with a wimberry pie from Fugistalls a few shops away, we went to the local cinema to see Mary Pickford, Charlie Chaplin, Tom Mix and Harold Lloyd in silent films. My father and I on Saturday afternoons in the twenties and thirties would walk a mile or so to Maine Road to watch Manchester City play. The team had a long history, beginning as a Church team in 1880. On one occasion we joined a record crowd of 84,000, beating Stoke City in the sixth round of the FA Cup. On the coldest days, for a penny, we bought a large bag of Dr Strong's cough pastilles, the strongest imaginable. My most memorable day, however, was when I was allowed into the dressing room and emerged triumphantly with the autographs of Eric Brook, Tilson and Toseland. They were in celebrative mood. Much later I was told the reason. Their weekly pay had been increased to five pounds, plus ten shillings for a draw and a pound for a win. (When they won the Premier League Championship this year, as I am reviewing this draft, the team's transfer price was reported to be £345 million.)

I did not follow the fortunes of Manchester United at the time but, thanks to C. P. Scott of the *Manchester Guardian*, I was given one of the best seats to watch cricket at Old Trafford. Later, I discovered that the friendly man in the seat next to me was none other than the legendary cricket and music critic, Neville Cardus.

On Sundays we took a bus for a day's walk to the lower peaks of the Derbyshire countryside. We went armed with a picnic hamper, which we filled at The Titanic – the kosher delicatessen, so named by the owner of the little shop near St Peter's Square who was a survivor of the sinking ship. For many years we spent our annual week's holiday in North Wales, boarding with a Miss Evans near Deganwy in her small house overlooking the Vadre. Our favourite evening walk took us over the Great Orme at Llandudno and into a deckchair for a seaside concert in the Happy Valley. Sometimes we went further afield to the Isle of Man, to enjoy music hall performances in Douglas of Florrie Ford and George Robey.

Our happiest times of all, however, were on Friday nights and Saturday mornings. Far removed from whatever worries the week had brought, all gloom disappeared with the sight of the gleaming white tablecloth and Sabbath lights, and with the prayers which my father recited. These occasions were wonderful. They lifted our spirits throughout dinner and the next day, when we all set off on our mile walk to the synagogue in Wilbraham Road.

When I was just six or seven we celebrated Passover Seder nights with my grandfather Eli Cohen and, since he had remarried, his large family in Cheetham Hill. Sometimes he would take me to his local synagogue, where I remember having to stand for ages with nothing to see and listening to the devout old men babbling away incomprehensively in Hebrew. I was only knee-height among them. The South Manchester Hebrew congregation in Wilbraham Road was the attractive new offshoot of the Great Synagogue in Cheetham. Its Byzantine features were the creation of a twenty-four year-old innovative Russian immigrant, who had anglicised his name to Sunlight. My sister and I attended Hebrew classes there, on Wednesday evenings and Sunday mornings. Our teacher, Gladys Besso, was inspirational and we never missed a class. In 1933 I celebrated my Bar Mitzvah in the orthodox way. Rabbi Louis Weiwow, addressing me, singled out the Fifth Commandment as the most comprehensive. 'If you honour your father and your mother, it will cover all the teachings of the

Bible.' At the party that followed I plucked up the courage to say to him, 'I thought 'all the teachings' were covered by 'don't do to others what is hateful to yourself.'' 'Yes, Rabbi Hillel did say that, but so did Confucius much earlier. The Commandments brought down by Moses were unique.'

I made the traditional speech, expressing thanks most respectfully to my teachers and parents and, of course, for all the presents from the congregation. No wallets, fountain pens or games, just books as far as I remember. Among my favourites were H.G. Wells and Howard Spring's *Fame is the Spur*. I still remember Spring's hero's climb to fame from a back street in the slums of Ancoats, where he met only the vulgar 'pilers up of brass', but never any of the educated Manchester families. And I still have, and read to this day, Wells' *Outline of History* and *The Work, Wealth and Happiness of Mankind* where he forecast, correctly as it turned out, that by 1940 Germany would be at war with Poland and, much more speculatively, that mankind would be forced to co-operate and create a world state by 2059.

Attending my Bar Mitzvah there were two or three refugee families newly arrived from Germany. Hitler had become Chancellor and immediately suspended all legal guarantees of their liberty. They were fortunate to have business interests to bring them to Manchester and decided not to return, leaving their larger families behind. We visited each other in our homes as they told us of the violent young men now in power – Goebbels, Himmler and Hess, all in their thirties, and Heydrich and von Schirach still in their twenties – and how the world was now in great danger. Back in Germany, many in their community said they were unduly alarmist and non-Jewish friends encouraged them to stay: 'You have contributed so much to our nation over two or three centuries; you have been decorated in war, you cannot be in serious danger.'

For the first time I heard the names of Buchenwald and Ravensbrück. Concentration camps were being constructed; Jewish shopkeepers they knew taken out into the street and beaten senseless. Soon after the 1938 Munich agreement with its hopeful message of 'Peace in our time' we had a special service for Kristallnacht. Our friends the Hertz and Feibleman families arrived in tears with the news that all synagogues had been burnt down and all their friends and entire communities rounded up and sent off to what became extermination camps.

I continued with synagogue classes until I was sixteen, when I was set a final essay to write, in the course of a year, on the Thirteen Principles of Faith, finding as many examples as I could to illustrate each in the weekly portions of the Bible. Amelia and I won many of the synagogue book prizes. Her Hebrew was at least as fluent as mine. She went on to be awarded the Chief Rabbi's prize and in due course became an accomplished and widely admired teacher herself.

My high school entrance examinations had come five years earlier. The staff of St Margaret's boasted no graduates, so they could not prepare us for the highly regarded places at Manchester Grammar School and none of us attempted it. I was granted a City Council award of £50 a year for maintenance to attend Manchester Central High School in Whitworth Street. It was an imposing red brick building with a polygonal corner turret. Our school motto, *Et virtutem et musas* was freely translated: 'We strive for manliness and culture'. Later, it became a Grammar School. Its only well-known alumnus was Robert Donat. There our headmaster, Robert Crosthwaite, had been teaching since 1905. His style apparently never changed.

There was nothing remarkable about my school performance. I was slow. On four evenings a week I brought back homework from school, nominally one and a half to two hours' work, but it always took me much longer. Lessons, however, were interesting and when, in 1934, a new young headmaster, E.F. Chaney, arrived he wrote to my parents saying my progress was very good. Oddly, I remember something of his opening speech, his reference to Barchester Towers, when he said he would try to fill the void for the sake of his predecessor. I enjoyed geography most, but did well mainly because of the mnemonics I made up. For the cotton spinning towns surrounding Manchester in clockwise order, all I had to do was remember 'Bill Bailey Riding On A Stag.' BBROAS stood for Bolton, Bury, Rochdale, Oldham, Ashton, Stalybridge.

In spite of this I won only two prizes, one for a small painting of a bowl of acacia which was exhibited – the curriculum did not allow me to continue with my art – the second awarded by the school's Literary, Scientific and Debating Society. That was a result of spending ages on an essay on Whipsnade, to win a book entitled *Heroes of Civilisation*, about the lives of famous explorers, scientists, engineers and doctors I admired. And in sport there was only one memorable performance. I completed the School Mile (under fifteens) when I was eleven: the School Magazine reported, 'Those who took no part in the race would do well to learn from the spartanesque efforts of the youngest competitor who, though almost a lap behind the leader crossed the finishing line to the vociferous cheers of all spectators.'

For me at high school, throughout most of the 1930s, it was a daily routine to take the tram to Whitworth Street, carrying my homemade kosher sandwiches, and join the other Jewish boys in my form. We were a pretty cosmopolitan bunch: Oleesky, Smolenski, Freedman, Jaffe, Oelbaum, Roussak and me. Three of them, I believe, went on to become doctors. In the lunch hour we walked the short distance to the town centre, and the Town Hall in Albert Square, with Ford Maddox Brown's painting of John Dalton collecting marsh gas from duckweed over a pond. More often we dived into Lewis' store in Piccadilly. There one day John Logie Baird was demonstrating, on a television screen in the basement, a concert that was being performed on the fifth floor. It seemed as though we were looking through a rainstorm; certainly we never dreamed it would become the medium of the future.

In the spring of 1939 I was about to sit my Higher School Certificate. My parents were convinced war was imminent, but they did not object when I asked if I could join a few sixth formers and masters for a week's holiday in Avignon. It could help my French. Travelling by train across beautiful countryside enjoying restaurants, learning a little of the history and the Palace of the Popes, my lasting memory was of a conversation at a café overlooking the Rhône, which shocked me. A French army crew in a boat was trying to row upriver, but being dragged down by the current. 'I hope they do better against the Germans,' I said.

At the next table a local man overheard us. 'Nothing to worry about, we won't be invaded.' He said that they had the guarantee of the Bonnet-Ribbentrop Declaration, and the Maginot Line.

'Don't you recognise Hitler as a menace?' I asked.

'Not really, we have one hundred million Frenchmen to defend the Tricolor. Actually Mussolini is the greater danger. Italy is a rival, a colonial power with real ambitions in North Africa.'

Just before my exams we took a week's family holiday in North Wales, this time sadly marred by a tragic disaster. We saw, off the Deganwy coast, the sinking of the submarine *Thetis* with the loss of almost the entire crew.

I did well enough in the geography, chemistry and maths exams to begin to think of a university. Which was it to be? Not one of my teachers was an Oxford or Cambridge graduate and none suggested that any of us should attempt their entrance examinations. Manchester itself had a good reputation, was my father's alma mater and, given family circumstances, there were advantages in living at home. But what to study? My father knew I loved the countryside and suggested Geology. I warmed to the idea of understanding how the landscape came to be what it was, and indeed, how life evolved.

Off I went to see Professor W.J. Pugh, and I was accepted for the Honours School of Geology, to specialise on the physical side, petrology and mineralogy. There was a staff of four, the professor and three lecturers, but only two students, the other being Bobby Price, a delightful Welshman, son of the village postmistress in Llandeilo. He specialised in palaeontology, had an incredible memory and could probably recount for the rest of his life every detail of some 2,000 fossils.

Term was about to begin in the first week of September. At home, my parents, sister and I were standing in the kitchen, gathered around our old Pye wireless set awaiting an announcement. Neville Chamberlain came on to make his brief, but momentous statement: 'Consequently this country is at war with Germany.' Then the King broadcast, ending with 'We [...] reverently commit our cause to God.'

I remember that day so clearly, exactly where each of us was standing. Just as we all now remember 9/11. My father, always against appeasement, was the first to speak: 'There are no winners in war, but if we are defeated by Hitler, we will all die.' And then he added, 'What will Russia do now? And America…?'

We did not discuss what I should do, join up or go to University. This decision, in any event, would be taken by the Government. The very next day I received a call from my school. I was needed immediately with other prefects to help the staff evacuate the entire school by train to Arnold School and elsewhere in Blackpool. Eight hundred boys and 600 girls were all labelled and provided with gas masks, carrying a small case of clothes, comb and toothbrush, and a bag of food. My job was to get as many as possible into boarding houses, tell parents where they were, adding reassuringly 'they are now safe from air raids.' This went on for three days. After they had gone to bed the evenings were considerably lightened. We prefects would trail off to the Tower Ballroom to drink and dance with the local girls. The mood was a strange mixture of euphoria and apprehension.

Beginning the following week, first year lectures and laboratory work in chemistry, physics, zoology and botany were given to large classes including the medical school. Though I studied zoology and dissected animals for just a year, Professor Graham Cannon was the star turn. Seeing many women in the lecture theatre he could not resist describing in great detail the behaviour of a prehistoric monster 'with a penis about the size of an Irishman's shillelah' to see what the reaction might be. Professor Pugh had been a professor when still quite young and, since 1919, specialised in stratigraphy. Without any handouts he covered the blackboard at high speed, too quickly for Bobby and me to take notes, so we joined forces, and left gaps to be filled in afterwards. He had taken on the additional role of Chairman of the Joint Recruiting Board for the three services and told us that there was no intention of our being called up at that time.

It was not until the second year that specialisation began, lectures giving way to tutorials, and I did well, luckily having read the metallographic research papers of Marie Gayler on intercrystalline boundaries. I was intrigued by comparing, under the microscope, the structure of man-made with naturally occurring materials and then seeing her research results offering an explanation for the similarities. In petrology and mineralogy I had almost private tuition. The lecturer was Stuart Olaf Agrell, a beanpole with a black beard, the son of a Swedish match manufacturer. Under his supervision for the best part of two years I was glued to a microscope, examining specimens. If at times it seemed laborious it was more than compensated by the sheer beauty of some crystal forms that I came across, that Nature could design something so breathtaking.

It was at about this time, that when I took my father on walks I asked him where his own ideas came from at the start of his research career. 'They began as a second year undergraduate myself,' he said. 'In Manchester, what was more natural than to speculate on the origin of rain?'

Joking aside, he felt that the generally accepted evaporation/condensation theory might not represent the whole story. Surely, at some altitude in the upper atmosphere the hydrogen generated bore the right ratio to oxygen necessary for the formation of water. This could be induced by electrical, meteoric, volcanic, radiation or other phenomena. He submitted his paper *A Chemical Theory of Rain Formation* to the University Colloquium. One of the adjudicators tried to calculate the consequences of his theory, but could not decide whether rainfall of such origin was equivalent to a tropical storm or only sufficient to fill a bucket. He did not win the ten shillings prize money, but was handed an envelope containing a special prize of a Queen Victoria crown, a five shilling piece, which he treasured for many years, and then left to me.

He was teeming with ideas and his next one as a student arose out of a lecture he attended, given by a Dr Wheeler of the Home Office Safety in Mines Department, on the combustion of carbon to form carbon monoxide and dioxide. He showed that the different products arose from the different structure of two forms of carbon, amorphous and graphite, which were allotropes. Knowing their properties, and that carbon was tetravalent, he worked out their molecular structures. When he presented this to the Manchester Literary and Philosophical Society, members of the university staff, keenly interested, came forward with offers of help. Weizmann even suggested he try to synthesise the most precious allotrope, diamond. The work was developed into a complete theory of allotropy, based on valency, and published.

Some of his ideas came to him at joint meetings of unrelated societies. One on vitalism, intriguing, but lacking any supportive evidence, led him to compare the mineral components of flora and fauna, the causes of periodicity in nature and the role of a colloidal medium. There was no let up in the stream of ideas and his will to publish. By 1925 his many publications brought him his Doctor of Science at Manchester. I remember how, returning home from the ceremony, he was so taken by his scarlet cap and gown that he refused to take them off.

Though struck down by ill health, his output of research, now mainly theoretical, expanded and grew in importance. Over the following thirty years it encompassed organic, inorganic and biochemistry, plant and animal physiology, cancer and influenza. During World War II he demonstrated practical methods of enhancing our agricultural production. Some two hundred publications appeared in all and these attracted a worldwide correspondence and recognition. The letters which I read out to him came from Rutherford and W.H. Bragg, William Crookes, Lord Horder and Alexander Fleming, from Ostwald in Leipzig and Liesegang in Frankfurt, and of course, from Weizmann. Little did most of them realise when they wrote to The Research Laboratories, Alexandra Road, Manchester, it was just a tiny attic over a shop. Weizmann wrote frequently, in a beautiful handwriting, usually in Russian or Hebrew, in purple or green ink, on paper in every colour, letters of sympathy for his incapacity, congratulations on his latest published work, never forgetting their earlier collaboration. And when my father told him I had been given the middle name Charles (Chaim) after him, he immediately became my unofficial godfather.

In 1932 all savings had gone. There was a dramatic slump and our income vanished too. Friends and colleagues rallied around. Offers of support followed from Eleanor Rathbone MP and Lloyd George himself. In March 1937, on the recommendation of Stanley Baldwin, my father was placed top of the King's Civil List. This assured him of a modest annuity for life. One morning, our postman arrived at the shop and saluted as he handed over an envelope marked 'Prime Minister'.

At first the war made little impact. At university we were blacked out with shutters and curtains, and students and staff operated a warden system during the occasional air raids. When we stayed on duty all night we were rewarded with breakfast. A few students and staff were called up. One member of the Economics Department was actually interviewed by the Home Office as an alien, just as the Ministry of Labour had selected him to undertake a Government survey. With all other science, engineering and medical students, I was told we must complete our course and only those who failed exams would be called up.

We joined the Senior Training Corps, donned battledress and went through the motions of army drill, supervised by Frank Swift, the celebrated Manchester City goalkeeper, and Bren gun exercises, under the command of Major Drummond, Professor of Botany. We also undertook weekly air raid precaution duties, sleeping in cold and musty underground corridors, equipped with a stirrup pump to tackle any incendiary bombs. One night I found Dr Tyson, Librarian and Chief Fire Officer, crawling over the roof of Whitworth Hall, drenching everyone within reach. On another, I was on the Medical School roof awaiting incendiary bombs, when a medical student arrived with a lacrosse stick determined to catch one and flick it over to the Dental School.

What's in a Name?

The traditional Shrove Tuesday Rag and procession continued for a while. Kitted out in fancy dress we made a major effort to collect money for our hospitals. They were not state controlled then and depended upon voluntary contributions. Being overzealous led me into trouble. I got the Art School to produce a 100 foot banner with the slogan 'We want money. You've got piles' and fixed it across the front of the Manchester Royal Infirmary. I was found out and marched off to the Police Station.

The University had two distinct unions for men and women. Occasionally they held joint debates. I took part in one, attracted I suppose by the motion 'Men are as clay, and women make mugs of them.' But such a combative attitude was exceptional. The women generally were quiet, and a little intimidated. They knew they would soon be paid less for doing the same job as men. And if they were teachers, for example, they would have to resign on getting married. How times have changed. Not long ago I read of a second year woman student, also at Manchester, who marched into her tutor's room shouting, 'You bastard. I never got a B for an essay in my life,' and threw it back at him. At home all we could do with incessant air-raid warnings was to take the pictures off the wall, fill up the bath with water in case of incendiary bombs, and wait.

The fall of France left us deeply worried. Hitler's armies had rapidly come to within ten miles of the coast and 400,000 exhausted Allied troops. The Dunkirk evacuation seemed miraculous, but surely invasion could not be far off? We read that Field Marshall von Brauschitz had been designated to rule Britain, with plans to transport all 430,000 British Jews to Eastern Europe.

On 22nd December, having just broken up for the Christmas vacation, I was returning from a friend's party south of Wythenshawe when I saw the searchlights and explosions over the City, then bombs and anti-aircraft fire. I wandered about for an hour or two, shrapnel raining down as I lay in the gutter. At home, to my great relief, I found my family huddled in the cellar, but safe. I went to my university post to be directed to help in Piccadilly. There I saw the Free Trade Hall and Royal Exchange on fire, the roof then the walls slowly collapsing. It was an eerie sight. The German bomber attack continued for two nights and then the bombing suddenly stopped, just as Manchester was at its mercy. Our anti-aircraft guns had run out of shells and all supply roads into the city were blocked. The following morning I went to visit a former schoolmaster whom I had arranged to meet, only to find a bomb crater where his home and family had been. In those two nights 363 had been killed and 455 seriously injured. Thirty thousand homes had collapsed or been damaged. The university, largely, had been spared. I felt I should be out there fighting, not studying, but the strict call-up timetable did not allow for this.

Our lectures and laboratory work continued unabated, interspersed with field trips in North Wales, two of a week each in Horton-in-Ribblesdale in Derbyshire, and an ambitious one in Argyllshire. In addition to two lecturers we had the valuable company of Dr Nockolds, a Cambridge petrologist. We scaled the mountains from Loch Awe to Loch Leven: Appin, Onych, Ballachulish, Kentallen – each with its own complex geology – mapping, collecting specimens and being examined by our lecturers. We walked a record forty miles in one sixteen-hour day from Ballachulish to Creagan by a circuitous route, Nockolds chain-smoking throughout. Early one evening we found a hillside covered with orchids, which warmed the heart of our landlady Mrs MacCallum when we presented her with a bouquet. At the end of my second year I took Part I of my Finals and managed to get a First.

Throughout 1941 and 1942 our fortunes in the war were suffering severely. We had faced the Axis powers in the west for a whole year alone. Churchillian resolve seemed our only source of hope. Distracted, it must also have put extra stress on my studies. We had five compulsory Papers to take and I must have been on edge in those last few weeks, overdoing my swotting, because I passed out cold before the last one and missed it. Without it, according to the rules, I would fail to graduate altogether. Thinking of the consequences made me more ill still. The powers that be eventually allowed me to be interviewed on the subject of this last paper by the external examiner, Professor O.T. Jones. We gathered around the notice board as the results were posted. Bobby Price had got a thoroughly deserved First. I managed to scrape by with a Second.

I can still see the expression on my father's face. The result was a great disappointment to him, his high hopes for me dashed. He knew all about adversity, no-one more so, and whatever he must have thought, all he said to me was, 'Well, now is the time to show just what you are capable of.' I could not have wished for a clearer challenge. He then turned to Bobby Price and invited him home for lunch and a celebratory glass of wine.

At last, I could join up. As science students on the Ministry of Labour's Register, Bobby and I were sent off to Reading University staying in the Halls of Residence for a six-week course in radio theory and practice in the Physics building. I remember it, oddly enough, for the foul smell of the local brewery when they were cleaning out their vats. We completed the course and then had to decide on our choice of Service.

I was away thereafter, apart from a few weeks' leave, for nearly five years. At the end of the war my parents sold the shop, moving to a small detached house at 1 Gildridge Road, with a garden on the Whalley Range side of Alexandra Park. The occasional letter still came from Weizmann, whose dreams and life purpose had now been fulfilled: the establishment of a State of Israel, of which he was its first President. It was at home in Whalley Range that my father died of a heart attack, aged sixty-nine. *The Times'* obituary referred to his fine bearing, his bravery and his kindness, and of his devoted wife as well as his distinguished achievements under conditions of great adversity. The Dictionary of National Biography entry expanded on the significance of his work. The writer, Sir Robert Robinson, was his brilliant former colleague at Manchester who established the structure of plant pigments, steroids such as sex hormones and antibiotics such as penicillin. His own deep insight astonished his scientific associates. By then a Nobel Prize winner and President of the Royal Society, he wrote: 'In the tragic circumstances of his later life it was impossible to bring much of his work to full fruition. This deprived the world of the full development of his undoubted genius.'

He and my mother were proud of their country. She survived him by nine years, continuing to be supported as the Civil List annuity was regularly reviewed by the Prime Minister's Office. By the end, I was in a position to support her financially, so I drafted a letter in which she offered to forego her annuity, but she was suddenly taken to hospital, where I was with her just before she died.

PUBLIC SERVICE
& PRIVATE LIFE

CHAPTER II

Defence of the Realm

In Uniform 1942–52: Radar in War

My brief, rather irksome square bashing OTC experience in khaki battle dress could not compare with the invigorating prospect of going to sea. I gave the Navy as my first preference. Though supported by the Recruiting Board Chairman, unbelievably there was no suitable vacancy, or so I was told. I was ordered to don the uniform of a Pilot Officer RAFVR and to prepare to become an RDF Officer, as radar was still called. Qualifications in geology were clearly irrelevant; presumably anyone technically qualified was qualified to do anything technical.

And so I began training at Compton Bassett and at Yatesbury with new graduates, mainly electrical engineers and, after a few weeks, was sent off to Stoke Holy Cross, in nominal command of Hopton, a tiny station in the vital chain of East Coast radar stations. My job was to supervise the radar plotting of the WAAF teams, its purpose to forewarn our protective fighters and help 60 Group intercept low-flying German aircraft. On just three occasions, and for a few seconds only, I saw the enemy. Luftwaffe fighter escorts suddenly swept over us, within a hundred feet or so, and vanished. My fellow officers were a Flight-Lieutenant, who was a technical trouble-shooter for the whole chain, an army Captain, concerned with coastal defence, and three WAAF Officers, covering around the clock radar surveillance. I was in nominal command because, though the most junior, I was there full time.

I had visits from a very engaging RAF technician who knew more about radar, and far more about ground controlled approach, than I. When he was recommended for a Commission, apparently, at the interview he held forth enthusiastically about interplanetary travel saying it was a certainty. That did not go down at all well. Some of the Board had served in the First World War and had a different mindset. There was some deliberation and quite a delay before he was interviewed by a more knowledgeable Wing Commander who had seen an article he had just published in *Electronic Engineering*. This time he was successful.

I was to remember this man, for he went on to found the British Interplanetary Society, become a distinguished science fiction writer, establish the concept of communication satellites and was eventually knighted. We even shared the same initials. It was Arthur C. Clarke. Years later he travelled from Colombo to London to receive a prize, and we met again. I had enjoyed reading his books and asked him what he thought of the science fiction of Jules Verne and H.G. Wells. He said Verne's passengers in his 'moon gun' would have been reduced to a thin smear, and as for Wells, his gravity screen violated the laws of conservation of energy. So I pointed out that technological forecasting, which he had promoted so well, had made many glaring errors and omissions. In his 1937 study of the prospects for 2000, he completely missed out computers, atomic energy, antibiotics, radar and jet propulsion. He replied, 'I will give you one forecast you won't be able to prove wrong. One day there will be more people living off the earth than on it.'

The fortunes of war were now just beginning to turn. We had captured Tripoli and the Russians at Stalingrad had annihilated 330,000 of the German army. I wondered, was I going to be too late to be of any use?

A few months later we were sent off to take a written and practical examination. I was busy fault-finding along the high tension line of a new transmitter when a Flight Lieutenant came into the hut, and left without a word. After a couple of days I was told that the Wing Commander wanted to see me. I knew I had not done well, but had no idea what was to follow. He told me I had failed. In particular, whilst I had been standing safely on a rubber insulated mat, by the transmitter, I had not locked the hut door. Anyone coming in and touching me would have taken the full 10,000 volts. I felt as though I had taken them. Total disaster.

For days I worried about what would happen. After my university experience, now this. I was dreading the consequences so I decided to telephone the Ministry of Labour before they might hear the results from the RAF to enquire what my situation would be. Then I received a call. A certain Flight Lieutenant Harry Hoff of the Technical and Scientific Register wanted to see me. He questioned me for half an hour. 'You wanted to join the Navy. I am proposing that you do, for an RN Commission as a Temporary Lieutenant.' I was to take a three-month course at the RN College and had to pass the Instructor's examination which included navigation, radar and meteorology.

My sense of relief was tinged with caution. It would be a promotion, but with higher risks perhaps. What was I letting myself in for? Switching uniform from Air Force to Navy would raise a few eyebrows, but failure then could well see me back in plain clothes. In the RAF I had not enjoyed my electrical fault-finding activities and obviously was not good at them. Perhaps the first was the cause and the second the effect? I needed to be interested as well as competent to have the best chance of success. This new prospect certainly appeared interesting and attractive. I saw no other, I had to stick with it and persevere.

I telephoned Harry Hoff. 'Good luck,' he said, adding, 'You may not know that Lord Trenchard failed his entry into Dartmouth, Sandhurst and Woolwich, but finished up as Marshal of the RAF.' I was directed to Gieves in Bond Street, naval outfitters since Nelson's time, to be fitted out and went straight off, somewhat self-consciously, as a sailor to report to RAF 60 Group in Cambridge, responsible for East Coast radar stations.

Group Captain Victor Tait knew of my name as a Pilot Officer, so he was flabbergasted. 'I assume it's all above board,' he said. We shook hands warmly and he wished me luck. Was it his charm that led him to become an Air Chief Marshal?

There were nine of us transferred from other services on that intensive course, in the end taking the practical and written examinations together. I came out joint top: better, I thought, than my performance deserved. I was forever grateful to Harry Hoff. He became a Civil Service Commissioner and our paths crossed again, twenty years later, over the Brain Drain enquiry. By then I discovered that he was none other than the accomplished novelist William Cooper. I had one further chance quite recently of telling him how much I owed to him, when his daughter invited me to have tea with him. It was just before he died.

Now, however, instead of being sent off to sea as I had hoped and expected, I was disappointed to be posted to HMS Collingwood and the Barracks in Portsmouth, to join the Instructor Staff. I asked why and was told, 'It's needed, and you should be good at it.' My job was to train specialist radar officers during their six-month 'Long Course' and give a few lectures and short courses to senior non-specialists, including Mountbatten, then a Rear Admiral. I burned the midnight oil cramming to make sure I kept just ahead of the classes.

The backwater into which I thought I had been steered began to turn out quite differently. Early in 1944 I asked senior officers about their operational experiences with radar; invited the junior specialists on their first sea-going appointments to carry out experiments on the detection performance of their equipment and, still informally, asked RN Air Stations to keep a Radar Performance Log. The reports that came from the Atlantic, Mediterranean and Middle East waters streamed in. I collated them, drew some tentative conclusions on the apparent effect of the meteorological and propagation conditions on performance, and in a short report showed the results to the Captain of Collingwood. He passed them to the Director of Radio Equipment at the Admiralty. From there they were circulated more widely – to the navigation, tactical and torpedo, meteorological and gunnery establishments. They were also reported to Sir Robert Watson Watt, who had done more than anyone to develop radar at the outset. He, in turn, wrote to Sir Edward Appleton, Chairman of the Ultra Short Wave

Panel of the Ministry of Supply's Scientific Advisory Council, attaching my report. The Panel's role was to review and apply for military purposes research results obtained in universities and government laboratories. I was now asked, formally, to get all further information I could based on sea-going experience.

A message arrived. I was to meet Appleton at the Ministry of Supply office in Glentworth Street, Marylebone. He greeted me warmly, 'Are you a physicist or an engineer?'

'Neither, just a geologist, masquerading as a sailor,' I said.

'I was a geologist too,' replied Appleton, 'at Cambridge, under Professor Marr. I opened up *The Yorkshire Post* one day to read I had won the Wiltshire Prize in geology – and I had never heard of it.'

He told me how his interest in radio communication came during army signals duties in WW1. Later in 1927, during a total eclipse of the sun, he discovered in the ionosphere the layer above the Heaviside layer, known today as the Appleton layer. He found that the layer and the eclipse changed at the same time, which meant that whatever caused the ionisation had travelled from the sun to the earth at the speed of light. 'That's how we went on to develop our theory of radio wave propagation.'

In October I attended my first meeting of the Panel, as the only serving officer. Welcoming me as a member of 'the team' I was introduced to Fred Hoyle, and other academics. At the December meeting I was able to report radar sightings of Elba from a distance of 115 miles, the Apennines, from HMS Scylla, at 370 miles and HMS Duke of York's detection of Foula, eighty miles away in thick fog. We compared these experiences with reports sent by General McArthur's Staff in the Far East, and in the Middle East. Between May and October, sightings of over 400 miles were made in the straits of Hormuz, when NW winds were blowing from Iraq over the Persian Gulf. Within a few feet of sea level these conditions had created a wave guide effect in which there was hardly any loss of signal strength over great distances.

Within the Portsmouth Command I arranged round-the-clock observation. We saw the low-lying French coast, beyond Cap Gris Nez, 130 miles away. Then I was asked, formally, to get all further information I could based on sea-going experience. Meteorological Officers began to take a direct interest. One of them, Lt Cdr Frank Westwater, and I took turns to lecture and recruit observers. I drafted a Fleet Order to be put out by the Admiralty which read, 'It was of paramount importance for tactical purposes to have knowledge of the probability of very long range warning of the enemy. According to the ranges of detection expected, new dispositions of craft in reconnaissance, search and patrol could be made. The range of detection of enemy search receivers too, needs to be known, for the most effective stationing of anti-submarine escorts and for mine-laying operations.' Reports arrived which proved valuable.

In 1945 a further half dozen Panel meetings were held, but in March an invitation from the USA came for a member of the Panel to participate in a conference and address members of the National Research Council in Washington. I was sure that Appleton would nominate Hoyle; he was the ablest and most knowledgeable of us. But he apparently had been there earlier, and Appleton proposed me.

I was well briefed by Hoyle. I was also fascinated to learn how his early interest in astronomy had arisen. As a boy living among the Yorkshire woollen mills, he had been given a small telescope and stayed up all night observing the stars. He became so fascinated that he set out to read all the works of Eddington and Jeans. Later, he went on to discover that our atomic elements on earth resulted from nuclear reaction in the stars and supernovae, which lived and died long before the solar system was formed.

With some excitement, I ventured on my first wartime trip abroad. It was late March; the war in Europe was all but over. Gen Eisenhower was advancing on Hitler's mountain fortress in Berchtesgarten, the Russians on Berlin. I was sent to Gouroch in Scotland to 'W62' the code for the RMS *Aquitania*. It was the mighty 'four funnel job', thirty years old, without armament. U-boats were at large in the Atlantic and still taking their toll. We depended upon our speed of thirty knots to avoid them.

Three other Royal Navy officers and I, all passengers on our way to take up duties in the USA, were called to the bridge. The Master explained he had his work cut out to get us safely across. He turned to me, the most junior: 'You are in charge of discipline aboard.' I said I had a speech to prepare. 'You can do that in the First Class Lounge. We are totally dry anyway, you shouldn't be troubled.' Those aboard were mainly wounded US Army servicemen, aircrew from the RAF Ferry Command, and forty ATS officers off to a staff course in Kansas.

I was handed a book on the rules of discipline and punishment. 'There are two things I won't tolerate,' the Master said, 'lights on deck and sleeping on sentry duty. Now I don't want to be disturbed.'

I was halfway through drafting my speech when I was interrupted. Two US 'snowdrops', as the military police were called, came down the ladder escorting two GIs. Apparently, a giant game of craps had been going on, the stakes were high, there were accusations of cheating, knives were brandished and these two GIs had been sleeping on duty.

I asked them what they had to say. 'We weren't sleeping, only pretending to be asleep.' I consulted the book for the offence, 'Sleeping on sentry duty' and read aloud: 'Punishment in time of war – death.' Shocked, all I could say to the military police was, 'Take them below and report back.' I decided to fine them both fourteen days' pay. The Master heard of it. I thought I would be told off for being too lenient, but he said, 'You shouldn't have done that. They are heroes and have been wounded.' As we approached the coast of America I was tipped off that the hat was going around, a collection to refund their fine. I relented, put the fine back in to the hat, and as we saw the thrilling lights of New York in the distance, added a dollar of my own.

New York, as we berthed, was a scene of amazement. After years of black-out at home, the illuminated city seemed like a dream. A women's military band on the quayside was playing *Sentimental Journey*.

A contingent of nylon-clad Red Cross Army and Air Force women came aboard, showering their menfolk with presents. A wonderful homecoming.

The war in Europe was just about over, but for the Americans thoughts of VE Day quickly turned to the prospect of a VJ Day, when Japan would be defeated.

I arrived at the National Academy of Sciences building for our conference and was called to give my address, on Britain's achievements, before an audience of 100 senior officers and scientists. Introduced as 'the British representative' I wondered just how I, a twenty-four year-old, came to be there. It all seemed so unreal. I recounted some of our naval radar experiences and ended by setting out the scope for future US/UK collaboration, not least to support their Task Force 37 in the Pacific, highlighting some of the problems still to be tackled. This was the theme of the discussion that followed. It was evident that our vessels, with long range radar installations, had proved themselves to be better than the Americans' for high air cover, but not as good for low cover or for fighter direction, where they could benefit from anomalous conditions.

At the end of the conference, the Chief of Naval Operations thanked me warmly, got in touch with a dozen service establishments and I was immediately invited to see their work at first hand. For nine weeks, placed on secondment to the British Admiralty Delegation I had meetings in fourteen US bases, university laboratories and institutes across the country and at St Hyacinthe in Quebec. I learned a great deal and reported at length to the Admiralty.

My visit to California was memorable for more than one reason. I went aboard the mighty USS *Indianapolis*, preparing to sail from San Diego, into Japanese waters. I had been a guest in the wardroom, so was shocked to learn she was blown up in July, in a submarine attack west of Guam; over a thousand of the crew perished at sea. Then at the Scripps Institute of Oceanography at La Jolla I met the Director, Professor Hans Sverdrup. The state of the sea and the prevailing winds had created ideal conditions for anomalous propagation over long periods. I found myself sitting on the beach with him whilst he, on the back of an envelope, was working out mathematically the radio-meteorological consequences of their recordings.

I also met by chance the only other British officer within miles, a Lieutenant McManus RNVR. We decided to spend the evening together travelling a few miles over the Mexican border to Tijuana. There we were given a twenty-four hour pass. It was then just a small shanty town and pretty sleazy at that. We managed to escape the persistent prostitutes, getting back to the frontier post after midnight, only to be held by four rough Mexican guards. Our papers were not in order. Our pass was valid apparently until midnight only. And so we spent the night in a cold dark cell. At about 7am they came in carrying an atlas, and asked in Spanish, 'Which Halifax?' pointed to my British Admiralty Delegation card with its facsimile signature of Lord Halifax, our Ambassador. They didn't understand. We were released at 8am, however, without having convinced them. Safely back on the US side we discovered the guard was changed at 8am and they could only go off duty if all cases had been cleared up.

Before returning to the UK I was able to take a few days' leave in New York, contacting friends of those back home. Lieutenant David Mountbatten (Marquis of Milford Haven) and John Edmonds, Captain's Secretary at Collingwood, had provided me with a list of night-clubs I should visit, and 'in order of merit' as he put it, were the Copacabana, El Morocco, Twenty-One and Lorne 'high class'; Leon and Eddie's 'low class' and the Stork Club and Diamond Horseshoe 'rather different'. Edmonds also asked me to look up his good friend Jane Watson, 'wearing my best suit, and sober'; to tell her he was being good. I arrived at a magnificent house at 4E 75th Street. In the drawing room were autographed photographs, 'To my dear friend Tom, from Franklin Delano'. Jane, four or five years older than me, came in. Her parents were away, so she took me to lunch at the River Club, where we were joined by Alice Marble, the tennis champion. I wondered why Jane had been rather subdued until she told me her terrible news that her fiancé serving in the Pacific had been killed.

She mentioned that her father Tom had founded a company called IBM, which I had not heard of. He was funding research at Columbia University, with Harvard's support, on behalf of the US Navy. His engineers were also building a computer at their Endicott Laboratory, which should prove a winner, commercially. 'If I were you, I would buy some shares in IBM.' I explained that my worldly wealth was my naval pay of twenty-one shillings a day, and I was staying at the Barbazon Plaza for three dollars a day, the equivalent of fifteen shillings. More than once since then, I have calculated the fortune I might have made if I had.

My return journey to England coincided with a tragedy. After visiting Canada and McGill University, I flew off from Dorval airport, but less than an hour later the weather had become so bad we returned to base. I had already sent a telegram to my parents with an estimated time of arrival. I shouldn't have done. They heard on the wireless news that an aircraft had just crashed in mid-Atlantic and that names of next of kin would be informed. Only after I was reunited with my parents, we learned it was Sir William Mahon, Colonel Capel Dunn and seven secretaries returning from the San Francisco Conference who had all been killed.

Back in London, I found that the Admiralty had been considering where further work on radio-meteorology should be carried out. My entire file had somehow been lost between Departments for months, but eventually it was found 'tied behind another file'. They had read my report and decided I should be released from further instructor duties, concentrate on this and report to Captain Garbett, Director of Meteorological Services. From my new office in Fitzmaurice Place, Berkeley Square, I continued to attend the USWP Panel, joined the new inter-departmental Admiralty Committee, took on one or two meteorological tasks and occasionally visited Portsmouth to supervise radar observations on installations operating on four different wavelengths.

Our most significant finding there occurred between 1st and 12th February 1946. I had advised those in the Portsmouth command to search all around them during a period of high sunspot activity. On the afternoon of 7th February, they recorded at two sites high intensity radiation bearing 350 degrees, i.e. magnetic north. This coincided with the magnetic disturbance and a display of the *aurora borealis* visible elsewhere. I reported this to Appleton. He said that no other searches had been made to the north and the results were significant. Sir Edward Bullard, the geophysicist, wrote to me on the 17th from Cambridge: 'The radio measurements sound most exciting.' They were recorded in the Panel minutes in June. It was in June in the following year he wrote to me, to say the Canadians thought they too had just got the radio noise from the aurora, so he reminded them of our observations and sent details.

Soon after Appleton was awarded the Nobel Prize he invited me to his house in Rutland Gate. He related how, in Stockholm, King Gustav had sent his horse-drawn coaches to convey Nobel Laureates to the glittering ceremony and ball. The coach door was slammed on his daughter Rosalind's hand and she was in abject agony. From the next coach the American prize winner in medicine, Dr Cori stepped out, saying he would take care of her. For the rest of the night they were seen dancing together, she oblivious of the injury.

By now, I was deemed to be a qualified meteorologist and was sent far north to the RN Air Station at Donisbristle in Fifeshire, to relieve another officer on leave. There I was briefing pilots on flying conditions, telling them where they should expect least turbulence and ice formation or not fly at all. I got a lift on one flight to the Shetlands where I made a rare find, a village shop with a dozen eggs. Carefully packed, I posted them to my parents. Two joyful letters arrived. It had been years since they had seen a fresh egg.

On another occasion, I was in a basement office beneath Admiralty Arch. I had been there hours, preparing a chart of flying conditions for a sortie high over Heligoland. The phone rang. 'When is this damned rain going to stop?' said the voice.

'What rain?' I said. Two minutes later the Director came in.

'Was it you who told the Admiral it wasn't raining? He wants to get out to play golf.' Then a Petty Officer came into our office, soaked from the downpour.

Demobilisation had been under way for some months when I was sounded out about joining the Navy as a career. A pleasant prospect, but it gave me food for thought. I had just become a Fellow of the Royal Meteorological Society, was about to join the Institution of Electrical Engineers and the British Institute of Radio Engineers, to add to my Fellowship of the Geological Society, and was well on my way to becoming a jack of all trades. I had been given the chance of gaining experience and some responsibility and I thoroughly enjoyed the companionship I had found in the Navy. I had been lucky to escape what befell some of my university contemporaries. Yet, somehow I did not see myself as a sailor for life. And, with a reputation as a specialist, my promotion prospects would be more limited than those of a 'salt-horse'. I had given no thought as yet to a career. I had no thought in fact of making any long–term commitment. Post-war changes were inevitable and might be rapid. Keeping options open, with an element of excitement and *not* knowing what might present itself was even appealing. I said, 'No'.

On the other hand, what should I do? I began to take stock. My research in colloid science seemed a thing of the past. Thanks to Pugh and Appleton, I had been nominated for a lectureship in Geophysics at Witwatersrand University in South Africa; I had also been tentatively offered a career oil prospecting, beginning in Borneo in off-shore exploration. Edward Bullard, a Reader at St John's College, Cambridge, had awarded me a Shell Fellowship in Geophysics, just for three years. Working in Cambridge was particularly attractive. This I accepted as a next step: it might be a springboard, whatever it might lead to.

A few days earlier, as it happened, I had spotted a newspaper advertisement. The Civil Service Commissioners had invited applications for established posts in an Office of the new Ministry of Defence. Candidates had to be born on or after 2nd August 1899, have research experience and, if women, be unmarried or widowed. I was intrigued. Without any idea of what it was, I wrote off, and for ages heard no more. I thought no more of it, so was pleasantly surprised to be called for interview. Partly out of curiosity, I went along.

I appeared at 11 Bryanston Square, W1 before a three-man board. The Chairman introduced himself as General Sir Stewart Menzies of the Life Guards. Only later did I realise he was 'C', with the formidable reputation of having built up and headed our wartime Secret Intelligence Service. On his right, Major General Kenneth Strong who had been General Eisenhower's intelligence chief; on his left Martin Watson, Under-Secretary in the Ministry of Economic Warfare.

Menzies, distinguished, courteous and charming, immediately put me at my ease. The Joint Intelligence Bureau, he explained, for whom Research Officers were sought, would be a critically important part of a new centralised organisation for defence. Its purpose, to brief the Planners and the Chiefs of Staff on any issue which could spell danger to our country, to the Dominions or the Commonwealth. 'We no longer have enemies, but need utmost vigilance and imagination to recognise potential mavericks and identify sources of potential trouble and targets.'

I must have looked bemused by all this. I wondered why my experience was relevant. The vetting process had been thorough, going back, I discovered, to my date of birth and my parents' naturalisation. Then Strong picked up the interview with a quite amazing question for a soldier. 'In Geology, powers of observation were essential, but you followed up with experiments and publications on silica gels. How did these two branches of science fit together?' I explained that by treating acids with waterglass, a silica gel, I had developed mineral structures in the laboratory, identical with those found in nature. The aim was to show under what geological conditions different forms of silica, such as opal, agate and flint might have been created. He seemed positively interested.

Eventually, Menzies asked whether I had any questions. Doubting whether I would fit into their organisation, I suggested that my scientific work might have been too remote and irrelevant. 'At your age,' Menzies reassured me, 'I was spending much of my time hunting with the Duke of Beaufort's hounds.' Even so, I assumed they would not choose me.

Weeks later, totally unexpectedly, an offer arrived from the Ministry of Defence. I had by then accepted the Cambridge post so went up to see Bullard and told him of the offer, a £700 a year starting salary, compared with an annual £300 for three years only, and the benefit of long term security of tenure for an established Civil Servant in the UK. I told Bullard that whilst I wanted to work with him I also wanted, in the long term, to help support my parents and hopefully, a family of my own. 'Of course, you must take it,' he said. 'Mind you, it's the Ministry of Defence. Think of the danger of twenty years of peace. What would that do for your prospects?' I didn't know, but felt confident enough to take the chance. I accepted the job. Since then I have never applied for any other.

The Navy always did things in style and they threw a farewell party in the Admiralty. Those attending included the Directors of Radio Engineering, the Meteorological Branch, the Captain, HMS Collingwood, and Fred Hoyle, standing in for Sir Edward Appleton – all for a departing Temporary Lieutenant, RN as I still was.

In my final month I had one last 'fling' and was sent off to deliver a lecture in Paris. This followed a Swiss skiing holiday with Ian and Brenda, friends from Portsmouth and their parents, Admiral Sir Arthur Davies and his wife, a fine landscape painter. They invited me to join them in Château d'Oex in the Bernese Oberland, where they had rented the villa Bon Acceuil. It was my first chance to learn to ski, and all thoroughly enjoyable. Coming home we took an extravagant detour via Milan where we went to the first opera performance at La Scala since the war. We sat in Box No 5 marked 'Signor Mussolini'. The production of *Samson and Delilah* was wonderful, but without heating we were frozen.

From Milan to Paris, reporting to the Bureau of Electromagnetic Detection in the Rue Royale, I gave my lecture on the operational capabilities of radar. I spoke in English, but those present did not mind –

the technical jargon, at least, was the same in all languages – and lacking operational experience themselves, they were delighted to have the opportunity of asking questions.

After lunch at the Ministry of Marine hosted by Admiral Kahn, I walked to the rue du Faubourg St Honoré to sign the Visitors Book in the Embassy. A military jeep was driving into the Chancery Yard and out stepped Winston Churchill wearing his 'British Warm' and his driver, a rather good-looking young woman, his daughter, Mary. She looked very smart in her ATS uniform. Churchill went up the steps to call on the Ambassador, Duff Cooper. Mary followed, making her way to the travel office. An old sports car then drove up with the Assistant Ministry Attaché at the wheel. It was Major Christopher Soames. He caught sight of some attractive nylon-clad legs. 'Was that Mary Churchill?' he asked. 'Where's she going?' Once he knew, he quickly made his way to the office too. Soon after, I read the announcement of their wedding. He had followed her by train to Rome. I was appointed to the Embassy myself eight years later. Green, still in the office, told me what had happened at the time. Forty years later when Mary visited us in Dorset, I told her the story. She was amazed to discover a witness to these events.

On Naval Patrol 1948–54

I was placed on the Regular Emergency List 'to be ready if needed' and given seniority as a Lieutenant, backdated by two years to April 1941. It meant I could be called on to don my uniform from time to time and get some sea-going experience. Over the next five years, I was to do this three times – welcome and rewarding breaks from being tied to a desk.

The first of my naval cruises in 1948 was a six-week venture into Arctic Norway aboard HMS Cygnet. She was a frigate with a crew of 180 leading our Fishery Protection Flotilla. I was to be let loose on Bear Island (Bjørnøya) to undertake a survey. It was a most welcome break, after eighteen months of desk work. The Admiralty had previously asked JIB to provide an intelligence questionnaire on Spitzbergen, Bear Island and Finmark. As my Emergency List duties allowed, I volunteered to go and try to answer the questions myself. I was given six weeks' leave to do so. It was a great escape and the sea air, scenery and duty-free gin were just what I needed. With five other officers we took turns to keep watch and I had a wide-ranging brief in radar, meteorology and navigation. My seniority put me temporarily second in command to Captain Ronald Mackay.

On 20th June we set sail from Rosyth, were entertained in Bergen, passed through the Lofoten Islands, saw the keel of our sunken cruiser Effingham, tragically lost in the evacuation of troops in the war, and on to Narvik. There we berthed for three days. Our Consul had telephoned us to tell us that Grimsby and Hull trawlermen had been poaching in territorial water and been arrested. They had antagonised the local community so we should expect to be unpopular on arrival. Captain Mackay decided to throw a party aboard for all the children. Our crew, in fancy dress, gave up their own chocolate ration, which soon made us popular with everyone. Our trawler men were quickly released from jail.

We sailed for Bear Island, sixty miles from North Cape, the most isolated island in the Arctic. It was desolate. Despite earlier Russian objections, Norway was granted sovereignty and had taken possession. We rounded small icebergs, approached 1400-foot black vertical cliffs and landed at the foot of the southern cliffs at Sorhamma, some 250 feet above us.

I was allowed to invite any fellow officer to join me in crossing the island on foot, a trek of 30 km, for which we'd allowed three days, so I asked Surgeon Lieutenant Murray, perhaps a little selfishly, in case there was an accident.

We scaled the cliffs with map, sleeping bags, thermos flask and sandwiches. All around us was bleak, desolate and soggy. Hundreds of skuas dive-bombed and pecked at us non-stop as we tried to beat them off with the rolled-up chart. It was exhausting. Clambering over sharp boulders we crossed the Russelva, skirted the forbidding Miseryfellet, crossed the frozen Englelskelya and continued north-west to Myggrabben and Nordkapp. It was there, a little to the west, we saw that our chart was incomplete. Supplied by the Admiralty, their latest, but their only one, it had been mapped by the Swedish explorer Otto Nordensjkjold back in 1874. A small lake, 1km to the south-west of Nordkapp was missing. I threw a rock into the water, marked it on the map (74° 30.5 N, 19° 21.3 E) and called it Lake Cygnet. Murray then sketched in the small cape just to the north and with friendly inspiration named it Cape Copisarow. So I added Murray Bay.

On we went in the mist to make out a small hut in the distance. To our complete surprise four men emerged. They were manning a weather and radio station. They were difficult to understand, but obviously surprised to see us. Over an unappetising strong drink, we gathered that they had volunteered to serve there so as to get remission from long prison sentences. We continued mapping the third day, followed some coal-bearing rocks and found a site in the permafrost which would allow aircraft to land in an emergency. From the top of a small cliff we saw our ship making towards us and she sent a skiff to pick us up from the strand below.

On 3rd July we were on our way to Spitzbergen, ominously surrounded by ice flows, when we received a message that the Norwegians had not approved our planned landing there. We turned east instead, towards Novaya Zemlya. The lines of longitude were now so close together, we had already got to a point east of Mecca. We met a fleet of twenty-five of our own trawlermen who gave us a cheer and unloaded more turbot and haddock than we could ever eat. Turning back to Varanger Fjord the Captain lent me the motor launch to do a twelve-mile survey of the local beaches. With Lieutenant Barton the engineer and a crew of three, equipped with empty cocoa tins, we collected specimens for later stability tests.

It was about 3am, and visibility off Murmansk was excellent. One of my ship mates entering into the spirit of our venture got me out of my cabin to photograph a suspicious Russian flying boat apparently photographing us. It was Lieutenant Tim Featherston-Dilke who wrote to me years later about the incident. He recalled how I had retaliated by concealing myself in the barrel of a signal projector to photograph the offending plane, and how we intercepted a radio message, transmitted by one of the trawlers in which they had wrongly identified us as a light cruiser.

Arriving at Kirkenes in a heat wave, mosquitoes everywhere, we were challenged to a soccer match by the local team and thoroughly beaten. Then rounding North Cape in the midnight sun I felt sufficiently light headed to signal the Commander-in-Chief Portsmouth, Admiral Lord Fraser of North Cape, sending our 'humble duty and respect to the Lord of the Manor'. He replied by telegram thanking his temporary residents and regretting he could not be with us to extend his hospitality.

We berthed in Tromsø where a party of Laplanders, men and women in traditional dress on the quayside, requested permission to come aboard. We asked them to join us for a drink in the wardroom. Only one spoke English, a pretty girl, who explained that they had come by reindeer and trap to do their shopping. They migrated seasonally from Hammerfest to Kautokeine and were returning to their village, Sorbmojok, that evening. If I had not visited a Lap community they would be delighted to show me, and get me back the following day. It was an invitation I accepted with pleasure. Getting there at 11pm we entered a large gloomy barn. The pretty girl handed me a flask of vodka whilst the others went to bed. I could just make out in the gloom a dozen or so narrow mattresses in a radiating pattern all now occupied but one. 'Where do I sleep?' I asked.

'Here with me'. It was cold. As we undressed, she slipped down alongside and put her arms around me.

'How did you learn to speak such perfect English?' I asked.

'Actually I am English. I'm only here for a year doing research in anthropology.' I did not know her name, and she didn't know mine. Later, I found out she signed the ship's Visitors Book, 'Joan Newhouse of Malvern Links'. I wonder where she is now.

Sailing south we entered Troll and Sogne, two picturesque fjords, anchored at Trondheim and went on to Bergen. We had a casualty at Balhomen. Captain Mackay challenged me to join him in climbing a giant statue of the Kaiser once presented to Norway. I declined. We all advised him not to, but he climbed it anyway, fell and sustained multiple fractures. We carried him by stretcher back to the ship and I phoned his wife who flew to Oslo to meet him. Strictly against regulations, we brought her back to England with us so she could care for him, and he recovered in Haslar Hospital.

On 21st July we entered Oslo harbour to receive an official welcome. We exchanged salutes at Fort Akershus, our Consul came aboard, and we paid official calls at the Royal Palace, signed the King's and Crown Prince's books and then met our Ambassador Sir Laurence Collier. He gave a reception at the Embassy where I met the Army C-in-C and, surprisingly, Professor Hans Sverdrup. It was three years since we had met, 6000 miles away in La Jolla, California. Now in Oslo he was Director of the Norsk Polar Institutt. We showed him and Captain Ryder, our Naval Attaché, our Bear Island photographs and annotated map. These Sverdrup warmly accepted, saying they would certainly amend their own when next reprinted. Captain Ryder also told us he would send us a copy. But that never happened.

Now that I came to write about this, incidentally, I realised I had never seen the revised map, so wrote off for a copy of it. In sixty years all had changed. The Polar Institutt had moved from Oslo to Tromsø; the documents and photographs could not be found; under current policy 'additional' personal names were no longer allowed, and the features themselves were too small now to be named. Sympathetically they wrote, 'It was perhaps unfortunate that in your trek you did not have available the 1925 (1:40,000 map) which would have shown larger unnamed lakes and headlands.' So much for the Admiralty's 'latest' 1874 map they had given us! For sixty years I had thought there had been a Cape Copisarow.

That evening our Naval Attaché gave a splendid dinner party. I had been tipped off in good time and, having no mess dress, sent a telegram to London requesting express delivery of my dress suit and white tie. I thought I might have been overdressed until I saw our host, Captain Ryder, resplendent in aiguillettes, the white ribbon of the Polar Medal and the crimson Victoria Cross awarded For Valour at St Nazaire. In 1942 he had destroyed the only harbour for the battleship Tirpitz, effectively changing the course of our war at sea.

We returned via Copenhagen, squeezed with inches to spare through the Kiel Canal and finally berthed in Portsmouth.

When Captain Mackay was fit again, he spent a year at the Imperial Defence College before going on to another Scandinavian cruise, where a further disaster struck. Thanks to his navigator, his ship was grounded in the Skaggerak. Repairs were costly and he insisted on taking all the blame and facing court-martial. Losing all prospects of further promotion, he retired and joined the Board of Foster Wheeler Corporation. We kept in touch. Whilst staying at Villa Captiva, their home near Cannes, he told me that his contemporary, Admiral Sir Charles Lamb, who came out top of his class at Dartmouth had, on his retirement, been turned down by his company on grounds of age. His own early retirement had turned out to be fortunate.

Back in my office, not only did I feel refreshed, I was delighted that my report on Bear Island and Finmark justified my absence and I was permitted to propose and undertake future trips. As well as the memos from my own Director Sir Kenneth Strong and the Admiralty, came a letter from Brian Roberts of the Foreign Office Research Department quoting Article 3 of the Spitzbergen Treaty of 9th February 1920. It made it clear we had equal liberty of access and entry for any reason or object whatsoever, of the water, fjords and ports of Svalbard (Spitzbergen). 'The Norwegians,' he said, 'had no legal right to make any prohibition.'

Two years went by. In 1950 I was preparing to embark from Scapa Flow on a second trip, this time for Fleet Exercises in the Atlantic and into

Norwegian waters, just as fighting in Korea began. My Department had to decide whether to allow me to go, as the Far East had now been added to my intelligence responsibilities. I sent off a signal to the C-in-C Home Fleet on 1st July, confirming I would join HMS Loch Alvie 'political situation permitting', which on reflection was a little presumptuous for a junior officer.

I did, in fact, join her for seventeen days. The train journey to Invergordon took twenty-two hours and I put up at the Royal Hotel. I signalled Loch Alvie requesting a pick-up, only to discover she was already on exercises 200 miles away. Not to be outdone I persuaded the King's Harbour Master to allow me to take his launch into the Firth, to board the tug HMS Reward about to deliver mail to the Fleet and then signalled the C-in-C aboard the carrier Implacable, asking if I could be transferred from Reward to Loch Alvie.

After fifteen hours in heavy sea we closed in on the 3rd Cruiser Squadron, dropped her mail, then on to the 2nd Cruiser Squadron and 6th Destroyer Flotilla. The C-in-C signalled Loch Alvie and Reward to close her at two cables and gave instructions for the boat transfer. The weather was atrocious. As we could not safely get alongside, a line was thrown from a rifle to haul over a heavier loopline with a chairbelt. This carried me aboard up high to be landed on to its superstructure. Watching my antics I thought hundreds of pairs of binoculars had been trained on me. I climbed aboard Loch Alvie to be greeted by Commander Hawke.

Following the exercises, and a brief excursion to Kirkwall, I was able to carry out some radar, meteorological and star sight navigation tasks. We continued to Egersund, with the destroyer St Kitts as our sole companion into Josingfjord, the site of the Altmark incident, before turning back to Amsterdam. There our Consul General had arranged meetings for me on JIB matters with the Naval and Military attachés, and finally we landed in Folkestone.

The third occasion, eighteen months later, was quite unexpectedly different. I reported that long after I had given up my radar duties I had been invited to visit the USA to discuss their further developments in radar research and operations with Prof C.R. Burrows of Cornell University and two US Naval Research establishments. I asked if I could combine this with a further brief stint at sea. The Admiral Commanding Reserves directed me to join the carrier HMS Perseus at Rosyth. She was setting forth for Norfolk, Virginia, on 30th December 1951 to demonstrate to the US Bureau of Ships, our new steam catapult. I arranged to take six weeks' leave.

Perseus was lying out at a buoy. The sea was so rough that I was ferried out. We sailed north to avoid the mined waters of the channel, then south, guided by the white light of Cape Wrath and headed straight for the Azores. There were now gale force winds and a heavy swell, and the ship rolled, but everyone was too busy with their duties to be ill. In the evenings we had cinema shows, the crew of about 450 being almost lost in the enormous spaces of the hanger deck. Back in the wardroom I paid 9d for four glasses of Louis Baron cognac, less than 1p per glass.

We spotted two lights about seven miles away and occasionally a third. They were on an American destroyer and a tug. At an 80-degree list we closed in on the Flying Enchantress, with her funnels below the water-line. There was nothing anyone could do to assist. We made for Bermuda, the weather improving, porpoises jumping all around us, kittiwakes diving on the quarter-deck and, as we entered the Gulf Stream, where the sea-water temperature had shot up to 71°F, eight-foot-long dolphins joined us, jumping off the port quarter.

I was busy with star sights and weather charts on 19th January when the Commander told me that Captain Poole would like me to give a talk to the ship's officers on 'Britain's Defence Effort'. Totally unprepared I tried to get out of it. 'It's just been published in Orders of the Day,' he said. There was no let out. Without any notes I just waded in, struggling to remember our defence commitments, the strength and cost of our Services which represented a sizeable part of our national economy. I had mentioned our ambitious three-year Defence Plan when I had an idea.

I said, 'Very few of our American allies realise what sacrifices Britain made in the war. When we arrive in the United States we are likely to hear impressive statements of their achievements. Our reaction should be one of admiration, but then we should ask whether they knew how we had fared, that our own casualties were a million, half a million homes had been destroyed, four million damaged, six million tonnes of merchant shipping lost, and 25% of our entire national wealth gone. Half of our national income was currently devoted to war purposes. If you have a chance, you might add it would take the combined efforts of both our countries to safeguard our future security. For half the officers and three-quarters of the ship's company, this is your first visit, yet we should all be our country's ambassadors in America.'

Approaching Bermuda, the swell had become so heavy we were concerned that the rails of the catapult built on the flight deck might buckle. We made straight for the Delaware River and Philadelphia, docking at Pier 6. Whilst I was with my colleagues beginning to train the US naval air crew on catapult launches, I received a message to go immediately to the Embassy in Washington.

Captain Poole had apparently reported my talk. Our Naval Attaché met me and introduced me to Sir Oliver Franks the Ambassador. He asked me to give an informal talk to the Governors and members of the English Speaking Union, along the lines I gave at sea. This I did on the 20th. Their hospitality was overwhelming.

My arrival in the Embassy happened to coincide with a very important visit by Winston Churchill. He was beginning his 'Indian Summer', as Prime Minister for the second time, and was making a brave attempt to do something to restore Britain's declining fortunes. We were economically weak and militarily becoming dependent on the US. He had travelled on the Queen Mary for talks with President Truman to address both Houses of Congress. On the 19th I met him for a moment as he was walking out of the Embassy with the Ambassador. He asked me how long I'd served in Washington. I said, 'This is only a short visit, but I was here in the Spring of 1945.'

'My first visit was in 1895,' he replied.

Franks then joined in, 'Is that when you met Mark Twain, Prime Minister?'

'No, that was five years later; he took the chair at my first public meeting. We were both living in sin at that time, I told him – America fighting in the Philippines, we in South Africa.' Churchill was looking old and tired, but he straightened himself, turned to me and added pugnaciously, 'I'm off to meet my friend Bernard Baruch now. I mustn't keep him waiting, he's older than me.'

The days that followed included my visit to Ithaca for discussions with research staff and industrialists at Cornell. I was suddenly offered jobs by two visiting scientists, one from RCA Victor Division in New Jersey, the other Convair in San Diego. That apparently was how spontaneously things were done in America. I had just been promoted in the Ministry of Defence and had no intention of moving so simply said I would have to think about it. Then I attended two Sessions of the 82nd Congress in the House and in the Senate, thanks to Senator Fulbright's sponsorship, and took a trip to New York and to Milford Haven's apartment at 510 Park Avenue. After only a brief conversation, once again, his other guest invited me to join his firm, Clark H. Getts Inc, head hunters! It was a lucrative offer, but I had no wish to become part of Britain's post war Brain Drain.

On then, to the Naval Air Station at Anacostia where more discussions were arranged, radar operations in the Pacific, and finally to Georgia and Florida.

Of all the Officer's Messes I have ever visited, that at Jacksonville was the most remarkable. It was at the water's edge, surrounded by walnut trees, palms, poinsettias, hibiscus, bougainvillea and sweet azaleas: a beautiful spot. It had deep carpeting and was expensively furnished. It was overcrowded with wives saying goodbye to husbands on their way to Korea. At dinner I sat down to a mighty T-bone steak and a whole pineapple filled with fresh fruit. It was preceded by a huge powerful cocktail, known as an Arkansas Stumplifter. I vaguely remember the barman carefully pouring out seven layers of liqueurs – absinthe, cointreau, kummel, crème de menthe, benedictine, chartreuse and grand marnier – I need no excuse for forgetting in which order, before he stirred them up! We were accompanied throughout the evening by two dance bands. For full board residence I was charged sixty cents a day.

I flew off from the McDill Air Force Base, Tampa, en route to the Azores with Bermuda as our first hop. Because the weather reports were so bad we had to stay overnight at the US Air Force Base in Bermuda. In the morning I saw a crocodile of schoolchildren walking into a church. As I entered Government House I noticed the Union Jack flying at half mast. The King had just died. I called on our Resident Naval Officer to pay my respects then went off to the airfield where our pilot, Wing Commander Frogley, had decided not to risk the Azores weather, but take off instead for Gander, Newfoundland. From there, where we refuelled and took off again, we had to return after 300 miles due to our engines seriously overheating. On inspection it was discovered that in Bermuda we had been given faulty lubricating oil. A heavy snowstorm then descended on Gander; the snowploughs were buried; visibility was virtually zero and all flights were cancelled. BOAC came to the rescue, making us guests at their Caribou Club. We were marooned for three days. Thinking back, we might have got away sooner had there not been so many attractive stewardesses marooned there too. It was not until 10th February that we landed in Lincolnshire, at RAF Manby.

So ended my immensely happy and rewarding association with the Royal Navy, begun in the war and ending in the Cold War. However, a year later, an unpaid wine bill from Gander arrived on my desk.

In Plain Clothes 1947–54

Whilst my intelligence duties kept me fully occupied I managed to pursue one or two additional interests. I had virtually lost touch with my old University, but learned in 1949 that a small London group of graduates had been founded in 1906, and had lapsed. With the Vice-Chancellor's (Sir John Stopford) backing I volunteered to re-convene it. Professor TS Ashton, now at the London School of Economics agreed to be its Chairman and Lord Woolton, the University Chancellor, its President, and as Secretary I arranged the functions. We dined for four years at the old Frascati Restaurant in Oxford Street, the Café Royal in Regent Street and once in the Tower of London.

As many as a hundred of us reminisced about our student days, in Owen's College as it used to be known. Ashton had argued with Christabel Pankhurst in 1906 about votes for women; ten of us had been there in Queen Victoria's reign, five having received knighthoods. Lord Webb Johnson had been a young physician and Professor Blackett told us how the work of Rutherford and Bragg attracted students from all over the world. At the time, the University had been surrounded by the attractive homes of rich cotton merchants and landowners, but following the devastation from wartime bombing the neighbourhood had become derelict and a slum – criminals squatting in roofless accommodation, the neighbourhood of Moss Side turning into an area where drugs, rape and murder were rife. Blackett commented on the fact that, in spite of this adversity, the University had maintained its position in the arts and sciences: 'it was a triumph of mind over matter'.

It was from Lord Woolton that I gained my first impression of the value of mobility in transferring experience from business to politics. His success in running a major domestic business, Lewis's of Liverpool, resulted in his appointment to Minister of Food in the War Cabinet, organising the supply and rationing of our food throughout the war. At one of our University Convocation gatherings over which he presided I asked him what was the most valuable thing he had learned, to qualify him? He said that after World War I he saw how they did things in America. He reached out for the menu and wrote something on the back. 'Excuse the doggerel,' he said, and I read it aloud:

It's not in devising a system that the fearful dangers lurk
It's not in devising a system but in making the system work.
For the working out of the system is not in the hands of the great
But rests on the shoulders of poor little clerks, like Mary and Jane and Kate.

It then fell to me to thank our President. I could not resist asking him to explain how, as a Manchester student and now its Chancellor he was ennobled as Lord Woolton of Liverpool – to some, a red rag to a bull!

'Actually, it was my third choice,' he replied. 'As Frederick Marquis, I had written to the King's Private Secretary, asking if I could keep my family name. He replied tersely, 'I am commanded to inform you that any more marquises, His Majesty will create himself.' We lived in Brook Street, Mayfair, but had an idyllic country cottage on the banks of Lake Windermere. I suggested that name to my wife. She was horrified! What would that make me? Reluctantly I turned to my Parliamentary constituency, which was in Liverpool.'

My Milbourne Grove digs were but a short walk to Imperial College and there, in the Royal School of Mines I was given the laboratory facilities of a PhD student. I had already published, jointly with my father in 1942, a letter to *Nature* describing our experiments on the structure of some forms of silica in a colloidal state. I now continued independently and went on to publish five more papers in *Nature*, *Science*, the *Journal of the American Chemical Society* and finally in the *Journal de Chimie-Physique* in Paris, all on the structure and mode of formation of naturally occurring forms of silica, flint, agate, opal and itacolumite, a sandstone, uniquely flexible, made up of interlocking quartz crystals, found near Itacolumi in Brazil. Its mode of formation had been explained in different ways on the basis of its characteristics in the field. I was able to show under what conditions they could be synthesised in the laboratory, by rhythmic deposition, known as the Liesegang phenomenon. The variables – temperature, acidity and fluxes present – determined which particular minerals were formed. The significance of this was the indication it gave of the geothermal conditions once prevailing naturally. One of the attractions of this work for me was that changes in a colloidal medium occur slowly, so for the next three years I needed to be in the laboratory only three times a week, at weekends and in the evenings.

My Civil Service career began in February 1947 at the Joint Intelligence Bureau, in the bedroom occupied before the war by the Duchess of Windsor's maid. The Duchess, to be accurate, was still just Mrs Wallis Simpson, otherwise known as The Kingfisher, a rare bird. She was living nearby in Bryanston Court.

I reported at Bryanston Square on 10th February 1947 to be shown, by lift, corridor and narrow staircase, up to a room in the attic – my new office. The building had been commandeered during the war and occupied by General Doolittle with his US 8th Army Air Force and the interior showed all the signs of their graffiti, which still adorned the walls.

The bedroom could never have been attractive; it was dingy, with a tiny window and now torn linoleum on the floor. A small cast iron coke fire gave out little heat, and its only redeeming feature was a solid mahogany senior officer's desk with twelve drawers. The steel filing cabinet in the corner was empty, apart from the bottom drawer which was jammed shut.

The following day, out of curiosity, I forced open the drawer to find confidential files compiled by Hugh Gaitskell, serving in the Ministry of Economic Warfare and Board of Trade, before becoming an MP. Naturally, I read everything in them.

I didn't make a note, but as far as I recall, in a file marked 'Neutral Countries' I found a memo minuted by Gaitskell to Hugh Dalton. 'The FO won't let us bully them; the Treasury won't let us bribe them. What shall we do?' More remarkably, in a 1941 file marked 'Atom: Developments', a manuscript note, 'Lindeman: Production by fission of slow neutrons would be too slow; its explosion would not affect the course of war. Thompson: a U235 bomb is a practical proposition. Churchill agrees.

Not for the Cabinet. Anderson in charge.' I sealed up the file and handed it all in, a little thrilled to have been privy to this knowledge.

A couple of days later a carpenter came up to my office toting a bag of tools. 'What do you want?' I asked.

'I'm from the Office of Works,' he puffed, and consulted a piece of paper. 'It seems you're only entitled to a six-drawer desk.' In order to achieve compliance with the rules, with minimum disruption, he proceeded to fix a block across six of my twelve drawers, damaging my one decent piece of furniture.

Under the direction of Kenneth Strong there were some 200 of us. We were organised into geographical divisions in the main, our duties to collect, collate, analyse and interpret information we received from all sources. This included reports from service attachés, international press and radio monitors checking for unintended leakages, interrogation and Security Service reports and air photographs. Information also came from our overseas offices in Singapore and Ottawa, as well as from British industrial and commercial interests around the world.

Apart from an early period when I was reporting to a Senior Research Officer whose editing and time-consuming improvements to my contributions I found highly frustrating, I respected my colleagues. I reported directly to Alan Crick, a jovial, slightly tubby man in his early thirties. He had a great sense of humour and wrote jocular little verses, which he would sit and chuckle over to himself. His easygoing demeanour hid a very quick mind, though, and he had great reserves of memory and analytical ability. At meetings I was struck by how clear and sensible his appraisals were.

He'd had an adventurous war. An able linguist, he went from London to Heidelberg University in 1938 to study for his doctorate. When war was imminent, he'd been recruited briefly as acting Vice Consul in Danzig. From there, issuing visas, he enabled many families at the last moment to escape from Nazi persecution.

Back in England he joined the army and as a major in North Africa, at great risk, he took on the identity of a young German officer, a research student friend who'd joined the Wehrmacht and was believed killed. In this capacity, Alan was incarcerated in a German officers' PoW cage. I do not know whether he had an escape arranged, but he was never suspected and succeeded in obtaining vital secrets of the German defences before El Alamein. Captured enemy documents later showed how his accurate reports had limited our casualties and conserved our resources.

Alan and I worked closely together. He peppered his conversation with many apt and pithy quotations relevant to our job. In a serious voice he would say, 'He who knows his adversary as he knows himself, will never suffer defeat, Sun Tzu, Chinese military tactician, 600 BC.'

When I married we all became the best of friends; their wedding present to us in March 1953, a set of antique silver napkin rings, is still in use. He was soon sent to the Embassy in Washington to deal with defence intelligence. When he heard I was visiting the American capital in August 1954, he invited me to stay with his family and meet many senior colleagues. Always destined for a big post, Alan later became Director of Economic Intelligence at the MoD. There were virtually no promotion prospects for intelligence officers beyond that.

Colonel Eddie Myers was concerned with another geographical area. He was the most dynamic member of staff, also with a remarkable war record. Dropped into Greece in 1942, he blew up the supply line to Rommel's Afrika Corps. The plan to rescue him by submarine failed, so he remained behind to pull together hitherto rival Greek factions into an effective group, and successfully sabotaged the Germans there. However, he then became embroiled in politics; a big mistake as it turned out. Churchill had wished to bring back the King of Greece as monarch. Myers warned the Foreign Office that without a plebiscite this would lead to civil war. Though not a very senior officer, he was hurriedly summoned to a meeting with Churchill, Eden and King George VI. He remained adamant, argued and was never allowed to return to Greece. But he made an excellent intelligence officer.

Edward Thomas, the Director's assistant, and two Assistant Directors in succession, Air Commodores Vintras and Woolley, and Martin Watson together made a strong team under Kenneth Strong. Once or twice Strong talked about his experiences and the personalities he'd met in Nazi Germany between 1937 and 1939, serving as Assistant Military Attaché in Berlin. He had spoken to Goering who was boisterous, Hess who was subdued, Jodl, 'an able planner' and to Rommel, then a Colonel and never expecting to be promoted, because he hadn't been to the all-important Staff College.

Strong told one or two of us about his conversations with German officers and, in 1938, of Kristallnacht which led to his report to London for the Cabinet and their decision to introduce conscription right away. Sir Nevile Henderson, then our Ambassador, did not share his concerns, but passed onto him a message from the Prime Minister, Neville Chamberlain, that his reports had played a large part in persuading the Cabinet to do so. He went on to predict that the German attack in 1940 would be made through the Ardennes. By 1943 Strong had become Eisenhower's head of intelligence in SHAEF and on 7th May 1945 in Rheims, he personally received the German surrender from Field Marshal Jodl. Such experienced colleagues inevitably commanded the respect of all of us.

Until I arrived at the Joint Intelligence Bureau, I'd had no experience of intelligence work and my vague impression of what it entailed may well have been formed years earlier when I'd read Somerset Maugham's *Ashenden*. However, I soon found that my job was entirely desk-bound. We had to collect information and judge its reliability as best we could. A great deal of material was reaching us from Germany and Eastern Europe, and we suspected that some of it was invented. There was a strong black market in information, including fake or doctored photographs. For some suppliers it was a sole source of income so even when the source was thought to be impeccable, we wanted to substantiate it. It wasn't our function to gather information in the field. Only once was I instructed to meet and interview an original source.

A call had come from the Home Office. A stowaway had been picked up at Tilbury, claiming political asylum. He insisted he had important information to divulge about the output of a factory in Central Europe where he was a senior manager. As I knew something about the factory, from our attachés' reports, it was decided that I should see him and assess whether or not he could be believed. I was taken to Wandsworth Jail, escorted by a Chief Warder past a procession of prisoners on remand in the exercise yard – one of them smartly attired in a waistcoat and spats: 'Five hundred watches in his car tyres,' I was told – and into a solicitor's room where I met the asylum seeker with an interpreter.

The information he had, if it were true, was significant. He confirmed what we knew and added to it substantially, but to one question he gave the wrong answer. He said that the factory Director to whom he reported, had arrived at a time, according to our information, well after he had departed, lost contact and could not have known. When I recounted this to the Home Office they were categorical.

'He was obviously well briefed, but not well enough. He's been planted and you've caught him out.'

When I realised what sinister consequences could be in store for him, I asked for more time to check our own facts. Getting back to our attachés, they found not only an error in the transcription of a date, but that information we believed had come from two independent sources had in fact emanated from a single originator by two different routes. I was never told what became of the asylum seeker and felt it better not to ask.

In international exchanges, notably with the CIA and other US agencies we usually benefitted even though in some cases, the reliability of data could not be fully tested; sources could not be revealed without endangering lives. After a year or two, we noticed a gradual reduction in the economic information coming our way, such as strategic raw material supplies, presumably because it was of potential commercial value. There also seemed to be sensitivity to other long-term domestic interests. Early in the 1950s, I noticed a definite improvement in the pooling of resources and assessments with the United States, which was after they recognised their own inadequacies once Korea became their principal target.

If there were problems in collecting reliable information, via our antennae, there were no fewer problems in the collation and analysis and in making inferences from the collation. I thought, at last, that my early observational experience and analysis in geology might not have been irrelevant after all! Individual items were rarely of critical importance. The value was created by piecing together and making sense of fragments, facts and views emanating from diplomats, bankers, mining engineers, journalists and others. For our part it called for teamwork, to enable our analysis and interpretation to assist policy makers concerned with national security. It also called for objectivity in analysis and judgement. There could be no cherry-picking of data, or wishful thinking to justify a particular stance or course of action.

We learned much about the capabilities of potential enemies, the terrain over which we might have to fight, the forces that could be ranged against us, the order of battle, the potential for danger and risk, the need to warn. Nevertheless, we and the Americans too, knew far less of their intentions. In fact, we hardly knew how to judge intentions. We had failed to predict the Berlin blockade, the Korean War and the Chinese invasion, in the same way that we were later surprised by the collapse of the Soviet Union.

Could we have done better? There were suggestions of our amateurism. I believe we could have got off to a better start in JIB. For two or three years we noticed that each of our three armed services were trying hard to retain their independence in intelligence matters. They were jealous of our centralising role. We might be strong intellectually, but retired senior officers in a civilian role should not be as influential as the top brass still on active service. From the start the services called us 'the exiles north of Marble Arch'. Perhaps we were a little less effective as a result.

However, this situation gradually changed. Kenneth Strong spoke persuasively of the importance of a co-ordinated, interdepartmental approach and the interplay between military, technological, economic, social and political forces. He also carried a particular authority in Whitehall and Westminster, annoying some senior politicians in the process by still calling Eisenhower 'Ike', long after he had become President.

On the rare occasion he mentioned Eisenhower to us, it was clear that their working relationship was admirable. Strong had direct access to him and Eisenhower wanted no detailed reports, but listened attentively to his evidence and judgement and usually acted on them.

Within our teams, we each had individual assignments. I had some responsibility for Europe, but my very first task, which seemed remote from any obvious national security concerns, was to construct a map of the geology and terrain of Afghanistan. It was required to show sources of rock for road construction, wells suitable for drinking water, caves for storage and possible oil reserves. A knowledge of Afghanistan was necessary, I was told, after our loss of India, 'to perpetuate our influence and power across the world; it might not be used for a while, but it could become important; having a geology degree, you are the best qualified to do it.'

In fact my geology had become quite rusty. The map was completed, later declassified, and a copy eventually found its way to the Anglo-Iranian Oil Company (later BP). *The Geological Magazine*, for publication purposes, however, also wanted the specific names of all the fossils in the oil-bearing areas which I didn't have. I was never asked about the map again. Twenty-two years later, in 1979, the Russian invasion of Afghanistan took the intelligence community somewhat by surprise. I have no idea if my map, later filed in the Public Record Office, was ever consulted again. I doubt it.

Within twelve to eighteen months the geopolitical scene had shifted, and so had our work. In Europe, the Czech communists had seized power in Prague, the USSR had cut all land links between West Germany and West Berlin and the NATO treaty came into being the following April.

In Asia, with the communist uprising in Malaya, we were losing the rubber and tin which formed such an important part of our dollar income. Now, included in my remit, was Korea. I was making progress.

The 25th June 1950 still stands out in my memory, not simply because it was my thirtieth birthday, but because it was also the day we learned that Soviet-supplied North Korean tanks had, without warning, crossed from North to South Korea. Unlike the Americans, we knew far too little about China and Korea, as it was not covered by the 1946 Anglo-American intelligence co-operation agreement, regarded as a matter for the US authorities. The all-important question was, if the US were to intervene by advancing on the Yalu River, would the Chinese counter attack to protect their electricity supply from North Korea? And would they do this even if it was undertaken by Korean forces?

The US was uncertain about the likely reactions of both China and the USSR. The Foreign Office, recognising the dangers, arranged an immediate meeting of the Far East (Official) Committee of the Cabinet. The head of my division, who was a member, was away and I was called to stand in. Thus, on 1st July, under the Chairmanship of Sir Esler Dening, with a dozen more senior civil servants around the table, I was confronted with the agenda 'To consider sanctions on Korea and an embargo on China'.

The others had views, but no facts. I had no opinions, but at least some information, notably Chinese industry's dependence on power supplies generated on the Korean side of the river. This I volunteered. On my return to the office I reported all this. The fact that I had been there on my own raised eyebrows. What had I let them in for? When the minutes arrived, Kenneth Strong seemed relieved and I was authorised to go to future meetings, though no longer on my own. By then Dening had been succeeded by Sir Robert Scott. This was my introduction to the gap to be bridged between Intelligence appraisals and political decisions and actions.

The Korean situation had deteriorated. By November General MacArthur had sought permission to bomb the Yalu River bridges, Chinese bases near the Suiho dam and airfields in Manchuria. The Russians had threatened to retaliate and American reaction was critical. MacArthur's plan was turned down. They were anxious days early in December when Attlee flew off to Washington.

In the office we were asked for any ideas to put to the Joint Intelligence, Planning, or Chiefs of Staffs Committees. I could think of only one small tactic. Could we get to their airfields surreptitiously and sabotage their aircraft to prevent take-off? Could we tamper with their stock of aviation fuel? It might at least provide more time for diplomacy.

I then remembered meeting Alexander Fleck at a scientific gathering; now he was a director of ICI. I rang and asked if I could see him. On 14th December I was ushered into his office. I explained that I couldn't reveal the circumstances in which this might apply, but technically, could aviation fuel be treated easily to make it useless? He smiled. 'Have you ever seen a honeymoon couple failing to get away from the wedding reception because someone had put sherbet in their petrol tank?' I reported back to my office with this flimsy suggestion and heard no more. I suppose it was nothing to do with the sherbet, but soon after that Fleck became Chairman of ICI and was elevated to the House of Lords.

The 9th July 1953 was a day to remember for quite different reasons. Although my 'territory' had been extended to the Far East, I continued to debrief our attachés serving in embassies across Europe. Group Captain Peter Townsend had been despatched as Air Attaché to Brussels, and on a visit to London, he was due to spend a short time with me, by now in our Northumberland Avenue offices. However, my secretary came in to report that a pack of newshounds and photographers had gathered outside the building and were waiting to catch him. Ever since Princess Margaret's formal announcement ending all prospect of their marriage, he had been trying to evade them. We sent out a message that Townsend had apparently already left the building by another exit, and after another couple of hours they finally disappeared.

Over sandwiches, meanwhile, he revealed a little more about his relationship with the Palace than had appeared in the Press. He told me that the King had actually encouraged him and Princess Margaret to spend time together. In fact, the King knew and approved of their wish to marry and he also knew that some courtiers did not share this view. Although the decision would eventually be his, the King, according to Townsend, knowing the mindset of courtiers, had no intention of expressing his approval prematurely. The abdication of his brother was still in everyone's mind. And then the King died.

One of my regrets, particularly after becoming a senior research officer in 1951 was how little we were told, after all our painstaking work, of how our reports might be used. Had we known of policy interests and concerns, to what uses our briefings might be applied, had there been some interaction and feedback from users – Chiefs of Staff or politicians – we might have been better able to focus on specific issues, answer particular questions and make more constructive use of our time and knowledge. Elements of risk, uncertainties, or probabilities usually entered into evaluations. What assurance did policy-makers need to act on our best appraisals?

We knew that intelligence was just one, though an all-important, element of decision taking, but we did not know how our carefully prepared analyses and recommendations could be influenced and even overridden by factors beyond our control, whether they were the beliefs of Ministers, attitudes of the electorate or the policies of our allies – or simply 'inconvenient'.

After nearly eight years in intelligence, I began to think of my own future. I was no longer receiving any job offers. This was hardly surprising. Our personal identity had almost vanished and our market value must certainly have fallen, as we could not discuss our work with anyone, not even our spouses. I had to ask myself whether there really was a long-term career for me in JIB. Internally, the problem was that retirements and resignations were few; staff numbers could not be increased and promotion prospects were therefore limited. I was fortunately, one of the minority to have received a step up, and had loyally soldiered on.

The Directorate recognised this lack of prospects, but were loath to lose any of us. It took, they said, ten to twenty years to mould first class intelligence officers and they intended to keep them. The trouble was that without inter-departmental mobility, career opportunities compared unfavourably with those elsewhere in the Civil Service.

Nevertheless, on balance, the pros of sticking it out outweighed the cons. The Cold War was essentially a conflict of intelligence. We felt needed; our joint efforts and our determination made for an amenable and stimulating working environment. The effect of bringing together the scholarly research approach of some with the operational, organisational, entrepreneurial and presentational skills of others was to create an environment and culture which produced results that were considered valuable in averting potential dangers.

This is not to suggest that intelligence officers or the intelligence community, as they came to be known, or the policy makers for that matter, always got it right. We had overestimated, as it turned out, Russian military capabilities in the late 1940s. The CIA's warnings on Vietnam, on the other hand, were apparently rejected by President Johnson. But much needed intelligence was lacking as a result of inadequate resources. Priorities had to be established under conditions of great uncertainty and funded over lengthy periods in the hope of bearing fruit.

I would have liked then to be able to contribute to the debate on what proportion of our national income we should allocate to our intelligence services, considered as the premium payable on an insurance policy. But of course, the sources and types of threats and our vulnerability were constantly shifting, so no natural ratio could be calculated. What proportion of our defence and security expenditure intelligence should command was obviously a political matter for the Chancellor and other Ministers. Sir Kenneth Strong's case was that the less Britain had to spend on material preparations for war, the more important it was to spend what we could on a first-class intelligence system. All the intelligence community could do, having made its case, was to demonstrate that their analysis was as accurate as possible, and their efforts were cost-effective.

CHAPTER III

Family Matters

At the end of the war my links with Manchester had become quite tenuous, brief visits limited to the few occasions I could join my parents and sister on High Days and Holy Days. I still had no thoughts of marriage, though no wish to remain a bachelor all my life. Any prospects in that direction would probably emerge where I worked and lived, but I had no suitable contacts in London.

My introduction to the London Jewish community came, not from any synagogue affiliation, but from a visiting speaker who came to address us at the RN College in Greenwich, Professor Norman Bentwich. He had once been Attorney General in Palestine during the British Administration. I introduced myself. When I told him of my father's scientific collaboration with Chaim Weizmann, he was so interested that he eventually recounted at length his own background.

'My father, Herbert, having heard Herzl speak in 1895 of his plan for a Jewish state in the Land of Israel, went there with the first pilgrimage of British Jews. I studied at Cambridge, Hellenistic and Jewish history and went out there myself when I was about your age, in 1909. I had no career but wanting to make it my home I joined the Egyptian Ministry of Justice. War came, I was a Captain in the Camel Corps and entered Jerusalem a few days after General Allenby's occupation in 1917. When I was appointed Attorney General to introduce the new legal system I aimed to bring equality and harmony between Jews and Arabs, but the political disturbances in 1929 made my position untenable. I accepted the Chair of International Law and Peace at the Hebrew University with the same aim, but spending some time in London.

'You must meet my wife's family,' he said. Helen ('Mamie'), who later became Chairman of the London County Council, arranged for me to meet the family – Ellis and Muriel Franklin and their five children.

As a result of this I joined their synagogue, the New West End in St Petersburgh Place, where their cousin Herbert Samuel was a lifelong member. When I met him months later he regaled me with his memory of the Day of Atonement in 1914 when three suffragettes came rushing in during the service shouting 'Votes for Women'. 'I don't believe they knew that a member of the War Cabinet was in the congregation,' he said. There, the rabbi Ephraim Levine was a star turn. Originally from Glasgow, as he read from the service in the 'Rejoicing of Law' of the death of Moses, it sounded as though Moses himself was speaking Hebrew with a Scottish accent.

There was an active communal centre over which Ewen Montagu presided and, within a year, I found myself elected Chairman. My supportive Vice-Chairman told me, 'That was only because the girls preferred your naval uniform.' Ewen Montagu himself soon became well-known through his wartime work in naval intelligence. 'Operation Mincemeat' was the successful top-secret plan to deceive the enemy and the origin of his book and film *The Man Who Never Was*, which were to bring him fame.

Bentwich, discovering my scientific background, recruited me as a British Friend of the Hebrew University, with a job to do. A Humanitarian Trust Fund had been set up to select and finance Hebrew University science graduates to undertake research at British universities, both Jews and Arabs. I interviewed many and, to those we made awards, most finished up occupying professorships in Israel and elsewhere. I was invited to become a Governor of the University, but had to decline as I was about to be appointed to Paris.

Elected to the Council of the Anglo-Jewish Association, I had met leading members of the community: Keith Joseph, Bernard Waley-Cohen, Philip Magnus, Tom Sebag-Montefiore and Henry d'Avigdor Goldsmid. They were a diverse, interesting and successful group. Most were second-

or third-generation immigrants who had prospered with the freedom they had found in Britain and enjoyed the most comfortable family lives. Some had arrived earlier, fleeing from the Inquisition or Pogroms in the successive waves of immigration from Spain and Portugal, the Netherlands, and others from Tsarist Russia. They survived their change in culture, gradually assimilated, some attaining high public office, and many tenaciously holding on to their Jewish practices. They made me welcome, to the point of inviting me to meet their daughters!

Many of the families I met were inter-related and became known as 'The Cousinhood'. To meet them, generally, was a pleasant experience. I say generally because of one particular occasion I had invited Leah, very young and vivacious, to a concert. I arrived at her large house and was greeted by her mother, a rather fussy woman dripping with jewels, when Leah came downstairs wearing a striking mink coat. 'Oh not that one, darling, your other one!' Up she went and came down in a magnificent sable coat. I knew enough about furs to estimate it would have taken me five or ten years at my salary to pay for it. A high maintenance woman!

In one or two cases I knew I would have received, as was then still expected, parental approval. But Jennifer, singleminded of purpose, as a distinguished academic in the arts, never married. Marion and Jane were just about to marry. At dinner one night Jane's mother apologised because her husband, a presiding judge, was still at work. When he got home she said, 'Did you finally sort out that divorce action? Incompatibility, wasn't it?'

'Yes,' he replied, 'It was simply a question of his income and her patability!'

And then there was Jean. I was already twenty-eight, perhaps over-cautious about marriage. She was six years younger, outgoing, very attractive and rather special. We had been introduced by a WRNS officer, a mutual friend in Portsmouth, now she was enjoying life in London. With a delightful voice, she was training to become a professional singer. And her parents, leading lights in the Jewish community backed her in this. I arranged for her to have an audition at the Royal Albert Hall, as

I was an honorary steward there. We met more frequently and began an exhilarating social round. Affection grew on both sides, I proposed, she accepted and we happily announced our engagement. Her parents came to Manchester to visit mine, wedding invitations were sent out, presents began to arrive and from a family trust her parents would give us a house in St John's Wood. Keith Joseph, Jean's second cousin, readily agreed to be my best man and the gossip columnists of the Press were complimentary.

It was only then I hesitated. I felt there was something wrong, something missing, something intangible. Whatever it was, we had to discuss it. We had spoken of love; our mutual affection certainly had developed to a degree that made going back a worrying prospect, but we discovered we both had doubts about a life together. As congratulations were being heaped on us, the wedding getting closer, our worries escalated. It was hard to make a break, but without total commitment we agreed we could not proceed. We made another Press announcement: 'the marriage would not now take place'. We returned each other's letters and were both thoroughly miserable.

My father wrote to me: 'If marriages are made in heaven, you should have to thank Providence for the timely intervention. Your future seemed to be based on quicksand and a happy married life doubtful. You have not impaired your character. *Gam zu letova* (may all be for the best).' It was, however, a real setback for us all.

Eleven years were to go by before Jean married, and then with the happiness she deserved. For my part it was four years. Then I discovered that Diana's mother's family motto was 'All for the best'.

One evening in 1951 I was invited to a Deb dance in Sussex Square, Hyde Park, for the eligible younger generation. In my thirties, I was almost past it. The small band in the drawing room had struck up and everyone rushed to a partner. I was slow off the mark and left standing, directly facing a wallflower. I had no idea who she was. She seemed surprised when I asked her to dance. Very gingerly, we took to the floor and said little. By the end of the evening all I learned was her name, Diana, and that she had just finished school in Cheltenham and was awaiting exam results. I knew, though it seemed unbelievable, this was love at first sight.

I soon found out that I had met her elder sister Susan Castello a couple of years earlier, but not her parents – fortunately, as it turned out. A friend and I had at the time taken Susan back home to Bucklebury only to find she had been locked out in the middle of the night. I managed to shin up a drainpipe and open a bathroom window, creeping down in the dark to open the door. I trod on the Bedlington's tail! A great hullabaloo followed whilst I escaped unrecognised. My identity was only discovered, purely by accident, many years later.

On Diana's birthday I sent her eighteen red roses. Over the next year Diana studied Italian at the University of Perugia; I continued work in Whitehall until Diana returned to take on a job with an Australian bank. Living in St George's Square we could at last see each other.

I wrote to Diana and kept her replies. I have never asked whether she kept mine. In any event they did not compare with hers. Her first one came in October:

Dear Alkon

The spelling of your most original name has quite beaten me.

Do you seriously want to come for a walk? After the dance you said you would like to, but after an evening of wine, women and song, one is inclined to say idiotic things. If you <u>were</u> serious how would Nov. 4th suit? I plan to go on a 5 or 6 hour hike – my last fling before exams!

Hoping to hear from you, but expecting not to.

On 16th May, her nineteenth birthday, when she was staying at the home of her elderly cousin at 3 Sussex Square, she wrote:

With thanks for the 19 red roses. Yesterday I was lying in the orchard at home sucking grass and Mummy sat beside me. I knew she wanted to say something, and she did.

She said that people of your age didn't normally pay a lot of attention to one girl, unless they were serious about her. She only wanted to warn me, so that I should never have to hurt you.

After tea Daddy, who's not usually very observant said how very much he liked my new coat, and the way I dressed. That was worth a thousand ordinary compliments.

We spent much more time together and announced our engagement on New Year's Eve.

I had already said, 'I imagine your father will be expecting me to get his permission to marry you as you are still only nineteen.'

'If I were you,' Diana said, 'I'd speak to Mummy first.' And this I did. I thought there might be some reservation because of our thirteen-year age difference, but it was never mentioned. Diana's parents happened to have been exactly our ages when they married. Her father had been a soldier and marathon runner and now they were living quietly in Bucklebury, Berkshire, content to give their time to good causes and voluntary council work.

Her mother's comment was memorable. 'You'll find Diana will give you her absolute loyalty.'

Her father avoided the issue. 'Do you go to the races?' he asked. I admitted I did occasionally. 'Never place your money with a bookie who's wearing running pumps.' That was the only advice I ever received from my father-in-law!

Ellis Castello had gone almost directly from school at Clifton into the Royal Field Artillery when war broke out, won a Military Cross, but claimed they had made a mistake – he hadn't deserved it. He retired as a young Major on finding that married life and army life in peacetime were not the ideal combination. He was recalled in World War II to train courageous volunteers to be dropped by parachute into occupied Europe and operate behind enemy lines.

He told me that in the first war, so little was widely known about the activities of Jewish servicemen, it was believed they had shirked their duty. Even though they were denigrated, he had no wish to broadcast his own role. But years later, I found a copy of a book compiled to refute this and when I presented it to him, he was embarrassed. Entitled *British Jewry, Book of Honour 1914–18*, it listed 60,000 service names and I read from his Military Cross citation:

> *For conspicuous gallantry … with the enemy on his flank and in rear …*
> *restored communications under constant machine gun fire and rifle fire …*
> *His fearlessness inspired all ranks.*

'They didn't realise,' he replied, 'there was such a hell of a noise, that I never heard them shout, 'Get Back. You haven't a chance'.'

I was fascinated to read in the book, incidentally, the social class distinctions that prevailed. From Polack's, the Jewish Boys' House at Clifton, there were 132 officers (twenty-four killed) and just six other ranks, but from the Jewish Free School in the East End of London, nineteen officers and 1210 other ranks.

Whilst I was busy in my office Diana and her mother were busier still preparing for a large wedding. Together we made a hectic round of visits, invited by a large circle of family and friends. On 18th March we were married by Ephraim Levine at the New West End Synagogue, where he had been Minister since 1916, and went on to a reception at 45 Park Lane, soon to be transformed into the Bunny Club! I don't think Diana enjoyed either the ceremony or the reception, she always preferred more private, low-key occasions. In any event we escaped as soon as we could to spend our wedding night at Great Fosters, the former home of a cousin, in a giant four-poster bed. Convenient for London airport, we left for Italy in the morning.

My Ministry of Defence colleagues had put me in touch with 'Leonardo' Walsh, an Irishman who, for forty years, had lived in a small picturesque locanda at Punta San Vigilio, perched on the bank of Lake Garda. There he took in a few 'guests' and we had a two-week reservation. We arrived to see *chiuso* hanging ominously over the entrance. From behind a lace curtain a face appeared, so I waved my letter. He seemed reluctant to let us in, had obviously been drinking, but took us up to our room.

I saw the minute hip-bath. 'I asked for a bath,' I said.

'Everyone wants a bath and not a shower,' he replied. 'The Duff Coopers were always complaining; Winston Churchill wanted a bath. There is no room for a bath, but I have just installed this especially for you.' Thereafter, we were treated to his delicious home cooking, lake fish and fine wines. When we were about to leave I asked for the bill and he changed the subject. Our departure was delayed by a round-the-lake cycle race, but eventually I said we had to pay immediately and go. 'No bill,' he said 'but you might call on an old friend living in London and give her my best wishes.' He handed me a card with a lady's Sloane Street address. We left without paying.

Once back in London, I telephoned her, she asked me round to tell her about Leonardo. I wondered whether I could give her a present, and not insult her if I put some money in an envelope. A good-looking woman, perhaps seventy years old, let me in – no doubt a pre-war girlfriend. Over tea I picked up courage, handed her the envelope and without opening it she said, 'Oh Leonardo is always doing something like this.' A thought passed my mind: there was exchange control in Italy at the time!

In London I moved out of Milborne Grove and we took a flat nearby in Lady St Oswald's house in Gilston Road, opposite Douglas Fairbanks' home in the Boltons, where we spent most of our first two years of married life.

It was at this time when, meeting Diana's extended family, I learned something of them and their fortunes. Descendants of successive waves of Jewish immigration into Britain, much earlier than my own – what difference time and culture make.

My parents' arrival from Tsarist Russia contrasted sharply with Diana's forebears, from the Inquisition, via Amsterdam in 1630 and from Prague in 1459. Among the more colourful characters was David Castello, born in London in 1790, building a sugar and quinine fortune in the Caribbean and then in New York and, financing Simon Bolivar, instrumental in achieving liberty and independence for Colombia.

Diana's mother was the granddaughter of Alfred Cohen (1836–1903) who was a great-grandson of Levi Barent Cohen, born in The Netherlands in 1747. In 1869 Alfred married Louise Marie Sophie Javal of France and, as a businessman, set up in Bevis Marks, whilst living at 8 Bury Street, SW1. He was the direct link by marriage between the two financial dynasties of Goldsmid and Rothschild and first cousin of Sir Samuel Montagu, the first Lord Swaythling (1832–1911). I was fascinated to read the two leather bound volumes of family letters we were given of the Cohens' family life in the 1880s. Alfred Cohen, in advising his son George at Harrow, wrote:

Remember, you come from a family of Jews that have held an unsullied reputation in England for 170 years – maintain our honour and prestige.

A few excerpts of his observations on education, contemporary politics, philosophy and his attempts to be funny give a flavour of the times:

Very bad news from Egypt. The Government have abandoned Gordon. For three months Sir E. Baring in Cairo has been imploring the Government to send help, Gladstone just sends fine phrases and telegrams, but no troops.

Sorry you lost your 'tails' – better than losing your head. But perhaps you lost your head, and therefore lost your tails.

Send your school account to Mamma to be audited. Ices £4-6-0, books ½d! You should see that the charm of an ice melts away, but that of the book remains.

I went today over the school with Lord Randolph Churchill, then School Dinner Speeches with Matthew Arnold.

The Russians have designs on Herat. Do not let your letters become 'erratic'; it requires a surgical operation to get a letter from you.

Egypt is a humiliation for an Englishman. Contrast the position this country fills today, with that of 1815. You would soon be cured of your liberalism if you read more.

'Station<u>e</u>ry' – Do not fall into slovenly spelling habits. Many a man has lost a fine civil service appointment by that. If you were to see what Lord Byron had written by the age of 17, you would be ashamed of your own ignorance.

I have sent you a copy of the Paddington Mercury containing a report of Uncle Lionel's speech. He and Lord Randolph Churchill have been selected as Conservative Candidates for Paddington.

The educated people of this country are ashamed of Gladstone. We are now governed by the Demos – as in Athens of old, led by the glib tongue of the brilliant orator and the smooth phrases of the rhetorician.

Netta Montagu is engaged to be married to Cousin Ernest Franklin. It is indispensible that you write a letter of congratulation – I send you this sketch letter. There was a grand ball at the Montagus' last night – a profusion of flowers <u>and</u> electric light.

Whereas Lord Beaconsfield bought back from Berlin Peace with honour, Gladstone has secured dishonour without peace.

Thomas has given me notice. He has been offered a place as first footman with some Lord who has half a dozen – very awkward in the middle of the season – at the same time as a kitchen maid is going to be married and William, the old groom, has to go to hospital.

What a very different background and relationship this was compared with mine with my father.

George, in spite of his father's criticism of his spelling, won a school prize in 1883. The full leather-bound illustrated copy of *Stories from Herodotus* came our way, still housed in mint condition in his father's bookcase.

Two memorable encounters I had in the 1950s were with Herbert Samuel and Rosalind Franklin. Herbert Samuel was the first practising Jew in the Cabinet, becoming Viscount Samuel of Toxteth and Mount Camel. He was Home Secretary in 1915 in the Liberal Cabinet and in 1931 in Ramsay MacDonald's National Government, but he turned down a further invitation from Neville Chamberlain to come back in 1938.

I first met him in 1950, before I knew Diana, at the twenty-fifth anniversary dinner in London of the Hebrew University of Jerusalem. He read out Churchill's message sent from Chartwell: 'As an unfaltering Zionist... I hope and believe... the University will proclaim to a distracted generation true progress, not only in literature, scholarship and science, but in those tolerant, comprehending humanities, without which all the rest is only mockery to human beings.'

On his eightieth birthday that year, the University designated a Professorship in his name. Unduly modest in accepting it, he said, 'I could never have been a Professor Herbert Samuel, but I am glad to think there will be a Herbert Samuel Professor.'

Three years later, he agreed to propose our health as bride and bridegroom, but unfortunately went down with pneumonia and missed the wedding altogether. Now that his great-niece was my wife I could tell him of my own conversation with Churchill in Washington. But his own association went back to when they joined the Government in 1905 and frequently walked to the Commons together, after dining at the Bachelor's Club.

'Winston would try to explain why, as the son of a popular Conservative leader, he aligned himself with the Liberals. He and I were quite different in character. He was a free spirit, and when in 1914 Belgium was invaded, roaring to fight, he arrived at a levee proudly besporting an impressive row of medals on his cavalry uniform.

'When I was trying to end the General Strike in 1925/6, I held some meetings in Bryanston Square – at Sir Abe Bailey's house – and Winston not only came along, but became my strongest supporter. It was only in the thirties, when he received intelligence reports privately of serious German rearmament that he disassociated himself totally from Liberalism.'

He described himself as an ameliorist, always expecting things to get better. I was flattered when he would discuss philosophy, ethics and morality with me. He sent me a copy of his book and paid me the compliment of asking for my scientific criticism of his 1950 *Essay in Physics*.

He was ninety-one years old when he and 'Aunt Bea' Franklin celebrated their sixty-fifth wedding anniversary with a large family gathering. 'Now I am approaching advanced middle age,' he said, 'I propose to speak for one hour only.' Then he went on: 'The finest and longest standing institution in the world is the Family – universal, with the exception of the cuckoo. I will tell you the secret of family success – I took only the big decisions.'

A great-grandchild asked, 'How do you decide what is a big and what is a small decision?'

'Your great-grandmother decided how many children we should have, where we should live and how much money we should spend. I decided how we should vote, how to end the Miners' Strike and our policy within the League of Nations!'

I first met Diana's cousin, Rosalind Franklin, on a whirlwind tour 'to meet the family' early in 1953. We were exact contemporaries and she spoke modestly of her early scientific research work in Paris. Now she was back in London I looked forward to hearing more.

On 2nd June, at my desk in the Joint Intelligence Bureau, the Coronation Procession was to pass below my office window in Northumberland Avenue and Diana and I could view it from there. Arriving early I took some magazines and journals to catch up on some reading when I spotted a letter from Crick and Watson in an April number of *Nature*. They stated they were stimulated in their work on DNA by knowledge of the general nature of Rosalind's unpublished experimental results and ideas. When we next met I congratulated her. She explained that working with Wilkins at Kings College London, her photograph No. 51 had shown the helical structure of DNA, and her measurements probably meant that the helix strands ran in opposite directions. Wilkins, apparently, had shown her photograph to Watson in January and the measurements, which she reported to the Medical Research Council in February, were passed on by Max Perutz.

'Is the credit for this going in the wrong direction?' I asked.

'Klug thinks so,' she replied. 'The pieces of the jigsaw I provided seem to fit perfectly, but one must be sure.' Klug's opinion was significant, he went on to win the Nobel Prize and receive the Order of Merit.

Five years later Rosalind died. She was just thirty-seven. Watson and Crick then jointly won the Nobel Prize for the work. Many believed she should have shared in it too. Hers was a vital contribution about which she was modest. Certainly, Watson's 1968 account in *Double Helix* was totally contradicted by Sir Aaron Klug. Rosalind's name was perpetuated elsewhere and in the National Portrait Gallery we can now see her photograph hanging alongside those of the Nobel Prizewinners. But for her, the ultimate prize, stretching for generations beyond her own short life, was the fundamental contribution she made to the Life Sciences.

When my parents arrived in England they embraced a new culture and a new patriotism to the country giving them asylum and opportunity. They could continue to espouse the Zionist cause. In October 1914, my father, now Chaim Weizmann's research assistant, received a letter from him as he was travelling back to Manchester University. He wrote, 'With a Prussian victory all Jewish hopes – including the Zionist – must fall. I conceive this as a struggle between Siegfried and Moses, and Moses withstood things worse than seventeen-inch guns.'

But the attitude of those long established here was very different. Diana and I came from two different camps. This disparity came to the fore over the Balfour Declaration. Weizmann, on the one hand, pleading for a Jewish homeland in Palestine and Edwin Samuel, on the other hand, convinced that a Jewish state would eventually send well-established Anglo-Jewry – bankers and politicians – 'back to the ghetto'. The Samuels and the

Montagus were supported by Curzon, Lord President and former Viceroy of India; Weizmann by Balfour and Lloyd George.

My father told me that Balfour had originally been introduced to Weizmann in 1906 by a Dr Dreyfus, formerly Chairman of the East Manchester Parliamentary Constituency, when Balfour was in dire need of a safe Parliamentary seat and that Lloyd George re-introduced Weizmann to Balfour during the war.

By 1920, when Britain held the mandate for Palestine, and Herbert Samuel was appointed High Commissioner he became, as he put it, 'the first Jewish Governor of Jerusalem for 1,850 years. Even though I was a member of the British establishment, most Jews were happy,' he told me. 'They called me 'Hanassi', the Prince! And whilst many Arabs were apprehensive, the Emir Feisal wrote to me in 1919: 'We Arabs, especially the educated among us, look with deepest sympathy on the Zionist movement. We wish the Jews a hearty welcome home. We are working together for a reformed and revised Near East, our two movements complementing one another.''

Before he left, and in spite of all the controversial decisions he had to take, he felt proud of the fact that Jewish enterprise there had supported the opening of 200 new schools for Arabs, and highly appreciative of the tribute paid to him by King Abdullah of Jordan. Five years later he returned to England by battleship.

By the 1950s I found myself sitting opposite him at services at the New West End Synagogue. He had a reputation for cool, dispassionate judgment. Certainly he was outwardly unemotional, but there were moments in the services when he was deeply moved.

As was customary, Passover was the time for family discussions. I conducted the Seder services, just as my father had done; Diana's invitations were keenly awaited and the children were enthusiastic participants. From the 1960s my themes would often extend beyond the Biblical one, the story of the Exodus. 'Can you imagine,' I'd ask, 'what it would have been like if you'd actually been there, in Egypt? Or persecuted in medieval times, driven out of Spain or Portugal, Russia or Nazi Germany, if it had been your family home for centuries?'

I told them of the Austrian refugee girl, who my parents sponsored when Hitler came to power. At our Seder service in Manchester in 1935, I think, she told us of the distinguished, patriotic service of her family throughout the nineteenth century, of their recognition for bravery in World War I, and now suddenly stripped of their status, deprived of their liberty, and awaiting the worst. They had long been assimilated, never thought of their identity, but others did.

As our children grew older and eventually left home, they have contributed their own experiences. Our younger daughter Rosalind was living in Amsterdam, close to where her ancestors lived in the seventeenth century. They were contemporaries of the Dutch philosopher Spinoza and we debated his ethics and radical ideas on the Bible. A man of remarkable intellect, considered one of the great 'rationalists', he was shunned by the Jewish authorities for his controversial religious ideas, which had none of the faith and hope or inspiration of the prophets – the keynote of our Seder service, upon which our survival over the millennia has depended.

It took years of repetition of our Biblical history recounted at our Seder Service, refreshing my memory, for me to grasp fully its significance. I began to appreciate what freedom meant. Life without oppression I had taken for granted. It took longer, having discovered how my parents had suffered, to realise the importance, especially in adversity, of living in hope. Through all this, my sister and I were left in no doubt about our identity, and our inheritance. She went on to teach children in England and America and, later became an influential Hebrew teacher, even to the grandchildren of her contemporaries.

For my part, before leaving school, in the essay I had to write on the Thirteen Principles of Faith, I had to find as many examples as I could to illustrate each of them in the weekly portions we read from the Torah in the course of a year. Then I went off to university to study science where I was to learn that belief required evidence.

What did I believe? I had learned the definition of an atom from Holmyard's text book on chemistry: 'An atom is the smallest indivisible particle of matter.' Even recent Nobel Prize winners had regarded that as sacrosanct. Yet within a few years, Einstein and a succession of leading scientists showed it was untrue. The atom had been split; matter was transformed into energy, wave mechanics dramatically supplemented classical mechanics and quantum mechanics implied that uncertainty was an integral part of the universe. Scientists' conceptions of truth were always changing. With all the reasoning that went into them they could never be regarded as final. Even the conclusions I drew from my own minor research efforts might well soon be disproved! How apt, the Royal Society's original motto, *Nullius in verba* – take nobody's word for it!

We continue to ask today the age-old questions on the creation, the origins of life, the nature of time, of consciousness and the origin and ultimate fate of the cosmos. Not just how, but why?

What was undoubted and what I admired were the wonders of science. In the garden, the beauty of a flower, through a laboratory microscope, crystals so fine in design, surely they could not have come about by chance. Given the natural laws of the heavenly bodies, we could predict the moment of an eclipse. In Professor Graham Cannon's zoology lectures I learned that a snake could detect a temperature change of one thousandth of a degree and that a spider could spin a stronger web than man could.

The literal account of the creation which we read in the Bible does not tally with the results of scientific research or philosophical thought, but then the systems of science and philosophy have themselves changed. I found it illuminating to read a little of the works of philosophers. Maimonides, in his thirteenth-century *Guide to the Perplexed* distinguished between the Divine Order and the Natural Order as systems of reference. He could not believe, for example, that man could create matter, given the state of knowledge at the time. Not until the twentieth century did we show that we could.

Whilst I wanted to continue to study and question my beliefs, work and family responsibilities took priority. In the war and on the move, my links with family and synagogue became more tenuous, Jewish chaplains to the forces were few and far between.

On one occasion we had taken our children to Bucklebury, in Berkshire, to see Diana's parents and their friends. Amongst them was the local Rector. He told me he had been reading in the Press about the controversy in the Jewish community over the beliefs of Rabbi Louis Jacobs. I said I knew him well. After the shortest of conversations he suddenly said, 'I don't suppose I could persuade you to speak to our Church Fellowship about your faith?' I was unprepared for that. I thought I had been sufficiently hesitant, but I was quickly asked about possible dates. And then a printed card arrived.

<u>Forthcoming Meeting</u>
Upper Bucklebury Church
Thursday 9th December 1965 at 7.45pm
Dr A C Copisarow
(Scientist and grandson of a Chief Rabbi)
'The Jewish Faith'

I didn't quibble about the exaggeration; I simply wondered what I could say. But I had time to think. On the night about thirty came along. The Rector introduced me warmly. After my talk there was a lively discussion.

Reading the notes I made at the time, they now seem more like a sermon than an informal talk:

Faith is our relationship with God and our faithfulness to fulfil His
purpose. The Torah encapsulates my beliefs, but it also presents a complete
way of life, showing what our obligations are, our duty to others, how to
distinguish between right and wrong — the choices then being ours.

I believe we are trustees — in possession, but not owners of the earth, responsible for sustaining the environment, allowing lands to lie fallow, for example, and trustees for the 'have-nots' too. The Old Testament calls for relief for the poor as a matter of social justice; 'charity' as we now know it, has a smaller compass. Our responsibilities to our fellow-man extend from the freeing of slaves to not cheating. In 30 BC Rabbi Hillel was teaching us 'What is hateful to you do not do to your fellowman'. Justice and mercy were two key virtues, but of these we should lean to the latter, for the former related only to what the law required, the latter to 'doing what was right' — not always the same thing.

We make no absolute claims for our faith, neither do we seek to attract others to it. Nor should we denigrate the different tenets held by others. What I look for is what in each tradition promotes peace instead of war, tolerance instead of contempt, self-criticism instead of superiority. In Icelandic sagas such people were called 'peace-weavers'. For me 'the return to Zion' is as much a return to our faith as it was to our ancient homeland. For the oppressed and survivors of the holocaust, it was in sheer desperation that they yearned for the Land of Israel and who knew when or where this persecution might occur again?

In my occasional discussions with fellow scientists many more see no inconsistency between science and their faith than the contrary. In the course of Jewish history there had been a succession of attempts to reconcile its contents with knowledge acquired later, to distinguish between the divine and natural systems of reference, and harmonise tradition with modern scholarship. For the past thousand years we had sought permanent truths, but could not find them. We had, however, tried to re-interpret the contents of an unchanging bible on the basis of up-dated scientific evidence. Unlike Christianity, Judaism provided no conclave or council to reformulate its faith, to reconcile it with modern knowledge.

In the course of the discussion I referred to the debate between the rabbis of old, arguing as to whether the study of the Torah was more important than the practice and whether good deeds were more important than prayer. In my case, sadly, I was deficient in both.

And on the issue raised by the Rector:

Rabbi Louis Jacobs was the most recent of those who could not accept the word of the Bible in its literal sense. With sincerity and a scholarly approach he examined God's revelation and the Torah as dictated to Moses. Like many before him, he challenged our tradition, extending back 2500 years. Most churches had their schisms; so had my congregation. The United Synagogue responsible for the designation of a new Chief Rabbi refused to accept him.

We were deeply divided and many of my friends in the congregation left to join him in an independent New London Synagogue. There they could speak 'in the contemporary idiom'. It was assumed, as I was 'reasonable', that I would go with them. But I had real reservations. Was reason sufficient? Had it not led us astray in the past? Faith required a dialogue with reason.

I hoped for unity in my religion, but in a world of diversity, did not expect uniformity. We had to accommodate a wide range of interpretations. There was a danger in not doing so. A tree that could not bend in the wind could break, but prevailing winds changed over the centuries, and the pendulum of perceptions and opinions which swung too far often reversed. All interpretations had to be very firmly rooted.

I was tempted to move with those who did, but there was too much at stake here. Were they looking through the wrong end of a telescope or was it heart over-ruling head? I decided to stay put.

In retrospect, this may unconsciously have been my first foray into risk analysis. For, oddly, in counselling a company chairman I thought back on my decision. I had advised him that a change of strategy ought to give him a 98% chance of becoming more profitable. 'So we go ahead,' he replied. 'But times change, and there's a 2% chance of going bankrupt,' I added. 'Bankrupt? No, I can't take that chance.'

Weeks after my talk, I was complimented, but by no means unreservedly. 'You know when Field Marshal Montgomery read the Lesson here at Bradfield School he was more succinct than you. He just strode into the pulpit announcing, 'And the Lord said – and I am inclined to agree with Him!''

Many years later, I was delighted to spot in my congregation an old friend, who had moved away. It was William Frankel, former Editor and Chairman of *The Jewish Chronicle*, who had been quite outspoken at the time. He had come simply to hear me recite from the Torah. By now I was eighty-three, the occasion of my second Bar Mitzvah, three score years and ten after my first. We parted in total agreement: we should be judged by our learning, motives and deeds and not by synagogue affiliations!

In a way we had already adopted this stance at home. Diana and our children had found Rabbi Hugo Gryn's services to be inspiring, more easily understood and enriching. To remain closer together when in London, though Diana and I have remained with the New West End, we all joined the West London congregation too.

My inheritance, both religious and cultural would always be with me. The atmosphere as a child at home was wholly English and Jewish. Russian, with elements of Yiddish, which my parents might have perpetuated, rarely arose. They did when a letter arrived from my father's brother, or when my sister and I asked to be retold a story. My mother provided the livelihood and was the home-maker, but the cultural background was that of scholarship and my father's academic contacts. Our national loyalties were progressively reinforced as my father's contribution in war service became recognised and hostile movements developed abroad.

I was attuned to those who had always aspired for a Jewish homeland, and later to those, from all over the world who I found praying alongside me, when I was at the Western Wall of Jerusalem. I wondered then how many of my ancestors, over the hundred generations since the destruction of the Temple, had had the freedom to come and pray there. The road to freedom had been unbelievably hard; it had been sustained by faith.

Faith called upon our memory. This I felt was the essence of my religious identity. I had the good fortune to be able to discuss these issues over the years with religious authorities and others: in 1997 in Cambridge with the Chief Rabbi Jonathan Sacks speaking convincingly on 'Survival to Heritage', and at the Athenaeum with Isaiah Berlin and Yehudi Menuhin with their more philosophical and spiritual perspectives, respectively, and with Donald Coggan and Robert Runcie, in turn Archbishops of Canterbury.

Runcie had welcomed me on having been appointed Chairman of the Club, as its first practicing Jew. We had both served in the war, but he in action being awarded the Military Cross, I at a safer distance. I said that I celebrated Hanukkah on the anniversary of a famous Jewish military victory in 167 BC when the Maccabeans fought for their liberty against the Greeks. And our celebration did not boast of victory, but served as a reminder, giving us cause for hope for the future of our people. Runcie replied, 'Nor did we, after the First World War, build an Arc de Triomphe, just a Cenotaph, and a Tomb of the Unknown Warrior.'

CHAPTER IV

A Scientist in Diplomacy

Paris in Revolt 1954–1960

My appointment as Scientific Attaché and then Counsellor at our Paris Embassy was a totally unexpected, life-changing move. My brief was to strengthen links with scientists and engineers, explore opportunities for collaboration between our institutions, governments and business, help British firms in a tangible way and advise the Ambassador on foreign policy issues arising. Duties were extended to Belgium, Holland, Switzerland and Italy, where we had no resident scientific representation, as well as multinational institutions. No diplomat is restricted in his compass, however, and I had the privilege of meeting personalities in all walks of life.

A retired French diplomat in his seventies told me he had participated in the *Entente Cordiale* meeting in London in 1904. 'That was *la Belle Epoque* of the diplomatic profession. Everything was so much easier fifty years ago. We had privacy, the power of the Press was in its infancy, the man in the street unquestioning, our profession was a *chasse gardée* for the aristocracy and well-to-do, we were one large family. One dispute we had with Britain had gone on for two centuries, over Newfoundland fishing and shore rights. We spent days on that, but finally agreed. The ultimate in diplomatic negotiation – it all hinged on whether a lobster was a fish.'

Until the Entente, it was the eighteenth-century Marlborough victories at Blenheim and elsewhere that led to a balance of power in European affairs and Britain and France beginning to emerge as colonial powers. In the nineteenth century the two most intense political passions were France's loathing for Germany, and Russia's longing for access to the

Mediterranean. This spelt danger. France sought to escape the web Bismarck had spun. She was Britain's rival in Africa and the Mediterranean and Russia, our rival in Central Asia and the Indian border. We also had strong Royal family links with Germany, so it was King Edward VII who took the initiative to end the disputes following a visit to France in 1903.

The Entente forged a bond between our two countries which in 1914 proved all-important. And it continued to dominate our relationship after Hitler's accession to power, World War II and the fall of France. This brought the little-known soldier Charles de Gaulle to London, claiming to speak for France. Churchill backed him. In 1941, standing in the House of Commons, de Gaulle declared, 'Britain and France are bound together, for life and death, by the same destiny, by the same ideal.' After the war, however, de Gaulle's notion of France was the beginning of a thirty-year drama.

There had been a rapid succession of some eighteen prime ministers when Diana and I arrived in Paris in what was called the Revolving Door Period. Our arrival coincided with the fiftieth anniversary of *l'Entente Cordiale*.

After all the excitement, my expectations of diplomatic life were dashed almost from the start. As we drove along the Champs Elysées in the cold, damp and fog, with Diana at the wheel of our blue Vauxhall Cresta, our first car, with a capacious boot and right-hand drive, we eagerly drank in those quintessentially Parisian sights that were to become part of our lives for the next few years.

As a set of traffic lights turned to red we came to a halt, then a cyclist trying to pass us in the narrow space on the inside caught his wheel in ours. Both he and his bike fell to the ground with a clatter, but fortunately he was not hurt. However, his reaction was to hurl abuse squarely at the driver. Responding to the urge to defend my young wife's honour, both as a driver and as a British woman, I wound down the window.

'Crétin!' I shouted. As the cyclist picked up his bike, he must have spotted the CD plates on our car. He remounted and started pedalling off furiously in front of us towards the Arc de Triomphe.

After a few yards, he turned his head and shouted back, 'Crétin Distingué!'

This unsophisticated exchange didn't offer the most auspicious beginning to a diplomatic career. I'm glad to say however, that this was as low as it got for me, for six memorable and quite wonderful years followed. We were supremely happy, leading the full life of a busy diplomat, enjoying the political side, whilst three of our four children were born in Paris.

But on the day our third child arrived, our lives were set to change. I was with Diana in her hospital room when Richard was brought in, pink, wrinkled and two hours old. Diana looked at her baby and raised a weary eyebrow. 'Oh no, not another Copisarow,' she said to the nurse. 'How is it that none of our children look like my side of the family?'

'Madame, you should be grateful. Most of the mothers who come here would give a lot for a baby that looked like their husband.'

Our move from London came about as a result of a chance meeting in the summer of 1952. Arriving at the Farnborough Air Show, I got off the train with another passenger whom I recognised as a senior military figure in the Ministry of Defence. I introduced myself. 'Don't you work with Kenneth Strong?' he asked. He held out his hand. 'Bertie Blount, Director of Scientific Intelligence.' Originally he had been a research chemist and I told him about my own scientific research.

'I'm on the Joint Intelligence Committee,' he declared. 'But you should be in Scientific Intelligence, not Joint Intelligence.'

In the course of the day, we saw more of each other and had a wide-ranging conversation, during which he was kind enough to take an interest in my career, appreciating perhaps, as I hoped he might, my liking for both the scientific and political intelligence aspects of my job. He was certainly an interesting man himself. Tall, lean, wearing ill-fitting country clothes that might have been his father's and with the unmistakable look of an academic, he could have been a character from Waugh or Sayers, or one of those legendary, inspiring prep school masters.

Over the months that followed I didn't forget my meeting with Blount. Could he provide the entrée to another appointment, I wondered?

In due course, Blount was promoted to become Deputy Secretary at the Department of Scientific and Industrial Research (DSIR). In 1954, I received a phone call from him asking if I'd like to be considered for the post of HM Scientific Attaché in Paris. It was, I learned, currently held by Tony Waterfield in his own Department. No doubt, in due course there would be nominations from the Ministry of Supply and other Departments with recommendations for the appointment to be made by the FCO.

There was a long, somewhat frustrating delay before I heard anything more. I couldn't deny that I was excited by the prospect of a stint in the Paris Embassy. Although Blount had first proposed me, I didn't know if he would have any say in the final appointment. I'd learned more about him since our first meeting at Farnborough. He'd had a remarkable and varied career, which seemed to have evolved by chance. After Oxford, he'd gone to Frankfurt for his doctorate, and had become Dean of St Peter's, Oxford and Director of Research at Glaxo by the age of thirty. During the War he'd served in the SOE, been dropped behind enemy lines in Greece and promoted to Colonel before serving with the Chindits in the Far East.

As I got to know him, I found that, like Diana and me, he loved to go walking, and we went together on three or four hikes in the mountains. He would cover the ground vigorously, leaning into a long, purposeful stride. The first time he came with us, we walked across into Andorra, and soon became used to his somewhat aloof, though always correct manner. We were amused by his scrupulous propriety when, every so often he would announce that his boot lace was undone, before disappearing behind a bush to relieve himself. He was a good companion with an impressive depth of knowledge, at times showing tremendous scholarly enthusiasm, especially for botanical specimens.

Diana and I got to know Blount pretty well and when we were in Switzerland together he told me about a top secret wartime assignment he'd been given – the unsavoury task of preparing a plan to assassinate Hitler. When it came to it, the plan involving anthrax or poisoned drinking water was not pursued. Blount was subsequently invited to become Director of MI5, which he declined. He became Acting Secretary of DSIR, but was never promoted.

Some maintained he was a maverick, that he lacked ambition, with the fortune he'd made from his Glaxo shares, and devoted too much of his time to the care of his garden in Tarrant Rushton. Although he gave this impression, he did want the job, and what was undoubted was that once he was passed over for promotion, his motivation was completely dissipated. When the DSIR was incorporated into the new Ministry of Technology, long before his retirement age, he quit public service altogether. I don't believe he ever forgave the Civil Service for what he considered shabby treatment.

I learned eventually that Blount had not been involved at all in my Paris appointment in 1954. Six candidates for the job – scientists and engineers – had emerged and were considered and the decision was taken by Dr Alexander King, DSIR's Chief Scientific Officer, a former Scientific Counsellor in Washington, in conjunction with the Foreign Office.

To my pleasant surprise, I was told that I would get the job, subject to a final meeting over lunch, to which Diana was also invited. We must have made a satisfactory impression because at the end of lunch I was advised I could now go ahead and order the formal black jacket and striped trousers that were de rigueur in the Embassy.

As soon as the JIB heard that my appointment had been confirmed they objected. They were short of experienced people, they argued, and couldn't afford to let me go. But the Treasury ruled that as I was being promoted, and my Department, with its limited complement, could not match this internally, I had to be released.

Within hours, I had ordered my diplomatic attire [photo, page 167] and signed up to the Berlitz School for a crash course to improve my French. I also cancelled the imminent purchase of our first home in Drayton Gardens, South Kensington, which turned out to be an expensive mistake. I'd agreed the price, but by the time we returned to London six years later on the look-out for a house it was on the market again, virtually unchanged, at more than five times the price.

In London, the JIB gave me a small farewell party in Northumberland Avenue, while in Paris our predecessors, Tony and Honor Waterfield, threw two parties to combine their own farewells with our introduction to their scientific contacts, Embassy colleagues and wide circle of friends. Tony had already written to welcome us and was tremendously helpful in settling us into our new home and job. While he had not perhaps as solid a scientific background as me, he was better qualified for the job in other ways. An Old Etonian, whose family lived in France, Tony was bilingual and had an enormous circle of friends, well beyond the diplomatic community, so fitted very well into life at the Paris Embassy. He gave us some sound advice, based on his five successful years there.

'This is a biggish Embassy with a reputation for being sticky, socially speaking,' he wrote. 'On occasion you will be having ten to dinner, and this will consist of soup, entrée, main dish, salad, pudding, cheese and fruit, so a large quantity of cutlery, china, tumblers and glasses is involved.'

I passed the letter on to Diana and her jaw dropped as she read it. I can still picture her face. She was after all just twenty, the same age as the children of some other Attachés.

In the weeks leading up to our departure from England I'd tried to prepare myself for the sorts of conversation I might be having with well-educated French people generally. To make up for some shameful gaps in my knowledge of European history and Anglo-French relations, I set myself some homework and read Brace and Weber's *The Historical Evolution of Modern France*, recommended to me by the FO.

For our first home in Paris, we took over the Waterfields' impressive apartment in an elegant nineteenth-century building at 25, Boulevard Flandrin near the Bois de Boulogne. Rented from Bernard Tricot, a career diplomat at the Quai d'Orsay, but then serving in Tunisia, we could have the place for as long as we liked, provided that he could have it back at short notice.

We arrived in Paris in the afternoon. It was 1st November, the feast of *Toussaints*, when everything was closed. There was no one to welcome us other than the concierge, who showed us up to our flat on the *piano nobile* and handed us the keys. It was huge, with high ceilings and almost empty. We knew we wouldn't have enough furniture to fill it. It was a cold day. Diana shivered and looked utterly miserable. She sat on the luggage, suddenly feeling daunted by the whole prospect. 'Let's go home,' she muttered. But she vanquished her fears; we moved in and soon found ourselves living there in style. Diana was by nature adaptable and eager to enjoy Paris. She also had some French cousins who rallied round and helped establish her there. It took her very little time to settle in and find her way around the superb shops and markets.

A year later we moved on. Bernard Tricot returned, having co-signed a Treaty with the Bey of Tunis and announced that he wanted his apartment back the following week! The Embassy quickly found us a choice of others and we settled for one, not many yards from the Arc de Triomphe at 15, rue Lord Byron, opposite Prince Louis de Broglie's maison particulière. It was well furnished, with an enormous painting by Jordaens. Below us lived the owner, Albert Neuvy, Chairman of Air Liquide, and his wife, the sister of the Duke of Palmella. Our maids had bedrooms on the sixth floor and on the ground floor lurked Mme Bouillac, the formidable *concièrge*. She was one of the 60,000 or so *guardiennes* in Paris who had a reputation for gossip-mongering and as agents in league with the authorities. They were known as *les cloportes* – woodlice.

Our new home was much more conveniently placed for my work, and a brisk ten-minute walk along the Champs Elysées and rue du Faubourg St Honoré brought me to my office and home for lunch.

The Paris Embassy, as one of the premier postings in British diplomacy, had had an interesting variety of successive appointees. Duff Cooper, a former Conservative Minister married to Diana, daughter of the Duke of Rutland, brought a bright, social sparkle into the first few post-war years. He was followed by Oliver Harvey, a career diplomat, urbane and charming, who gained popularity among his staff by inviting them to dinner and Scottish dancing on Saturday nights.

Gladwyn Jebb, to whom I was to report for the next six years, was followed by Sir Pierson Dixon, just before the end of my stint. Dixon had previously been our representative at the UN and was running early negotiations with the Common Market in Brussels. Selwyn Lloyd decided that he was the only person qualified to take over from Jebb, but asked him also to continue his work in Brussels whilst running the Paris Embassy. It was as a result of conscientiously performing two testing and very full-time jobs that he died, I believe, quite simply from overwork and exhaustion.

Gladwyn himself was a highly intelligent, well-connected and impressive individual, always elegantly turned out, but for most not an easy man to know. He had a natural aloofness and apparent disdain, even contempt, which did not encourage familiarity or small talk. He also had an appalling memory for names of people who were not important to him professionally. On one occasion after we'd been in Paris for years, he was introducing Diana to someone at a big reception. 'And this is er…er…this is er…This is the wife of my Scientific Attaché.'

On the other hand he had immense experience, been Acting Secretary General of the UN and had attended all the major post-war summits. He had met almost everyone of significance on the world stage and had the stature to operate on equal terms with Secretaries of State.

The Ambassador's official home, the Chancellerie, to which we were invited, usually 'on duty', was a block away from the Elysées Palace. It had been built in the 1720s for the Duc de Charost, tutor to Louis XV. After the Revolution it was sold to Napoleon's younger sister, Pauline, who married Prince Camillo Borghese. She added two substantial wings to the house, lavishly decorated by Visconti, who created a magnificent Salle de Bal. In 1814 the house was bought by the Duke of Wellington on behalf of George III and became the first British Embassy. Visconti's ballroom was used as Queen Victoria's throne room during her visit to

L'Exposition of 1855. Somewhat jaded after the German occupation of Paris, and temporarily put in the hands of the Swiss, the building and all its First Empire furnishings had been restored to their former glory.

Behind the house was a huge and glorious garden, with superb trees and acres of lawn, which had been kept in trim by grazing sheep during the Revolution.

Diana and I arrived for our first party there, bang on time, when Diana was buttonholed by Diana Beith, who was twice her age and whose husband was Head of Chancery. 'Didn't you know, staff should arrive ten minutes early?' We had not been given Marcus Cheke's book on how to behave. Protocol was as stiff as it comes in Paris. It didn't take long, however, to learn for example that waiters should not offer trays of alcoholic drinks to the Begum Aga Khan, or that we should bow and curtsy to the Duke of Windsor, but not to the Duchess.

We soon learned to love the city, and so many Parisians too, with their intellectual snobbism and obsession with their liver, which they talked about just as we discuss the weather. We indulged in their passion for food and wine. Life was meant to be enjoyed with a style and elegance which were seductive and hard to resist. The city was as vibrant and beautiful in the winter as it was in the summer when, on *le 14 juillet*, the mood would change dramatically as everyone fled to the coasts and the countryside.

The people we met were friendly and hospitable, I quickly took to my embassy colleagues, but it wasn't so easy for Diana with their wives, in the most *protocolaire* of embassies. For a time she was self-conscious about her age, but everyone soon made friends with her and took her to their favourite patisseries and hat shops. After all, one could not be seen in the same headgear more than once!

My own spoken French, undoubtedly with a marked English accent, was improving. Diana was born with a musical ear and was already very fluent, adept at spotting regional accents she heard among sellers in the cheese market – Breton or Provençal – and she would recognise and happily chat with any of them. On 1st May when the French traditionally give *muguet* (Lily of the Valley) to each other, a stall-holder to whom Diana regularly chatted, presented her with a small posy.

'But it's plastic!' she exclaimed before she could stop herself. 'Ah yes, but it will last much longer, like my Love.' So much for French pragmatism. The French shopkeepers liked her and looked after her, so when she was pregnant and they spotted her waiting at the back of a long queue, they would call out to those in front, 'Madame has six little children; she must be served quickly!'

My own grasp of scientific French was more than adequate, but by 1954 English was so much the lingua franca of science that most French scientists were glad of an opportunity to practise their English on me. However, I did address conferences and made a few lengthy speeches in French and even publicly defended my doctoral thesis at the Sorbonne in French, fielding questions from all quarters. That was in 1960 when I eventually found the time to pull together my half-dozen publications on colloid science and present them formally for my Doctorat de l'Université.

I also ventured into wider discussions. I had thought it would be helpful, if not essential, to have some grasp of French politics, so I could talk more confidently, but a little to my surprise, I found the French didn't encourage this on formal occasions. Politics to them, I discovered, was too much a matter of dogma and argument; they wanted intellectual discourse. History had the attractive quality of always being ambivalent, depending on whose version you'd read, but it was philosophy that lit them up most. This, they felt required a more direct application of intellect. It was after all, the country of Descartes, and now of Camus and Jean-Paul Sartre.

When the conversation turned to deep philosophy, I tried to confine myself to listening, which probably saved some embarrassment, but I enjoyed talking about literature. A broad understanding of the works of Balzac and Flaubert could go a long way at a dinner party, particularly as the other guests were all too ready to tell you what they thought of an author. And when the wine flowed and the conversation became more animated and indiscreet, on one occasion, brushing sensitivity aside,

I asked my neighbour about French collaboration under Nazi occupation. She said, 'We lost two million males but never lost our patriotism. Some girls were called *collabos horizontale* and one, defending herself in court at the end of the war, was adamant, 'mon cul est international, mais mon coeur est toujours français!''

My diplomatic colleagues at the Embassy who made us most welcome from the outset included Tony Duff, a heroic wartime submariner already in command at the age of twenty-three, who went on to become head of our combined security services. On retirement, his compassion turned to helping London's homeless, those sleeping on the streets. He and his wife Pauline, living modestly in the West Country, used to visit us in Dorset. Murray Maclehose, a future Governor of Hong Kong; Eddie Tomkins, Press Counsellor, later Ambassador in Paris; and Michael Palliser, a First Secretary who went to the top as head of the Foreign Office, were all convivial, hard-working colleagues. They and the Naval, Military and Air Attachés in particular ensured that Diana and I enjoyed the social scene.

Senior to us were Patrick Reilly, Minister, formerly Chairman of the Joint Intelligence Committee, a future Ambassador in Paris, and Gladwyn Jebb. I had regular weekly meetings with Reilly, a quiet, friendly, brilliant Wykehamist in predominantly Etonian surroundings. The Etonians tended to be more extrovert, at ease with those in all walks of life, whilst those who excelled intellectually within French society seemed to be more interested in those who came from Winchester.

After some months I began to see Jebb more frequently. My medium sized but dingy office was very close to his palatial one, so occasionally when he wanted to get away from a less than edifying visitor, he came into mine, unannounced, taking possession of my one armchair. Although to many he was aloof and intellectually arrogant, he could be charming and I got on well with him. Reporting to London as well as to him, I enjoyed a little more independence than my colleagues and once or twice he would mention his former conference experiences in Quebec, Cairo, Teheran, Dumbarton Oaks, Potsdam and San Francisco.

'At the UN,' he said, 'I found that the only way to counter a blatant Soviet challenge was with irony and that is how I confronted Malik.' We had wide-ranging discussions over French aspirations in atomic weaponry and energy production where Britain was so strong. He said obviously we must withhold any information for defence purposes, but on civil developments, be as cooperative as possible.

'We must take care,' I countered. 'We may soon become competitors in the civil field. They will advertise their ambitions with tidal power generation, but with quiet determination go all out for a national programme of nuclear power generation.'

'In that case, I agree,' he said. After that he would introduce me to others as 'the scientific tool in my diplomatic kit-bag.'

Gladwyn could be imaginative and resourceful in the way he utilised his attachés. One day in May 1956 he called me in following a visit from the Duke of Windsor. The Duke had complained to him about the risk of radioactive contamination emanating from the Saclay nuclear research laboratories some twelve miles to the south-west of Paris. He said they were polluting his home and had asked, somewhat naively, whether his estate could not be designated British territory, like the Embassy. He somehow thought that such a change would allow him to control the activities of his neighbours. Jebb noncommittally agreed to look into it.

'Of course, it's not a question of sovereignty,' Jebb told me. 'This is a technical matter. You know the Commissariat well; you deal with it.'

I quickly established, as I'd assumed, that there was absolutely no danger, but in any event the Commissariat promised they would continue to ensure that this would be the case, so I phoned Waddilove, the Duke's secretary, to say I had good news, and was invited to tea.

The Duke and Duchess received me warmly. The Duke, though looking pale and tired, was charming. Exquisite tea paraphernalia, complete with cucumber sandwiches, arrived on a trolley. I explained the solution to their concerns, which was not at all the constitutional change they'd been hoping for. As I talked, their faces clouded. The Duchess stood up, and without another word, walked from the room. It was clear, too, from the Duke's demeanour that our meeting was over. More courteously, he carried on with some inconsequential conversation for a few minutes and then simply stood up and escorted me to my car. A few days later I received a polite letter of thanks for my visit. Curiously, it was typed on Buckingham Palace writing paper, twenty years after the Abdication! [photo, page 168]

Jebb had been right in saying that my links with the Commissariat à l'Energie Atomique were close, for I learned a great deal about their civil and military programme. The main factor behind French success in nuclear development was sheer determination, and the appointment of joint heads, scientific and administrative, charged with sorting out all problems. Francis Perrin, an outstanding and excitable scientist, son of René, the Nobel Prize winner, fulfilled his technical role with complete competence. Pierre Guillaumat was a politician with outstanding industrial experience and a true patriot whose regard for France was greater than for his own personal ambition. He was also a loyal supporter of de Gaulle who later made him his Army Minister. It was not easy to draw him into a conversation, but on one occasion he did reveal, quite quietly, 'I was inspired by my father,' he said, 'a general in the First World War. He was totally dependent for his transport on American petrol supplies. I want to ensure France's self-sufficiency in energy.'

He was, effectively, the father of the French nuclear power programme. Despite his elevated position, he was always helpful and gave me his views when I asked to meet him from time to time, clearly appreciating that it was my function to look out for Britain's interests. He went further too, when on the Queen's birthday, for which the Ambassador threw a party, I heard that he had been complimentary about me to my Embassy colleagues.

Though Perrin and Guillaumat worked together effectively, they were by no means personal friends. When my secretary phoned theirs to discover when they and their wives could both join us for dinner, she was told they never showed up together; they took it in turn to accept.

In time I became quite close to the Commissariat. One day Perrin came to my office virtually unannounced with his Director, Bertrand Goldschmidt. We knew him and his English wife, Naomi de Rothschild well. Bertrand, once a laboratory assistant to Marie Curie, had got to Ottawa in the War and convinced de Gaulle that France must have atomic weapons of its own. Perrin told me in the strictest confidence of French plans for exploding their first test bomb in the Sahara. 'But I've already read about that in the newspapers,' I told them 'and the date has been published.'

'Yes, we have a tiny but worrying technical problem. If it fails to go off, the Arab world would laugh at us. We are not asking for any information from the UKAEA, but would someone come across secretly and help – just in case?'

'Are you serious?' I asked. 'I'm sure that our mere presence would be a non-starter under the terms of the Anglo-American agreement. It would probably not remain a secret in any event, and then you would be thoroughly humiliated.' Anticipating my response, they asked, 'Would you put it to your Ambassador?' To this I agreed and reported the conversation to Jebb.

'I might tell the Prime Minister,' he remarked casually. I was amazed he'd said the Prime Minister. Later his secretary Irene Durlacher told me he was still on the look-out for some excuse to talk to Harold Macmillan. He had had little opportunity because the PM knew that Jebb had always been an R.A. Butler supporter for Prime Minister. However, when Jebb did next meet Macmillan, the matter of our assistance at the French atomic tests, I gather, was never even raised.

Contrary, perhaps to the perception of others in the Embassy, Gladwyn Jebb was very family minded. When I mentioned to him how warmly his wife Cynthia had been welcomed at a reception attended by some leading French engineers, he was delighted, though he added with habitual dryness, 'I think the French pay higher regard to her as Brunel's grandchild than as Britain's Ambassadress.'

'And they call her the pocket Venus,' I replied.

He was concerned about his son, Miles, who was stuck out in East Africa in 1959, working with the Hunting Aerosurveys Company and wondered whether I had any ideas about management opportunities for him nearer home. He also asked whether I knew anyone at the Sorbonne who could tell him about a science student called Joel de Rosnay. 'Our daughter, Stella, wants to marry him!' I was able to obtain a comprehensive CV.

Stella's wedding went ahead at the end of the year. Among the 600 guests at a glittering Embassy reception were Pierre Mendes France, Pol Roger, Claude Cartier and Nancy Mitford. De Rosnay went on to become French scientific attaché in Washington and had a distinguished career thereafter.

When de Gaulle became President in 1958, he held receptions twice a year at the Elysées for the diplomatic corps. Now I was Counsellor, Diana and I were invited. On arrival, I was announced by the *houissier* as 'M le Conseiller Scientifique de l'Ambassade de Grande Bretagne'. I stepped towards de Gaulle's extended hand and walked forward a little too soon as the *houissier* added loudly, 'et Irlande du Nord'.

It was a Soirée Musicale, in full dress. I was standing near Cynthia Jebb who was resplendent as always, when one of the Elysées staff approached her to say that the President would be delighted if she would sit on his right at the concert. I caught Cynthia's eye and nodded. Then she moved closer, much closer. 'Oh, I'm so short-sighted; until I'm close enough to kiss someone, I'm not sure who I'm speaking to!'

De Gaulle's return to power was the third of three especially memorable events in successive years, which began with Suez in 1956, followed by the Queen's visit in 1957 and the constitution of the Fifth Republic in 1958.

Although I was only a spectator of the Suez debacle, Bobby Isaacson, the Minister (Commercial), as a member of the Suez Canal Company Board, had told me in July what Nasser's nationalisation could mean, in economic terms, with 5,000 British ships a year then passing through the canal, and potentially in geopolitical terms.

In October, I was witness to the comings and goings that followed, the visits to Paris of Eden and Selwyn Lloyd, and of their counterparts, Mollet and Pineau to London and the arrival of Macmillan, still then Chancellor of the Exchequer. British and French forces had landed in Port Said and Port Fuad and Bulganin had threatened to intervene with Soviet Migs.

Throughout it all, Gladwyn Jebb was obviously frustrated and thoroughly miserable, especially after the threat of Soviet intervention. Normally cool and imperturbable, he came into my office. 'I'm angry,' he said. 'We're being totally ignored. They need to be told what the French have been up to and what the American and UN attitudes might be to an attack.'

He knew the French attitude, seeing Nasser as the principal supporter of rebellion and arms supplier to Algeria, that Israel wanted both to stop Nasser and, if possible Soviet support of Pan-Arabism, whilst our interest was to keep the Canal open and protect the rights of the Suez shareholders. But, more importantly, we had to realise what Soviet interests in the Mediterranean were. He made no secret of his disgruntlement at being left out of the mid-October meeting, doubted whether Selwyn Lloyd was at all interested in his opinion, and was not surprised that he'd used the excuse of FO questions in Parliament for not coming to meet Pineau.

My interpretation of Gladwyn's posture was that he felt humiliated. His own experience and that of his able staff, looking to him for a lead, was being ignored. Both the Foreign Secretary and the PUS Sir Ivone Kirkpatrick 'who knew little about France' hardly communicated with him at the most critical time. He left his diary blank for almost a week and wrote privately to Kirkpatrick in a friendly but unproductive fashion.

I cannot judge whether better communication would have made a real difference to the Suez debacle, but as the military situation was changing by the hour, it is just possible it may have done. And so much was at stake.

Many years later over drinks, after a meeting of the Governors of the English Speaking Union, Sir Patrick Dean (formerly Ambassador in Washington) who was chairman and I, as deputy, were discussing the importance of international communication. I remarked that the failure of communication between the Roman Emperor and his far flung Empire contributed to the fall of Rome. Quick as a flash, Patrick retorted, 'At the Foreign Office, when I was Assistant Under-Secretary, it was failure of communication between No 10 and the FO that had the most disastrous effect.'

After the withdrawal of all Allied troops from Egypt, Gladwyn Jebb told us that Dillon, the American Ambassador, had told him he did not consider that British action had been unreasonable, but that Foster Dulles took the opposite view. In rapid succession, Dulles came to Paris for a NATO meeting in December and Macmillan succeeded Eden as PM in January – both of which upset Jebb considerably.

Throughout the entire period, however, I felt there had been another dimension to Gladwyn's unhappiness. He realised he was no longer in line to become PUS and in his Paris post he would see the end of his diplomatic career.

Happier times for all of us came with President Coty's invitation and the prospective State visit of the Queen in April 1957. The preparations were lengthy, but thorough. In the ten days leading up to it, the sense of excitement was everywhere. For the French, this was the occasion which finally shook off their hateful experience of wartime occupation. Diana and I had met some of them and people began to talk. Our friends were telling us how, despite the danger, they had eagerly listened to the radio call, 'Içi Londres, içi Londres' and Anglophilia everywhere rose to the surface.

The chestnut trees along the Champs Elysées were all in flower; the Union Jack was flying from the Eiffel tower. The shops in the rue du Faubourg St Honoré vied with each other for the most dazzling display. The resplendent guard of honour of the Spahi, the Algerian cavalry, led the procession.

On the Monday evening, Diana and I were invited to the immaculately restored Petit Trianon theatre in Versailles, which had been inaugurated for the Dauphin's marriage to Mary Antoinette and closed for a hundred years before its Royal reopening that day. The performance of Rameau's ballet *Les Indes Galantes* succeeded in convincing us all that love triumphs over evil! For the banquet, the Queen, young, dignified and beautiful, was wearing a sensational Hartnell dress and among the myriad of embroidered fleurs de lys, was sewn a tiny gold bee, Napoleon's symbol of industry. The Queen spoke in French. 'Vous fûtes le berceau de nos rois' (You were the cradle of our kings.) The following morning, splashed across the papers were the ecstatic headlines 'The Queen Conquers France'.

On the Wednesday morning in the Ionian room of the Embassy, the Queen presented me with an engraved box of gold cuff-links with royal cipher and two silver framed autographed photographs of herself and Prince Philip. Then off I went with the Prince to Saclay to visit the atomic energy laboratories. We drove along the Champs Elysées with crowds cheering our procession of cars. Their waves travelled along the route like a giant Mexican wave. I told him I wasn't used to this. 'And this is a little different from my start of the year' he said, 'on Deception Island in Antarctica.'

Before going to join the Queen at Malmaison after lunch, he asked about my time in the Navy. I gave him the highlights and then went on to tell him of my interest in the Duke of Edinburgh's Award Scheme which he had just started up. 'I don't know how well it will go,' he said, 'but if anyone can make a success of it, it will be John Hunt as Director. You should meet him.' It was many years later, through Diana, actually, that I did so.

Back at my office there was a note of appreciation from the Commissariat. Their status had been raised, they said, by the very favourable press coverage of the Prince's visit to Saclay. [photo, page 167] There were further benefits too, as co-operation became noticeably easier after that. Royal visits, I realised, were not just social occasions.

Perrin thought that the visit had been arranged at my instigation, which in truth, was not the case. I had been responding to a Foreign Office suggestion. Even so, long after the State visit, whenever I asked Perrin for anything, he always made sure it was done, and members of the UKAEA were given far greater access to the French programme than the Americans.

May 1958 found us caught in the midst of a revolution. Arising in the colonies, it was happening literally on our doorstep. The French Algerians were planning an invasion of Metropolitan France; the Arc de Triomphe and Champs Elysées were bursting with Anciens Combattants, and outside our front door in rue Lord Byron, Jacques Soustelle, ex-Governor General of Algeria, was lucky to evade a threatening crowd. The mood was ugly and the demonstrators, tens of thousands of them, swarmed the streets around our apartment. Our *bonne à tout faire* was looking for somewhere to hide, and Diana in the very last stages of pregnancy urgently needed to get to hospital, but we simply couldn't get through the noisy rabble filling the Etoile until the Police came to the rescue.

The Prime Minister, Pierre Pflimlin, with the support of Michel Debré, foresaw the prospective disintegration of the State, as the President had no power to intervene, and considered that de Gaulle's return might be its only salvation. Mendès France and Mitterrand opposed him. President Coty threatened to resign, but was told that no President of France since 1875 had done that. De Gaulle himself did nothing to oppose the rebellion.

The Fourth Republic's administration had become powerless, with the disintegration of its colonies. Tunis had gone; Algerian nationalists wanted nothing less than total independence with no compromises, while the old guard, colonial French *pieds noirs* were determined that France would not abandon them. These rebels had considerable support from the armed forces and many of the elements of a civil war were in evidence.

In the Assemblée Nationale, there was pandemonium. I had a ticket to attend what was likely to be the pivotal session, but couldn't get into the building. The Prime Minister tried to make a critically important statement, but the Speaker André le Troquer, who had the authority, would not allow it. Finally, de Gaulle, regarding himself not as a politician but almost a sovereign, agreed to come forward.

He had done so once before to save France when overrun by Germany. Now, in order to avert civil war, he accepted President Coty's invitation. He was requested to return as Prime Minister, prepare a new Constitution and after seven months succeed to the Presidency. He accepted with the simple announcement. 'I am ready to assume the powers of the Republic.'

It was all high drama. In the Embassy, while there was some relief at the easing of tension, we couldn't help reflecting on Churchill's difficult relationship with de Gaulle during the war. It was with great pleasure, therefore, we were told that one of de Gaulle's earliest pronouncements was to invite Churchill to Paris and invest him with the Croix de la Libération.

On 7th November, Diana and I were among about twenty guests in a small salon in the Matignon Palace, with a few photographers to record the event. De Gaulle, towering over Churchill, arrived with him linking arms as they made their way towards a chaise longue across the room. Just as they reached me, a mighty shove in the back sent me bumping into both of them. I looked round and saw it was Randolph Churchill with a large camera and a badge: PRESS – Europe No 1. 'It says Press, not Push!' I protested, in earshot of everyone.

One further notable event took place in May 1960. I was in my office after lunch writing a card for Diana's 27th birthday the following day. The door was closed, but the voices outside unmistakable. The Jebbs had given an Embassy lunch to Harold Macmillan and his entourage, and were all now on their way to the Elysées for their summit meeting with De Gaulle, Eisenhower, Adenauer and Kruschev. My telephone rang. It was John Henniker-Major, head of Personnel at the Foreign Office. 'Can you find Gladwyn? It's urgent and personal.'

Whilst Macmillan hovered in the doorway Gladwyn took my phone. 'I think you should take this call, Prime Minister, the Office say I shouldn't accompany you; I'm past my retirement age.'

Macmillan took my phone. 'What's this nonsense? Gladwyn knows De Gaulle better than anyone else.' As he put down the phone he turned to Gladwyn. 'John said 'Of course it's your decision, Prime Minister, but he's not eligible to receive a salary any longer'.'

I never discovered whether Gladwyn continued to receive his salary beyond his official retirement age, which was three weeks earlier. Kruschev, however, cancelled the Summit Conference altogether – it coincided with the U2 spy plane disaster, shot down over Russia.

Between these diplomatic highlights, our social life was unflagging. Diana and I were hosts at least twice a week and receiving as many as four invitations a day for conference receptions, embassy national days, art exhibition *vernissages* and friends' dinner parties.

It seemed that it was impossible to live in Paris without developing an interest and real liking for art. I thoroughly enjoyed my visits to some of the most wonderful exhibitions, mounted in Paris at the time. One of the first was a retrospective of the works of Henri Matisse, shortly after his death in 1954. Another was a selection of Picassos. There was no stopping me. I went to the Bernard Buffet exhibition, Paris Cadavre and in 1955 the British Council put on an exhibition of Ben Nicholson's work.

At the preview for this show, a dozen or so of us were gathered around one of Nicholson's complex abstract paintings when I heard a man's voice behind me.

'That one's been hung upside down!' Everyone pretended not to hear. 'That one's been hung upside down!' repeated the man.

'No it hasn't,' came a flippant reply.

'Yes, it has!' Nicholson insisted.

Occasionally I dropped into the Crillon bar for a drink, where I got to know a couple of the journalists: Sam White of *The London Evening Standard*, who was always propping up the bar on the look-out for gossip, and Art Buchwald who wrote for the European edition of *The New York Herald Tribune*, such entertaining pieces as 'Throwing a children's party'. 'The birthday boy opening the door to each guest with 'What have you brought me?' He checks the parcels against the number of guests...the squabbles and fights...pandemonium when the party is over, everyone crying simultaneously...father returns home to count the cost...cleaning of Aubusson carpet, re-stringing of Steinway Grand...'

One day in 1957, walking back to the Embassy after a meeting, I bumped into Art who was with his luncheon guests, a man and woman I seemed to recognise. They just happened to be Elizabeth Taylor and Mike Todd, her latest husband! Art said they were on their way to buy a Cézanne at a sale of Impressionists and he invited me to join them. Mike failed to get the picture she wanted, so we ended up in Hermès, buying her a mere crocodile handbag in consolation.

There was more picture excitement that year when Robert and Lisa Sainsbury, friends of Diana's family in Bucklebury, came to visit us. They had returned to Paris where they spent their honeymoon in 1937 and, with their legendary eye for art, had picked up a pair of small Modiglianis for £30. They'd lent the paintings for a retrospective being put on in Paris and, at the end of it, the curator had contacted them to say he had been offered £30,000 for them. They would never contemplate selling and the paintings are now worth many millions.

Of course, it was always enjoyable to join in a friend's excitement over a new and well-judged acquisition, but how we wished we'd bought more pictures ourselves. One day, we went off to the artists' *quartier* in Eze in Provence. In one of the studios a jocular fellow broke away from his easel and introduced himself as Georges Doussot. We were delighted with the small painting we bought, of children drawing graffiti on a wall, which hangs in our daughter's house. Since Doussot died a generation ago, his very distinctive pictures have become highly regarded.

Diana's distant French cousin, Louise Weiss, lived in great style in Avenue Président Wilson and gave us the entrée to quite a few politicians and academicians. Tante Louise, to us, was then in her sixties.

In her youth she had struggled for the political rights of women in France, as did Mrs Pankhurst in Britain. She became an influential journalist and was offered a post in Léon Blum's pre-war Cabinet, conditional on her abandoning her suffrage campaign, which she declined. She won her first Légion d'Honneur in 1924 for rescuing 126 French school teachers trapped in the Volga Basin. In occupied France she was Valentine, Agent 1410, and at Strasbourg had the honour of chairing the inaugural meeting of the new European Parliament. The building opened by President Chirac in 1999 bears her name.

At elegant salons in her home she told us of the statesmen she had met: Briand, Streseman, Trotsky, Masaryk and Pilsudski. She showed us the poster Lenin had given her. On the walls around us were works of Paul Valery, Raoul Dufy, Vlaminck and Dunoyer de Segonzac.

At one of her lunchtime salons, she sat me next to a man in his seventies whom I hadn't previously met. Glancing at his name card, I read 'Robert Debré'. He told me he was a paediatrician. He spoke of his father, who was a rabbi until he converted to Catholicism when he married. I asked if he was in any way related to Michel Debré who'd recently been appointed Prime Minister by de Gaulle. He inclined his head a fraction, 'Michel is the younger and less intellectual of my two sons, so he has become Prime Minister.' He did go on to give credit to his less intellectual son for drafting the constitution of the Fifth Republic in such a way that it would both satisfy de Gaulle, and make continuity possible after his departure. Indeed, that same constitution is still in force.

Louise Weiss went on to establish a private Foundation, L'Institut des Sciences de la Paix. I was flattered to be asked to join its Council, alongside Pierre Pflimlin, Jean Rostand, Guy de Rothschild and other members of the Academy. When I was invited to attend an election ceremony of the Immortals on the death of Paul Claudel, the distinguished gathering included Marshal Juin, General Weygand and Jean Cocteau, who was one of the candidates.

Guy de Rothschild's cousin, Baron Edmond, invited me to lunch one day and told me how his father Maurice had voted 'Non' in the French Senate against Petain's 1940 alliance with Germany, and made a beeline for Switzerland. Their home was taken over by the Luftwaffe. He suddenly noticed the cuff-links I was wearing. 'I'll do you a swap,' he said. They were identical except for the engraving – his 'E de R', mine 'E II R', a present from The Queen.

We were entertained too by a talented artist, a student of Chagal, once a Benenden schoolgirl, Beris Lindner. Having come to live and study in France she'd met and married Prince Kandaourof, after his father had sent him abroad at the outset of the Russian revolution. Their house was situated between a horse butcher and brothel, in rue des Martyrs in Montmatre, where we joined them for a dinner-party one evening. 'Do you still have the Marie Antoinette earrings?' someone asked my neighbour. He said he did, and I was prompted to glance at his name card, Prince Youssoupof. Naturally I grasped the opportunity to delve for details of the Tsar's final days.

He told me that everyone knew of Rasputin's murder, but not the events that led up to it. Russia had been shamed by the disastrous war with Japan, and by then Germany had become a more serious threat still. Youssoupof said, 'German spies were everywhere, their sympathisers in the Duma. The Tsar (Nicholas II) unlike his father was inexperienced, dim and weak and his young bride nervous and vulnerable. She welcomed Grigori Rasputin's services, offering to heal their son, a haemophiliac, even though he was a Siberian vagabond with a mixture of coarse debauchery and spiritualism who had wormed his way in to royal circles.'

I asked, 'How did you meet him?'

'It was in 1909, just before I went up to Oxford. He had repulsive, colourless eyes, a huge head, tangled hair, bald in front as a result of a beating for horse-stealing.

'After I married Irina, the Tsar's niece, he said he would like to meet me again. By now he was a protégé of the Tsarina, becoming most dangerous. He told me he could make me a Minister and dissolve the Duma. I pretended to feel depressed so he offered to heal me by hypnosis, and almost succeeded. 'How do you do it?' I asked. 'I'm guided by people from afar,' said Rasputin. 'From Siberia?' I questioned. 'No, from Sweden!"

He went on, 'I was so alarmed by 1915 when we were already facing disaster in the war that the Grand Duke Dimitri Pavlovich and I, and a co-conspirator, planned to shoot him. It was many months later that we finally had the chance. I drove to his home, brought him back to dine with us, put Prussic acid in the wine and cakes and waited. It took two hours. He got a vice-like grip on my arm and then collapsed. We thought he was dead, but he murmured, 'I'm thirsty, give me some tea.' I took Dimitri's revolver and shot him through the head. Suddenly, incredibly, he was crawling away into the courtyard. We shot him there again and drove his body to the river, dumping it in a hole in the ice! In case the police, who found the body, spotted the blood in the courtyard, we shot a dog and put its body in the snow there. Our servants, always loyal, upheld our alibi in the face of police suspicions. But the Tsar ordered Dimitri to leave for Persia and I was confined to our home near Kursk.' Around the table, the other guests listened attentively. They said nothing. I had the impression they had heard it all before.

After dinner, I was taken into the Kandaourof cellar to see their large vodka still. We were not allowed to leave without a stone flask, beautifully painted by Beris, of their powerful homemade spirit.

Most of our Parisian acquaintances were less extraordinary, but there was one notable exception. Tommy Yeo-Thomas came to dine with us when he was the representative of the Federation of British Industries. He'd become famous through his code name The White Rabbit and book, which recounted his spectacular wartime exploits in the resistance and in the British SOE (Special Operations Executive), activities for which he had been lavishly decorated by both the British and the French. He turned up looking, it has to be said, pretty peculiar. He apologised for having put on the wrong suit. I told him it didn't matter at all; we were very informal that evening, but I did notice that his jacket was several sizes too large for him. Over dinner, he explained.

He was only nineteen in 1920, when he was sentenced to death by the Bolsheviks for fighting for the Poles, but he had managed to escape. He'd made his way back to Paris where, in time, he became manager of Molyneux, the couture house, where he was when World War II broke out. Having grown up in France he was totally fluent in French, and he joined the Resistance, but was moved to London as General de Gaulle's interpreter. The British SOE quickly spotted his potential, drafted him into the RAF, and dropped him back into France as an agent. After several successful sorties, he was caught by the Gestapo, taken to their HQ in Avenue Foch and tortured almost to death. After that he was taken to Buchenwald, from which he managed to escape by means of a mock funeral, passing through a column of German soldiers guarding a delivery of rockets, to board a waiting Lysander. Not surprisingly, as a result of his treatment by the Gestapo, his health had suffered greatly. The functioning of his glands had gone completely out of control. His weight would fluctuate violently between nine and thirteen stone, with the result that more often than not, his clothes didn't fit.

We were told by Steven Hastings, then serving in the Embassy, later a Member of Parliament, that although Yeo-Thomas was a multi-decorated hero, he couldn't be invited to The Queen's birthday celebrations because he wasn't married to Barbara, his lifelong partner.

Our visitors' book from that period serves as a marvellous reminder of lifelong friends and the stream of scientists, civil servants, diplomats and industrialists who came to see us. A civil servant at my level in London would never have been so fortunate, to have had the opportunity of lengthy discussions with the likes of Plowden, Cockcroft, Roxbee Cox and so many others.

Victor Cavendish-Bentinck came twice to see me when he was with Rio Tinto, trying to locate additional sources of uranium. He'd had a dramatic reversal in his meteoric career. In the 1920s he had attended the Lausanne and Locarno Conferences, was a brilliant Chairman of our Joint Intelligence Committee throughout the war, ensured that the

Foreign Office took the Chair thereafter, advised the Chiefs of Staff when in possession of the ULTRA decrypted cipher material, and went on to become Ambassador in Warsaw. It was there in 1948 after a divorce scandal that his public services came to an end. Ernest Bevin, then Foreign Secretary, decided he should leave without a pension. He told me that had his name been Smith, and not the next Duke of Portland, the outcome might have been different. So began his new career in business, mainly establishing Anglo-German trade links.

Over lunch at the Crillon early in 1959, we were discussing the war. I told him of the atrocities recounted to me by German Jews in Manchester who had escaped from Hitler's regime and asked him what the JIC knew of the events leading up to the Final Solution. What did he know of top French civil servants under Petain putting their Duty to the State, as they saw it, above their personal consciences, in sending Jews off to the extermination camps? 'Yes, we did know what people like Papon were doing. We received many reports from the continent. At first they seemed so extraordinary as to be incredible.' He paused. 'How could any of us have been expected to believe reports that millions of women and children were being put into gas chambers? We waged all out war with the Germans, but even then, what was unearthed at the concentration camps was beyond belief!'

French cousins apart, of all those Diana and I knew in France, our longest lasting friendship was with Marcel Boisot and his family. We had met through Embassy colleagues who had served with him in North Africa. Marcel was an enthusiastic sportsman, mathematician and philosopher with immense charm. Captured by the Nazis, escaping and flying with the Free French and the RAF with distinction, his two ambitions were to become a full professor at l'Ecole Polytechnique and also French Open Golf Champion. He didn't quite make either, but did write erudite philosophical papers whilst living the life of an imaginative Walter Mitty.

His first wife, Hélène Cordet, a close friend of Prince Philip's since childhood, ran the fashionable club, the Saddle Room in Hamilton Place in Mayfair and introduced us to the up-and-coming Paul McCartney, with his then-girlfriend, Jane Asher.

We saw more of his second wife, Denise, who was a highly influential intellectual in Cairo where they'd met, and their daughter, Christina. It was the Boisots who threw a farewell dinner for us at Maxims. I remarked on the Salvador Dali style of dress of our neighbour, who was wearing a flamboyant shirt of many colours. 'That is Señor Dali,' said the waiter.

After Denise died we rather lost touch until 1990, when Diana threw a surprise birthday party for me at the Orangery in Holland Park. I couldn't guess who the mysterious figure in a white dinner jacket and harlequin mask was until he spoke. It was marvellous to see Marcel again. Tragically, when well into his eighties and driving at great speed to deliver a lecture, he crashed his car and was killed.

At the end of the war, Winston Churchill had a dazzling vision of a Great Britain at the centre of concentric circles, a Europe that would unite, a Commonwealth that would adhere and a United States in an all important partnership.

Five years had elapsed by the time I had arrived in Paris and new forces had come into play. With the onset of the cold war, NATO and OEEC (later OECD) were established, both with headquarters in Paris. The latter, with Marshall Aid, subsidised eighteen European countries to generate their economic recovery and hopefully guard against totalitarian regimes.

France itself had changed greatly whilst we were there. There were only three cities when we arrived, Paris, Marseilles and Lyon; the colonies became independent whilst the provinces grew rapidly and began to boom. For France, even more dramatic than the Suez crisis was the birth of the Fifth Republic. Anglo-French relations burgeoned during that time, with a healthy mutual regard for each other's strengths and a degree of tolerance for weaknesses. But my concern was with the prospect of a gradual decline in Britain's own competitiveness.

Leading French businessmen and politicians emanating from the same mould, a meritocracy with an esprit de corps second to none, had a new mission, a plan for the modernisation of the country's infrastructure. Their government's priority was to support business by all possible means. In the UK, many in business believed they were actually under attack. Was there any role for me in alleviating this situation?

My responsibilities did not include NATO, but I participated in some OECD affairs, accompanying the UK representatives, Sir Hugh Ellis-Rees and then Lord Hankey at conferences. More importantly at the time, there were the early moves of a few countries towards economic and political co-operation. With a new-found confidence leaders began to realise how, if barriers could be removed, a new vitality could spread across Western Europe.

My main focus from the outset was with science and technology in France. In 1954 the country was at the start of a new phase in its national development. For although she had always had her quota of outstanding individuals, from Ampère and Pasteur to the Nobel Laureates of the interwar years, the national effort since the wartime eclipse had never got off the ground. There was a lack of funds, laboratory facilities, and little postgraduate training. Pierre Mendes France, on becoming Prime Minister, was the first to act, recognising that with growing international industrial competition isolation was tantamount to backwardness. The principle of Descartes, deeply ingrained in the French educational system, encouraging the solution of a problem by pure reasoning rather than experiment, was no longer tenable. There was the often repeated quip of a French industrialist, 'Well, that may be fine in practice, but it will never work in theory.' Spurred in no small measure by the publication of *Le Défi Americain,* highlighting how the USA was bringing new products to the market in one third of the time, convinced that science and technology were essential elements in national strength, Mendes France attracted support in new circles. He appointed Henri Longchambon as his first Secretary of State for Technical Progress. Formerly a Professor of Mineralogy, as well as Senator, I discovered we had a research discipline in common in mineralogy and so I was off to a flying start.

Our two countries, of course, were different in so many ways. France was predominantly agricultural, self-sufficient in food, had more very small businesses, and was not pressed to export manufactured goods. The few large businesses, notably in aeronautics and motor vehicles were excellent, but the infrastructure had been comprehensively destroyed in the war, including two thirds of the railway system, and nothing less than a national programme for recovery was called for. Britain's infrastructure had not suffered to the same extent. In fact we were already supplying half of the world's turbine power and civil aircraft.

The French slogan 'Modernise or decay' was coined by Jean Monnet, a brilliant strategist who had begun his career running the family brandy business in Cognac. Under successive modernisation plans, twenty-five committees had been set up, tackling problems extending from higher education to re-equipping the railways. Special attention was paid to key components: the development of reversible turbines to harness tidal power, new welding techniques enabling six-inch steel vessels to be made for nuclear power generators, and so on.

The French government regarded planning as a political necessity and they adopted it in the way they saw the influential role of US Congressional Committees, setting out alternative options for evaluation, decisions then being taken on economic criteria. Initially these were left to the planners, but they could be far-reaching decisions when they tried to decide what the best balance was between economic growth, investment of capital and labour, the size of the labour force and the length of the working week. When Pierre Massé became Director General of the Plan I asked him how effectively the politicians and technicians worked together. He ducked the question: 'Politicians describe those technicians who disagree with them as mere technocrats. The technicians describe politicians as those who think they can both have their cake and eat it.' They realised they could do better and after a while they closed ranks, the Government invariably consulting the Economic and Social Council before giving instructions formally to the Director General of the Plan.

British companies who sought our help increased in number, in competition with the USA and three continental rivals. On occasions like that we did not feel that the cost of our diplomatic lifestyle was an unreasonable burden on the tax payer. In fact, after three years and a promotion, I was given the services of an Assistant Scientific Attaché, reinforcing our joint efforts thereon.

It was to atomic energy that France, then an also-ran, devoted most resources and gave top priority. She depended for about 40% of her energy needs on imported fuel (compared with 12% for Britain) and felt vulnerable. Her escalating electricity demands could not be met in any other way. Furthermore, she regarded nuclear weapon manufacture as a means of restoring political prestige. She was not allowed, however, to share British and American secrets useful for military purposes and so put great store on a five-year programme aimed at exploding two or three bombs. She constructed power reactors at Marcoule and built a controlled thermonuclear fusion plant at Pierrelatte. In Britain we were way ahead of them, having nuclear reactors in operation or on the way at Harwell, Windscale, Calder Hall and Dounreay.

In 1955 Sir John Cockcroft came across to sound me out on how France might respond to an invitation to participate in a multinational conference to be held in Geneva. President Eisenhower, addressing the United Nations General Assembly, had proposed the theme, 'Atoms for Peace' for a world conference under UN auspices. I said that if British and American companies were prepared to exhibit their wares, if some confidential information was declassified, and if the US also agreed to supply a little fuel, the French and others would come along in large numbers. We were both surprised by the huge actual turn-out. In the light of what followed eventually, it was the birth of a new world industry. A second conference followed in 1958.

The French programme for generating energy by nuclear means, begun in 1953, had got under way. Heading the joint commission, Pierre Ailleret of EdF had said, 'One cannot do other than follow the line taken by the

British.' For France, slowly at first, there was no looking back. By 1973, 8% of its electricity was nuclear, but after the Arab Oil Embargo, the price of oil trebled within three months, so they went flat out to replace oil fired generation as quickly as possible. Today, more than three quarters of France's electricity is nuclear and French companies are actually supplying five million of us in the South of England.

Throughout the period of my involvement there was virtually 100% rapport between our two countries. In fact, the only discordant note came unexpectedly from the medical world. Sir Ernest Rock Carling, a Medical Research Council adviser to the Home Office raised the prospect of genetic mutations producing a genius with the startling remark, 'One Aristotle, Leonardo, Newton, Gauss, Pasteur or Einstein might well outweigh ninety-nine mentally defectives.' The argument was never resolved.

Alliances have been crucial throughout history. In Europe particularly, countries have sought to become stronger by merging their essential interests. Post-war recovery came through France's Comprehensive Plan, Germany's Wirtschaftswunder, and Italy's Miracolo. Each wanted to collaborate with Britain, but each had a different economy, social history and tradition.

Britain favoured multinational cooperation in science and technology. In supporting it I had to show the limits of what was practical. The role of scientists was in some ways a privileged one. Scientists used a common language, no less widely accepted than was Latin centuries earlier. This was a source of unity and strength. But military developments affected national security, industrial processes and products competed for markets and national prestige increasingly influenced foreign policy. For this reason, inevitably, NATO, the OECD, the Council of Europe and the Common Market each adopted different approaches to cooperation.

In fundamental research the advantages to all were easy to recognise, not least for the largest projects. No single West European country could afford to build CERN, near Geneva, and equip a 27 km circular tunnel for universal nuclear research exploration, which now employs more than half the world's 13,000 particle physicists. It was proposed originally by two Nobel Prize winners, Louis de Broglie of France and Isidore Rabi of the USA. The UK was given the honour and Lord Hailsham, as Lord President of the Council, arrived at Meyrin to cut the ribbon. This he did in style and with all due ceremony, stepping out of a vintage Daimler, wearing his grandfather's morning dress and wielding a pair of silver scissors. After the ceremony, he embraced his brother Neil who had turned up in a pair of lederhosen, and arm in arm they walked off until this extraordinary looking pair was out of sight. The following year, incidentally, on coming into power, de Gaulle paid a visit too, but he stipulated he would not enter by the main gate which was in Switzerland, but by the side gate in France.

Most Western European countries moved closer together, after Bruges and Maastricht and the fall of the Berlin Wall, when membership of the European Union widened to the east. The rationale for it now changed from Peace to Power – a more powerful continent – if only policies could be aligned. Crucial steps in bringing this about were the monetary union with the creation of the Euro, the growing strength of Germany and agreements on public spending. But, given the subsequent financial disasters, a 'two-speed Europe' and the complex relationship between the European and national Parliaments, federation is out of reach.

There are those, however, ruled perhaps more by their heart than their head, who still share the views of Jean Monnet, in his *Mémoires*:

The European idea is a deep and powerful movement on an historic scale.... Like our provinces in the past, our nations today must learn to live together under common rules and institutions freely arrived at. The Sovereign nations of the past can no longer solve the problems of the present: they cannot ensure their own powers or contain their own future. And the community itself is only a stage on the way to the organised world of tomorrow.

We shall see.

Being formally accredited to Italy, Belgium, Holland, and Switzerland gave me the opportunity to make comparisons between our respective Ambassadors. Unlike Sir Gladwyn Jebb, Sir George Labouchère in Brussels I found truly delightful with his old world courtesies and, among other interests, a love of antique furniture. He admitted almost proudly, 'Science is a subject I *never* studied at school.' Sir Paul Mason in The Hague, keenly interested in all I was up to, simply 'looked forward to learning.' Sir Lionel Lamb in Berne and his slightly eccentric successor Sir William Montagu-Pollock could only be described as 'enthusiastic amateurs', whilst Sir Ashley Clarke in Rome was positively constructive and questioning, arranging for Italian industrialists I wished to meet to come to the Embassy to do so.

One weekend, when Diana and I were briefly in Bournemouth, a message arrived from Ashley Clarke. 'Can you be here at nine o'clock on Monday morning to meet Enrico Mattei, head of AGIP Nucléaire?' Diana, with her love of Italy, volunteered to drive me to Rome in her Vauxhall Cresta. At great speed she negotiated the narrow coastal road from France near Imperia, overtaking the continuous stream of huge Supercortemaggiore oil tankers, to arrive triumphantly at the Embassy with minutes to spare. As I went into the meeting, she said, 'Now will you let me enter the Monte Carlo Rally?'

I had read that Mattei also headed up the Italian Energy Ministry and, as such, had just awarded a large grant to his own company. I asked him whether that was true. In the UK it would be regarded as a clear conflict of interest. 'Yes, it is true,' he said. 'You see, you can afford to take that view. In Italy we have so few qualified and capable people at the top. We are obliged to share out a large number of appointments between us.' I think he spoke only half in jest.

On one occasion in Berne, Leo Lamb, as he was known, told me of his childhood years. A diplomat's son, born in Erzerum on the Black Sea, miles off the beaten track, he went on to live in China for thirty years. Rising from student interpreter in the Peking Embassy, he held consular appointments in most cities, became fluent in many dialects and was Minister in Nanking when HMS Amethyst was attacked by the Communists' Yangtze River shore batteries. He asked me to dinner together with the Australian and Canadian Ambassadors in Berne. Over coffee the Chinese Ambassador to Switzerland joined us. He had brought with him a document he could not understand and Lamb immediately translated it into Mandarin for him.

On a later visit, our Consul General in Zurich told me about Lamb's successor. William Montagu-Pollack had survived an early setback to his career in Rome when, as a twenty-four year old, he was arrested for being disrespectful to a fascist policeman. In Lausanne Montagu-Pollock introduced me to the Swiss President and then, in 1958, arranged for me to address the leading Swiss industrialists gathered together in Zurich. The occasion was sponsored by Escher-Wyss, engineers from the time of Napoleon. I was able to tell them that after their founder Hans Caspar Escher had seen an English spinning machine in operation in St Gallen, he sent his son Albert to England to be trained in mechanical engineering, so setting the company on course for its great development.

He and I subsequently had conferred on us the Freedom of Schaffhausen, being ceremoniously kissed on both cheeks by the Stadt President and then the Kanton President, before joining in a long procession on a hot summer's day to a celebratory reception. Whether anyone remained sober, I don't remember! Montagu-Pollack went on to be Ambassador in Copenhagen, where Diana and I were invited to stay, before he retired to a life of comparative seclusion at the sandy tip of the Playa Blanca in Lanzarote.

The scientific organisation and activities of each of 'my' countries differed widely. In France, research and development were largely divorced and the national organisation was less effective as a result. In Belgium, the government's role was minimal, and institutions were fragmented and often duplicated between the independent Flemish and Walloon communities.

Local allegiances were all-important. I was asked to give an address in English on the centenary of the Ecole des Mines in Liège and, over lunch, the Mayor asked me whether I recognised what the orchestra was playing. I thought it might be by César Franck and said, 'Ah! A Belgian composer.'

'Absolutely not' he replied. 'A Liègeois. There was no Belgium until 1830.' Years later, after my return to London I was given the task of appraising Belgian scientific policy officially. Some of my recommended improvements were put to Théo Lefèvre, who had become Prime Minister, and implemented. The divided nation has still not been able to unite its institutions, however.

In the Netherlands, more emphasis was placed on the selection of projects to be supported in the interests of the economy. I paid frequent visits, notably to Philips of Eindhoven, with its worldwide reputation, and the applied research and development laboratories of the TNO, comparable to our own DSIR. I arrived at their Waterloopkundig (Hydraulics Research Establishment) in Delft after the serious flooding of the country, which caused so many deaths and enormous damage. It coincided with their Queen's visit. She asked Dr Thysse the Director, 'How high would you have to build the dykes to prevent this from happening again?'

He replied, 'Anything is possible in nature, but one metre would prevent a recurrence on average every ten years and two metres perhaps every forty years.'

When I visited the laboratory again a year later I asked Thysse what had been decided. He said, 'We were allowed to spend whatever the government had left over, after all other commitments had been met!'

Switzerland was renowned for its specialisation in 'niche' areas, such as precision engineering and optical devices like radio theodolites. They excelled in these and in speciality chemicals and sophisticated pharmaceuticals, competing with the best in the world. They were strongly supported by the ETH (the Zurich Polytechnic) with a reputation second to none for teaching its students to incorporate from the outset the economic and marketing factors relating to their science and technology programmes.

In Italy, by contrast, government support for teaching and research was among the lowest in Europe. The country's achievements were almost entirely those of the few large research companies, Fiat and Montecatini in particular, and with emphasis on the building up of the under-developed south, the *Cassa del Mezzogiorno*. On a visit to Florence, calling on Professor Giordano, I met one of his young postgraduate staff and asked him about his own research project. He said he did not have time for much experimental work. As a quid pro quo for helping the relatively poor Giordano family with secretarial and domestic duties, the Professor would eventually sign him up for his PhD!

Attempts to rationalise the applied scientific effort in Europe had met with some success where complimentary facilities could be shared. The OEEC, for example, arranged for the study of corrosion of ships' hulls in which Norwegian ship builders using British anti-fouling paints could use warm Italian harbours for their investigations. Again, for aircraft safety purposes, investigations on metal fatigue were successfully made with tests on forty-three million pieces of metal in nine different national laboratories.

On a wider industrial front, by setting up an operational branch of the OECD, the European Productivity Agency, 'best practice' was being promoted. And even in the sensitive field of nuclear energy, the Dragon Project was initiated when Sir John Cockcroft, Sir William Cook and Sir Leonard Owen together – over lunch in our flat – discussed the approach to cooperative development internationally.

Some of the more ambitious members of the OECD, usually reflecting the wishes of their respective governments, went on to seek an overall 'policy for science.' But its purpose was interpreted ambiguously. Two well-publicised conferences were attended by Ministers of Science, but they made little lasting impact. As time went on, in matters of cooperation in Europe, OECD was no longer the focus of attention. The OECD began to turn to the broad global issues of overpopulation, education, the environment and poverty.

The Soviet Union's launch of Sputnik in 1957 was a major spur to joint scientific endeavours in Europe and in the USA. But a bigger influence still on European cooperation came as a result of the successive measures towards economic integration already begun by The Six.

As is widely known, at the Messina Conference in 1955 two schemes had been put forward which led to the Common Market and Euratom. Without consulting Britain, Robert Schuman, in collaboration with Jean Monnet, then heading up the French Planning Commission, set out a plan in which they were joined by Paul-Henri Spaak of Belgium and Alcide de Gasperi of Italy, to set up economic and military institutions between The Six. Their strategy was not indicated, but very much in their minds was their wish to forge forthright Franco-German collaboration, leading to long-term unification in Western Europe. I had the opportunity of discussing all this with Michael Palliser, then a First Secretary in the Embassy, from his diplomatic perspective.

The European Coal and Steel Community had already been set up in 1951. Controlled by the High Authority in Luxembourg, under the Presidency of Jean Monnet, it formed one unified market and produced one sixth of the world's hard coal. Being accredited to Luxembourg, where Sir William Meiklereid was Ambassador to the ECS Community, I accompanied him to their headquarters, the former office of the Luxembourg Railways. They certainly did a valuable job in technology, but the political context was never far away. I remember the Dutch representative taking me aside and whispering, 'We must prevent the Ruhr once again making bombs to destroy us.'

When it came to establishing the Common Market, Mendes France had actually opposed French membership. Guy Mollet's subsequent coalition government was a little more favourable, as was Konrad Adenauer's, so the Treaty of Rome which was signed in 1957 aimed at removing all barriers to the movement of goods, capital and labour.

The UK was disturbed by the prospect of a federation and countered with a Free Trade Area of Seven. However, there was little confidence that it would be realised. Negotiations dragged on for almost two years before it was stopped abruptly once de Gaulle assumed power.

The call for Euratom was for an agency with its own Parliament and Council of Ministers, to bring together all the resources of The Six and generate as much atomic energy as possible. It followed recognition that Western Europe was becoming dangerously over-dependent on imports for its total energy needs. The UK, by comparison, imported only 11% and had already built Calder Hall, the best reactor in the world.

I reported some possible export opportunities for British firms and in October 1958 the Board of Trade called me to address this issue comprehensively, before a large audience in Whitehall. I spoke about the opportunities both to export and to collaborate with continental firms and institutions, stressing the need to act urgently whilst we still had a commanding lead. Cockcroft had supplied me with some of his calculations. Reactor capital costs and fuel costs together would soon be less than costs for coal-fired stations, but the future costs of waste treatment, decommissioning and disposal were still uncertain. At the time my talk was commended as being 'invaluable' and there were indeed a few early collaborative arrangements, but the will to win was lacking and too little follow up in the next couple of years. By then I had been called to return home to a new appointment.

Throughout the second half of the 1950s, as a price for the deployment of US troops in Europe, Germany, now within NATO, was being re-armed by the USA. Considerable US funds were available to support agreed projects. With its headquarters then in Paris, our successive Ambassadors Sir Christopher Steel and Sir Frank Roberts took little part in its Science Committee, but Sir Solly (later Lord) Zuckerman with considerable authority made frequent visits. From time to time he told me of their proposals to strengthen the Western Alliance and to some extent developing countries too and of how, too often, strategic considerations and the scientific merit of intended projects were mutually incompatible. Some of the participants regarded their agenda as 'pursuing science against others'. Some merely tried to make good their own national scientific deficiencies. The brief of some foreign ministries was, in effect, 'Give in a little on science, if there are political benefits to be gained,' whilst finance ministries were saying, 'Do co-operate, but your projects must be financed out of the national science budgets you have.' Frank Roberts and his wife invited us quite often to meet other NATO Ambassadors. On one occasion he expressed his concern that Jebb was not content with his limited role in France following his wide UN experience and asked me, 'Why does Gladwyn want my job as well as his own?'

I was fortunate to find myself as a witness and occasionally a participant in events involving the interplay between science, technology, diplomacy and foreign policy. The Council of Europe Secretariat had invited me in 1956 to apply for a Council Research Fellowship. Guy Mollet was then President of the Council, hoisting its flag in Strasbourg. I was asked to present a paper on *The Possibilities and Significance of European Collaboration in Scientific and Technical Research.* As it involved no extra work on my part, but gave me a welcome opportunity to interview others, it was approved in London and I was granted a small Fellowship award by the Secretary General.

I had thought about this topic a year earlier. In August 1955, at the UN Conference on the Peaceful Uses of Atomic Energy, 1,260 official delegates from seventy-three countries came to Geneva to meet under the Presidency of Professor Bhaba of India. I was one of the five official British representatives then led by Sir John Cockcroft.

From the political point of view, the most stimulating aspect of this and a second conference in 1958 was the interaction between the unifying forces of international co-operation and the disruptive ones, where delegates competed for national prestige. At times, positions became polarised. On the one hand most of the fundamental scientists, the smaller national delegations and the UN specialised agencies aimed to create an atmosphere of wholehearted collaboration. They lived up to the high hopes of the UN Secretary General, Dag Hammerskjøld, in his opening address. However, in the exchanges between the United States and the Soviet Union and in many of the Press reports the competition for technological, commercial and political prestige predominated. At the Second Conference, the hopes of the scientific community rose when we and America agreed to declassify fusion research reports and Russia donated a hundred of its own unpublished research reports in this field.

As seen by impartial observers, the UK almost alone emerged with its status enhanced. We lent our weight to a policy of co-operation in science, but competition in commerce. France did not. Though contributing well to the technical discussions, the French delegations took an independent, somewhat provocative line and certainly failed to be sufficiently sympathetic to improve their immediate prospects of joining the exclusive Nuclear Club, as they would have wished.

The ideas beginning to develop in my mind about a job to be done were quite exciting. The interplay was growing in complexity and importance. No institution or individual to my knowledge was responsible for studying it. Historically our government had failed to recognise the foreign policy implications of scientific achievements and their consequences, and now the timescale for this to be acted upon had shortened.

We had missed opportunities before. We had failed to recognise during World War I that Haber's synthetic ammonia process could be the basis for all explosive production, so that the Allied blockade intended to cut off Germany from the Chilean nitrates was rendered ineffective. The Netherlands and Britain once held a virtual monopoly of the world's rubber. Again, had we realised the possibilities for synthetic rubber production on a large scale, immediately before World War II, we could have avoided serious political friction, particularly with the United States.

Then in 1939 Hahn and Strassman showed that when a neutron collided with a uranium atom, the nucleus could be split with a loss of mass and as Einstein showed, to produce a large amount of energy.

Very few then imagined it could quickly lead to a devastating weapon. Two years later we did recognise it and in just four more years the Hiroshima atom bomb ended the war with Japan.

Now it was clear to me that as an ingredient in foreign policy formulation geography was giving way to technology and geo-politics to techno-politics. This would dramatically shift the equilibrium in international relations.

With the rise and fall of our economic, military and political aspirations over the years, it is a wonder that we and France could so recently be celebrating the centenary of the *Entente Cordiale*. We have had our disagreements, over the European Constitution and Iraq, for example. But we trade vigorously with each other; three million French people visit Britain each year and twelve million of us go in the opposite direction, thanks, no doubt to the weather. One hundred thousand Britons have homes in France and the same number of young French people come over each year to learn English.

Our greatest joint achievement in engineering has been the construction of the Channel Tunnel. Incredibly, it was first proposed 200 years ago, but within a year we were at war. With the signing of the *Entente Cordiale*, a new impetus was given for the Tunnel, but again the prospect of war in 1914 held it back. When the possibility of joining the Common Market arose in the sixties, it was agreed that a rail tunnel would be a good investment. Ernest Marples, our Minister of Transport in 1964 asked me to discuss it over lunch in his flat. I remember the occasion for one reason alone. I had been studying the bottle of Fleurie on the table between us. 'What do you think of this?' he said, 'I bottle it myself.'

'I see the label reads *mis à bouteille,* M Ernest Marples. I think that should be *mis en bouteille,*' I replied.

'Oh, should it? Well, the people who drink this won't know the difference!' [photo, page 167]

Looking back over the past century there have been times when the Entente might have been better described as Glaciale than Cordiale. Very often, national pride was at the heart of the problem. We all applaud our victors and heroes – Henry V and his bowman at Agincourt, Nelson and his band of brothers at Trafalgar, Churchill and The Few in the Battle of Britain. They have indeed been an inspiration. But strength in the longer term is never a matter of fleets and armies and politics alone. Our institutions, the character of our people, their alliances and mutual trust are critical.

There would be a need not only to adjust our policies, but so far as possible predict and prepare for the consequences of technological capabilities to come. The main obstacle to solving this was the lack of communication and adequate understanding between the parties involved and the absence of a framework for an effective dialogue to inform judgements.

The USA and Soviet Union had both begun to consider this issue, but it raised discordant views. When in 1957, President Eisenhower appointed James Killian as Special Adviser and moved him from the Office of Defence Mobilisation to the Executive Office of the White House, there was an outcry, the theme of which was that by promising miracles, self-interested scientists were able to obtain large funding without proper public accountability. However, by February 1960 Dr Kistiakowsky, Special Assistant to the President, re-emphasised the importance of an effective dialogue and a framework for it, in a Department of State Bulletin. The US Senate Foreign Relations Committee had also become sufficiently interested to ask the Carnegie Foundation for International Peace in New York to undertake a one-year study selecting its own team of scientists and diplomats for this purpose.

For my part, I set out my thoughts in a short memo for Patrick Reilly and Gladwyn Jebb. They backed it up and forwarded it to Paul Gore Booth, head of the Foreign Office. The Foreign Office in turn supported them, and all three encouraged me to pursue the subject. I was asked in particular to demonstrate how scientific and technological advice could contribute to diplomacy and policy and how I thought they could affect the balance of an increasingly precarious East-West equilibrium.

My view was that calling for advice from practising scientists, on an ad hoc basis when needed, was inadequate. This view was supported by the Advisory Council on Scientific Policy, whose Chairman, then Sir Alexander Todd, pointed out, 'Scientific Attachés had acquired a unique view of the interplay. Their continuity as official representatives was better than scientists, no matter how eminent, when problems were becoming increasingly orientated towards applications relevant to many Departmental responsibilities.'

I saw a need for a Foreign Office appointment at a senior level, a scientist or technologist of wide experience for this role. Todd's decisions usually carried the day, not least after he had been ennobled and awarded the Nobel Prize and Order of Merit, but there was no decision for some time.

It was at that moment after six years away, that I was suddenly called back to the UK to be told by Sir Harry Melville, head of DSIR, that I was to become Director of the Forest Products Research Laboratory (FPRL) in Princes Risborough. This came as a complete surprise. I was puzzled as I knew nothing about trees or timber. On the other hand I had become enthusiastic about the chance of developing what I believed would become an increasingly important matter for the government in formulating foreign policy.

I had already been tipped off that if I wanted to transfer to the Foreign Service at my present level I would be welcome, but my next appointment could be anywhere. I saw no way of applying my specialist experience in Phnom Penh, nor did I believe that if I were to join in this way, I would have begun early enough in diplomacy to emulate my Paris colleagues with up to twenty years of successful Foreign Service experience behind them. I had learned from them how many factors they took into account – national aspirations, economic necessities, strategic and material possibilities, traditions and personalities. I was greatly impressed by the understanding and contributions in meetings and dispatches of my Embassy colleagues, Michael Palliser, Anthony Duff, Murray Maclehose, Brooks Richards, all then in mid-career, all eventually going to the top.

I was still on the books of the Department of Scientific and Industrial Research. 'We are quite content to leave you in Paris indefinitely, if that was your wish,' Melville said, 'but this post is a promotion and to an executive role for the first time. With a staff of 162, you would have the chance to demonstrate any leadership qualities we believe you have.' I said I would like to think about it overnight.

I quickly read the Annual Reports of the Laboratory and recognised that the high quality and volume of their research publications was hardly matched by valuable applications. Perhaps, with a change in programme, the Laboratory could help British industry do better and conceivably, do more to justify its support from public funds. I also liked the idea of running something. Then I thought of what it would mean for my family, returning to England. Our children would soon all be of school age, my father had recently died and my mother was now on her own. I accepted what I regarded as a risky job with enthusiasm, and we all prepared to pack and leave for Princes Risborough.

Diana and I had been so happy in Paris; we could have stayed forever. We absorbed the culture, loved the social whirl, and had the good fortune to encounter the most interesting people of distinction and achievement, of working with talented colleagues and friends. It opened up a new international perspective for us as a family. But after our first, second and third child were born in Paris, the telegram I received from my boss read, 'Congratulations, once again. But that was not the purpose of your mission. Return to London immediately.' Those six years seemed like a lifetime.

Within weeks of beginning work at the Laboratory I received a letter inviting me to take part in the Carnegie Science & Foreign Policy Project in the USA and naturally I could not pursue it. Then Patrick Reilly wrote to me. On becoming Ambassador in Moscow he had cited his successful experience with me in Paris to get approval for the appointment of a Scientific Attaché to his own staff. Now he asked if I would prepare a short paper on what we had proposed to the Foreign Office earlier. I sent him an outline reiterating the growing number and importance of issues on which the Office could benefit with the appointment of an in-house scientific advisor. I gave examples of how my office, using the language of science, had helped to achieve wider cooperation and expand our overseas trade already. As we had a lead internationally we should exert our influence and carefully select partners with whom we could collaborate.

This was seen by Sir Paul Gore Booth, who wrote to the Royal Society, asking them for their comments on this. Their Fellows had maintained our international scientific relationships with distinction, through war and peace, for three centuries. The reply, a personal one from D.C. Martin, effectively their chief executive, was that though the matter should be treated very seriously indeed, it was a somewhat intangible one. Would I therefore meet a small group of Fellows of the Royal Society who had expressed an interest at Burlington House to prepare the ground? It was to be an informal meeting but a formidable group – Sir Patrick Linstead, Sir John Cockcroft, Lord Fleck, Sir Charles Dodds, Sir Willis Jackson and Sir Joseph Hutchinson. I had checked my draft paper with my fellow Scientific Counsellors, E.S. Hiscocks in Washington and Brigadier Spedding in Bonn and reported all this to Sir Harry Melville.

A few days later, however, Melville wrote to me: 'I am disturbed about the request you have had to attend the Royal Society on 7th December…I think you should not go to this meeting. If the Royal Society wants information in this field, it must either go to the Foreign Office, or make contact with our organisation centrally, so that the official view can be put.'

I had to apologise to Martin, saying this subject would no doubt be taken up officially. I also had to write to Melville to confirm that the meeting had been cancelled. It was never rearranged.

Two years went by. I was engrossed in my new work, when Sir Patrick Reilly wrote again, asking me to return to the same subject, in the two-week Foreign Office Summer School for Senior Officers to be held in July 1963 at Peterhouse, Cambridge. In the previous year, Sir Humphrey Trevelyan had presided, when the general problems of foreign policy in the next five years were considered. Now under the Chairmanship of Sir John Nicholls the subject was 'Science, Technology and Foreign Affairs'. Sir Harold Hartley, Sir Solly Zuckerman, Sir Harrie Massey, Sir Harry Melville, Sir Harold Himsworth, Sir Andrew Cohen and Lord Todd were principal speakers. I was delighted to see this topic at last getting the attention and debate it deserved, especially when the earlier exchanges were revealed! Eventually it led, as I hoped it would, to a rearrangement of the Foreign Office's internal organisation to deal with this issue.

I was still being called upon personally, from time to time, to speak at International Conferences, in Teheran in 1963 at a meeting of CENTO (the Central Treaty Organisation with Iran, Pakistan and Turkey participating), then in Ankara, Brussels, Washington and in Turin where my speech on European co-operation attracted the attention of the lead writer of *The Times*, and finally in September 1967, at the request of the Foreign Office, at the European Parliament in Luxembourg. There, with David Owen, I addressed the subject of a European Technological Community, which had been floated by Harold Wilson in his Guildhall speech the previous November.

From time to time the government gradually realised the range and importance of topics and international organisations involved. They included satellite broadcasting, uranium enrichment, environmental damage and non-proliferation issues, and work in conjunction with the UN, EEC, OECD and NATO Departments. By 1970, the FCO had established a new Science and Technology Department to deal with them, with a staff of six under Ronald Arculus, who was later knighted. After 1972 this was extended to two Departments reporting to a Super Director. It had taken long to materialise and now I was too busy to remain involved. It was reassuring, though, that over the years that followed, the contributions of our Royal Society Fellows and others became of great importance, the FCO recruited one of their all-rounders to be Chief Scientific Adviser, and that my original judgement for the need had not been unjustified. I had just got there too soon!

CHAPTER V

Science and National Prosperity

Research Director 1960–62

It was a culture shock to be transferred from the elegance of diplomatic life in Paris to a tiny cottage in rural Naphill, and for me from affairs of state to the dedicated backroom scientists and down-to-earth craftsmen. Sir Patrick Reilly wrote to me, 'As a test of character it must be comparable to my shock on moving from Paris to become Ambassador here in Moscow, at the height of the Cold War!'

I arrived at Princes Risborough with no knowledge of trees and no acquaintance with the timber industry, to direct a long-serving and well-qualified laboratory staff. Editors of the trade journals were scathing about my appointment: 'He is ignorant.' They were right. How could I demonstrate the rationale behind my appointment? In academic circles, the Laboratory was held in high regard. I had succeeded Professor Frank Henderson, formerly of Imperial College, and Sir Ralph Pearson, who had established it originally to promote the more economic use of timber. It did much to support the 'Buy Empire Goods Campaign' in the 1930s and, during the war, advise on the use of unfamiliar hardwoods arriving from Africa and South America.

The return to peacetime production in a period of stringent shortages brought a need for soft currency timbers in place of hard. There was a new need to assist the Forestry Commission with a policy to invest in home-grown plantations. One of our aims therefore was to help foresters produce better quality timber in larger quantity, and to find uses for the thinnings and lower grades both from state and private ownership. A second purpose, to help British industry, seemed to have been neglected.

I took an early opportunity to address the industry on the national problems we faced. We had to import nine tenths of our timber. Its cost was comparable to our entire balance of payments deficit. How could we extract the maximum value from it? This was the big question.

Almost every day I took a walk around the establishment, which was spread across many acres of countryside. I looked in on specialist laboratories and workshops and chatted with everyone. Soon I realised that in a rather academic environment, whilst motivation for research of real quality was admirable, abstracted from the commercial world, they took a rather leisurely approach. There were no rewards for successful practical initiatives, no promotion prospects other than vacancies due to retirement, key research staff were ageing and there was little opportunity to get close to industrialists, other than the local furniture manufacturers in High Wycombe. This had to change, but only in a way that was widely acceptable. I invited more ideas from staff at all levels.

Our first steps were to open the doors widely to industry. At our Open Days, all activities were on display and explained; visitors crowded in and they increased sevenfold to 8,000. We set up an Intelligence Section to deal with the volume of practical problems that industrial companies began to raise with us. They came from companies across the public services. The Central Electricity Board had to increase the life of the timber fill of its cooling towers and there were 415 of them. The treatment cost only 10% of the timber, but could extend its life from ten years to thirty years, equal to the life of the power stations themselves. British Railways had 105 million sleepers on the tracks and the Post Office millions of poles. They were all treated less expensively with preservatives derived from the laboratory's research. In financial terms the most remarkable results arose from our seasoning investigations.

I learned that it took as much as five years to import logs, season and hold them for treatment and manufacture. It was this delay that incurred much of the cost – the cumulative interest paid on stocks held. We set out to reduce the seasoning time by studying the physical characteristics of each species so as not to harm them, carefully changing their kiln drying schedules, the design of the kilns and the training of the kiln operators. The time required was reduced to one fifth. And so in time were the national stocks of timber. It was calculated that within three years, tens of millions of pounds were saved in interest, representing over a thousand times the entire cost of our R&D programmes and perhaps, according to Sir Stuart Mallinson, one of the large beneficiaries, a hundred times the entire cost to the industry of implementing the change. In addition some of our timber yards could be sold off. We were given the credit for being one of the earliest to start at the far end of the industry's supply chain, looking into its economics, and adopting what was quite an unorthodox approach for a government research laboratory.

There were opportunities both for interdisciplinary projects within the Laboratory and for multilateral collaborative work with our counterparts abroad. Of the former, by combining the joint efforts of our wood structure, chemistry, physics and preservatives sections, we could modify the cellulose content and harden the wood. When asked how I hit on that idea, I had to admit it was based on schoolboy memories of dipping conkers in vinegar!

The collaboration with Scandinavia, the most important source of our timber, was more significant. We invited the four research directors, from Denmark, Finland, Sweden and Norway, for joint talks in Princes Risborough, which lasted a week. Our subsequent joint efforts proved successful and less costly.

One fascinating outcome of this collaboration was an invitation to inspect the submerged Swedish warship Wasa, which was being resurfaced in Stockholm harbour. It was a sixty-four gun man-of-war, built in 1628, intended to control the Baltic. Owing to a faulty top-heavy design she keeled over in the wind and sank as she began her maiden voyage. After many earlier attempts to salvage her, unsuccessful except for retrieving the guns, she was finally brought to the surface and pulled in to dry dock. The seamen's chests were full of clothes and drinking vessels and personal items were scattered around. The ship's timbers were in very good condition after 333 years on the bottom, but if allowed to dry out they would rapidly shrink and split. Action was needed urgently. I was present at the beginning of the cleaning and preservation process. They were using polyglycol, a Swedish product, but agreed that the addition of boric acid and borax that we had already tried out in our laboratory would provide further protection against decay.

Professor Siimes and his wife asked Diana and me to visit them in Helsinki. Whilst the others went shopping, Siimes introduced me to the Sauna Society, of which he was President. As we entered this imposing building he warned me, 'In the next three hours you will lose the equivalent of half a bottle of whisky. Let's order some. Waiter, a bottle of Scotch!' It was only just beginning to take effect after half an hour in the sauna, when an Amazonian 'bath-lady' came in, picked me up by an ankle and wrist and threw me out into the snow. I got up like a scalded cat.

Then Siimes appeared. 'How do you feel now?'

'Terrific,' I said, 'as though I weigh two ounces.'

'You've definitely lost the equivalent of half a bottle of whisky; we'd better order another one,' he said. 'Waiter, a bottle of Scotch.'

In the course of our Open Days a few companies asked us to undertake particular investigations for them, so we agreed terms and entered into contracts to do so. We used the first fees to recruit two scientists and one engineer for that purpose. The Treasury objected. Because they controlled the funds they sought to control recruitment. But when I maintained we were not asking for additional public funds, they gave way.

The industry's trade journals began to warm to what we were doing. They reported: 'A new spirit abroad at Princes Risborough.' Among the staff, the more academic members who had no deadlines for completing their work saw others hurrying down the corridors to complete R&D contracts on time. At a Royal Society Conversazione our first radioactive carbon 14 dating method was on display. And a boost in the morale of our craftsmen quickly followed. Having nominated Bill Waterman, our Saw Doctor for the Imperial Service Order, in recognition of his thirty-four years of service to the Lab, I was asked to present it at a large gathering.

Our links with the Forestry Commission remained close. Twelve members of its staff worked on our site. I joined their Advisory Committee under the Chairmanship of Lord Radnor and accompanied them to Scotland for the inauguration of a ten-year coastal planting programme on Culbin Sands, between Inverness and Elgin. The area had not long been above sea level, but preliminary results showed that spruces would flourish and the plan was to plant millions of them and take the thinnings to the pulping mills of Wiggins Teape in Fort William. The Treasury had undertaken to match industry's own contribution, if we could obtain the first £7 million.

As our small plane touched down in a field near Nairn, Radnor and I could see that a huge breakfast had been laid on for us by the local landowners and foresters, whose families had lived there for centuries. We sat down and tucked in. Radnor turned to me and said, 'Now's our chance, ask them for the money.'

I'd hardly struggled to my feet before my neighbour stopped me. 'Och man, sit down, you've got the money.'

'Surely it can't be as easy as that?' I asked.

'It grows at 7% compound while we're asleep,' he replied. We received the money and the matching grant. Over the years the plantation developed to become the well-established Culbin Forest, nine miles long.

I was asked to participate in the eighth British Commonwealth Conference, held in Nairobi in June 1962. The delegates came from Australia, Canada, Kenya, Malaysia, New Zealand, Tanganyika and Uganda. Though still a 'new boy' I was Chairman. In the course of three days, we were able to agree on where new, small forest product laboratories could best be established, what they should do over the next five years and submit a proposal for coordination by the Department for Technical Co-operation.

Arriving at Nairobi airport, I was met by a member of our East African High Commission who told me, Jomo Kenyatta wanted to see me. I said, 'You must have the wrong man. Anyway I thought he was in jail.'

'No, he's out now, he's Prime Minister. It won't be long before he's President and, for some reason, he wants to see you.' So after flying through the night, I was rushed off to his office to be greeted by a broad grin and a handshake so powerful it hurt for ages.

He flicked me on my chin with his silver fly-whisk and said, 'I'll tell you how to plan the future of your country.'

'Are you mistaking me for someone else, Prime Minister?' I asked.

Handing me a page of *The Times*, two months old, he said, 'Tom Mboya kept a file for me. This is you, isn't it?' The cutting reported my appointment to the National Economic Development Council (Neddy) as Chief Technical Officer. Well what could I say? 'Well thank you, we will need all the help we can get.' I put it down to euphoria on his release because I didn't get any advice, just another excruciating handshake and a promise to 'keep in touch'.

With experiences such as these, I was really sad to be leaving the Laboratory. Work had only just begun. It was some consolation to read the editorials of the trade magazines that had protested about my appointment, now eating their words. I was awarded the industry Federation's 'Palm for the Speech of the Year'. *The Master Builder* which, in July 1960, had originally announced my appointment: 'Naval geologist, radar, intelligence, chemist for FPRL' was corrected by *The Timber Trade Journal* in 1962: 'We were wrong when we cast doubt on his appointment – he is the sort of man needed by the timber trade. His stay with us is far too short.'

Lord Hailsham, my Minister, wrote to me: 'I sincerely wish you good fortune in your new and extremely important work astride the new quadruped (Neddy) – not, I hope long-eared!' After earlier setbacks I had found relief in this unlikely appointment. To be at Princes Risborough in the early Sixties was to be in the right place at the right time with a great team.

I was still to discover how limited my perspective had been. I was critical of 'stand alone' science when I quoted John Jorrocks: 'Science is the ticket; everything should be done by science' (addressing his fellow farmers on the merits of *nitrate o' sober,* in Surtees' novel *Hillingdon Hall*), but I still regarded the innovative process as a chain of events, in sequence, and had not been challenged. I was to learn differently. So many inputs, interlinked, interdependent, and running in parallel were needed to succeed.

National Economic Development Council 1962–1964

The telephone call came from Sir Frank Turnbull who headed Lord Hailsham's office. 'What are you up to at the moment?' he asked.

'I am with our mycologist, before he visits HMS Victory,' I told him, 'seeing how he will deal with wood rot in Captain Hardy's sea chest.'

'Well, this is perhaps a little more urgent. Will you come here tomorrow afternoon? Sir Robert Shone would like to meet you. It's about a job in his office.'

'I have a job,' I replied rather lamely. I was intrigued, because Shone was Director General of the newly established National Economic Development Council. Far from my own laboratory world, I wondered 'why me'?

After a few hours in a library I could pretend to know more than I did. I took the train to London, calling first on Turnbull for any advice, then on to see Hailsham in his office, who was with David Eccles, President of the Board of Trade. Eccles told me something of the background and the questions they expected Neddy would be addressing. 'Why was Britain's wealth growing much more slowly than Europe's? Was it balance of payments constraints, stop-go policy, lack of incomes policy or the power of the trade unions? How could we be more competitive, increase exports and gain full employment?' All a far cry from what I had been concerned with.

He went on: continental competition would be a stimulus but, whether we were in or out of Europe, we had to raise industrial productivity and develop the new methods which technology could bring within our reach. The relative contribution of R&D was still a matter of argument, but this was one aspect of interest to Neddy. How could I contribute?

Arriving at Shone's office in Bridge Street, just opposite the House of Commons, I found him with Sir Donald McDougal, the economist who had accompanied Churchill to the Potsdam conference in 1945 before retiring to academic life in Oxford. Shone seated me in the third armchair with a cup of tea and came straight to the point. 'We have asked you, and one other person has been nominated, to see who might join us as Chief Technical Officer. Is this something you could do?'

To bide my time, I asked, 'Why me?' Shone replied, 'We will be developing plans for economic growth. You have seen something of Jean Monet's planning system in operation in France, and now your laboratory is beginning to develop activities to generate results which should benefit the economy.'

'So far as planning is concerned,' I said, 'I cannot see the French plan as a model for us.' I added that France did have a fast expanding economy, but that was because an agricultural country being industrialised and modernised grew fast. In addition, their powerful bureaucratic institutions regarded planning as the logical way of doing things. However, as far as our economy was concerned, I firmly believed technological innovation was essential for growth and expanded on this.

I was rather startled when Shone told me the make-up of the all-embracing Council: the Chancellor of the Exchequer, Minister of Labour and President of the Board of Trade, all without officials; the heads of the TUC, TGWU and AEU (Woodcock, Cousins and Carron respectively); Robens (NCB), Beeching (BTC) and Oliver Franks. I wondered where the leadership and sense of direction might be found – or would they simply be fact-finding and relieved to find some common ground? After a few minutes' silence, McDougal looked at Shone who suddenly said,

'We propose you join us, and as quickly as possible. I'll speak to Turnbull.'

I returned to Princes Risborough in something of a daze. Surely I was out of my depth? Surely another risky venture? But I could learn a great deal and I would be promoted. I was still wondering what on earth I could deliver and had not yet accepted, when my appointment was suddenly announced in the Press. Our children returned home from school very excited that their Daddy was working with Noddy!

It was months before I could be completely free from the Laboratory. I continued part-time until a new Director could be appointed. Happily they accepted my recommendation of promoting my Deputy. He had served loyally and well and, I believe, was half expecting to be given the job instead of me in the first place.

McDougal, Fraser (the Industrial Director) and I, supported by a well qualified staff from the public and private sectors, set out to prepare two reports. One was *The growth of the UK economy to 1966* (the Green Book) and the other was *Conditions favourable to faster growth* (the Orange Book).

On the first report there was argument about the assumptions made, and consequently about the value of its conclusions. The all important 4% growth objective was itself a compromise. Shone much preferred 3%, Selwyn Lloyd was holding out for 5% and Alec Cairncross seemed to be the broker who brought him down to the 4% figure.

Apart from growth rate, we entertained alternative assumptions: whether or not we would be within the EEC, seek to balance our payments and bring unemployment down to below 300,000. When Maudling succeeded Selwyn Lloyd as Chairman, I asked him informally before a meeting, 'If we can't achieve all of these, what are our priorities?'.

'We just have to do the best we can,' he replied.

Shone said to me afterwards: 'Typical of the man, not a patch on Selwyn Lloyd.' It was not until later I learned that Selwyn Lloyd was Shone's brother-in-law.

The second report, on the conditions that would be required, was of greater influence. It tackled the issues of prices and income policy, mobility of labour, training and redundancy, capital investment, the need to stimulate technical progress, touching on the contribution of research and development, the scale and distribution of its funding investment allowances, and regional policy. All of these sooner or later should enter into the legislative process. That was the intention.

Our studies underlined how serious the economic situation was. Government, industry and labour all agreed we had to be more competitive internationally, but that's all they seemed to agree on. To achieve this, the Treasury wanted to restrain incomes, because wages were growing faster than productivity, damaging our exports and balance of payments. The TUC said that wages were not the problem; import controls and export incentives were needed. Industry blamed the stop-go policy which undermined confidence and held back investment.

The FBI (later CBI) had advocated a government initiative which would allow for tripartite talks with a view to some type of planning. There was disagreement over the nature of any body that would be set up. The Treasury did not wish to see an independent office or industrial commission co-ordinating investment plans. Independent forecasts might cast doubt and undermine government forecasts and authority. Peter Thorneycroft and Reginald Maudling favoured a weaker body, but the Prime Minister wanted a tripartite council with a substantial degree of independence, especially as it would be backed by George Woodcock of the TUC.

Occasionally I attended Council meetings when the issues of productivity, innovation and the role of science and technology were raised. What was the correlation with economic growth? What time lags were involved? How could they be reduced? How could we improve skills, training, the contribution of engineers, arrest the Brain Drain, make more effective use of the Government laboratories?

Should high technology be supported to enhance exports, or existing technologies to improve the performance of the backward sectors and smaller firms? Would fiscal incentives help? When the 'little Neddys', the individual development committees, were set up – nine initially, I chaired three of them for electronics, chemicals and chemical plant and electrical engineering industries – we looked into specific problems.

We moved from our antiquated Bridge Street offices into the resplendent Millbank Tower, even before construction was completed. Then *The Economist* commented on Neddy's two reports in a critical review: 'There's no need for a hundred pages on this. Ask any of the door keepers down Whitehall, 'what are the obstacles to growth' and they'll tell you precisely, behind which desks they are sitting.' The debate that took place was of value as a forum for education, in better informed exchanges and in helping to explain to Council members, notably trade union leaders like Frank Cousins and Bill Carron, some of the harsh economic realities. It did not change their entrenched views, but it seemed to introduce an element of optimism. We thought we would soon be joining the European Community and enjoying their economic growth too. We were wrong. It was a mood that was to change with the loss of confidence in sterling.

I was finding this new experience useful in understanding the process and place of innovation. I read a little about its history. Much had not changed.

Britain had had the reputation of teeming with ideas, discoveries and inventions, but of being poor in exploitation. Dr Lyon Playfair reported critically on this, after the 1851 and 1862 Exhibitions. But after World War II experiences we hoped our situation had changed. Yet there had been countless examples since then, where we failed to capitalise on our technical success. The Colossus computer had to be destroyed and those who worked on it were forbidden to talk about it; the X-ray scanner designed at EMI could not be made because of their 'medieval' electronics department; polyester was a British invention but we sold the patent to Dupont, who blended it with cotton to make Dacron and Teflon; penicillin and the structure of DNA were not patented at all. We did build up the world's leading helicopter industry, but lost it to become totally dependent on imports.

Alongside our Ministries of Supply and Aviation, the well-established DSIR was an ideal vehicle for supporting some industrial research. But more was necessary for innovation to succeed.

I was able to obtain direct inputs from top industrialists on the Council, from Boots, Dunlop and Ferranti, on the practical problems they faced and on management education too, from Oliver Franks, then Provost of Worcester College. With him I discussed the need to train management to be more forward-looking and to establish business schools in the UK on the lines of the MIT Sloan School and Harvard. I was able to pursue this topic further following my 1964 visit to the USA, at the invitation of Walter Heller, Chairman of the Council of Economic Advisers.

The Treasury was restricting the information it was giving Neddy, but I had the benefit of straightforward access to documents from committees dealing with the organisation of the Civil Science (Trend), expansion of higher education (Robbins), engineering design (Fielden) and the social sciences (Heyworth). I had meetings with Zuckerman, Lockspeiser, Willis Jackson, Trend and Blackett and was appointed to the Scientific Manpower Committee by Lord Todd.

My two clear impressions were how many of our best qualified people were preoccupied with academic and defence work and how many more were remote from those in industry. The little Neddys themselves were identifying a range of specific obstacles that had to be surmounted. They also demonstrated a widespread ignorance and lack of concern about the competition they were facing. On this last point, at a joint meeting I held of the chemical and chemical plant companies we found that the main export competitors for our chemical manufacturers were our own successful chemical plant manufacturers, exporting to the same countries. Our machine tool manufacturers complained that though 59% of our machine tools were more than ten years old, users would not re-equip, believing the poor designs available did not make it worth their while. The value of speed was not appreciated when we suggested that a particular market could well be captured at no extra cost by applying more resources for a shorter time. Philips had concentrated its four year R&D programme into two years, in spite of the protests about cash flow and risk, to overtake the competition and increase its profits.

Across UK industry as a whole, the causes of reluctance to innovate appeared to be due, in descending order of importance, to management weaknesses, lack of information, understanding the marketplace, risk assessment, lack of skills and lack of incentive. Less common causes were lack of capital, apparent unprofitability of equipment replacement and lastly, union attitudes.

In April 1963 an article appeared in *The Financial Times*, in which Sir Harold Roxbee Cox (later Lord Kings Norton), maintained that as a nation we should concentrate our efforts on particular products, processes and projects, just as we did in war, when the government was the customer. Shone called me in to a meeting with him, Sir Harry Melville, Sir Leon Bagrit and McDougall to discuss this. On what principle could a central body do this? If profit were a motive industry, surely, would do it for itself? In my view there was much the government could do to help, but not a central body. We were concerned with the appropriate scale of our effort nationally and how resources should be broadly distributed. We could not tell how much extra growth might result from a given increase in R&D expenditure, but theoretical work in the United States demonstrated a positive contribution. Its importance would depend on the capital investment, the marketing, the training and so on that went with it. In Britain over the previous six years, there had been a 50% increase in our total R&D expenditure, growing twice as fast as that on education and four times as fast as capital investment generally. For civil purposes, growth in R&D should certainly continue to be at least as fast as our national income, but some redistribution was essential. Exports of conventional products were still four times as great as those incorporating high technology.

We came forward with some practical proposals for industry, in electric power generation, natural gas processes, automatic telephone exchanges and building mechanisation and pointed out how novel combinations of existing technologies could sometimes be more successful commercially than the development of new leading edge discoveries.

The financial aspects of some of these issues were debated at a conference on 'Science and the City', sponsored by Hambros and *The New Scientist*. Almost for the first time, the question of risk was debated. In the reports that followed, however, it was John Hambro's opening remark that struck a memorable note among some would-be investors. 'There are three ways of losing money,' he said: 'gambling, women and backing inventions, and the least pleasant is the third.' My comments on the process of innovation were summarised as 'R&D could be the goose that laid the golden egg, but shut away, it became a broody hen.'

I came out strongly in favour of economic and social criteria being set out fully from the outset in selecting projects. It had been done exceptionally with the proposed Victoria underground line. The receipts expected from users would not only cover the investment costs, but bring major benefits to the improvement of overground traffic and reduce journey times. This procedure soon became normal practice. I reported on effectiveness studies carried out in the USA. The National Research Council had calculated the probable return from oceanographic research, better weather forecasting and conservation policies in terms of fish supplies, minerals and agricultural output, to obtain larger budget approvals from Congress as a result. In our case I suggested opportunities for the use of our more public funds where individual companies would not be the main beneficiaries, as in lessening noise or pollution and in improving our balance of payments by substituting domestic materials for imports.

We had to focus and show the way by identifying some promising fields, sometimes using government purchasing power and larger civil development contracts. Aubrey Jones, Chairman of the Prices and Incomes Commission, warmed to this, but in 1957, when Minister of Supply, he had proposed a Ministry of Technology to tackle this very problem, yet found little support.

A more general issue was our weakening international competitiveness. I advocated more capital investment, commenting on my six-year experience on the continent. When France surveyed her wholesale wartime destruction with the loss of two thirds of her railways, she made large capital investments. When the Netherlands lost Indonesia and her central European market, and also suffered widespread flooding of her own territory in the Fifties, she launched a major capital construction programme. Belgium too, shocked by the loss of the Congo and its wealth of minerals had a new incentive for capital investment at home.

For our part, we had lost most of our overseas investments and our exports alone now had to pay for our imports. Eighty-six per cent of our exports were manufactured goods, but the competition we were meeting was more severe and the developing countries were becoming more self-sufficient in the simpler products.

In addition, our own investment policy had been haphazard. In the coal industry, for example, we set out to increase output rather than efficiency and our railways were being starved of capital, so the freight they should be carrying was now helping to congest the roads.

One of the questions Shone put to me was on selectivity. Why could not the United States be left its dominant role in the computer and aircraft industries? If Switzerland could live prosperously by selling watches and machinery and buying motor cars and steel, why could not Europe buy computers from America and sell whisky and small cars in return?

'In my view,' I said, 'quite apart from European passions and political arguments, there were powerful economic reasons for us to concentrate on industries where a high content of skill and ingenuity would add value to minute raw material costs. Ultimately, the decision was a political one as well as one for business. We might of course simply work longer if we could sell more. The French chose to take some of the benefits of their national income in the form of a shorter working week and actually did better in terms of GDP per hour. The United States had the greatest proportion of highly skilled, college-educated people, followed by the UK, France and Germany.'

Shone and I each addressed different audiences at about the same time on these themes. Talking to the Institute of Personnel Management at Harrogate Shone suggested that the return on educational investment was comparable with that on physical investment. One of our limitations was to think of growth in terms of machines and physical capital, but in advanced industrial communities the stock of capital invested in education and training should be no less than the total invested in roads, railways and factories.

At the Institution of Electronic and Radio Engineers and then the Council of Engineering Institutions, I made a plea for a broader education for engineers. I asked, 'How many engineers can read a balance sheet?' And I ran into trouble. Some of the institutions already required members to know something of elementary economics and social studies, but not the Electrical, Civil, Gas and Structural Engineers. 'Accountants should do their job, while we do ours', they said. 'In any event we need many more engineers to do engineering than we have. Vacancies cannot be filled and there are many empty places in our University Engineering Departments.' The public image of engineering and of an engineering career did not help; its esteem was low relative to science, and consequently its inferior status and remuneration. Nor were the talents of qualified engineers being fully utilised.

Estimates of these shortages were sought by the Committee on Scientific Manpower. I emphasised the need for qualified scientists and engineers to be helped to gain wider knowledge, experience and responsibility in their formative years to facilitate better communication and integration with non-technical management. They should be able to calculate and balance technical against commercial or economic considerations and improve decision-taking. They were more likely then to find their way to the top.

In the course of my visit to Washington DC, I was impressed by the way in which American engineers, economists and finance staff jointly assessed the value to the nation of a possible $1,000 m supersonic transport project. Similarly engineers, statisticians and economists were called together to make value analyses of alternative water resource policies. Acting together they recommended how Federal Funds should be distributed in, I believe, five States in the Mississippi-Missouri region, between the provision of new water supplies, the improvement of old ones and the removal of water pollution. In Britain, both at the national level and at the company level we had far less experience of this detailed type of appraisal.

Yet many disagreed with me. 'Take away an engineer's slide rule, equipment and proven formulae, and you've taken away his competence.' Certainly, courses in subjects such as industrial economics, and a variety of management techniques were beginning to be established. The two Business Schools being set up in London and Manchester would give a fresh impetus to their application. I advised Sir Oliver Franks that engineers had to be adequately represented from the outset at these Schools.

I had advised a large gathering of professional engineers on 'Enhancing the contribution of the engineer to the economy', whilst at Neddy in 1962 and in a lecture published in 1973 asked, 'Is the management challenge too much for engineers?' A third of a century later the issue arose again, the very same arguments for and against, being made. The new editor of the journal decided to take an online poll of members, asking, 'Are today's engineers better equipped to face the challenge of management than they were twenty years ago?' Twenty-eight per cent said 'Yes', 38% 'Probably'. The improvement had been very slow to materialise.

No clear sense of direction emerged from Neddy, only a list of specific, potentially valuable recommendations. All that was required was for them to be better implemented. If half of them were, I estimated, we would have achieved something.

Unplanned Journey

Ministry of Technology 1964–1966

We had been in our superb Neddy premises in Millbank Tower for almost a year in October 1964. My office door was open and in walked Frank Cousins. 'I do like your office,' he said, 'I'm looking for a new one.'

'What's wrong with Transport House?' I replied.

'Well, I've just come from No 10; Harold has asked me to set up a new Ministry of Technology.'

I shot to my feet, 'Are you in the Cabinet?' I asked.

'Yes,' he said 'and I have been offered Gwydir House in Whitehall. It is a fuddy-duddy old building. I want something like Millbank Tower, in pristine condition, in keeping with the 'White Heat' election campaign.'

I had met Cousins at Neddy meetings, where he was an outspoken representative of the Transport and General Workers Union; a bluff Yorkshireman, who went into the coalmines at fourteen and became a lorry driver at nineteen.

There was a figure lurking at the door.'Charles, come in. My Parliamentary Secretary.' As he introduced me to C.P. Snow, I gulped. Why was an author joining the Government with a seat in the House of Lords? Recovering, I said to Cousins, 'Congratulations, but you can't pinch my office, it's the best I've ever had.'

'I have an idea,' said Cousins.'Join us and keep your office.'

'The system doesn't work like that,' I added, rather lamely. But it did.

Two days later I had a call from Sir Charles Cawley, Chief Scientist, Ministry of Fuel and Power. 'The Treasury has asked me to have a talk with you. You have been nominated by Blackett and Cousins to become a Chief Scientific Officer in the new Ministry. The Treasury think you are moving up too fast' – it would have been my seventh civil service promotion in fifteen years – 'They require a formal appraisal both of what the prospective job requires and your suitability for it.' We had an hour together. Cawley must have reported favourably enough, as the appointment was confirmed. I kept my office and a new nameplate duly appeared on my door. Sir Donald McDougal, newly installed in the Department of Economic Affairs under George Brown, telephoned me to wish me well.

The machinery of government and how this Ministry in particular came into being I will expand on later. In this case it was party political considerations that overruled all others. At MinTech there were just a dozen of us at first, led by Sir Maurice Dean, a mathematician and Treasury mandarin, as Permanent Secretary. As his special adviser, Patrick Blackett, Nobel Prize winner, prospective President of the Royal Society, Order of Merit and Peer, but Dean saw him as a maverick. On my first day, Dean took me aside. 'A good civil servant,' he said, 'is one who can stop a Minister or his adviser's half-baked schemes from materialising, or else convert them into practical propositions.' He did not revert to this theme.

Snow's appointment was very surprising. As author and playwright, he was famous for *The Two Cultures*, about the breakdown of communication between the sciences and humanities, and for *The Corridors of Power*, which became a phrase in the English language. However, his only knowledge of politics was the internal politics of a Cambridge college in *The Masters*, the subject of the Godkin Lectures he delivered at Harvard. But he did know Blackett well. Once or twice, passing my office, he would look in for a chat – a ponderous figure, bald, with heavy spectacles, always interesting. 'When I worked at the Cavendish on infra-red spectroscopy and crystallography,' he said, 'it was the Golden Age for physics. If one wanted to know the sweetness of scientific life, one had to be young in the ten years before 1933. There were just three great centres – Rutherford's Cambridge, Niels Bohr's Copenhagen and Franck's Göttingen and we moved from one to the other as though we were on a lawn tennis circuit.'

On another occasion he said, 'Like you, I admire the beauty of crystals, but I enjoy equally reading Balzac and Proust. A couple of years ago, I had a mighty row with F.R. Leavis, ten years my senior, because he insisted that art was the dominant culture and to read science would be to condone it. He and his wife Queenie, a literary critic, condemned my novels as 'pedestrian prose'.'

I could not help contrasting my two ministers – Cousins, with little education, a forceful and effective trade union leader; Snow, highly educated and an able presenter. Neither, however, made any impact in Whitehall or Westminster.

The Ministry's remit was to guide and stimulate a major, all-embracing national effort to bring advanced technology and new processes into industry. Initially it would extend the award of civil development contracts (expanding the NRDC, set up originally in 1948 by Wilson when President of the Board of Trade), make more effective use of some DSIR laboratories and those of the Atomic Energy Authority and, as recommended by Neddy, provide an industrial intelligence service, spotting technological weaknesses and investment opportunities. In the longer term Wilson clearly wanted a comprehensive Ministry of Industry, but in the short term it would concentrate on just four industries: machine tools transferred from the Board of Trade, telecommunications from the Post Office, electronics from the Ministry of Aviation and computers from the Treasury.

We had problems from the start. First we had to recruit staff laboriously, then wait four months for Frank Cousins to get a seat in Parliament, to speak for the government. For the best part of a year we did little. The economy was worsening and Cousins came in to complain that he was expected to revolutionise the computer industry in one month.

I was put in charge of the Electrical, Chemical Plant and Material Industries Division and also the International Division. Internal admin-istration led to confusion. More seriously, the prospect of departmental mergers was attracting all the attention, not the service we should be giving to industry. Meanwhile, the Estimates Committee was repeatedly asking us to account 'for what we had achieved'.

To be successful, the new Ministry had to be powerful. It could have been, in conjunction with the Board of Trade, or the new Department of Economic Affairs, if given early responsibility for sponsoring major industries. It was wrong to have a Ministry of Technology with no say at all in the government's largest stake of all in technology, our aircraft industry. All four of our industries – machine tools, electronics, computers and instruments – were low down the list of our exports. The German machine tool industry, for example, had a net export ratio of 41% of their output; the UK's was only 8%. We had far fewer qualified scientists, engineers, designers and technically qualified salesmen. Furthermore, whilst our machine tool exports cost £800 a ton, our imports were more sophisticated and cost £1,300 a ton. Analysis also showed that our manufacturing runs were usually too short to get prices down. The proceeds of sales could not pay for quicker innovation. Most companies were far too small to succeed in new product development.

We suggested how, when and where government money might be injected and identified firms that warranted closer attention. NRDC gave financial support to International Computers and Tabulators (ICT) for four years and to Elliott Automation for three years. Sometimes, however, our discussions tended to put us, as civil servants, in the position of salesmen, offering Government investment to induce technological advances that we proposed. This approach was very different from that adopted in the defence field. Civil projects had to remain under the essential control of the companies themselves; those in defence had a captive customer in the Ministry of Defence and had to accept a substantial degree of detailed government control.

Changes at the top came quickly. Dean retired as Permanent Secretary and within three days Frank Cousins resigned, following his disagreement in Cabinet over incomes policy. As a trade union leader he had carried some weight, but as a Minister, he was neither comfortable nor successful. They were succeeded by Sir Otto Clarke and Anthony Wedgwood Benn (later, Tony Benn). Benn was thrilled to have inherited Blackett and Clarke. As Permanent Secretary, Clarke was the antithesis of the traditional civil servant, with the earlier experience of being a leader writer on

The Financial Times and his was a first-class appointment. He ably supported Blackett's endeavours to create scientific centres of excellence, and worked well with Benn. He also admitted to us that he never quite understood how to administer a system where the government was the customer, but was also free to intervene in the financial control and management of the supplier. When he in turn retired, incidentally, he went on record to say, 'Government grants may just push a marginal decision over, but managers only succeed when they do what they want to do.'

Some of my senior colleagues told me of their dilemma in being torn between the need to intervene with management, discrimination to reinforce the more successful companies and having to defend themselves against claims of unfairness by MPs representing neglected constituencies. Worse still, businesses were paying less attention to what their customers and the market required, than to what the government thought should be done. I remember discussing this with Clarke in his office one afternoon. He agreed then he suddenly stood up, saying, 'I must go. I'm due to talk to my son's headmaster.' Charles Clarke, the future Home Secretary in Tony Blair's cabinet, must have been fifteen at the time.

My colleagues were highly competent. They worked hard and served loyally. From time to time however, their frustration showed with our lack of progress. Some had been approached with job offers in industry, but were not tempted. I was asked too, and began to wonder. I looked back to the earlier promise of tackling the national issues raised in our Neddy reports. Managerial effectiveness, the attitudes of labour, inadequate skills and training, the size and structure of firms and under-investment were all issues hardly addressed. We did have a few modest achievements, such as setting up a Programmes Analysis Unit, in collaboration with the Atomic Energy Authority to provide cost-benefit evaluations for the RB211, but we certainly were not focusing on the central issue of improving our competitiveness by innovation and higher productivity.

Sir Ieun Maddock came in from the AEA as Controller and I now reported to him. He constantly supported me, but I was inevitably becoming a smaller pebble, in a Department led by seven Ministers, two in the Cabinet, and three Permanent Secretaries. Whilst my meetings with Frank Cousins had been fairly regular, now with Tony Benn, a popular successor, they were few, and I was just one of a large group. More importantly, I became further removed from the industrial leaders I should have been meeting. The 'White Heat' election manifesto was a winner, but in office it amounted to little. We were not being well governed.

My views on what was needed for success were now crystallising. The key was to translate our knowledge, ideas and technology into the products and processes which would make industry competitive and managers to be dissatisfied with the status quo. I wanted to analyse situations more closely, solve the problems involved and help implement the solutions agreed.

From a totally unexpected quarter, I was then invited to do just that. Though I had prepared as best I could to be of potential value to others and to be seen as such, the likelihood of being offered a position at an appropriate level seemed remote. But I was. I resigned from the Civil Service on 1st December 1966, and was appointed to a new job the same day.

My paternal grandparents, Elkanah and Deborah, Uncle Joseph (standing) and my father 1897

My maternal grandfather, Eli Cohen 1920s

Alcon Charles aged one and parents, Eda and Maurice 1921

*Dr Chaim Weizman in his laboratory
1913 Photo: Maurice Copisarow*

My sister Amelia, 1953

Father, Maurice Copisarow DSc

Father-in-law, Major Ellis Castello MC

RMS Aquitania – My first Atlantic crossing, 1945

On watch at Midnight in the
Arctic, HMS Cygnet 1948

Instructor Lieutenant Alcon Copisarow
RN 1943 Photo: Guttenberg

Now we are six! 1966 Photo: Ron Haddock

The new Mr & Mrs Alcon Copisarow 1955

Cheers! 1974 (L–R) Richard, Rosalind, Katharine, Edward

At home with Diana, 1992 Photo: Mo Daoud

Mis à bouteille! *Ernest Marples*

'Off duty' in formal attire, Paris 1957

With Prince Philip at CEA – Saclay, Paris 1956

BUCKINGHAM PALACE

May 14th 1956.

A.C.Copisarow Esq.,
H.M.Scientific Attache,
British Embassy,
Paris.

Dear Mr, Copisarow,

Moulin de la Tuilerie, Gif-sur-Yvette.

     Many thanks for your letter of May 8th, regarding
the above property and the activities of the Atomic Energy
Commission's in the immediate neighbourhood.

     The Duke of Windsor is gratified with the
satisfactory result of your approach to the Commission, and the
assurance that they will respect His Royal Highness's property.

     The Duke and Duchess hope to take an early
opportunity to visit the Commission's properties at Saclay, and
will communicate with you when they are able to arrange this,
with a view to your accompanying them, if you can fit it in.

        I am,
         Yours sincerely,

         Victor A. Saddlene

        Private Secretary.

Letter 'from Buckingham Palace' twenty years after the Abdication!

HOUSE OF COMMONS
LONDON SWIA OAA

To help young people is one of the most important things anyone can do. The Prince's Youth Business Trust aims to help young people to set up in business on their own. The success of their businesses will help them *and* the people they will employ as their businesses grow.

We support this most imaginative venture and we warmly commend the Appeal. We particularly hope that people who have already made their way successfully in business will take this great opportunity to give real practical help to the next generation.

November 1986

All Party Agreement

Caught at home by The Times *Photographer 1968*

Cartooned by Trog in The Daily Mail

THE McKINSEY
EXPERIENCE

CHAPTER VI

Consulting at its Best

As the first non-American Senior Partner of McKinsey

In 1965 I had been asked to take part in a conference at INSEAD, sponsored by Harvard University and IBM, held in the beautiful surroundings of the Palais de Fontainebleau. Prince Bernhard of the Netherlands presided and the speakers included Olivier Giscard d'Estaing, INSEAD's Director General, Pierre Massé, Commissaire Général du Plan and Pierre Ailleret, Head of Electricité France. I spoke, but I was particularly attracted to another contribution from David Hertz, then a director of McKinsey in New York, because of his analytical approach to problem-solving. He had joined the firm as a junior partner, having previously been in the US Navy's Post-Graduate School and President of the US Institute of Management Sciences. Apparently he was interested in the contribution I made too. We dined together. I enjoyed both the dinner and his company. He asked me what I knew about McKinsey. I said, 'Very little'. I knew of its reputation that it had done most of its work in the United States and had begun to expand to Europe. We agreed to keep in touch. That chance encounter was to change my life.

Many months later, I was approached by two or three of McKinsey's senior partners in turn. Dick Neuschel said he was coming over to London and had heard that I'd had an interesting chat with David Hertz. Could we meet for breakfast at the Connaught at 6:45am? A former Harvard Business School Baker Scholar, then with Sperry Gyroscope, he had joined the firm in 1945. I enjoyed my conversation with him too. Then, a telephone call from Gil Clee, formerly serving with the World Bank, who looked forward to a meeting and then lunch with Hugh Parker, in charge of the firm's small London office. All rather intriguing. It was not lost on me that they were thinking of recruiting me.

David Hertz telephoned and said: 'John Macomber is coming over from Paris and has also asked to see you. Look, I don't suppose there's any prospect of your joining McKinsey?'

I said, 'When you're a civil servant you stay. It's a career and I have fifteen more years to go.'

He said, 'Well, I think that you might consider it; there's a great deal you could do for McKinsey and I believe there's a very great deal that McKinsey could do for you.'

I decided to take this approach more seriously. Why me, I asked myself? Why should clients be prepared to pay handsomely for my services when I knew less about their business than they did? It was obviously risky. How secure would I be? I needed more information. Where to begin?

I dipped into Frederick Taylor's *Principles of Scientific Management*, in which he made the case for modern factories to be manned by operatives taught to be obedient and abide by the rules. Then I turned to another American, John Dewey's different views, the need for thoughtful creative problem-solvers to manage our affairs. Such was the choice, a century ago. Should education be about doing what we are told, or learning to think for oneself?

Initially Taylor won the day, influencing Henry Ford to adopt his approach to improve manufacturing efficiency, stealing a march thereby on his competitors. Then a report of the Bedaux System appeared measuring work and payment by results. Bedaux seemed to attract his clients by hosting lavish parties at his Loire château – and his demise was due to the disclosures of his links with high-ranking Nazi officials. My first impression therefore was of a profession with a chequered early history, calling for few qualifications or barriers to entry.

Subsequently, with the growing demand for improved labour productivity, four British companies sprung up to cater for the need:

Urwick Orr, PA, PE and AIC. In the US at the same time the nature of consulting assignments shifted from efficiency improvements to organisational and strategic issues. The four companies leading the field there were A.D. Little – strong on operational research, Booz Allen – on manufacturing control, McKinsey and A.T. Kearney. Between them they were tackling wider problems faced by large businesses in a changing world.

James O. McKinsey had previously taught at the University of Chicago, published his *Budgetary Control* in 1922, became Chief Executive of Marshall Fields and died within two years of founding his own company. Tom Kearney had managed McKinsey's Chicago office and Marvin Bower his small New York offices. Bower himself was a Harvard trained lawyer who decided to concentrate on Chief Executive-level problems. He purchased the exclusive use of the McKinsey name, became its first Managing Director and with his few partners began to build up the firm. Dewey's approach to learning was now back in favour – a much more attractive professional prospect for a consultant.

This was all I could glean before I received a call in my Whitehall office from Marvin Bower, in New York. 'Would you be free for a chat at home tomorrow (Saturday)?' I said: 'Yes, but I live out at Amersham in Buckinghamshire, though not far from the airport.' He said: 'I can be with you in the morning.'

I asked him to lunch and told Diana. 'Oh,' she said, 'how do we divide two small trout into three?'

After lunch, he came to the point. 'I came over to discover whether you would join us?' 'That's already been suggested, most attractively,' I said, 'but I'm an established civil servant; I don't see how I can move. Incidentally,' I added, 'I was once asked to join Arthur D. Little in the US, but I gave them the same answer.'

Marvin replied: 'The demand for professional services is growing fast. A.D. Little have appointed General James Gavin, formerly Commander of 82nd Airborne Division and head of the US Army's R&D Directorate, to join them.' He went on, 'The work for US multinationals alone does not really justify a permanent presence for McKinsey in Europe; what is needed is a domestic client base and that in turn calls for consultants with a highly successful track record, personal reputation and important contacts in Europe too.'

'Look, if ever you *were* to leave, how would you decide where you would go?'

'I would be very much influenced by the calibre of the individuals I would be working with,' I replied.

'What do you think of my partners who you've met?'

'They're outstanding,' I said. 'You ought to come along and meet the others, they're all outstanding. We have eighteen directors, thirty-eight principals and over 300 other consultants. The partners own the firm. The directors are the senior partners. We are asking you to join us as our first non-American director. You could be based in any office you wish, on assignments of your own choice.'

'You will appreciate that I have grown accustomed to the culture and ethics of the British Civil Service. How would that go down with your ambitious business clients?' I asked. He turned on me. 'We are a profession, with professional values, not a business, out for money. When Howard Hughes called me wanting us to take on Paramount Pictures I went straight off to Los Angeles, where he entertained me in great style. But what he said and his approach to business was so unacceptable, I told him so and turned down a lucrative assignment.'

We had been walking for over an hour and returning home I said, 'I'm honoured, but it's a terrible risk you would be taking,' and he said, 'Yes, and so would you!' There was the challenge. I agreed to consider it carefully, it would have been churlish not to. I was certainly tempted, but then I thought about giving up the security I had. I would also have to pluck up courage to tell my Minister, Anthony Wedgwood Benn.

It was obvious that Marvin Bower knew about my work on the management of technology in public services, of my relations with British and European companies, experience with Neddy and my very short stint with the Council of Economic Advisors in Washington. Directors had asked others about me too, without my knowledge. I learned later that Hugh Parker and Roger Morrison had called on my Deputy Secretary at some stage for a meeting in confidence. I was impressed with the professionalism of it all. Marvin Bower had returned to America and wrote thanking Diana for his 'two thirds of a trout.' He also enclosed a first class open-dated return ticket to New York. 'Come and discover more about us,' it read.

Now I could not resist. Arranging a free day or two I went off to New York. I was expected to dinner with Ev Smith, another director, but was held up by fog, landed in Boston and finished up in Smith's apartment in Sutton Place South at half past two in the morning. Gil Clee was with him. They were wide awake and pleased I could still keep my eyes open and talk shop. Over the next couple of days I had thoroughly interesting discussions with them and other partners covering the contribution I might make, how I could widen my own experience and horizons and also adapt to a change in lifestyle. From their point of view I felt they were aiming to attract someone with greater external experience than hitherto, with the prospect of a successful, harmonious partnership.

I asked how my performance would be judged. They said, in effect, 'The world's your oyster, we simply expect quality, the ability to serve clients well and to set an example in expertise and professionalism to the younger consultants.' Not once did they refer to the income I would be expected to generate or the financial rewards.

I had been curious at the outset, even intrigued, but now I was beginning to view the opportunity as a remarkable offer of a new lease of life. I agreed to give them a definite answer on my return to London: 'If I were to resign and join you I would wish to be with my family, based in the UK.' That was agreed.

Back in Millbank Tower when a few of us joined the Permanent Secretary for a meeting with the Minister, I stayed behind: 'Can I speak to you about a personal matter? I have been invited to take on a substantial job in the private sector and would really like to feel that no official obstacles would present themselves.'

Wedgwood Benn looked surprised. 'Are you negotiating some job with a company we have links with?' I said, 'No, I've been invited by Americans.'

Recovering somewhat, he said, 'You've been overdoing it. When did you last have some holiday?' I said, 'They're serious, I'm keen and I'm very impressed with the work they're doing.'

'Who is it?' 'It's McKinsey.'

'McKinsey? Well, when I was Postmaster General they did a very good job for us. You could certainly learn a lot from them. If you are keen why not join them, but for two years only, then you should come back? You would be more valuable still.'

I said, 'I'm very attracted by the idea of making a permanent move.' 'What about approved employment terms?' he said. I knew that that was a scheme the government could offer to facilitate transfers into some other public service, a nationalised industry, the Bank of England or the BBC, for example. It allowed pension rights to be preserved and return to the civil service at the end of two years.

I said, 'Well, it wouldn't apply to the American private sector.' 'I'm not sure that it couldn't,' he said. 'What are they asking you to do?'

'I would come straight in as a director.' 'Oh then, you must accept.'

It was at that moment I decided to make a clean break and resign. I think he assumed I would return and swiftly turned his attention to more pressing matters of that day.

At home I tried to explain to Diana the prospect of longer working hours, absences abroad and the risk I was taking. When Richard, who was then six, overheard me say, 'It's possible it will turn out to be something of a cowboy business', he became quite excited: 'And will you wear a hat like John Wayne?'

Diana said, 'Whatever you think is right, I go along with.'

At my farewell party on 30th November, colleagues were generous with their remarks and with the drinks, but convinced I was crazy. 'All you need to do is to stay here, you're totally secure, honours will come along, and now you take this risk; you ought to have your head examined.' I arranged a handover and said goodbye to Otto Clarke, but walking out of Millbank Tower rather in a haze, I felt as secure as a trainee pilot might have felt, taking off on his first solo flight.

I was surprised when Approved Employment Terms came through a few weeks later. *The New Scientist* in its editorial was delighted to see this courageous example of 'much needed mobility for senior civil servants' and they wished me luck, if only *pour encourager les autres*.

A year later I met some former colleagues at a conference. Morale in my old Department was not at its best and views there were changing. 'You seem to be making out all right,' they said. 'If you ever hear of anything interesting going on outside…' I said, 'Don't leave it too late.'

Two years after my departure, I was asked to return. By now I was hard at work, in the midst of four McKinsey assignments and enjoying them immensely. I knew I had made the right move and declined.

My McKinsey appointment had been confirmed to begin on 1st December, but I was asked in advance to address the entire firm at the New York Hilton. It was the last occasion when the rapidly growing firm could all meet together.

I was welcomed warmly, spoke for forty minutes as requested on the management of technology, rather dangerously I thought, not knowing anything of McKinsey's clients or their needs. However, it seemed to strike the right note at the time.

Looking at my notes today, it is all redolent of a bygone age. I began:

Twenty years ago there was hardly a scientist or technologist who confidently expected that by 1966 rockets would be landing on the moon and men walking about in outer space, that computers would be squeezing the work of months into seconds, or that chemists would be wrestling the secrets of heredity from nucleic acid and proving that even woman's beauty could be merely a matter of chemistry, pure and applied. Nor were there many businessmen or politicians who could appreciate then, that the demand for automobiles would soon multiply at such a rate, that choices would sometimes have to be made between complete redesign of city centres, a major limitation of road traffic, or inevitable self-imposed chaos.

I went on to explain why earlier predictions had been falsified by events, the dramatic rise in the scale of research and development, the full impact of which was still to be felt, and the new demands it made on management faced with the threat of worldwide competition. And I concluded with a forecast of what the future might bring, raising eyebrows at the time but, in retrospect, quite inadequate.

The management of technology problem has, since then, changed out of all recognition. No longer is it simply a matter of scale and the proliferation of scientific disciplines. The problem to be solved is the all-embracing one of managing innovation, of which technology is a component. Technological change has been inexorable, but there has also been a remarkable development in the innovative process itself.

The rise of information technology since then has changed working practices. Virtual conferences are held instead of travel. There are touch-screen airport bookings and 'pay-as-you-go' tickets on trains; for shopping, online shopping, comparison websites and entertainment devices at home. Now the promise of the Internet of Things, that by connecting people will allow us to track and count everything, reduce waste and costs and make changes with profound implications for the future.

Creativity and innovation have provided the new opportunities and sources of demand. Innovation remains the lifeblood of the economy. The process may call for new alliances and close customer relationships are critical. In most cases the orchestration of many individual performers and teams with a diverse range of talents is the crucial management challenge. Thirty years after my 1966 lecture I had the opportunity of helping put this 'orchestration' into effect, in establishing the Eden Project in Cornwall and after forty years, I expanded on the theme in my 2005 Churchill College Archives lecture.

I was at my desk in the new *Economist* building facing St James's Street early on 1st December 1966. Greeted by Hugh Parker, brought a cup of coffee by a cheerful young secretary, I was then left alone. Standing by the window I looked down on the traffic, back at my desk, and suddenly realised there were no papers. One couldn't be a civil servant without papers – nothing inherited from one's predecessor. Nor, of course, could I be a consultant without a client.

At the weekend I attended an office training session where I met the whole of the London office, about fifteen consultants in all. I discovered what they were up to. The very first note I jotted down was, 'It's not what the consultant knows; it's what the client does that counts, and its consequences!'

It was in fact during my first few weeks, that I gained most of my main impressions of the firm. They did not change much throughout the next ten years.

The consultant's job was to solve client problems and help create the conditions that would enable them to enhance their performance. The first requirement was to collect and collate all relevant facts and subject them to thorough analysis. Their interpretation formed the basis of initial presentations and eventually, recommendations to the clients. Consultants had to learn to listen to their clients, challenge them if necessary, and relate to the realities of the business or organisation – resources, staff capabilities, regulations and politics. They had to see the big picture. Each McKinsey consultant too, was different in some respects, so building the best team was important. And occasionally brainstorming sessions, based on logical, structured and persuasive presentations, open to argument between team members, could prove invaluable.

Just like the civil service, McKinsey and most consulting firms provided professional careers and both were meritocracies, but in most other respects they differed totally. In government, Ministers had the responsibility, being accountable to Parliament, but senior civil servants had a great deal of power.

Those senior civil service colleagues I had worked with were good strategic thinkers, generally less successful in developing the skills of their staff, tending to give instructions rather than eliciting ideas, and were little concerned with the delivery of services. Admirable in drafting memoranda, precedent was important, process all important. Innovation and change could be dangerous – I had seen proposals thrown out for fear that 'something might go wrong.' Public monies could not be put at risk. It was patently unfair to support one enterprise without giving an equivalent opportunity to another. The key to a successful career was to avoid mistakes and gain the reputation of a 'safe pair of hands' and perpetuate the established order. Yet somehow, the top posts, almost without exception, went to the ablest people. Whatever level was attained, forty years of service was normal, security of tenure assured, and a generous non-contributory pension paid on retirement.

How different in McKinsey, and also in business, as I was about to discover. Businesses were governed by markets, their prosperity and their very survival depending mainly upon satisfying their customers and rewarding their shareholders and staff. McKinsey was in some ways in an intermediate position, a firm of professionals, a service, run in a businesslike way. Standards required of everyone, at all levels, often surpassed what would easily have been acceptable to the client. The firm prospered when satisfied clients recommended them to others and when our best consultants could continue to learn, enhance their value, and in turn help attract others of the highest calibre to join them. And not just the Baker scholars, Rhodes scholars and White House Fellows, or PhDs in nuclear physics, but people with common sense, who could be trusted.

Now I found myself among highly educated, talented, ambitious young people, 99% of them men with on the job training, eager to learn quickly, build on the analytical skills they had already demonstrated in the recruitment process, be creative and show what they were capable of. They had the best opportunity to address key management issues in strategy, productivity, profitability and risk-taking, and need to balance flexibility and firmness of purpose in managing a human enterprise. They had no security of tenure, but once they had qualified for greater responsibility and advancement they were not held back awaiting a vacancy in the establishment. They were constantly encouraged to become more knowledgeable, to put forward ideas, to be critical and not hesitate to dissent if they believed they had spotted a better solution, or way ahead. If they did not do well enough to scale the progressive promotion levels the 'Up or Out' policy meant early separation from the firm. Those who remained became partners in their thirties, and some directors in their forties.

Compensation was directly related to personal performance in whatever capacity. Directors would retire between the ages of fifty-five and sixty, being obliged to forego one-fifth of their shares each year. Acquiring these in turn was part of the motivation of the younger partners. The system applied across all offices. It was rigorous, appraisals being made by a rotating panel of directors and, in my experience, totally fair. As the only non-American, a special arrangement was necessary to enable me to buy my shares without having to pay the prevailing 26.5% dollar premium. It required the legal services of three firms. Slaughter & May and Sullivan & Cromwell for McKinsey, and Freshfields – on my behalf – to set up McKinsey International, so that I, and UK nationals who became partners in future, could obtain Bank of England permission.

Within two hours of my arrival, McLain Stewart, a director, had flown in from America to tell me of a prospective assignment involving the management of technology with North American Aviation in California. They wanted to acquire a high-tech European company, which would be a 'good fit.' Had I any ideas? Would I think about it and come to a meeting arranged in the Dusseldorf office?

I thought about it. Could any European company then be 'a good fit'? According to the influential publication *Le Défi Américain* Europe's concern was that the United States was a machine uniquely geared to exploit the flood of achievements pouring from richly endowed laboratories of industry, universities and government throughout the developed world.

Its serious content was Europe's underlying fear that excessive dependence on America – for the most sophisticated research, advanced technology and consequently most of the associated key decisions – would lead to a permanently second-hand economy, one in which Europe would be obliged to buy, if it could, the results needed.

This point of view, concentrating on the technological gap, was certainly valid to some extent. American firms operating multi-nationally were the first to acknowledge that while their European laboratories were fertile in ideas, these ideas frequently took two to three times as long to apply outside the United States. In many cases they were not applied at all. Now I was being called in to help the Americans, with the possible participation of the Germans.

The time had come for my visit and perhaps my first assignment in the management of technology.

The Assignments – The Management of Technology

At our Dusseldorf meeting Jack Vance, of our Los Angeles office, asked me to be Consulting Director to his team, assembled in California. I met them in Los Angeles, three young Americans, very bright and highly enthusiastic. Their client, North American Aviation, was a giant military aerospace company employing 220,000. Now that US Department of Defense contracts, upon which they almost wholly depended, were being drastically cut back, what should they do? They quickly convinced me that NAA was living in a 'cost-plus' environment, profits being directly related to their scale of operations, and that the company knew nothing of the marketplace. They explained that a potentially beneficial merger with a small German company initially identified had been ruled out because 'NAA didn't speak German'. Two British companies, tentatively suggested, were also unsuitable.

In my own experience, attempts to acquire companies simply to diversify rarely succeeded. I knew of only two exceptions, with limited success, both in the redesign of products, SAAB and Dornier. The many attempts, all of which failed, included boat building, commercial gas turbines, aluminium walls and building panels. The reason for failure was either a lack of understanding of the market place or inadequate coupling of the research, development, manufacturing, marketing and financial functions, or else they tended to assume, wrongly, prospective management compatibility.

I spent three intensive weeks in California visiting the company campuses, hopping from roof to roof by helicopter. Twice a week I called for team meetings to confirm that our interviews and analyses concentrated on the key issues and to discover any problems in implementing recommendations.

The best civil application agreed on was the use of the Atlas Moonshot technology to facilitate oil exploration in the Gulf of Mexico. It was technologically risky, but potentially highly important. Petroleos Mexicanos was rapidly increasing its drilling activities to 500 wells a year, but on a 'hit or miss' basis. The most suitable company for NAA to be associated with was Rockwell, a dynamic medium-sized engineering company. It had been founded in 1919 with the launch of a new bearing system for truck axles and built up by Willard Rockwell of Pittsburgh. We prepared a proposal for collaboration leading to a full merger and, even before I left, it was accepted, but I was called back to California urgently. There was a critical stumbling block to the merger. Lee Atwood, President of North American Aviation, and Willard Rockwell both insisted on being Chairman of the combined company. There was an impasse. If not resolved all our work might be wasted.

I invited them to dinner, in turn, on two successive nights, first, to discover the reasons for their insistence and secondly – with that in mind – hoping to conciliate and negotiate a compromise to achieve the merger.

Atwood, who was sixty-one, wanted to continue and retire on a high with a long track record of profitable growth. Rockwell, who was fifty-one, just could not envisage becoming a number two. I told them that in 1959, Professor Parkinson, in a highly entertaining book, had calculated the ideal age for a Chairman to retire and his successor to be appointed – in the interests of the business, of course. More seriously, Atwood acknowledged there would soon be a downturn and was prepared to depart early to become President, perhaps eighteen months later. Rockwell, recognising the difficult times immediately ahead, admitted he had much to learn to prepare for a dynamic future. If briefly second in command, he conceded his Chairman would be in the public eye to face the music. The deal was done. The combined company became known as Rockwell International. It came about not because of any technical expertise on my part, but rather by my acting as a general counsellor and conciliator. Underwater drilling is always hazardous; environmental disasters demonstrate the operational needs of highest professional standards and for many years they were highly successful.

No sooner had I returned from my first visit to California, I received a call from the managing director of Mullard, an important subsidiary of Phillips of Eindhoven.

'I have a problem,' he said, 'my Research Department is teeming with ideas and proposals. Some of the most exciting will take ages to materialise, but Phillips want results now and profits without delay, whilst the research staff, with different criteria of success, object and obstruct.'

They had a reputation second to none in supplying high quality mass-produced components for the radio and TV industry, but demand was now changing. Semiconductors and integrated circuits were replacing valves and American competition, notably from Texas Instruments and Motorola, required a different strategy.

The new equipment was complex and specialised; the life cycles of products were shortening. There was no time to lose. They had to accelerate innovation, reassess the suitability of their extensive R&D portfolio, make better use of scarce scientific manpower and prepare for a changing market. The periodical forced ranking of their portfolio of research projects with an eye to the market would enable the most promising and rewarding projects to be supported, at the expense of the least attractive commercially. This system was soon adopted widely, most notably in the pharmaceutical industry.

In the course of this assignment we learned about product life cycles more generally. Through other McKinsey offices we obtained comparative information, including Columbia Broadcasting System and Du Pont, which was hit hard by the rapid decline in the price of nylon. We were surprised to see how quickly life cycles were shortening, the effect on Gillette's razor blade market, of Wilkinson's innovation when its Super Blue blade lost out to the stainless steel blade, or the more rapid maturity of commercial aircraft – the DC3 holding its position for fifteen years, the DC7 and Electra for just five years, then the DC8, Boeing 707, 747 and Lockhead airbus in rapid succession.

What surprised Mullard was that they had two products in the late growth phase, nine in the early obsolescence phase and none at all which they could soon introduce. Phillips, in turn, was concerned. Much of our work therefore was to set out detailed arrangements for their technical, marketing, manufacturing, and finance people to work more closely together from the outset.

Probably the most prevalent single reason for failure in the planning of new products and processes was top management's failure to understand what the research staff were doing. The crucial issue in maximising the investment return was the effective coupling of the scientist and general manager.

It was highly significant that certain innovative companies as, for example, Hewlett Packard and Canon in the USA, succeeded in getting two or three times the number of new products and processes to the market, compared with others. And they incorporated two or three times the number of new technologies in half the time in twice the number of geographical markets.

On the basis of this study we contributed to McKinsey's important Practice Development activities on innovation strategies generally:

(a) Breakthrough or 'first to the market': risky, but potentially very rewarding.
(b) 'Follow the leader': development intensive, exceptionally rapid response time.
(c) 'Application Engineering', less innovative perhaps, but more precise planning and careful return on investment and cash flow calculations, and the
(d) 'Me too' strategy, without R&D: rapid delivery, modifications only to reduce costs, competing on price with a low margin. This approach could wreak havoc on others as it shortened the period of their own profitability.

Quite a few of our later assignments had a substantial technological component.

Sir Henry Jones, Chairman of the Gas Council, who I'd known for many years and whose advice I had sought initially on the advisability of joining McKinsey, asked if I could help with the entirely new problems and opportunities that lay ahead for his industry, which was now being nationalised. He was the fourth generation of gas men, distinguished, immaculately attired, a former young Brigadier serving in Burma: he certainly did not look like a gas man! We often travelled together by train into Marylebone Station and he told me how his great-grandfather, early in the nineteenth century, had illuminated Pall Mall.

Now he was about to steer the industry through a revolution. How could the industry's growth rate be doubled, whilst supply was being extended from local gas plants to natural gas, following the dramatic North Sea oil discoveries? We spent a year helping to establish British Gas. Liaising with former civil service colleagues, obtaining Parliamentary approval for major change, without resorting to new legislation was helped by my earlier career. On Jones' retirement, we continued to work with Sir Arthur Hetherington, his successor, who had the job of converting thirty million domestic appliances across the country.

And then there was the Inter Container Company. Without any expertise in the transport field, but with the knowledge and skill of Rodney Leach, as engagement manager I directed the firm's first nineteen-country multinational assignment. Based in Basle, the UIC (Union Internationale des Chemins-de-Fer), had to develop a new freight transport system across Europe.

The European railways had long faced increasing competition for general freight from road transport. Diesel engines had improved, new roads were built and no sidings or trans-shipment facilities were needed. As a result, the freight carried by rail had fallen dramatically.

But road transport also had two disadvantages; it was labour intensive and, where cargo was carried onward by sea, a second trans-shipment was required at the ports. The railways began to recognise that the transport of modern, high-capacity containers by block trains justified considerable investment in automated handling equipment at the rail terminals and for transfer to container ships.

In our Amsterdam, Dusseldorf, London, Paris, and Zurich offices as well as the USA, we evaluated the commercial opportunity and prepared the strategic plan and organisation to exploit it. It was our first step towards creating a global approach to consulting.

As we went on to determine routes and volumes and the resources needed in East and West Germany, I went to meet the Ministers of Transport in East and West Berlin, luckily with a driver allowed to cross at Checkpoint Charlie. However, I was held up so long by the Russian guard, I called out: 'It's easier to get from Moscow to Washington than to cross these few yards.' 'Moscow is only 100% Communist; here in East Berlin we are 200% Communist,' was the deadpan reply.

The net effect of the completed project was to speed up European freight transport dramatically. Fresh produce from the Balkan and East Mediterranean ports arrived in Rotterdam still perfectly fresh, whilst more valuable packages – such as precision instruments which were sealed – were no longer being damaged on frontier inspection or pilfered. As a consequence, insurance costs were reduced. Rodney Leach was great to work with and I made sure he was promoted.

As a token of our work I was given an inscribed paperweight – a one centimetre section of the actual new railway line we proposed, linking Paris and Cologne – now adorning my desk.

Banking

I could never have guessed what would happen just a month after my arrival. On 2nd January 1967 I was thrown headlong into the world of banking. Sir Edward Playfair, my former civil service and Neddy colleague, now a board member of Westminster Bank, said to me, 'Westminster needs some help.'

Duncan (Golly) Stirling, his chairman, came to my office. 'I wanted to see you away from the bank to avoid premature publicity. I'm concerned,' he said. 'The scale of the bank's operations has doubled over a decade and our services have been extended to meet the competition, but costs have mounted faster still; for premises alone they have quadrupled in five years. We also need to address the new competition coming from credit cards, and from overseas banks attracting deposits from some of our customers. We need help.'

I said, 'The firm's experience of the banking industry in Europe is limited and mine is non-existent.' But he was not deterred.

A fortnight later Stirling invited me to lunch in Lothbury to meet selected directors and senior managers. There was no doubt as to their need to clarify their aims and their strategy and organisation to achieve it. I suggested a study along these lines, homing in on a few immediate improvement opportunities.

McKinsey had done some work with the Bank of Ireland and in the USA, in retail marketing and customer profiles, in General Foods, Heinz, Coca Cola and Marshall Field. There had been nothing quite like that in the service traditions of British banking. Assembling a team of four, with David Griffiths as manager, we analysed the economics, customer profiles and the adequacy of Westminster's capital base. We measured performance on the basis of what managers were allowed to control directly, rather than on overall bank performance. Some of their best people had the least attractive opportunities.

In those days, clearing bank directors were not professional bankers, but a bevy of aristocrats and illustrious gentlemen 'who could be trusted'. It was their standing and achievements in many walks of life which gave a bank its reputation for probity, and its customers confidence in its stability. By contrast, most of the staff had come straight from school; not one had been to university. Top management was separated from the directors by the proverbial green baize door. Ralph Elliott, Westminster's Chief General Manager stood to attention before the Chairman seated at his desk, before being invited to sit. A year later, when I said to the Senior Personnel Manager Ralph Hoppes, 'at least you share a Christian name with Lord Clitheroe', he replied, 'In his case, it's pronounced Rafe.' They cautiously went along with most of our recommendations, in time developing their own management skills and confidence.

Towards the end of the year Stirling told me that the Governor of the Bank of England, Sir Leslie O'Brien, had informed the 'Big Five' (Barclays, Lloyds, Midland, National Provincial and Westminster) that Martins Bank, one of the 'Little Six' would consider takeover offers. 'I presume you would support a Westminster bid?' Given our views on the need for more capital we did, and he invited us to calculate what the bid should be. He brought in Hambros, their merchant bankers, with us. We quickly calculated 'the right price' to offer, as best we could, considering assets, profitability, the competition for deposits, synergies, and the 'pre-emptive' worth to compete against other bids. There was no full disclosure of information for a careful calculation in those days.

We knew of no other fast growth strategies. Other banks thought the same, however, so within a month the market price of Martins' shares had doubled. They now looked poor value for Westminster. Stirling showed our calculations to Jocelyn Hambro. We had to move fast.

On 3rd January, with Stirling's agreement, I went to see Sir William Armstrong, Permanent Secretary of the Treasury. Stirling, in any event, could not go to the Treasury directly, only through the Governor as intermediary. Armed with an *aide mémoire* prepared by Westminster, I covered the limited brief. Then Armstrong asked my views on the steps required to strengthen the competitive position of UK banks generally. I pointed out what Aubrey Jones had told me the previous May, as Chairman of the Prices and Incomes, that there were merits in some amalgamations to face overseas competition. Armstrong said, 'Mergers are not illegal.' He knew that bank deposits held by UK clearers had declined rapidly, largely lost to more aggressive overseas banks. His only comment was, 'I will speak to the Governor.'

As I had to leave for California, I told Stirling I would be returning on 17th January, whereupon Stirling called a special Board meeting for the 19th for McKinsey to make a presentation.

Martins, in our view, was now probably worth more to Barclays than to Westminster. The Board was divided, but after a long debate they agreed, and finally recorded a consensus. I did not know then that two days earlier, David Robarts, Chairman of National Provincial, had told Stirling they would not be bidding and believed a merger with Westminster would be better than an acquisition of Martins – a view he had actually held for some years.

Stirling asked, 'What's the McKinsey view?' I said, 'The climate for major mergers has become more favourable, since GEC had bought AEI, British Leyland had merged and so had Thorn with Radio Rentals. All of these created demands for larger loans, easier for larger banks. The services and resources of Westminster and National Provincial (which included District Bank) were complementary and allowed a rationalisation of the branch network to release funds for other purposes. Together they could compete more strongly against Barclays, Lloyds and Midland. However, the Colwyn Report of 1919 had specified that in order to maintain adequate competition all five banks were needed. Was this still the case?' The Board of Trade could refer any merger proposals to the Monopolies Commission and they might well disapprove.

On the 23rd, Stirling and Robarts went together to see the Governor and to seek his approval for the merger. Stirling was still armed with our 'fallback' bid if the merger was not approved, but the Governor had spoken to Armstrong who, with Board of Trade agreement, obtained the Chancellor's approval, without reference to the Monopolies Commission – all in the space of three days. The two Chairmen never met the Chancellor.

When a public announcement was made, without any premature leak, the other three major banks were shocked. Stirling had telephoned their Chairmen and they didn't believe him.

The following Monday we were invited for discussions with Midland and Lloyds, and then with Barclays and Lloyds, who all thought a further merger still might be possible. I had to say it would have been a direct conflict of interest to work with them, but in any event there would be no more mergers. NatWest would be the last. The Monopolies Commission confirmed this in July 1968: the merger terms were agreed by 99% of shareholders, announced after the Stock Exchange had closed, sanctioned by the High Court and enacted by Parliament.

The merger, in terms of deposits, had created what was then the fifth largest bank in the world. It included Travel Card and Diners Club, the unit trust interests of Westminster, Commercial Union and Hambros,

Mercantile Credit, North Central Finance, Coutts, Ulster, County, Yorkshire Banks, ICFC and the Agricultural Mortgage Corporation. Huge savings would be achieved by rationalising the branch network. Our first full meeting with Robarts was on 8th February and with District Bank the following day. We found that the three banks – Westminster, National Provincial, and District – each had its own set of Rule Books. Throwing them aside, a combined team introduced a single set.

The 3,600 existing branches were divided into seven geographical regions, each with its own Board and support divisions, and into eighty-one areas. By then we knew all the senior managers and as we could compare their respective aptitudes we were asked to advise on their suitability for some of the main positions to be filled. Then we all went off for a week to Middleton Park, the country house near Bicester, which was National Provincial's Senior Training Centre, to discuss how the new bank might best be run.

To meet the deadline, the team had worked every day of the week. The bank staff never guessed that delineating the eighty-one areas across the country was only done the previous day on the basis of an AA book, which in those days noted the population of each major town, and which Christopher Stewart-Smith, a key member of our team, happened to have in his car.

Six of the seven regional directors had misgivings about our operational proposals, but one showed more courage – 'I believe it will work.' So it was agreed we would start working in his SW region, as a pilot exercise. In due course he was totally satisfied and persuaded the others in turn.

Of all the decisions that had to be taken, slimming down the main Board was the most ticklish. It was readily agreed that Stirling would be the first Chairman and David Robarts, as Deputy, would succeed him. Stirling then turned to me: 'We are more than sixty directors in all and the Boardroom table only accommodates twenty-two. What should we do about this?' he asked.

'Who is the eldest?' I replied, 'Shouldn't he be the one to set an example and resign?' 'It's Sir George Schuster, he's eighty-seven, but he's terrific and he was a school friend of my father.'

'If he remains,' I said, 'others will say they are not too old to continue.' Stirling gave me permission to speak to him about 'my' suggestion. Schuster invited me to lunch at Brooks Club. When I got round to asking delicately, 'What criteria do you think we should apply in appointing directors to the new slimline Board?'

'Not too young and not too old,' he said. 'What's too old?' I asked. 'When I was five years old,' he said, 'I thought boys of ten were old. Now at eighty-seven, I think ninety-two is getting on a bit.'

At that moment Lord Aldington coming into lunch waved. I said to Schuster, 'I see he has just been elected a Fellow of New College.' 'Yes, as a Fellow myself I was one of his supporters.' I asked him what he remembered of those early years. 'The occasion that stands out was a night in 1901. I was a Classical Exhibitioner then and the news of the relief of Mafeking came through. There was a loud brass band and a rowdy procession of students marching round a bonfire. A first-floor window opened up and Warden Sewell, in his nineties, wearing a white nightshirt and cap shouted, 'Stop that row. We didn't even allow that sort of thing when the news of the victory at Waterloo came through.'

Schuster retired and Board members, including seven Lords and six Knights, were drastically cut to twenty-two. And in a historic change, among them were a few of the most senior managers. When I advocated that one or two younger members came from outside after a Board lunch one day the Marquis of Exeter came over to me carrying his coffee and brandy. 'You know I can thoroughly recommend my young stepson Robin.'

'Two members of one family together?' I asked.

'But I am due to retire in April. I will send you his CV.' It was impressive so I mentioned it to Stirling. It was Robin Leigh Pemberton. Beginning on a regional board he became Chairman of the Bank, and rose to be Governor of the Bank of England and a Knight of the Garter.

I told my team I was sorry they were missing out on such high society, but then discovered that they themselves were lunching every day with General and Assistant General Managers. There was a whole hierarchy of dining rooms and the continuous exchange of information and views was invaluable in building up an atmosphere of friendship and trust. Stewart-Smith told me that, with the Assistant General Managers, port and cigars were served every Friday and, rather than smoking their cigars, they would pop them in their top pocket for later.

Our successive assignments continued with a first attempt at long-range planning, always somewhat academic because future bank rates, interest rates and money supply were all uncertain. In my presentation 'Fortune visits the prepared mind' – a title I borrowed from Louis Pasteur – we showed the consequences of different scenarios and options that might arise, allowing decisions to be taken more quickly whenever they might be needed.

We were making the first comprehensive approach to modern business management methods applied to a British joint stock bank. Financial journalists acknowledged this. For much of it we had to thank the American business schools. I also made sure that David Griffiths became a partner of the firm.

When Stirling retired, he wrote, 'I've never ceased to be thankful for the fruits of my first visit to you in St James's Street.' As Chairman of the Committee of London Clearing Bankers, he had told the Governor too. David Robarts and then John Prideaux succeeded him and were equally complimentary.

A new era dawned in 1971. The Eurocurrency market provided business for merchant banks and the newly arrived thrusting US banks; building societies came into their own in the property boom and finance houses, offering attractive personal loans, all entered the competition.

The risks were escalating. Institutions were being encouraged to be more aggressive and expansionist and inexperienced bankers were making loans without time for security checks on customers. The popular saying was, 'A genius is a banker operating in a rising market, with a short memory.'

The clearing banks, offering a narrower range of services on a huge scale, with an inflexible interest rate structure, had to decide whether to compete for deposits by offering higher interest rates still, or else to diversify, with the additional strain of over-extended, inadequately experienced management. NatWest recognised the dilemma. They chose to extend their presence globally, targeting big business and incentivising successful salesmanship. Then traditional culture and prudence of a service run in a businesslike manner was being changed to put short-term profits first. In a new highly competitive business sector it began to spell danger.

The worst was to come long after my departure when in, 1988, I was asked to a Celebration Dinner Party in the NatWest Tower, of the twentieth anniversary of the inaugural Middleton Park occasion. Many of the original Board members and senior managers in retirement attended. I had the honour of proposing the Toast, which I did with reminiscences galore. But I also guaranteed that banking would continue to change – probably out of all recognition – as new technologies and institutions emerged. Continuous review was therefore vital.

Over forty years have elapsed since our first assignment. Perhaps twenty years since it began to lose its way. Facing growing competition it hovered between excessive risk-taking and sclerosis. Then, pretty cheekily, it was taken over by its smaller rival, the Royal Bank of Scotland. Catastrophe struck. Some lessons in management are never learned – or too easily forgotten.

Bank of England

On 11th September 1968, Hugh Parker received a call. Would he and I come and see Sir Leslie O'Brien, Governor of the Bank of England, later that day? In his Parlour, the Governor explained that the Bank in its long history had always adapted to change, but there had never been any comprehensive appraisal of its affairs. Deloittes, their auditors, advised on their computer systems, but they needed an objective review of their efficiency and effectiveness overall. There were many consulting firms the Bank might have considered, but he simply asked, 'How could you help?'

Quietly excited, I pointed out the political sensitivity of such an assignment as American consultants. Would we be privy to all the information needed? 'Yes,' said Sir Leslie. And I was invited to direct the assignment personally.

When the Bank announced it had retained us, there were startling reactions. 'McKinsey plum chokes Britain's own consultants,' announced *The Sunday Times*. *The New York Times*: 'Rivals cannot describe their rage and frustration that such an essentially English institution as roast beef and Yorkshire pudding should go to the Americans.' *The San Francisco Chronicle*: 'Intruders on Threadneedle Street,' and, by way of explanation, 'a quiet word from the Governor is likely to get as much action in the financial district, as an Act of Congress.'

The cartoonists made great play of it. JAK in *The Evening Standard* showed me being challenged by the doorkeeper of the Bank, who is saying, 'How do I know you are not Al Capone?' And another: 'Excuse me Ma'am, would you be the Old Lady of Threadneedle Street?' referring to the soubriquet first given to the Bank in a Commons Speech in 1797. It originated with the Gillray cartoon 'Political Ravishment', showing Pitt trying to get hold of the gold from an indignant old lady, seated on a strong box marked 'Bank of England'. Trog, in *The Daily Mail*, depicted us as gangsters and generously sent me his original cartoon [photo, page 170]. In *The Sunday Mirror* the Bank staff were turning away their historic defence patrol saying, 'Sorry chaps, our consultants suggest an electronic burglar alarm instead.'

On the Sunday before work began, an enterprising *Times* photographer tracked me down and caught me in waders in the stream, which ran through our garden in Denham, trying to clear plant debris lodged in the weir. *The Times'* caption read, 'Dr Alcon Copisarow, who will soon be wrestling with the Bank of England, yesterday tackled much less involved problems at his home.' This attracted a letter to the Editor advising that the correct way of using the rake was not pushing from above the weir, but pulling from below. Then a second letter, 'Mr Dobson overlooks the fundamental point of the McKinsey method. What does he suppose would happen to the dislodged debris if he were to be standing downstream?' [photo, page 170]

The second reaction, a serious one, came from Parliament. Ian Mikardo, Chairman of the House of Commons Select Committee on Nationalised Industries, believed this was an opportunity for Parliament to get in on the act. The Select Committee wanted more information and analysis of the Bank's affairs, than they might get otherwise for their own enquiry into prospective nationalisation. Neither Treasury officials, nor the Chancellor wanted Parliamentary debates on interest rates, foreign exchange rates or sterling parities before decisions were taken, largely because of the effect they would have on market expectations. The Committee complained that Parliament was being kept in the dark. It wanted to know how much did Bank thinking influence the Treasury and, more to the point, how much did Bank actions in the money markets and in relation to foreign central banks distort the Government's intentions? The Select Committee was suspicious that the Bank had called us in to pre-empt what they themselves might propose, but the Governor told the Committee that he wanted us for quite different reasons.

So Mikardo telephoned and asked me to meet him on 27th November. He implied that the Treasury liked to protect the Bank on sensitive issues and the Governor, in turn, reciprocated when it came to government policy. But Parliament expected more transparency and the Select Committee would look to me to respond to questions. I said I couldn't be of any direct assistance; my professional duty was to our client and, in any event, I was just about to learn about the Bank's affairs myself. He was not happy with my answer. I told the Governor, reassuring him that our responsibility would be to him and I hoped that if there was any question of my being arrested for disobeying Parliament and brought to the Bar of the House, he would defend me! He said, 'Leave that to me.'

A further reaction came when the Governor was criticised by the Chairman of the Management Consultants Association for not approaching one of their members.

In the House Roy Jenkins, the Chancellor, was questioned. How could we be given access to matters concealed for centuries from outsiders? Judith Hart, the Paymaster General, replied that the choice should rest with the client, based on the suitability of the firm and the individuals engaged on the assignment. All she could add was that McKinsey was very carefully considered out of a number of firms. It was the recommendation, I gather, of James Selwyn, one of the Governor's advisers.

Before meeting the Governor on 3rd January 1969 I began to read a little of the history, 274 years of it by then. I recommended that my colleagues did the same. It was a fascinating example of how a great national institution could evolve through turbulent times and it put into perspective how our own small contribution might fit into its future.

Briefly, following the Glorious Revolution, a group of investors were given a charter to operate as the Bank of England, in return for financing William III's war against Louis XIV. So was born the Funded National Debt. It survived the Jacobite plots which led to the Riot Act and the South Sea Bubble, the greatest disaster until the Wall Street crash of 1929. Thackeray and Trollope wrote about the troubles that befell those who gave guarantees as a friendly gesture. Gladstone strengthened the Treasury at the expense of the Bank and Bagehot went on to develop the idea of the central banking function. Montagu Norman became Governor in 1920, and by sheer force of personality, was re-elected again and again until 1944, when throughout two decades of economic crisis, he created a fully fledged State bank. He argued vehemently with Lord Catto, who succeeded him. Naturally, they became known as Doggo and Catto. In 1946 the Bank was nationalised; the Radcliffe Report of 1959 on the

Working of the Monetary System set the scene for the next decade. Now we were being called in to recommend and make improvements, as complete outsiders. My small team, like me, knew nothing of central banking, but they were very good analysts.

We started work in February 1969 and continued for a year before a short break and a follow-up engagement. In thinking of how we could measure effectiveness, we were breaking entirely new ground, for only a few of the Bank's activities had business counterparts with financial objectives. An organisation undertaking a service normally charges a fee, but for two thirds of the Bank's work, it received only a nominal sum, and nothing at all for its important advisory and representational services. In some ways it was an intermediary between the Treasury and the general public. As bankers to the Government it had to cater for continuous changes in their needs, issuing bank notes, controlling their circulation and registering governmental stock. They had to supervise the financial community; they were the government's agent in managing Exchange Control and the Treasury's Exchange Equalisation Account. The Bank's income derived mainly from clearing bank deposits, the size of which it could not directly control but its knowledge of the industry, the financial community and their impact on industry generally was wide-ranging too.

We set out to demonstrate how sound management practices could improve the efficiency and effectiveness of the Bank's activities. We conducted about twenty in-depth interviews. At the top level, in addition to that of the Chief Cashier, John Fforde, the most valuable inputs came to us from three Executive Directors; Jeremy Morse (later Chairman of Lloyds Bank), Kit McMahon (later Deputy Governor and Chairman of Midland Bank) and Jasper Hollom (later Deputy Governor and Chairman of Eagle Star). Morse had been a Fellow of All Souls and McMahon a Fellow of Magdalen, whilst Jasper Hollom, who had joined the Bank staff from school in 1936, told me how lucky he had been in the timing of his recruitment. Until he arrived, everyone had had to count silver coins for two years, because the weight was unreliable. His was the first entry after 'silver' coins were mixed with nickel so he only had to count them for two months before moving on to gain wider experience! Jack Davies, the director responsible for Personnel, had been Secretary of the Cambridge University Appointments Board. A keen cricketer, he not only became President of the MCC, but had the unique distinction, when the University was playing cricket against the visiting Australian test team, of bowling Don Bradman 'out for a duck'.

One issue was a question of service quality. It did not call for three waiters to serve the Governor with afternoon tea. We sought more disciplined, less casual budgetary control procedures and recommended the appointment of a Financial Controller, new to the Bank. This was all agreed and done quickly.

A better appraisal system to plan and develop careers and clarify roles was then introduced. Demands being made on the Bank had been changing continuously. The Chief Cashier's remit as successor to the former Chief Executive of the Bank was most in need of redefinition, for two thirds of his time had been devoted to activities which were not really a central banking function.

We studied particular Bank operations, such as the Note issue and use of the provincial branches and were able to improve their productivity. In the course of all this we helped put in train big staff reductions. These continued long after we had left.

To limit risk, supervising the liquidity of the joint stock banks' assets, the Bank required 8% to be in cash or other liquid forms. They checked this on the same day each week. But when we investigated, taking samples throughout a week, we found they averaged below 4%. From then on the times when returns were required were simply chosen at random, and the liquidity figure soon moved up to the 8% level.

The Overseas Department, traditionally dealing with questions of international trade and balance of payments through a proliferation of interdepartmental committees, was now having to cope with the new multilateral organisations. We set out our thoughts on risk diversification.

There was a limit to the help we could give in the way policy advice was formulated. Much of the decision-making was in relation to the Treasury and they were not our client. When for example, the Governor asked if we could study credit control, with the alternative options of changing private sector lending rates, variable asset ratios or imposing new ceilings, we were stopped dead in our tracks by the Treasury because that issue entered into the Chancellor's forthcoming Budget Speech.

But simply to understand how the Treasury and the Bank worked together with a view to regulation, I benefitted from the explanations of two former civil service colleagues. As fiscal policy was the main regulator of the economy, the initiative lay with the Government. When unemployment went up too far, government spending and borrowing rose. The Bank as its agent lent to the private sector, but the interest it charged – the Bank Rate decision was taken by the Chancellor – as advised by the Governor. The problem lay in relating the Bank's recommended actions in the short term, reflecting market conditions to longer term objectives, like reducing the cost of Government borrowing or increasing foreign exchange reserves.

Whilst the Treasury kept their distance, the Select Committee on Nationalisation could not get the information they sought, and the Chancellor, Roy Jenkins, wished to avoid any debate which could affect market expectations. Both Sir Douglas Allen and Robert Armstrong were most helpful. I chanced my arm with one further question on policy to Sir Douglas Allen. 'So who's right?' I asked. With a twinkle in his eye, demonstrating his consummate skill, he replied, 'The question is not who's right, but what's right.' And left it at that.

Bank Rate changes, obviously, were a matter for absolute secrecy. One afternoon, however, I was summoned urgently to see the Governor. Very severely he said, 'I hear you knew in advance of today's Bank Rate announcement?'

'No,' I said, 'I just guessed.' 'And how did you guess?' 'I saw workmen arranging the chairs for a Press Conference. You only do this when an announcement is to be made.' O'Brien was shocked. He ordered them to be set out regularly thereafter. I told the Bank's archivist of this episode, but he was adamant, it was impossible!

Wherever the Bank could not initiate action, all we could do was to establish a more systematic framework for their policy planning. This we did by setting up a small Internal Policy Review Committee, chaired by the Governor himself. Its purpose was to provide some focus and analysis to the work of the intelligence and advisory services. It would evaluate, for example, whether sterling would be restricted for financing third country trade. We had to steer clear of politically sensitive areas, but were able to assist, for example, in the Ghana Debt negotiations. Here was a country that owed the UK a large sum, but if it was extracted too quickly it would put a brake on its economic development and reduce its ability to repay. The Foreign Office advocating patience, and the Treasury wanting to be reimbursed, had rather different objectives here. We developed with the Bank a mathematical model to calculate the value to them of different sets of terms offered – down payment, repayment period, period of grace, and rate of interest – and showed that it was possible in negotiation with the debtor to forego up to three of these terms as long as the fourth was accepted. The Bank went on to use this approach elsewhere.

Though tradition for the Bank held as much sway as innovation for us all it had proved to be a worthwhile assignment. The Governor wrote to us appreciatively in August 1970, the results of our work were reported internationally and Marvin Bower phoned to say, 'We are now getting approaches from the Federal Reserve here in New York.'

More than a quarter of a century later Eddie George, by then the Governor, in the course of a Thanksgiving Service address on Lord O'Brien's death recalled, 'The McKinsey consultancy had a lasting and positive impact on the Bank, and its success owed a great deal to Leslie O'Brien's strong support.' To my mind it was the Governor's strong support, as in all client relationships, which was paramount.

Consulting at its Best

In 1973 I had been asked to speak about the bank to the Keynes Society at Eton. By then, most UK clearing banks, offering a limited range of services on a huge scale, with an inflexible interest rate structure, decided to expand globally, targeting big businesses with less regard for their capital base and liquidity. The consequences were immense. In December 2009, months before the General Election, I was most surprised to be asked to repeat the talk there to the Political and Keynes Societies as the Bank was so very much in the news, I felt that after thirty-six years just a little updating would not be out of place!

Colonial Government

Murray Maclehose, a colleague with whom I had served at the Paris Embassy in the 1950s, was First Secretary (Commercial), then Counsellor, before he went off to Hong Kong as Political Adviser. We next met in London in 1965, in his office as Principal Private Secretary to the Secretary of State, George Brown. Six years later, in November 1971, following his time in Vietnam and Copenhagen as Ambassador, Murray came up to me, at the Athenaeum. He knew what I'd been doing recently, mentioned he'd spoken to the Governor of the Bank of England and said, 'You know, Alcon, I'm off to Hong Kong shortly as Governor.' 'Congratulations,' I said.

'I'm not so sure,' he went on. 'Ambassadors are not Governors. Any ticklish problem is just passed to the Office and Secretary of State; you report and act on instructions. But in Hong Kong the buck stops with the Governor. If there's a typhoon, it's the Governor's problem, or too few hospitals, schools, or housing, or widespread corruption, there's nobody else to refer to. Hong Kong has management problems we need to solve; they will be my problems and I don't know the first thing about management. Come out and help.'

'What I think you ought to do,' I replied, 'is to go out there and see for yourself. You may take a different view of the need for us when you do.'

I thought his was an ideal appointment in so many ways. Earlier in his career he had served in Amoy. He understood the Chinese mentality not least from having once served with the guerrillas behind Japanese lines. Then I received his letter:

After two months here I'm convinced. You can imagine what problems the fantastic growth of both the population and the economy have thrown up for the techniques of government, particularly when these are limited along traditional colonial lines. That is, the Governor acts on the advice of a nominated Executive Council, recommending laws to a nominated Legislative Council, administered through a Colonial Secretariat and a series of large outside departments. There is no getting away from the constitution, but the machinery of administration is worth a very close look indeed. One of our problems is that we're simply not getting enough of the right sort of people. We must make sure those we do have use their time to the best advantage and that the balance is properly struck in the distribution of decision making and effective control between the Colonial Secretary, Secretariat and the Departments in formulating and implementing policy.

What I would very much like would be for you, yourself, to come out here for a fortnight to have a look at things and discuss with us the scope, timing, and I suppose, the cost of a regular consultancy exercise. The task will involve considerable tact as well as imagination and could be quite counterproductive if mishandled. I would feel reluctant to recommend the operation unless you yourself could manage it. Can you confirm you can come over for preliminary discussions?

I arrived in February 1972 to find 300,000 refugees from the mainland squatting in huts, crime rampant. On my way to stay with the Governor in Government House, I noticed a banner crossing the approach road:

'Danger, Trenchworks ahead', but 'Trench' had been altered to 'Maclehose' – Sir David Trench had been his predecessor. Trench's Financial Secretary, Sir John Cowperthwaite had for many years conducted a laissez-faire economic policy which, linked to the innate entrepreneurship of the Chinese, generated attractive business opportunities. He was admired internationally by monetarists such as Milton Friedman. However, very little was spent on welfare. Gambling funded the limited hospital facilities, housing was totally neglected and corruption was rife. And then Cowperthwaite retired.

It had only been a year or two before Maclehose's arrival that Communist inspired riots were widespread. Godber, the Superintendent of Police, had led the telling counter-attack against the protestors and then claimed he had never been rewarded 'for saving the Colony'. Wanchai was still wild when I arrived, death from drug overdoses commonplace. The US Sixth Fleet was constantly in and out of harbour, America now realising it was losing the Vietnam War. China, after Mao and the barbaric Cultural Revolution, was beginning to look outward.

There was such a hive of activity that everyone visiting Beijing stopped off in Hong Kong. Heath, Mountbatten and Kissinger were among those staying at Government House, when I was there. Murray Maclehose, in his meetings with them, kept his finger on the pulse of world affairs.

So far as our work was concerned I had to recognise the delicate political situation we faced, both because a Colonial Government run on traditional lines was being called upon to manage a dynamic economy, and because of the deeply entrenched attitudes of its 93,000 civil servants. The entire government machine had evolved very gradually out of the early colonial model, providing for security, a legal framework and an environment in which private business could flourish. It had failed to adapt to deal with the infrastructure and services now urgently needed. Everyone seemed to have a legitimate interest in everything done, so even the simplest decisions took forever. I began by conducting key interviews.

1st of March was Budget Day when the Colonial Secretary Sir Hugh Norman-Walker and Philip Haddon Cave who, as Financial Secretary, was presenting the Budget, were much in the news. *The China Mail*, however, with an exclusive report and front page spread revealed the probe that the Governor initiated. I was 'the British expert' who, following our Bank of England experience, he had called in. Two days later *The South China Morning Post* reported officially that my ten-day visit was an exploratory one, to decide whether we would be recommending a full scale investigation.

Before I had to leave, the Governor called an extraordinary meeting of the Council – one to gain approval, including a vote, to pay our fees. 'Our system will only allow for expenditure previously voted,' he told me. I made a rapid assessment; more of a guess in fact, of the prospective cost for a team of three or four that I hoped we could field, how long it would take to arrive at our recommendations, get them accepted and begin to implement them. I had to consider whether the high cost and problems for McKinsey of working so far from home were worthwhile all round. With an hour to spare, all was agreed in principle. It was only possible with the Governor wholeheartedly behind it.

I asked Roger Holland to move to Hong Kong to join me as Engagement Manager. He would be in charge when I was not there. It was an ideal arrangement. From the outset his work was admirable, as were his relationships with Government staff at all levels and, with his wife Angela, they fitted well into Hong Kong life. The full formal interviews began with the Governor himself and extended to his staff, Executive Council and Advisory Committees. Their comments and opinions were not always consistent.

The Governor's concerns were about archaic administrative procedures, the heavy workload on the most senior staff, objectives being compromised when responsibilities were unclear and about the independent advisory bodies, which were often regarded as part of the government hierarchy.

The scope for vetoes by the staff led to underspending in departments where the need was dire and where the Government just had to deliver.

Sir Hugh Norman-Walker had previously served as Governor of the Seychelles Islands and did not seem entirely happy now as second in command. He wanted to be interviewed at his home. I was shown into the drawing room, where a huge Labrador occupied the whole length of the sofa. 'Get down, Prowse,' he called. 'How did you come to call him Prowse?' I asked. 'You know, Keith Prowse – 'You want the best seats, we have them."

Norman-Walker cited the shortage of talent and lack of experience. 'Forty per cent of the Secretariat is under twenty-one years of age,' he said (a figure we later found to be wrong). 'Many will not take decisions in case they prove wrong and would lose face. The abler Chinese that we do succeed in recruiting are immediately sought by the business community. Budget surpluses are encouraged because they can attract 8.5% interest deposited in London.'

Philip Haddon Cave had the key responsibilities that covered both financial decisions, administration and economic policy, where land sales and social expenditure – housing, health and education – were paramount. Transport and power were privately run. He was especially concerned about the incompetence of departments in putting up proposals seeking his approval. 'They should be seen to be believed,' he said. The Deputy Secretary shared this view: 'Thirteen officers were involved with a file relevant to only three.' The Deputy Economic Secretary's budgets always seemed to come up from departments more or less on the same basis as the previous year. They hadn't the benefit of new statistics in a time of rapid change. The Director of Education simply commented, 'If you are angry enough, you can get what you want.' The general tenor was that fifty per cent of the time was spent in routine committee work, the remaining fifty per cent in training or redoing the work of others. Delays were interminable.

The police were particularly frustrated; the major 1964 plan for the Tzensan Station was still awaited eight years later, although 180,000 people had resettled there in the meantime. As for the myriad of minor matters, the saga of the Kai Tak departure lounge ice machine was typical. It broke down in the midst of the summer heat wave. Options had to be evaluated – replacement or repair or ice supply contracts with quotes sought from every possible supplier. A dozen different departments had to have their say and eighteen months went by before the machine was in operation again.

Our interviews with some of the unofficial Members of the Executive and Legislative councils were no less illuminating. There was a lack of supervision in the lower and middle grades and lack of direction from the top. Sir Sidney Gordon maintained that members were overwhelmed with the volume of papers and often focused on the wrong things, an extra clerk or a Xerox machine, but not the dire need for a reservoir. And papers were presented in such a way as to make it impossible to say 'yes' or 'no'. The comments of Sir Yuet-Keung Kan, of the Bank of East Asia, on the paperwork included the memorable 'two paragraphs for a sixty million dollar project and three pages for one typewriter'.

It may have been Sir Douglas Clague, Chairman of Hutchison International, and one of the other Unofficial Members, who told us we needed visiting cards, printed in English on one side and Chinese on the other. We had them done. The translation was based on finding the best phonetic equivalent in Cantonese. McKinsey, romanised as *MA Kin-si* meant healthy and timely. Copisarow romanised as *KO Shing-nok* meant keeps promises truthfully. Holland *HO Lai-tak* meant renowned for good deeds. They all appeared so complimentary, especially when the Chinese said they reflected the character of the individual. But then we discovered that Sir John Keswick was translated as *Chiang Kai-shek*, whilst a prominent visiting British businessman proudly presented himself as 'the man with the droopy penis!'

By 10th May, the *Hong Kong Standard* was able to announce that we would study how the Government's staff resources could be better utilised and decision taking improved, and that a team of three would be arriving from London for a six-month initial assignment in June. Following our report, a further six-month assignment, continuing until July 1974, was devoted to helping implement the changes in key spending departments. We then left the Colony for a few months so that they would not become overdependent on us and returned to tackle their immense housing and law and order problems.

The Governor had readily agreed at the outset that I could speak freely at a press conference at my discretion. This I did with Roger Holland. It took senior staff by surprise and initially they were somewhat reluctant, but Murray Maclehose's diplomatic instincts proved right. *The Standard* was able to announce that the President of the Chinese Civil Servants' Association and the Chairman of the Senior Non-Expatriate Officers' Association both considered that our work was welcome and it would benefit the community at large.

The Government's role and criteria of success had to cover both legislation and policy making and the execution of policy. The former involved qualitative judgments beyond our competence. On the latter, however, we were able to apply more factual criteria, akin to those in business, to respond quickly to changing needs.

An underlying problem was the need to expand services whilst skilled and experienced staff were becoming fewer. A complication was the fragmentation of responsibility across many departments inhibiting change. For example, in crime prevention, a dozen departments were involved and when it came to more specific factors, such as police recruitment, most were beyond the control of the police themselves. In the overriding interest of law and order, however, the police, the courts, the prisons and welfare departments, each of which had its own budget and acted independently, were persuaded to release funds, share objectives, pool resources and work together. Collectively they were better able to tackle the pervasive narcotics and corruption problems.

Occasionally there were emergencies. A riot broke out whilst I was in a meeting with the Governor. The Colonial Secretary came in to announce that a menacing crowd of investors in the four Stock Exchange buildings – as there were then – could not sell their shares. There had been no time to register them; dividends in any event were not important, it was quick capital gains they were after in an unbelievably volatile market. They threatened to set fire to a building. The Governor gave instructions for it to be evacuated and shut down and the fire brigade to use force if necessary. Within half an hour the stock market operation continued in the street, the jobbers and the brokers behaving as though nothing had changed.

The Press was always curious. *The South China Morning Post*, perhaps seeking to gain easier access to me, as early as March 1973, had reported our team effort as 'the Copisarow reforms'. I soon put a stop to that, but I also promised them as a quid pro quo more entertaining details for their readers, as events unfolded.

The following October the Governor, in addressing the Legislative Council, spoke of the intense activity there had been over the previous year. There was the stock market's dramatic rise and fall; the loss of reserves due to the sterling float; the prosecution of Godber, Superintendant of Police, and his escape, highlighting the problems of corruption; shortage of raw materials and import prices escalation. All of these occurring simultaneously, placing a considerable strain on the machinery of government. But he was proud of the response of the public service. The progressive implementation of McKinsey's recommendations would, he hoped, strengthen the Government's machine and planning processes and eliminate the need for any repetition of such a mammoth operation.

No sooner had we left than the Colonial Secretariat was reorganised. Forty departments gave way to six; branches were created for economic services, environment, home affairs and information, housing, security and social services retrospectively, and two for resources. Seven of the eight

Secretaries were appointed and our recommended system introduced across the board.

In the six months that followed, the Press persisted with questions about progress in implementation, but the hard-working Secretariat was often too busy to respond. As a result the *China Mail* speculated that there must be difficulties. I didn't like the publicity:

Reading between the lines, they reported on 31st January 1974, *one only needs to look at the life and style of Alcon Copisarow to realise that the problems must be quite severe. He is a rather Kissinger-like figure, winging round the world from project to project, keeping all the pots boiling, and coordinating developments with head office. He arrived in Hong Kong on January 19th after various high level talks during the preceding few days in London, New York and at Los Angeles airport, to enable immediate onward transit to Singapore and Malaysia. The plan was that he would remain in Hong Kong only until 22nd, before whirling off again on urgent business back in London. At Sir Murray's personal request he stayed on an extra two days, spending most of the 24th in deep discussion with the Governor out at Fanling Lodge. Dr Copisarow is discreet about these matters.*

I had to admit to myself that being described as a 'Kissinger-like figure,' which might go down well with American readers, was not the type of publicity I or McKinsey welcomed, even if it captured something of the truth.

I had visited Hong Kong almost every month for two years, for four to ten days each time, suffering from jet lag because I was working in the USA and Europe at the same time. Throughout I could rely on Roger Holland to lead the small team, which included Mark Weedon and Martin Beresford, both out of our London office. Three members of the Secretariat were effectively team members too: Mike Clinton, Deputy Colonial Secretary, Peter Lee, later Commissioner for Narcotics, and David Forde, later HK representative in London. Unforgettably, there was a Mr Brimmiscombe-Wood too, who doubled as 'Colony hangman'. He maintained he thoroughly approved of 'suspended sentences'!

Though working relationships were excellent, the Financial Secretariat presented a specific problem. They had attracted over the years the brightest people and they knew that the changes envisaged meant losing some of their power. Other staff, who were less able or were lazy, had reached their positions by waiting and keeping their slates clean. Now they were nervous about change and not over-helpful. Philip Haddon-Cave, however, who was highly capable had the most to lose as Financial Secretary. The Governor's advice to me was to use what diplomatic skills I could, in addition to his, to encourage him to accept that organisational change was imperative.

He soon retired, appropriately honoured with a knighthood. The Colonial Secretary also retired and was succeeded by Sir Denys Roberts. Hitherto Attorney General, he was a talented barrister as well as an accomplished author. With a fine sense of humour, he entitled his book *How to dispense with lawyers*.

What I had not expected was for minor problems to arise in the team's relationship with McKinsey's own administrative staff in New York. Assignments in Hong Kong were a totally new experience for them and led to confusion. They mistook the $HK for the $US more than once and, unable to understand the International Date Line, delayed an entire month's expense claim because it included two bills 'for the same night'.

One unchanging feature for the team as a whole was the social scene. I occasionally stayed at Government House, but usually in the same suite at the Repulse Bay Hotel, with its famous 'noonday gun', and when Diana was able to join me once or twice we were guests of Lawrence Kadoorie at the Peninsula Hotel.

Diana's mother's family had known Sir Elly Kadoorie, Lawrence's father, who had come from Damascus to Shanghai to build up a giant business empire in Hong Kong. He showed me his priceless collection of antique jade, including the mighty anointing spoons of the earliest Chinese Emperors, and was impressed more than anything else, by my knowledge of the mineralogy of jade, which I had gained thirty years earlier as a student.

When I stayed at Government House informally, we all went, the Maclehoses, their dogs and a detective, cruising around the islands and walking in the hills of the New Territories, Murray with his huge strides always out in front. Gaunt, austere and sometimes tense at the start, with weighty problems on his mind, he returned relaxed and affable. At other times there was strict formality, and then the correct dress was essential. Murray told his tailor to come to measure me in my room and he completed two suits and six shirts in a matter of hours, at a total cost of about £4. At dinner, Squeak, as Murray's wife Margaret liked to be called, took great care to ensure that protocol was properly observed in arranging a complicated seating plan. And after dinner, I was invariably invited by other guests to go on to some other function or event.

Michael Sandberg, about to become Chairman of Hong Kong and Shanghai Bank, asked me to join him in his Box at the Jockey Club for the major annual event at Happy Valley. He gave me a tip to back the favourite in the big race. Before I could, an elderly Chinese industrialist, Sir Sik'nin Chau said 'He can't win.' There was a friendly argument; I had no time to bet, Sandberg lost his and tore up his ticket.

I asked, 'How could you be so sure the favourite would lose?' 'He could not possibly win. Traditionally the winner is led into the Winners Enclosure by the wife of the owner. He is sitting there, not with his wife but with his mistress. She just could not lead him in; it could not win,' replied Sik'nin Chau. He was keen to get all the publicity he could. Years later, at Kensington Palace, Princess Margaret told us that on her visit to Hong Kong, he had popped into every photograph taken of her: 'He gave me a thoroughly Sik'nin time.'

I was taken one night by the Superintendent of Women's Police with an armed guard, to see a gangland area of Wanchai. Provided with an old raincoat, I arrived at a gate to be 'rubbed down' by a wizened old man with greasy hands. Two Alsatian dogs leaped out, but on sniffing us they turned away. The grease was apparently to distinguish us as 'friends'. Roger Holland willingly joined in raiding drug dens and brothels and told me they identified underage girls by their molar development – 'an acquired skill', he assured me.

The most important factor contributing to the effectiveness of our work in Hong Kong without doubt was the personality, experience and motivation of the Governor himself. Consultancy at its best involves working in collaboration with the most competent clients. Murray Maclehose was clear in his objectives, utterly determined to succeed. Walking in the hills one Sunday, he said to me, quite confidentially, 'Regardless of Treaties, China could take Hong Kong over whenever it wished. I hope they realise they could have much to gain if the takeover was peaceful, a partnership as it were, under Chinese sovereignty. I think they do. It would benefit their overseas relations if they were seen to be preserving Hong Kong's way of life. To be the powerhouse for finance and trade in South East Asia, Hong Kong needs to have the best education, housing and healthcare with the cleanest, least corrupt and least criminal population. What is needed is something that did not exist when I arrived here – a government machine that would deliver.'

He took his oath to The Queen as Head of the Commonwealth very seriously. Despite all previous loyalties, the interests of Hong Kong put those of Britain into second place. When Hong Kong left the sterling area and aligned itself to the US dollar, the British Government was not pleased. But Murray, with absolute authority, was single minded of purpose, self-confident and courageous. His humanity also shone through. This, I once saw for myself as he struggled with a decision on whether or not to commute a death sentence, which he detested.

Roger Holland told me he had been invited, whilst I was away in London, to 'fill a spare seat' at a Governor's dinner party for Desmond Plummer, head of the GLC (Greater London Council) who was passing through. A telephone message was whispered into the Governor's ear. Apparently an irate Ted Heath had missed a vital Commons vote because a traffic jam had held up his car from Downing Street. 'Desmond,' the Governor said to him, 'the PM has been on the phone wanting to speak to you about a traffic jam. I assumed you would prefer to enjoy your dinner in peace. We told him you are not available.' Then another course, another whisper in his ear, but no comment; dessert brought yet another whisper and the arrival of an aide to receive brief inaudible instructions. Later over coffee Murray said, 'Desmond, apparently the PM called several times. He sounds in a bad temper over something. The lines to London appear to have gone down, so I don't think you will be able to talk to him tonight and unfortunately you will have left for Beijing before he is awake...' The Governor was reappointed twice, to popular acclaim, and elevated to the House of Lords.

Whilst in Hong Kong we were asked to work with others there. On each occasion I mentioned this to the Governor and we agreed there could be conflicts of interest in an environment where every business wanted to know more about the Government's intentions.

However, I was surprised to be approached by China – specifically by the Chairman of the Hong Kong branch of the communist Bank of China – on behalf of its Central Government. Would I meet a Vice-President of China to discuss a possible assignment with them? I knew it would not please the Governor, so I first telephoned Marvin Bower, McKinsey's elder statesman in New York for his reaction. He began by asking for my views. I said it would be momentous, but required setting up and staffing a Beijing office of the firm, and that was not part of our current strategy.

He replied, 'And how long do you think it would take China to implement your recommendations?' 'Many years,' I replied.

'Yes,' he added, 'and would you be satisfied with so little to show for your efforts for so long?' We took no further steps there. I could only guess why we were being approached. Perhaps the Chinese Government wondered what they could learn from us for contingency planning before Hong Kong was returned to China. We should only take on the right client at the right time.

We did however compile a list of other prospective clients we might work with when the time was right, including the Hong Kong and Shanghai Bank. The private Kowloon Motor Bus Company was one we could take on with just two consultants, without delay. Introduced by its Chairman, P.C. Loo, an Unofficial Member of the Council, the Governor had no objection. We were interested to discover how it could charge the lowest fares in the world, be a good employer, and invariably pay a dividend of 15% out of profits. They were clever enough to be able to achieve higher productivity still, and more rapid expansion, following our study.

It was time for our team, wanted elsewhere, to leave. Roger Holland, on promotion to Principal, returned to London. I addressed the colony's Management Consultants' Association. The Vice Chancellor of Hong Kong University (Dr Hueng) asked if he could incorporate the substance of our work for the Government into his book, to be published by the Oxford University Press. This was agreed.

Our services were being sought elsewhere in SE Asia, at the same time. The early results of our Kowloon Motor Bus Company assignment came to the notice of the Minister of Communications in Singapore, Mr Yong Nyuk Lin, who wanted to improve Singapore's own bus company. We put that on hold. Then I received an invitation to call on HH the Sultan of Johore, the most southerly state of Malaya, just across the Causeway from Singapore, for some undisclosed purpose. The Sultan received me in his Palace so graciously I felt sorry not to be able to help him, but his was a political problem. He wanted Singapore to provide his small fleet with dock facilities. However over a family lunch, which included most of his grandchildren, he regaled me with stories of polo matches with Lord Louis Mountbatten.

From his military aide, I learned how he received the Japanese officer who had come to take him prisoner when Singapore was surrendered.

The Sultan had told his aide, 'Tell him I'm asleep and cannot possibly be disturbed.' Trembling, he delivered the message and then, unbelievably, the Japanese officer saluted, turned about, marched away, and did not return for another year. The elderly Sultan sent me Christmas cards regularly. He had not been to England since he was six years old and wouldn't travel now, 'because of the English climate. My grandfather was staying at Bailey's Hotel, South Kensington when he died. They said it was rheumatism, but he wasn't in bed on his own at the time!'

In 1974 with the prospect of more approaches to extend our activities in South-East Asia coming our way, I set out my views to the firm's Development Committee on the pros and cons of a permanent presence. In its favour, was the chance of an important assignment with the Hong Kong and Shanghai Bank. More generally, we were attracted by the dynamism of the people throughout an area growing in world importance, with some of our multinational clients contemplating expanding their interests there. Against this, however, the area was scattered; large companies were still few and life for consultants was expensive. Our immediate competitors would have included strongly entrenched accounting firms, some unethically combining their role as company auditors with management consultancy. Nor was bribery unknown. It was a question of priorities. The time would come when we would have to be located there, but in the near future, other centres might be more attractive.

I did not disagree with the firm's decision to forgo South-East Asia for the time being, for Europe and the USA needed more attention. But other consulting firms were quick off the mark to spot the opportunity, not only those extending the services of public accounting firms, but indigenous firms too. SGV, the largest SE Asian management consulting firm with twenty one offices and two thousand staff members soon formed a successful 50-50 joint venture with Sun Hung Kai Securities, taking over the twenty-sixth floor of the prestigious Connaught Centre.

Personally, I was asked to stay in the Colony by Lawrence Kadoorie, to join his Boards – China Light and Power, the Peninsula Hotel Group and

Star Ferry – and I warmed to this approach. Kadoorie had a remarkable life. A son of Sir Elly Kadoorie, he was imprisoned by the Japanese in 1941 and his properties confiscated. He set about rebuilding and electrifying Kowloon and the New Territories, made huge charitable donations to medical and agricultural projects and eventually received a knighthood and a peerage. Adding his encouragement for me to join was George Nelson (Lord Nelson of Stafford) Chairman of English Electric, who knew me well. He was there bidding to construct an atomic power station at Castle Peak on Kadoorie's property, where we all met. Kadoorie was a member of a highly respected Jewish family. Both he and Nelson assured me I would get unbelievably rich too! I had a stark choice. It was the most significant occasion when I came face to face with the issue of work-life balance. Riches were certainly attractive, but with a young family I did not imagine myself as an expatriate. More importantly, Diana was firmly opposed to a life there. She could not contribute as much as she had begun to do at home, nor be miles away from our children at school. We were already comfortably placed to finance the expensive higher education of our four children. I turned down the invitation, and have never regretted it.

After 130 years of British rule, Hong Kong was our last remaining major colony. We could not foresee in 1974 how the handover to China, due in 1997, or its consequences would unfold. The formal handover ceremony was attended by a newly elected Tony Blair and The Prince of Wales, who apparently called it 'The Great Chinese Takeaway'. The first act of the Chinese government was to paint the traditional red pillar boxes fluorescent green with a purple base, in line with their own postal service. The second was to delete the Royal prefix to the Jockey Club and Police Force. The most welcome improvement, long overdue, was the construction of the new airport, replacing Kai Tak. On each of my visits I had the frightening experience of all passengers, landing under the washing lines linking the tenement blocks.

Most significantly for us, however, after the Chinese regained sovereignty in 1997 the new regime, according to McKinsey's partners in the office established later, continue to this day to act on our 1970s recommendations for reorganisation. They have withstood the test of time under a communist regime.

Values

I have often been asked, how valuable are consulting services? I have discussed this widely, but have found no unanimity. A few dismiss management consultants as outright charlatans. Very few of these survive today. There is no doubt however that some clients are dissatisfied with their work. Some of these clients just do not have the 'will to manage'. McKinsey's assignment for the National Health Service suffered from the argument between the Minister, Sir Keith Joseph, his officials and the service itself on what was needed and what could be accomplished. When this happened, consultants sometimes blamed the clients for their inadequate brief. Some assignments could get well underway before it was recognised that full implementation lay beyond their client's control. In the case of the Bank of England both Parliamentary challenges and Treasury reluctance to cooperate were potential obstacles, but were bypassed largely by the good fortune of personal relationships. On other occasions cost-cutting proposals, invited and delivered, proved too unpopular to be adopted.

There were successful businessmen who would not retain them on principle. Arnold Weinstock, a highly successful Managing Director of GEC, would not use them as his style of management was simply to concentrate on closely monitoring seven performance ratios and reacting quickly when they were not satisfactory. In my Neddy days, I had met him in his office early one morning. He was calling the manager of one of his component manufacturers. 'Why has your sales/output ratio gone down 2% in two days?' The word got around. It kept all managers on their toes.

In one case I found it impossible to discover why we had been asked. Our Los Angeles office tipped me off that John Paul Getty would like to get in touch with us because his Tidewater Oil interests in California were extending to Europe. I went to see him at Sutton Place, his sixteenth-century home in Surrey, where Henry VIII had met Anne Boleyn. When I arrived, the door was opened by the Duchess of Argyll. 'We are being economical with the heating', she announced. It was bitterly cold inside. I admired the magnificent Aubusson tapestries. Getty appeared, coming downstairs at almost midday, wearing two dressing gowns. 'How well do you know Armand Hammer?' he asked. I told him I didn't. He just switched off and said no more. Breaking the silence, I commented on his patriotism – taking seriously the national fuel shortage – and I noted a momentary change in his expressionless eyes. There was a red public telephone kiosk in the corridor; his visitors had to pay to make a call.

Before he showed me out, I plucked up courage to ask, 'Mr Getty, have you ever gambled?' 'Only with other people's money,' he replied, 'but if I were to, I would buy a casino.' When I related this episode to Hugh Parker, he told me of his own strange meeting with him in Scheveningen. Getty had queried the breakfast bill, because marmalade should not have been an extra.

More than compensating for these rare events, however, was the immense value that could develop over the years of building a strong relationship with an influential business leader. This was exemplified by Lord Aldington's role. He recommended us to the Stock Exchange Council's Chairman, George Loveday, following the economic disaster which struck them, serving them in 1973/4 and, as Chairman of National and Grindlays Bank, Sun Alliance and The Port of London Authority (PLA), he called us in to each in turn. Once he had seen some results of our activities he explained in one annual report that we actually 'changed management attitudes'.

Toby and Araminta, his wife, became good friends. I cheered him up considerably one day in his office because Charles, his son and heir, on graduation had done badly and I told him that precisely the same had happened to me!

The problem for PLA's management was that in the previous decade the number of ships coming into the Port of London had halved and the cargo tonnage had dropped by more than a third. This decline occurred in spite of an overall growth in traffic to and from SE England, because of uncompetitive high prices, under-investment, unreliable labour and equipment and poor marketing. Industrial relations were at a low ebb.

From having a largely administrative function, somewhat akin to that of a local authority and landlord, the PLA had become primarily a dock operator and one of the largest stevedoring employers in the world. Yet its staff, management structure and processes all reflected its earlier role. Experience of managing dock operations and understanding shippers' requirements was lacking. Reversing the decline would not be easy.

Working with the Authority, port development was switched from the upper reaches to the newer berths close to the Thames Estuary. This left the PLA with much redundant but valuable land. It included 96 acres of London Docks, 372 acres of Surrey Commercial Docks and 320 acres of Beckton. Together with the under-utilised buildings overlooking the Tower of London at St Katharine Dock House, the Press described it as 'the biggest asset-realising opportunity in London since the Great Fire'. So far as client value was concerned, our fees paled into insignificance.

Tragedy struck Aldington's final years on a personal level. After a fine career as a scholar, then soldier, he rose to become a young Brigadier on the General Staff in 1945, advancing with the allies from Italy into Austria. Entering Parliament at Toby Low, he attained Cabinet rank. In 1945, under the Yalta Agreement, in exchange for the return of our prisoners of war, Stalin required the repatriation to the Soviet Union of tens of thousands of his 'enemies', which included entire families. Aldington was instructed to organise their return. On arrival they were all murdered.

A generation later, Sun Alliance refused to pay out on an insurance claim to a relation of Count Tolstoy. Ten thousand copies of a leaflet describing Aldington, then chairman, as a war criminal were distributed. Although he won his claim for libel, he was never compensated. The episode brought great unhappiness to his family.

On a lesser scale, 'value received' was recognised perhaps uniquely by Duncan Stirling, about to become Chairman of the merged National Westminster. He telephoned about the invoice I sent to him. We had had only three days in which to calculate the price that Westminster should pay to acquire Martins Bank, but we had not negotiated a fee. My invoice simply reflected our normal billing practice. 'Is that what you think it was worth?' he asked. 'I'm sorry,' I said. 'We should have discussed it in advance. Please destroy it and send us a cheque for what you consider fair; I'll send an invoice to match.' The next day, with a most appreciative letter, we received a cheque for three times the amount. The word went round the firm. 'Value billing', as it came to be called, rather than time-related billing, was encouraged. This applied both ways. I have thought about this carefully, but in my experience over a decade, the value that my colleagues delivered to clients far outweighed the bills presented.

Leadership

McKinsey provided its consultants with the chance of learning continuously and of demonstrating their leadership potential. In my ten years in the firm, I learned much about leadership, both in acquiring knowledge and with the general principles of management. In the former case it could be finding new applications for sophisticated military products and capabilities, discovering their value in civil markets, the competition they would have to face, and then developing new strategies, aligning the applied research, design, manufacturing, marketing and financial functions to achieve them. Where there had been a revolutionary change in an industry, such as natural gas, North Sea oil supplies and global transport facilities by container, the boundaries between industries could virtually disappear and new opportunities arose, calling for judgement and forthright action. To be effective, it was necessary to combine technological expertise with the management of information, of assets, risks and wider relationships.

I soon found that the principles of general management encompassed not only science, but art and included different styles of leadership – the pathfinders, the decision makers and those who could best motivate and revitalise their workforce.

Many leadership qualities were common to the public sector, private sector and in professional and voluntary institutions. Leadership called for innate personal qualities, an inspirer and developer, one with vision, drive and courage, with a capacity to communicate and to gain the support and commitment of those led. Some individuals could adapt their style to their following easily, without compromising principles. In many cases, having a reputation for leadership tended to develop a momentum of its own and lead in turn to further success. However, the latent capacity to lead frequently showed only when particular circumstances arose.

In McKinsey, all our leaders were men; it took decades to change that. I mentioned the omission when I spoke, at our Directors' conference in Madrid, the first to be held outside the USA. One of our oldest directors said, 'Women as leaders? Don't forget the final scene in *My Fair Lady*. When Professor Higgins called for his slippers, it was Eliza who fetched them!' It took almost twenty years for this to change.

Every director of McKinsey was a leader in some respect. It was essential in relation to his consulting team or presiding over development committees or firm offices. Five Managing Directors in succession, all American, had prime responsibility for leading the firm in my time. In our partnership, they had less formal authority than that of a company or institutional chief executive. Their power and effectiveness derived from personal credibility, to influence, inspire and create the best conditions for the firm's success. Each director was asked who he perceived to be the person most needed at the time, nominating two or three who had agreed to stand, one being selected by secret ballot.

Marvin Bower was unique. His vision, his ethical principles, his sense of mission, standards of professionalism, energy and selfless commitment established a firm that would thrive long beyond his own lifetime. Colonel Urwick, who created Urwick Orr with a sure touch, was seen by some as his counterpart in the UK. Both had quite different personalities and approaches – Urwick was autocratic, Marvin wholly collegiate.

Gil Clee, as his natural successor, upheld all Marvin stood for. Quiet and thoughtful with a warm personality, he invariably brought the best out of his colleagues. His previous World Bank experience ideally equipped him to expand the firm internationally and his untimely death, so soon after his appointment, was an immense loss. Even during his short tenure, he made the crucially important change, to incorporate the firm, and by doing so allowed partners to accumulate their earnings until they chose to retire, a key incentive to remain in the firm.

Gil's successor was Lee Walton, 'the tiny Texan dynamo'. He had an intellectual grasp second to none, and was a by-word in having both political flair and total integrity, providing much of the momentum for the firm's early international expansion. After my Bank of England assignment, he discussed with me the problems faced by central banks more widely, and towards the end of our Hong Kong work, the opportunities for expanding geographically in South-East Asia. He was in favour of this, but the firm Development Committee considered that at that stage our first priority lay elsewhere.

He went out of his way to oppose the sale of McKinsey's shares even though we would all be offered a large multiple of their book value. In this, he and Marvin Bower – by now in semi retirement – were in absolute accord, both dedicated to putting the interests of clients ahead of the firm's. Lining the coffers of existing consultants would be a betrayal of their predecessors who built up the firm, and possibly render them less objective in the advice they gave. Later, when I told Lee of the contributions we could make in the non-profit sector, he encouraged me to do so and accept any welcome invitation I received. 'Others might not share this view until we are in a stronger financial position,' he said, 'so it cannot yet be firm policy generally.'

Al McDonald was elected on the second vote by the narrowest of margins, at a time when our finances were under pressure and some cost cutting essential. He was a tactician, ambitious and opportunistic, who came to the rescue when the demand for services was briefly in decline. This did not make him universally popular, but by reducing costs he helped pave the way for successors to reinforce the enduring qualities of the firm.

And finally in my time, Ron Daniel, the ideal all-rounder, whose understanding and encouragement of all raised morale, by rebuilding confidence when it was needed, from the time when he headed the New York office until his election and re-election. He elevated standards of competence, recognised the value of intuition as well as deduction in problem-solving, invested in practices and training, and re-emphasised Marvin Bower's philosophy of long-term client relationships.

One or two directors who would have made outstanding managing directors chose not to stand. Some wished to concentrate on serving their clients; Max Geldens in Amsterdam was one. He had established a formidable reputation, unrivalled in the business world, and a confidante of all in the Netherlands government. Other directors were a perfect fit, heading the firm's offices. Hugh Parker, in London, never regarded himself as a great problem solver, but he had the stature, social and business connections and easy approach, to make him the perfect national representative in the UK of an international firm.

Other directors were different still. Roger Morrison was the ablest analyst. He would shepherd his team into his office, close the door for hours on end and emerge with a recommendation for the client, invariably demanding and hard to implement fully, but impossible to argue against – and wholly necessary.

I was different again. I had criticised excessive analysis with the phrase 'Analysis, analysis, paralysis' – at a time when we should have sat back for thought and counselling. Years later, Brigadier Harry Langstaff, our London Office Manager showed me an early appraisal made of me by my then co-directors. 'Not single minded on analysis,' it read, 'but the quickest to absorb and home in on the key points; his teams are usually foremost in fastening onto the few issues essential for the client.' If there were less generous appraisals I wasn't shown them!

I certainly sought to deal with the most important issues, those with the chance of making a real difference and giving clients 'best value for money'. All directors contributed to firm leadership by encouraging dialogue and helping to build the firm around a shared agenda. As we expanded geographically most adapted well to the wider range of cultures. John McDonald in Germany and Max Geldens were outstanding examples. In cultural terms however, though otherwise highly accomplished, some transfer between the US to Japan proved less successful. Some chose not to make McKinsey their whole career. One or two directors left early to take on full-time leadership positions in charitable or voluntary bodies where they did well. Those who chose business disproved the old adage, 'If you can't manage successfully, you consult.' Their ambitions led them to the executive roles of Chairman or Chief Executive of major corporations such as American Express, Westinghouse and IBM. Lou Gerstner became IBM's highly successful Chairman. He had always enjoyed the intellectual challenge, fast pace and top level relationships as a consultant, but thought it obsessed with analysis. He left, initially to run the American Express Card and Travellers Cheques service. He told me of his IBM interview much later. Asked, 'What do you rate your prospects of turning this company around?' he replied, 'About one chance in three.' 'If that's all, why do you think you should get the job?' 'I know the others on the short list,' he said. 'They haven't one chance in a thousand!'

Mistakes were made by the firm in one or two new appointments. Within a few months of my own arrival, the directors were sufficiently emboldened to go further and recruit three well-known Americans to join as directors. They did not fit in and did not remain long. Sam Gould, a New York University President and Charles Leigh, a highly regarded business specialist covering South America, remained for a few months only, whilst Neil Harlan left after just a year, to preside over a Californian pharmaceutical company, where he thrived. They had excelled in their own fields hitherto, but were not sufficiently versatile and could not really adapt to the particular leadership role required in a management consultancy. So I remained as the sole survivor, following the risk McKinsey had taken with me ten years earlier. Nor did they attempt to recruit any more. Perhaps the strike rate of success was too low!

All in all, my decade with McKinsey gave me far more in terms of understanding and skills than I envisaged possible at the outset. Building on my previous experience, there was the need to incorporate the management of technology into general management, recognise and calculate the many aspects of business risk, in the context of the politico-economic scene, the roles of government in contributing to prosperity and social welfare, and aspects of co-operation and leadership. It gave me insights into other issues, such as the time scales involved to bring about change, the critical differences in the culture and competitive strengths of other regimes − and more personal confidence. Other well-known consulting firms had certainly been successful, but for my relationship with McKinsey and our relationships with clients, this was consulting at its best. There could not have been a better foundation, or tool kit for the twenty tasks I was invited to tackle thereafter.

Chance for youth in small business

From Dr A. C. Copisarow

Sir, The Government's "Action for Cities" programme is a departure from the past for it will command a four-year budget of £12 billion, whilst delegating to others — without abdicating overall responsibility — tasks best done by others.

Ten years ago, after a loss of 15 per cent of all jobs in the big industrial cities in a decade, the Urban Programme was introduced and attention then turned to the interests of small businesses. Large businesses, more or less independently at first, recognised their own social responsibilities.

The multi-faceted enterprise agency movement was born and momentum gained when the professionalism and leadership of more company chairmen was attracted, notably under the auspices of Business in the Community. The voluntary sector paid most attention to the needs of individuals.

The measure of success of all endeavours, as seen nationally, is the cumulative effect. But locally it is perceived as the impact on individuals who are seeking to improve their own lives and their immediate neighbourhood. To achieve success budgets, whatever their size, must be used productively. Quantity is no substitute for quality.

Not many are as successful as the young woman three years ago given advice and £1,000 for milk-testing equipment by the Prince of Wales's Youth Business Trust, who now has an annual turnover of more than £3 million. Yet, under this trust alone, with its 2,000 experienced volunteers, 4,000 small businesses in 23 regions of the country have been set up — and most are prospering. The young people selected and advised lack experience in preparing business plans and judging risks, but they do have "street sense", courage and determination and a profound influence on attitudes in their communities.

We know that many more are capable of setting up and successfully running their own business than get the chance. Each year an additional 20,000 at least in the 18-25 age group who wish to do so could succeed. Some of them are disadvantaged; one fifth have at least one A level; but though some literacy and numeracy is needed, the record shows that the potential for wealth creation is independent of intellectual potential.

The voluntary sector could do more. Even if the Prince's Youth Business Trust, for example, were to continue to grow at over 40 per cent a year, as it has over each of the past six years, it would take a further seven years before it could fully cater for its own age group.

Many firms have contributed money and seconded staff. The Government has recently begun to match some of these donations on a pound-for-pound basis. It has also helped the young directly through the Enterprise Allowance Scheme and considerably improved training facilities through the Manpower Services Commission.

The most cost-effective schemes should be enabled to do more. One per cent of the Action for Cities budget could dramatically accelerate results. Without intervening in the management of voluntary organisations, a more careful monitoring of performances would be needed — the survival rate of business start-ups, the cost per job created, and success in attracting funds (including the EEC's European Social Fund) — to identify the most successful practices and means of recognising and launching those individuals prepared to help themselves.

Yours faithfully,
ALCON COPISAROW
(Former Chairman, The Prince's Youth Business Trust),
25 Launceston Place, W8.
March 22.

Letter to The Times *1988*

Presenting the first Copisarow Award

Trustees of PYBT   Photo: *Tim Flach*
Back row (L to R) Sir Matthew Farrer, David Richards, Stephen O'Brien,
Sir Michael Quinlan, Anthony Everett, Peter Mimpriss, John Pervin (YBI)
Front row (L to R)
Lord Boardman, Sir Angus Ogilvy, Dr Alcon Copisarow, Sir Hugh Dundas, Howard Phelps
(Chairman)

On North Sea oil rig 1982

Roald Dahl
letter 1979

TELEPHONE:
GREAT MISSENDEN 2757

GIPSY HOUSE
GREAT MISSENDEN
BUCKINGHAMSHIRE

5th January, 1979.

Dear Alcan,

    I don't want to shower you with bumph but before
you go in to see Bob Bernstein you might want to glance
through the enclosed letter from my New York Literary
Agent, together with a bit of background. Most of it
is to do with contractual negotiations which is not what
you are going to talk about, but I think it will help
you.

        Yours sincerely,

TELEPHONE:
GREAT MISSENDEN 2757

GIPSY HOUSE
GREAT MISSENDEN
BUCKINGHAMSHIRE

12th March, 1981.

Dear Alcon,

    I thought the enclosed would interest and

amuse you. My break with Knopf was probably

inevitable from the time when we had to fight

them so hard to get our just desserts. But it's

a big thing in my life. There won't be any problem

in finding another publisher.

        Yours sincerely,

        Roald Dahl

Roald Dahl letter 1981

Reunion of Prima Ballerinas – Violetta Elvin (Savarese) and Moira Shearer

*On top of the world – in Provence
with John Peyton 1997*

Philosophising with Marcel Boisot

With my boss Dr Bertie Blount, 1963

Putting the world to rights with Fernando Savarese – Taormina 1994

A captive audience for Robin Day on Golden Cap

Hats and Dogs – the Dorset walk Boxing Day 1996

With friends at Forde Abbey
(L–R) Robert Armstrong, Lucy Faithfull, Paddy Armstrong, James Miskin

Unplanned Journey

Still Geologising: Canary Islands

Still Studying: Churchill College, Cambridge 2005

Still at sea: aboard 'Elissa' 2012 with Richard, Wendy, Justin, Emma

Still married: Diamond anniversary 2013

Home – Moss Side from 1922

Home – Denham Village from 1968

Eden Project Biomes 2000

OPPORTUNITIES
KNOCK

CHAPTER VII

Royal Connections

By the time I had reached the approved retirement age my combined experience over thirty years, across the public and private sectors, at home and abroad, offered me many future options. Pure leisure was not one of them.

Now was the time to step back and take stock. I had been fortunate to have enjoyed everything I had done. I was also thrilled by any new challenge. Where could my varied experience make a difference? What was I best qualified for? What interested me most? What were the opportunities at hand? How would they complement my other work? Above all, what was most worthwhile and also fit into my family life?

We, as a nation sought security, economic prosperity, environmental integrity and social welfare, both at home and for the poorest in the world. I had an interest in all of them. I had not been involved in defence matters for a quarter of a century, so was rusty. But in the civil field, perhaps a non-executive industrial directorship or two might come my way. I considered a few.

The pharmaceutical industry was certainly attractive. It had evolved beyond expectations, quickly developing globally. Its manufacturing was not capital-intensive. It depended critically upon large research and development programmes, publicly funded medical research and the protection of patents of groundbreaking drugs. A fair balance had to be struck between safety and incentives for innovation. Inward investment allowed tested products to get to market more quickly and government price control in the UK provided for stability – very different from the French arrangements, where many government departments intervened.

I discussed this with Sir Alan Wilson of Glaxo. In 1972, the Monopolies Commission had not let Beecham and Boots acquire Glaxo. But keener competition and a weakening export market forced Glaxo to take the initiative.

Wilson, a former Research Director, had played a key role at Glaxo in integrating the work of R&D, medical and commercial departments, encouraging lively debates, even arguments between them, but always insisting that scientists had to be convinced that what they were doing was worthwhile. His leadership led to the recognition of the changing economics of the industry, higher development costs, the need for more sales outlets, new strategies and reorganisation. With the incorporation of Beecham and Smith-Kline, Glaxo stormed ahead.

But political intervention could have a dramatic effect. When the Government had to reduce public expenditure, it sought to force drug prices down once patents had expired and insisted on the more extensive use of generic drugs. The National Health Service did not protect British suppliers, so companies had to expand internationally. Success was heavily dependent on the high quality of its bio-technological research, its close collaboration with universities and the application of information technology to reduce the time for clinical trials and filing submissions. It also depended on flexible financial markets, entrepreneurial venture capital and a congenial regulatory environment. This was an industry of real interest to me, but I came to the conclusion, and Wilson agreed, that I would need to give it my full time in an executive role, to make a major contribution.

My next thought was of possibly entering the civil aviation industry. I read the Plowden Committee's 1965 report which was revealing. Government funding for the industry was much higher than economic benefits could possibly justify. It was in the national interest, however, to support it to provide employment, cushion the decline in defence orders, realise some technological spin-off if possible and, above all, by diplomacy and politics, attract some national prestige. Could I help it to become profitable?

Only two projects out of thirty-five, I noted, had ever repaid our public investment: the Viscount and the Dart engine. The Treasury was strongly opposed to greater support. One of their principal arguments had been that they starved other industries of the limited supply of scientists and engineers. Edmund Dell, whose unique perspective came from three appointments – as Secretary of State for Trade, in MinTech, and as Chairman of the Public Accounts Committee – told me that disproportionate support for the aerospace and nuclear engineering industries had substantially weakened the total performance of our postwar industry. No one seemed interested in further recruitment to the industry.

Then, among my technical qualifications were electronics and electrical engineering. A major structural change had taken place in 1969 with the merger of GEC, AEI and English Electric, promoted by the IRC (Industrial Reorganisation Corporation), to bring together heavy electrical, process control, automation, radar and electronic components. In Hong Kong, I met Lord Nelson again, emerging from the Colonial Secretary's office. I had known him as Chairman of English Electric, since my Neddy days. Now the merged company was bidding for the major contract for the first nuclear power station at Castle Peak. Before we parted, he asked, 'What do we have to do to get you to join us?' 'I'm a McKinsey man', I replied.

In any event, my thoughts now were turning towards increasingly important social issues, both at home and abroad. With so many others I shared a concern for the disadvantaged, for those in extreme poverty and I thought of the widening and increasingly dangerous gulf between the rich and the poor of the world. Could I not find a role for myself in which technology and good management could reduce the inequality?

I had touched on aspects of this issue at conferences in Teheran, Ankara and Nairobi. When Blackett then asked me who was best qualified to initiate further studies of the opportunities for technology in the developing world, I had proposed Sir John Cockcroft.

I had met Cockcroft first in my Paris days, when he enjoyed recounting, quite diffidently, his earlier years in Lancashire and then on course to splitting the atom, being told off by Rutherford for paying the Americans ten dollars for just one gallon of 2% heavy water! Then, as a member of the Tropical Products Advisory Council, I was in touch with him again, able to tell him of Blackett's proposal and provide him with documents and an office in MinTech, where he wrote a useful report.

In 1970, at a wide-ranging multinational conference held in Los Angeles, on 'The Application of Management Principles to World Economic Development', I was asked to be opening speaker. All present were agreed on the growing importance of this issue, but what struck me was that none of those who recognised and had proposals to resolve the problems, neither the developing countries themselves, the donor nations nor the international development agencies, had in place any effective management processes to do so. It was difficult, of course, to incorporate social science and political inputs into economic analysis, but little attempt had been made to entertain even the most basic management thinking.

I spoke not only about the prospects of transferring and translating certain technologies into the means of generating a higher standard of living, but the importance of tackling a host of unrelated, even minor practical problems, to be effective. I quoted from a report I'd read, presented in Vienna by a UN official:

A factory is completed, but it has difficulty in importing spare parts. The price of a commodity has fallen on the world market, so earnings of foreign exchange fall and imports have to be curtailed. The young engineer sent abroad for training decides not to return. The installation of the laboratory equipment in a new college of engineering is delayed for three years because the donor country's foreign assistance budget is cut. The funds set aside by the government to stimulate local businessmen go instead to speculators. Negotiations with a potential foreign investor are delayed six months when the Minister of Industry is forced to resign. The feasibility

*study for a new cement plant cannot be undertaken until next year,
because of the difficulty of recruiting foreign consultants.*

I concluded that for technology transfer to be successful, a cure also had to be found for the problems of fragmentation, discontinuity, delay and conflict of interest, all requiring better management. Only then might it begin to attract external resources and inspire internal commitment. Blackett went along with this, saying, 'Science is no magic wand to convert a poor country into a rich one.'

Important as it was, however, I did not see myself as the ideal person to concentrate on this complex problem. To make a practical contribution, one really had to work long and hard with the indigenous population in remote places. It called for the prolonged and dedicated services of the young and energetic. Apart from that, I was still troubled by the stance of a principal speaker at that conference, who had disagreed with my views. I had raised the question, 'How could East Pakistan (now Bangladesh) allow thousands to die in the recent flooding of the Ganges, claiming they did not have the funds to build up the river banks, yet choose to spend much more on rearmament and the development of nuclear weapons?' He, a government minister, replied, 'We are taught that the more we suffer in this life, the greater the reward in the next. If we are attacked, however, we must be prepared to defend ourselves, and that is costly.' It took almost forty years, in fact, for the country to tackle the problem seriously.

I decided I had left it too late to get immersed in all this, important though it was. I should try, in any event, to spend more time at home with my family. I was neglecting them.

The limitless task of sustaining the environment appealed, as a no less worthy cause nearer to home. It would become increasingly important. As a student of geology, on field trips to Yorkshire, North Wales and Argyllshire, I developed my interest in the evolution of the landscape. Then, thanks to the Forestry Commissioners and their counterparts around the Commonwealth, my interest in the environment grew. Learning more about the dangers to plant life that lay ahead, I wanted to play some part in helping to protect our environment. I remembered what I was taught. I was a trustee of the environment. It would not be for many years, however, that an opportunity would come along. When it did, in the shape of the Eden Project, to be completed for the Millennium, I took it readily.

In the meantime, I had been being asked and agreed to take on three or four less demanding voluntary activities. Each of these was worthwhile, but taken together they would over-fragment my time. I mentioned this to two former senior civil servants whose opinions I valued, Sir William Nield and Sir Douglas Allen (Lord Croham). They reacted in the same way: 'Given your subsequent roles, have you thought of returning to the Civil Service for a few years? It really does need more of the wider experience you could certainly bring.' They were not recommending it, but inviting me to form my own judgement.

There was certainly a need for additional perspectives, and new skills to introduce best practice into the operational delivery of public services. For this, management consultants, specialists and academics were already being recruited, sometimes too many of them, and not always in appropriate roles. But the service was now on course to changing its ethos and its nature. Ministers were appointing, in larger numbers, political advisers imbued with their party orthodoxy. Their policy recommendations were becoming increasingly independent of those of civil servants in their Departments. To some extent they were in competition. There was the danger if perpetuated of objective advice being overruled. Furthermore, with a service that I felt was already too large, a suitable appointment would be difficult to find.

It did not take me long to decide against going back. I still looked back with an element of nostalgia on my more productive years in the Service, but any attraction to return did not compare with one exceptionally deserving cause, enhancing the prospects for the young. I had been introduced to this by Prince Philip. I had thought about it over the previous decade and even before leaving McKinsey. A key component of our social welfare, it was inspired and guided by Prince Philip and then the Prince of Wales. Thanks to my previous well-paid appointments our savings would now allow me to work unpaid for the foreseeable future. I committed myself to it to over the following twelve years.

The link to the Royal family went back to the last year of the war, when briefly I was instructing David Milford Haven, Prince Philip's cousin, a Lieutenant RN, and Lord Louis 'Dickie' Mountbatten, then Rear Admiral.

At HM Signal School, Portsmouth, in the intervals between 'Long Courses' I held forth on the operational performance of radar under different meteorological conditions. David was clearly interested, but he told me that unlike his most able father, whose mathematics was strong enough for him to become a specialist in gunnery, he was directed to signals.

Dickie Mountbatten's command of almost any subject, on the other hand, as I found later was formidable. I had covered the blackboard trying to work out the answer to the question – at what range could a particular transmitter with a given aerial height expect to spot a specific target? After a couple of minutes he stood up, saying, 'Perhaps I can help.' He strode to the front of the class, took my chalk and calculated the answer in a flash. To ease my embarrassment, over lunch he revealed he had been a Senior Signal School instructor fifteen years earlier, and had written much of the two-volume *Admiralty Handbook of Wireless Telegraphy*, still in general use. Others in the class told me, 'He also knows the names of every telegraphist in the Mediterranean fleet.'

David Mountbatten was friendly. He told me that those in the class with hyphens in their surnames had given me an honorary one, Copis-Arow. It was meant as a compliment! He then asked me to join him at a party in St John's Wood. He had a tank full of petrol. As I thought of him driving back seventy-three miles to Portsmouth a little worse for wear, I advised him to take the train. He wouldn't hear of it. Eventually I was tempted, and went along, both of us in uniform. Returning in the early hours and giving a lift to a girl living near Sloane Square, we were stopped. David had not drunk too much, but he was driving fast down the Hyde Park east carriageway. As we were waved down by a police car, David said, 'Leave this to me.'

A police sergeant came across and, removing his gloves began, 'I don't suppose you know what speed you were doing, Sir?' 'That's quite alright, Officer,' said David, and then, in a whisper, I thought he mentioned Princess Margaret, and drove off. We were not followed. I never knew whether he was recognised, or what Princess Margaret, only fourteen at the time, had to do with it, but it was never mentioned again.

After his reign as Viceroy of India, 'Dickie' Mountbatten returned to the Navy, and we met again when he had become Chief of Defence Staff. In April 1964, ten of us on the Council of the British Institution of Radio Engineers were invited to a private dinner in the Mikado Room at the Savoy Hotel, where the CDS, who was also our President, would join us.

The only Signals matter we discussed all evening was when I asked him about changes in his lifetime – how the speed of communication at sea, for example, had changed during his fifty years in the Navy. He said in some ways it hadn't improved in 150 years. 'If Nelson, from his flagship in the Bay of Biscay, wanted to send a message to the Board of Admiralty, he would dispatch it by fastest frigate; it would be rushed by a relay of cavalry to Whitehall; the Board would immediately pen their reply and the document would be returned in the same way, reaching Nelson a month from the outset. Today the sophisticated electronic signalling system would transmit the Admiral's message instantaneously to the Ministry of Defence and then, in the same way, four weeks later they would send their instantaneous reply.'

Throughout most of the dinner, we were regaled with his reminiscences of the splendour of his own forebears – he obviously loved the panoply of state occasions. As a great grandson of Queen Victoria and son of Princess Victoria of Hesse, he told us about his aunt, the wife of Tsar Nicholas II, who was assassinated about the time he was midshipman. 'She was indefatigable. On one occasion, within a day or two of giving birth, she stood erect for four hours to receive a procession of about a thousand members of the estate staff.'

We were interrupted towards the end of the evening, when a manager came in to ask if all was satisfactory. Mountbatten said, 'I don't suppose you ever knew the assistant hall porter here in 1917?' 'Oh yes Sir, he's living in Rottingdean now, he must be well into his eighties.' 'Well, send him my very best wishes and tell him I remember his advice to me and a US Navy midshipman.'

Mountbatten told us what had happened. He was in London to receive a new posting and stayed at the Savoy that night. 'The American came up to me asking how one could find some female company here. I said, 'Let's ask the hall porter' and we went across to his counter.'

'In Theatreland, with its concert halls, they are called singers.' 'So where do I find a singer?' With a dismissive wave of his hand, he replied, 'just across the road.'

'We crossed the Strand to see a Singer Sewing Machine shop directly opposite, and through the window a pretty girl.' 'Strange customs you have here,' said the American. 'In we went; she surprised to see two young Naval Officers.'

'I would like a Singer,' said the American. 'What sort of Singer?' she asked. 'We have this model fixed to the table, propelled with the hands, and this fixed to the floor, propelled with your feet.' 'We are looking for one fixed to a bed, propelled with your hips,' said the American.

Mountbatten tried his best to persuade us it was a true story, one he had not retold for nearly half a century. Probably the first time I retold this story was in 1957 to Prince Philip himself, when we first met. In the course of the three-day state visit to Paris, he mentioned on the car journey his recent appointment of Brigadier John Hunt, as the first director of the Duke of Edinburgh's Award Scheme. He thought I should meet him. But it wasn't until we were back in England that I was able to do so.

We were living in Amersham when Diana joined the Buckinghamshire Association of Youth Clubs as a volunteer, and was later its Chairman, then President. She helped recruit volunteers as instructors and prepared candidates for their Bronze, Silver and Gold awards. She also produced a film, *Beyond the Gold*, featuring Gold Award holders to demonstrate the attractions of the scheme and inspire others to follow their own example. John Hunt came to its premiere in 1966, cutting the celebratory cake. He was enthusiastic about achievements in the County and he joined us for dinner at home in Shardeloes. Our six-year-old son, discovering that the Everest conqueror was with us, crept down in pyjamas to meet him. Animated conversation with John continued for an hour in his bedroom. It was my first indication of John's enthusiastic interest in and support of the young, and Prince Philip's commitment to the Award Scheme.

I remember that, at a meeting on education I had in Whitehall with the Minister, Sir Edward Boyle, the subject of the Award Scheme came up. 'Surely,' he said, 'Hunt could find something better to do with his time than simply duplicating what children learn at school.' I told him I did not agree. Among its aims was a balanced development of character and physique. Before the scheme was launched, in fact, Prince Philip had discussed this with David Eccles, Minister at the time, and in the year after, a very constructive meeting with Lord Hailsham, his successor, at which Sir John Hunt was present.

I noted that if the Trustees of the scheme were ever to run into trouble, the Minister of Education could have a role – he nominated an observer to the Advisory Committee. I need not have been concerned. Yet I did wonder whether the scheme, now growing rapidly, was actually reaching the individuals who needed it most, some without any self-motivation. John's aim was well-directed. The young needed new experiences and challenges – adventure, enterprise and service to the community – to attain maturity, gain confidence and a sense of responsibility. Too few had the opportunity to discover what they were.

I now had sufficient time to offer to examine the scheme's performance, its problems and scope for improvement and this was warmly accepted by the new Director, Sir Alfred Blake.

My study confirmed its remarkable success. There was scope for improvement, but in terms of cost-effectiveness, for example, it was incomparable; at an annual cost of less than £3 per head, over 100,000 young people were gaining the services of 50,000 volunteers. The foundations laid in the first eleven years of the scheme established its future. At home and throughout the Commonwealth, the benefits could be seen, not only in the disproportionate success of the young participants in job applications, but also among adults, assessors and skilled advisers, many of them former Award Holders themselves.

The report itself was based on a series of twenty-four interviews at all levels, comprehensive questionnaires addressed to 870 individuals, a careful analysis of the 78% who responded in full, and valuable comments in amplification. Whilst I was working at the same time on a McKinsey assignment for the Port of London Authority, I was supported admirably by three volunteers from the London Graduate Business School and the Tuck School, Dartmouth College, USA.

In brief, the report's diagnosis and recommendations were:

> The Award Scheme had spread to forty countries of the Commonwealth, attracted well over 1,000,000 participants and 500,000 awards had been gained and eighty per cent of all participants had been introduced to new activities and interests, with more than 400 to choose from.
>
> One in every four participants had been asked about the scheme at job interviews and one in eight said they would not have obtained their present employment had it not been for their involvement in the scheme.
>
> More than 22,000 adults provided direct help to the scheme, contributing a total of 6,000,000 hours a year.
>
> The majority of participants were at school so the scheme had gained a school-based image and four out of seven dropped out of the scheme each year, with or without awards; mainly at school-

leaving time when they were seeking an adult environment. Emphasis should therefore be placed on continuing participation after leaving school and on recruiting new entrants from among young working people.

The scheme's image did not reflect the realities: participants were regarded as having higher-than-average academic qualifications, middle-class backgrounds, club orientated and were using the scheme as one more symbol of their ambitions. The real picture was that entrants were not significantly above average in intelligence, they came from all levels of society, nearly a quarter of all participants did not belong to any club and the prime attraction of the scheme was the challenge it offered.

Many more volunteers were needed and it should be shown that it did not demand a lot of time, money or skill. The scheme would benefit if presented on a more localised basis, with the creation of regional award centres and industrial group operating authorities.

When the Directorate examined and approved my report, they passed it to the Trustees for review; Sir Alex Abel Smith and Brigadier Dame Jean Rivett-Drake, and then Prince Philip. He called for a full press conference, to be held at Buckingham Palace, where the 'Copisarow Report', as he designated it, would be presented. It happily coincided with the scheme's twentieth anniversary, so the Press turned out in large numbers.

A stage was set up in a large ground floor room overlooking the garden. We approached along red-carpeted corridors with black leaded grates filled with neat paper crowns. The décor was Egyptian; on one side of the room was a large wall painting of Queen Victoria driving to her Diamond Jubilee, on the other a huge graph showing the scheme's twenty-year record of growth.

In presenting the report, Prince Philip said the scheme was now nineteen years older than he expected it to become. 'At first, they thought

I was trying to start up a Hitler Youth Movement,' he said. 'In my view a civilised society depends on the freedom, intelligence and civilised behaviour of its members. The problem is how to turn this philosophy into a practical programme.' He referred to one of our findings that four out of seven entrants dropped out each year. 'One girl who was asked why,' he said, replied 'she was giving up the Duke because the nights were getting shorter.'

At the following Trustees' meeting, all agreed on the desirability and feasibility of the recommendations and proposed to implement them, in consultation with the Operating Authorities. The plan appeared under the rather ambiguously worded heading 'After Copisarow'. Prince Philip then asked if I would join his Board of Trustees, for a six-year term, if possible. This, I was very happy to do.

I learned soon after, that there was a movement afoot to inaugurate a similar scheme in the United States. The initiative came from three Irish Gold Award holders who persuaded two Senators and a Congressman to propose a Congressional Award Scheme, modelled on ours. Prince Philip offered advice and legislation was prepared by a Committee of Senators and Representatives. They asked for copies of my report to be sent over to help make their case. No Federal appropriations were being sought, but the active help of business leaders was essential and my introductions to supporters who served on US company boards and my presence in Washington to speak to key Congressmen desirable.

I was able to introduce Sir Richard Dobson, who was on the Exxon Board and Lord Aldington on the Board of Citicorp, and drafted as requested, two letters to promote the cause, for them to send to Rosalyn Carter, the President's wife, and Senator Edward Kennedy.

Eventually to ensure its success, Prince Philip generously made a special private visit to Washington in October 1978. When I was sent a copy of the Senate hearing of 24th April 1979 by Tony Culley-Foster, one of the Irish Gold Award holders, I was surprised to see they had faithfully recorded, for all time, in the ninety-sixth US Congress Record, the contents of the 'Independent 1976 Evaluation – The Copisarow Report'.

For some reason I never understood, one of the protagonists, Clement Stone, a direct descendant of Mark Twain, made me an 'Honorary Knight of the Mark Twain Society', of which Winston Churchill had become a Knight in 1937!

Over the following six years, under Prince Philip's active leadership, the scheme continued its healthy growth throughout the Commonwealth. In 1979, I was fortunate to find that Ronald Gardner Thorpe, a personal friend, was likely to become Lord Mayor of London. He agreed to make the scheme his Charity of the Year. For a short while, I chaired the fundraising committee and this is where personal contacts, three in particular, were so valuable. Michael Randolph, who was at the time on the Press Council with me, had become Editor-in-Chief of the *Reader's Digest*. He agreed to publish a lengthy article about the scheme on its twenty-fifth anniversary. Then a scientific colleague, Sir Harold Thompson, who had just become Chairman of the Football Association, decided that all the proceeds of the England v Spain match at Wembley – to which Lord Carrington and I were invited – would go to the Award Scheme. The Chief Executive of American Express, while a McKinsey partner, told me that our anniversary in 1981 coincided with their European centenary. To mark this, every time a card member used his card in the UK during October and November, American Express would donate 2p to our appeal. We had both the international publicity we wanted and donations beyond all expectations. By 1981, 1,500,000 young people had entered the scheme. One of the Trustees, the delightful Myra Butter, told me that she always knew Prince Philip 'could achieve something important', and she had known him most of his life. It was only later I discovered they were both great-great grandchildren of Tsar Nicholas I.

Our celebrations extended from a national 'standing room only' St Paul's Cathedral Thanksgiving service, to a local Buckinghamshire project where Gold holders with Diana's help, staged and enacted the scheme's history in the Elizabethan setting of Chenies Manor, once Henry VIII's Chenies Palace.

In the following years, there were many memorable moments for us – helicopter trips of the Queen's flight from the lawns of Buckingham Palace to Hever Castle and the Home Counties – and, at the same time, important steps were being taken to coordinate the scheme globally.

We held an impressive International Forum in 1982 attended by American as well as Commonwealth representatives. In November that year I reported on a meeting I had been asked to attend in New York. The Foreign & Commonwealth Office and Department of Education & Science approached me in connection with a United Nations initiative for an International Youth Year in 1985 and the need to set up coordinating machinery in the UK. I had since 1978 also been involved with the Royal Jubilee Trust (RJT) and 1985 happened to be the Jubilee of King George's Jubilee Trust as well as the Girl Guides, so I commended this UN initiative to my colleagues.

In December 1983 my time was up and I formally retired from the scheme. In the course of a Palace luncheon given by Prince Philip, he mentioned that perhaps he too should give up his patronage. He was shot down vociferously on that one and I added, 'You are younger than me.' I proposed, however, that when the time came, perhaps Prince Andrew might be given a role. Richard Davies, Prince Philip's Secretary, wrote to me: 'I am advised by the Queen's Private Secretary… it would not be possible for Prince Andrew to play an effective part as Patron without interfering with his Naval duties.' In fact, Prince Philip had not considered Prince Andrew then, as he was serving full time. He had nearly got a Gold and later took over Outward Bound. Prince Edward got his Gold in 1986. Prince Philip remained the ideal patron and responsibilities eventually went to Prince Edward, where they continue to this day.

The RJT was the combined body, supporting the young and disadvantaged with monies raised for the 1935 King George V and then for The Queen's Jubilee celebrations. Lord Remnant asked me to join its Administrative Council. A small staff, directed by Harold Haywood, was making grants in response to approaches from ethnic minorities, trade unions and regional bodies, for the general welfare of the under twenty-fives. It was also supported in due course by the Prince's Trust.

The Prince of Wales proposed, following a visit to Toxteth and Merseyside in 1981 and after speaking to many unemployed youngsters with ideas and hopes of setting up in business for themselves, but with no opportunity of doing so, that they be helped to achieve this. The Royal Jubilee Trust agreed to set aside one tenth of its annual income for this.

My arrival coincided with the retirement from the Jubilee Trust Council of Sir John Partridge, who had attracted the valuable sponsorship of important businesses. I was asked to explore the opportunities for youth business enterprises. Apart from my McKinsey experience, I had some involvement in the venture capital industry, becoming in 1981 Chairman of two investment funds. I therefore set up a panel which included government representatives, staff of the Department for Education and Science (DES), the National Children's Bureau, the Manpower Services Commission, UNICEF (Europe) and the Van Leer Foundation. We began to consider what was missing in meeting the needs and capabilities of the unemployed and disadvantaged young. On my return from the UN Committee meeting in New York, Jimmy Remnant told me that closer collaboration was being sought with the Prince's Trust which was making direct grants to these young people. This was exactly what our panel had hoped for, so I was delighted to be asked by Prince Charles to join the President's Committee that he would chair, to take the proposal forward. Within a month, a new structure was agreed. Lord Lieutenants would nominate, but Prince Charles himself would approve, the leaders of the joint groups in ten cities across the country. We all recognised his real concern and were thrilled when he told us he committed himself to this cause as his principal interest.

The Committee was expanded: Sir Kenneth Durham, Keith Sutton, Bishop of Litchfield and Baroness Carnegie of Lour joined us, and I was asked to set up a scheme. This we called the Youth Business Initiative. It would enable selected youngsters with ideas of their own to start up a business with the aid of grants we would make. The need was clear. In early March 1982, writing under the heading 'The Caring Society', hearing many of the young say, 'We've got nothing to do,' I had urged for a major reinforcement of our voluntary efforts to find something that suited their capabilities and interests.

One difficulty was political – the sponsorship of officially recognised services was fragmented between four government departments, Local Authorities and Trade Unions. The National Council for Voluntary Service had a co-ordinating role only. I raised this at the time with Peter Morrison, Minister of State – we should bring together complementary bodies for greater impact. The Regional Offices of the Award Scheme knew of opportunities. I hoped that some public funds for expenses could be found. Morrison, with some responsibilities for the Manpower Services Commission warmed to the idea and indicated the likelihood of funds becoming available for a pilot scheme. When I reported this to the Palace, Lord Rupert Nevill said that Prince Philip thought the Prince's Trust might also be able to be closely involved.

I was keen to show that, with the right kind of help, even the hardest hit of unemployed youngsters might have the ability and determination to set up and run successfully their own companies. In national terms, of course the scale would be small, but for the youngsters themselves it would be a major achievement, to their sceptical neighbours a forthright challenge and to so many others, who had fewer obstacles in their path, exemplary. When the Prince of Wales agreed to be our President, I knew that YBI would develop rapidly across the country.

From the viewpoint of the young I talked to, it was a most appealing prospect to set up in business alone, taking risks, committing everything, and a far cry from the continuous rejection at interviews and the depressing effect of standing in dole queues. But there was a huge challenge to be faced. What YBI did through its national network was to receive applications from unemployed eighteen to twenty-five year-olds who had worthwhile and imaginative business propositions, consider their plans, their needs and prospects of success, advise, select and make grants of up to £1,000 each and provide two tutors in every case to give advice. To satisfy charitable requirements, the monies had to be used for tools and equipment, rates, insurance and transport, and not for stock or raw materials.

All applicants had been unsuccessful in getting help elsewhere. Apart from lack of money, there was almost always a degree of hardship or disadvantage in their family, social, economic or ethnic background, or even physical disability. In some regions of the country, as many as a third of the recipients were from Afro-Asian communities. In every case, however, a viable plan had to be presented, admittedly with some help from YBI, and skill, entrepreneurial talent and determination demonstrated. So in each enterprise we were sponsors, supporters and go-betweens. YBI also made recommendations for the Business Enterprise Allowance of £40 per week at the outset for living expenses and, at a later stage, supported the applications for loans from other sources for some who were expanding.

Evaluating the performance of these small businesses was all-important. In the early years, 80% of them continued into their second year and beyond. An additional 10% provided their owners with such experience and confidence that, for the first time in their lives, they successfully applied for full-time jobs elsewhere.

YBI was quite clearly in the risk business. On the one hand its policy, conforming with its President's wish, was 'if in doubt pay out'. On the other hand, a track record of success had to be established that positively encouraged donors to contribute. 97% of all funds received went to the youngsters. It was thanks to the goodwill of industry and commerce – the services of the fifteen full-time officers they seconded, secretarial help and office facilities and the advice for a few hours each week of some 2,000 voluntary tutors, all at no cost to YBI – that administrative expenses were limited to some 3%. About a quarter of all applicants received awards and the 'near misses' were advised, given some training and reassessed with a view to their being reconsidered later.

The real measure of the scheme's success was the difference it had made to the lives of so many young people. There were some remarkable, heart-warming stories of transformation, from enforced idleness, frustration and potentially dangerous youngsters, into determined, hardworking, responsible and optimistic members of the community.

David Wood in Birmingham had spent three years on the dole whilst undergoing numerous operations on a cancerous shin bone and was feeling pretty low. Deciding that boredom and feeling sorry for himself were a recipe for disaster, he took a course in upholstery at Walsall College of Technology and a further short commercial course, found premises at a Local Authority Workshop and, with a grant from YBI for his van and equipment, set himself up in business, which went from strength to strength, and soon employed others.

Colin Harding was one of the better off. He set up his carpentry business by selling all his treasured possessions – stereo, electric guitar and so on, raising just £500. He needed more and also help in dealing with the accounts and solving marketing problems. YBI gave him £1,000 and frequent advice. His company, Barry Cabinets, making fitted kitchens and bedrooms of a high standard, achieved a turnover of £45,000 within a year and then orders from abroad started coming in.

We were told that Chailey Lambert, a silversmith aged twenty-one, had won several commendations for precious metalwork, but could not get a job anywhere. With YBI's help, a £1,000 grant for a kiln and casting equipment, and advice in getting his business systems worked out he began to produce superb model cars for Aston Martin, aeroplanes for the RAF and received commissions from the British Museum and the Bowater Group.

There were hundreds of examples. Mac's bakery in Glasgow for instance, soon employed fourteen people and planned further expansion. One of the most interesting cases was a centre in Bristol where company personnel were trained in outdoor pursuits. All four of its owners had criminal records. With advice and a total grant of £3,000 an impressive, useful and totally law-abiding business venture was established.

The tenor of the appreciative letters we received was conveyed by Derek Coffee: 'If hard work and dedication is what it takes to make a business work then I promise I won't let you down.'

Crucial to all these operations were local coordinators in fifteen regions of the country, officers with expertise and experience, seconded usually for two years, with responsibility for administering the scheme regionally, screening applicants and recommending those they thought could succeed to their local YBI Board – members of business, local government and educational establishments.

The Regional Officer asked them why they thought the business would work, what their competition was, how they would go about promoting their business and helped them develop their first year's budget. They would have to do most of the research themselves.

Regional Officers also selected suitable tutors or mentors to ensure the continuity of their training, and an adequate understanding of management. It was the continuous personal advice from the same two tutors that was so important. National Westminster Bank set a wonderful example in providing over thirty of them. Their Community Affairs Manager commented: 'It was very interesting for the tutors; they came into contact with young people, sometimes from very different backgrounds, unemployed with no track record, 'high risk'.'

The bank's Area Advances Officer for Bromley told us he spent his day lending sums of up to a million pounds. On his way home from work, he dropped into a tiny fashion design business run by Marilyn Smith and gave a hand with the accounts. 'She's very talented, but wants to pursue the bits she enjoys – she must become a complete business person.'

Once a product was made or a service developed, the problem of marketing needed more attention. We recruited a National Marketing Adviser from ICI's Fibre Division. Her job was to advise on how best to advertise within a strictly limited budget, build up good relations with the local Press, and so on.

A few major companies became so enthusiastic about the scheme that they instituted a collaborative Business Bursary Scheme, accepting youngsters we recommended to set up businesses in their own factories and offices, with all the available facilities and advice, and paying them up to £1,000.

Unlike many other schemes, it was not one for job seekers, but for job makers; it did not aim to select the most promising commercial prospects, but rather the most deserving, on social and humanitarian grounds, so long as the commercial prospects warranted it. By striving for a balanced approach – of a caring society, self-help and wealth creation – it avoided political controversy.

The demand at home was inexorable. Millions of pounds were needed to cater for just a fraction of it. The young bursars themselves could contribute a little and the Royal Trusts one fifth at the most. Happily the Lord Mayor of London-elect, David Rowe-Ham, generously agreed to make Youth Business Initiative his 'Charity of the Year' in 1986. With that in mind, I went to St James's Palace for a talk to Angus Ogilvy, Chairman of the Youth Enterprise Scheme. This had been set up in 1984 by the National Association of Youth Clubs and provided low interest loans for a similar purpose as YBI made grants. I suggested there would be some merit in a merged Trust under the Prince of Wales's patronage. He thoroughly agreed. Apart from the all important leadership of Prince Charles that we would obtain in a merged Prince's Youth Business Trust, he welcomed the prospect of cross-fertilisation of our respective appraisal systems and joint fundraising efforts. In YBI we had developed some risk assessment guidelines for making grants, which might be more widely applied for the loans.

We had problems in the beginning. One particular objection came from Sir Kenneth Cork. As a Trustee of the long established Fairbridge Society, which was closely associated with YES, he saw a conflict of interest. Getting agreement on the chairmanship of the merged body was another. Fortunately Sir Charles Villiers, formerly Chairman of British Steel, was thoroughly supportive, had much influence and we went ahead.

Leading up to the merger, YBI obtained funds from the Manpower Services Commission for three pilot studies to explore more thoroughly the needs of the young unemployed in West Yorkshire, West Midlands and Greater London. Armed with the results, I proposed in a letter to Lord Young, by then Secretary of State for Employment, that joint funding by the public and private sector would be highly beneficial. He was enthusiastic, highly supportive and his permanent secretary, Sir Michael Quinlan, became one of our most valued Trustees – especially when substantial sums had been offered by certain businesses only if we could obtain matching public funds on a pound for pound basis.

In the formal announcement of our establishment as the Prince's Youth Business Trust (PYBT) under Prince Charles' presidency, and the appointment of its Trustees, Angus Ogilvy and I were designated Joint Chairmen. I thought it more appropriate for him to be sole Chairman, but he wouldn't hear of it: 'You should take it on; I can chair its Advisory Council.' The Trustees agreed and on that basis, we carried on for the best part of two years [photo, page 232].

Sir David Rowe-Ham's Mansion House reception was a conspicuous success. We arranged a programme of other fundraising events for 1986. One of the earliest offers came from the *Reader's Digest* who awarded ten bursaries in each of the twenty-five counties across the country – at a cost of a quarter of a million pounds. There were also sporting occasions. In June, Prince Charles took part in a polo match sponsored by Guinness at the Guards Polo Club with the award of the Bell's Scotch Whisky Trophy. We received a handsome cheque from the Guinness Chairman, Ernest Saunders.

Photographs were taken, and we were just about to cash the cheque when I saw a Press report alleging financial offences and criminal proceedings against Saunders. Concerned that Prince Charles could inadvertently become associated with 'ill-gotten gains' I telephoned him, saying we had some worries. 'What do you suggest?' he asked. 'In my view,' I said, 'the ends cannot justify the means; ethically a positive commandment cannot be fulfilled by transgressing a negative one.'

'Yes, but we are not sure that it is tainted money, what would you advise?' 'That's right', I said 'we're not sure.' Then I probably gave the wrong advice – that we should keep it. Prince Charles went along with this, adding, 'and we can certainly make better use of it than they can.' With hindsight I think we should have accepted it conditionally, with provision in our accounts to refund it if guilty verdicts were reached, as eventually they were.

On 6th August, Prince Charles had to bow out of a charity football match at Old Trafford between Manchester United and Flamenco of Brazil. Not only was I asked to stand in for him, but the United Chairman, Martin Edwards invited me to kick off, which I did as a Mancunian. I received a trophy, but was then obliged to make an after-dinner speech.

In June 1987, among many other polo matches, HRH played again for our charity, on Smith's Lawn for the Pimm's Cup. Three years later, unfortunately, he broke his arm in two places in a fall between two horses at Cirencester. In reply to my letter of sympathy he wrote with his left hand, '...forgive me for not being very humerus (pun)!...' describing his awful writing as rather 'sinister'.

My visits to America to help set up a YBI in Boston, in preparation for a visit by Prince Charles in September, together with the Congressional Award publicity resulted in another welcome cheque coming our way. The American Ambassador in London, Charles Price, persuaded the organisers of their Golden Eagle Ball to donate the proceeds of that major event to us.

Then Diana had the idea of compiling an anthology of witty contributions from friends, with cartoons by David Langdon, entitled *Compliment Slips*, and royalties would go to the PYBT. Prince Charles' Foreword announced that the proceeds would provide an annual Bursary in my name for a disabled young person. [photo, page 231] For years thereafter, I was called on to present the award. One especially deserving winner was a paralysed young man who started up a cow chiropody service. Once on holiday in Holland he had seen one. Because cows with bad feet could not graze, they sat and produced no milk. He was much in demand to help raise milk productivity.

The work of the Trust was going from strength to strength. Then it was decided, in October 1987, that the Chairman should be independent of YBI or YES. Sir Hugh 'Cockie' Dundas, a Battle of Britain hero flying with Douglas Bader, succeeded me and developed a great reputation thereafter. Our handover was a most pleasant occasion and to be able to look back on the difference we made to some young people's lives was rewarding beyond measure. I only wish I could have continued. As it was, all I could do was to write a letter to *The Times* in 1988, 'A chance for youth in small business' [photo, page 231], which helped to build on its success.

Angus Ogilvy, travelling in India at the time, wrote to me from the Prime Minister's house in Rawalpindi: 'When we agreed to merge I had considerable reservations as to whether it would work in practice. I really believe now this will become one of the UK's major charities. If it does, the credit will be entirely yours because you are the person who laid all the foundation stones.' Had he written later surveying the subsequent track record he would have described it as a true measure of Prince Charles' unique achievement.

I have been asked by friends more than once since then, 'You have known three generations of our royal family. How different are they from one another?' The short answer is that my informal contacts have been relatively few. In the case of David Milford Haven and 'Dickie' Mountbatten, there were incidents which were indicative, but my contacts with Prince Philip and Prince Charles were more frequent.

Some of Prince Philip's and Prince Charles' beliefs, convictions, ideas and aspirations, reflected in the schemes and activities they committed themselves to, and their responses to needs and the extent to which they have sought and received advice, have differed significantly.

Philip's approach, predominantly rational, Charles' more intuitive; Philip's judgement in balancing exploitation and conservation, or tradition and modernisation contrasting with Charles' concern to redress the balance and throw his weight behind the policies and causes he espouses. Both, however, have sought to enable the young to flourish, bureaucratic obstructions removed and voluntary, altruistic efforts supported. In their unique roles their achievements have in both cases outweighed their own original expectations.

Over two generations, our expectations and court attitudes have changed. Many traditions have given way to modernity. When there was a prospect of Prince Philip, a bright, energetic moderniser, 'not steeped in our traditions', as some put it, acquiring a constitutional role on marriage to the Queen, there were concerns. Unlike his uncle 'Dickie', his naval service and career were cut short, but he was not prepared to take a back seat. Churchill invited him, unexpectedly, to become Chairman of the Coronation Commission and he made a conspicuous success of it. I happened to cross the Atlantic in 1965 in RMS Queen Mary with Peter Dimmock, a TV presenter for the occasion, who told me how much this surprised the doubters.

In the absence of parents at hand in his upbringing, Prince Philip, like others in such a situation, I think became more self-reliant. It is that aspect of his character which provides a clue to his Award Scheme and its objectives – at its heart, 'set your sights on a purpose and achieve it'. Prepared to face a challenge, his personal philosophy has always been action orientated.

From his behaviour, and from what he does not say, rather than otherwise, it is clear he instinctively recognises his first duty, as Consort to the Queen. Much else has been the stuff of newspaper reports and commentary. On official engagements when I accompanied him, the tiresome intrusion of the same reporters and cameras repeatedly flashing in our faces, at the French Atomic Energy establishment, for example, all came with the job.

His general approach may in no small measure have been due to the basic naval training of a Midshipman. I did not see his Journal, which always had to be presented for the seamanship examination and promotion to Lieutenant, but I saw others and he would have had to demonstrate powers of observation, a habit of orderliness, and powers of expression.

He places human ethical and moral values and human behaviour way above sophisticated technology. We discussed this over lunch when Lee Kwan Yew, Prime Minister of Singapore, was visiting Cambridge University. On that occasion Prince Philip as Chancellor, and President of the English Speaking Union, invited him to try out the new computer for translating Techspeak. Dr Peter Nancarrow who, with ESU funds, devised it, managed to put technology in its place by feeding in a phrase he'd selected to be translated into Chinese and then back into English. 'Out of sight, out of mind' emerged as 'blind idiot'.

As for politics, on a visit to the RAF in Falconbury, when I asked if he now saw any merit in government involvement in the Award Scheme, he simply said, 'The art of good government is to make individual ambitions and self-interest coincide with the national interest.' I reflected on this in a letter I wrote on 'Action for Cities', which *The Times* published in 1988.

In 1982 our youngest child, Edward, as his own idea after gaining his Gold Award, presented me with a copy of Prince Philip's *A Question of Balance*. One sentence read, 'There could be no more admirable ambition than to bring up and educate a child to be a responsible and decent citizen.' Prince Philip, when I told him, congratulated me on how well we had brought up our son, that he had bought his book for me!

Prince Charles, for his part, has always shown deep concern for those suffering the effects of long-term unemployment, the impact on the disadvantaged who do not qualify for financial support, latent talents being wasted and loss of confidence without reason for hope, for those who deserve better. These are timeless problems, but he long agonises over finding workable solutions. On other subjects he has no problem putting the sanctity of life issues, for example, way above the values of modern science.

The questions Prince Charles raised with me concerned how to organise and manage schemes dear to him, so as to win over supporters and beneficiaries, how to measure success, to demonstrate cost-effectiveness and raise growth rates and survival rates of business start-ups. At times apprehensive – 'Will the Government really keep its promise of matched funding? And for how long?' Recognising that many good ideas and initiatives do not live up to their promise, he asked, 'How long can YBI last?' On that occasion, I said, 'In one form or another, for a quarter of a century.' That was well over thirty years ago!

He was teeming with ideas on topics as wide-ranging as free banking services and 'shop front' publicity, to a European network of community volunteers who might learn from us. This we discussed with the King Baudouin Foundation in Brussels. At times he did not receive appropriate good advice from those with experience, though he sought it. At other times, advice could be given that was not asked for, even wrong, but it was welcomed all the same, not least when he was called upon to speak. On my return from talks in the United States with the Chairman of YBI Boston, in advance of Prince Charles' visit in September 1986, I found there some adverse criticism of youth entrepreneurship. According to the Press, the US Administration was advocating this as a substitute for Federal expenditure on employment and training programmes, which had already been cut from $9 billion to $3 billion and likely to be cut further. It was quite widely held that support for young entrepreneurs was just a 'red herring', to distract attention from economic policies, which themselves prevented young entrepreneurs from operating successfully. There was little sympathy for the disadvantaged 'who had only themselves to blame'.

I wrote to advise Prince Charles that these were the editorial views of the influential *Washington Post* and *New York Times*. There was a danger that if he was unaware of them, his intended remarks would come over heavily in favour of the Reagan economic policies. Hence my advice: (a) it was within a sound general economic environment that young entrepreneurs could do best, (b) support for them was no substitute for other policies (the Enterprise Allowance scheme we had in the UK catered for just this situation) and (c) the training schemes we had arranged with financial support of the Manpower Services Commission generated employees as well as entrepreneurs.

Prince Charles' speeches in Boston and at Harvard took note of this and were well received. Had he Queen or a member of the Government been invited to speak, they would have been well briefed officially. At that stage Prince Charles had no such help. The help he most sought from Government, apart from money, was quite simply the elimination of 'red tape'.

He knew that his views would often be the stuff of controversy. When needing assurance he would ask for advice, but not always. I assured him he could not avoid politics, almost every issue had some political dimension, but party-politics was quite another matter. When the Press in 1986, at the time of our PYBT Appeal, quite unfairly charged him with meddling in party politics, it coincided with my being a member of the Press Council and I told newspaper editors they were wrong. They said to me, in effect, prove it! With John Pervin a PYBT colleague, I went to the House of Commons and obtained the signatures on its writing paper of all four party leaders – Thatcher, Kinnock, Steel and Owen – to the same text [photo, page 169]. This we sent to the editors of the national papers. No reference to his party politics appeared for years thereafter.

It was twenty-two years later on his sixtieth birthday in 2008 that I sent Prince Charles this unique document together with birthday wishes. I received a lengthy characteristically appreciative personal letter in reply.

Both father and son have revitalised the spirit of volunteerism, so easily overshadowed either by the state or by individual self interests. Prince Charles' crucial achievement has been to forge an invaluable role in the monarchy whilst still 'in waiting'. It is based on the important principle that charity can be allied to commercial skills to transform the prospects of deprived young people. Serving in this way, with faith in our future society, Prince Charles has, with humility rather than the flamboyant personality of his great uncle, Lord Louis, carried out the time-honoured duty of heir-apparent to the throne – *Ich dien*.

CHAPTER VIII

British Industry: Sink or Swim?

Those who may have thought that, given a track record of being helpful elsewhere, I could when asked do much to help in solving the problems of British Leyland and the British National Oil Corporation, were wrong.

British Leyland

In 1976, Sir Edward Plowden and Sir John Partridge told me that British Leyland Motor Corporation's (BLMC) problems were serious and escalating. They needed new Board members urgently. They knew I was still busy at McKinsey, but would I be prepared to serve on a part-time basis? Partridge said he wanted me to meet Sir Richard Dobson, their new Chairman, who was asking one or two 'carefully considered individuals' to join him as non-executive directors. The company needed all the talent it could get.

Before seeing him, I read through the Central Policy Review Staff think-tank report. It was scathing about the British motor vehicle industry generally and British Leyland in particular. The UK industry performance had already been overtaken by France, Italy and Germany; imports of vehicles had risen from 5% to 50% and poor profitability no longer allowed for the capital investment long overdue. We had a poor reputation for quality and reliability. False economies with old designs resulted in escalating manufacturing costs. We paid less for less skilled labour. Productivity had dived so far that, once the highest in Europe, we were now the lowest – it required twice as many hours to assemble a car as it did on the Continent. Typically managers were being replaced every twelve months, but the shop stewards remained for ten years. The Amalgamated Engineering Union sought recognition of the skills of its members in their pay, whilst the unskilled Transport and General Workers Union insisted on second-to-none agreements – i.e. there were to be no differentials. The shareholders in BLMC would have liked to put their company into liquidation, but the market value of their shares had fallen to just seven pence, one-sixth of the value of the assets.

The think-tank report had been commissioned by the Callaghan Government which was now determined to control the fortunes of the newly formed British Leyland. The Government therefore acquired nearly 95% of its shares and ordered the dismissal of the CEO, appointing Sir Ronald Edwards to take over the chair from Lord Stokes. Sir Ronald sadly died soon after.

In April 1976 Sir Richard Dobson, whose entire career had been with British American Tobacco and was now its president, became Chairman. He told me that Sir Dennis Greenhill, recently retired head of the Diplomatic Service, Ian MacGregor the distinguished American industrialist and Sir Richard Clark, a banker, on the Court of the Bank of England, had all just agreed to join the new Board on a part-time basis. 'Given your experience,' he said, 'you would complement the team admirably.' He himself had spent all his working life, RAF service apart, in the private sector, but he felt it was now his public duty to take the lead to restore what was still the third largest car manufacturer in the world. 'It's a difficult job, but I hope you will regard it a public duty to join us.'

British Leyland's needs were urgent. I was allowed to join them a month before leaving McKinsey, in time for their Board Meeting in October. It was at that first meeting I fully realised how perilous their situation was: unconstitutional disputes and strikes, many management resignations, rapidly diminishing productivity, production targets being missed by more and more. Lord Ryder, Chairman of the National Enterprise Board, as intermediary on behalf of the Government, insisted that we produce 948,000 cars a year. The most the company could hope for was 850,000 and this only reflected the best outcome in an uncertain situation. Unable to attain targets which were acceptable, government finance would be withheld. The Leyland Board relayed this to Eric Varley, Secretary of State. In February 1977 Varley told us he anticipated great pressure from Parliament and from Cabinet colleagues to review the size and nature of the Government's commitment to British Leyland.

A few days later the head of the Cars Group, Derek Whittaker, introduced Eric Varley at a large motor industry conference. Whittaker's speech was hardly picked up by the media. The essence of it was that the failure that year would inevitably mean a closure of plants, new models being cancelled and large-scale unemployment. He listed the models which had either been stopped already or were just about to be stopped – the Mini, Marina, Maxi, Princess, Dolomite, Jaguar, Rover, Triumph 2000, TR7 and Spitfire – and the closure of the huge depots in Cowley and Cardiff, where parts were stored. As for the competition, Whittaker reported that Vauxhall, Ford and Chrysler were rapidly expanding sales in our markets, of cars being manufactured on the Continent. Quality, output and industrial relations were the three cardinal problems, and they were interrelated.

The Government for its part stood firm. No further money would be loaned for modernisation without a pronounced improvement in industrial relations and output. The National Enterprise Board, as intermediary, did nothing more than reiterate the Government's position. We maintained that the conditions required to reach these targets depended upon factors beyond our own control. Furthermore those parts of the business with most of the workforce needing the most capital investment, notably Austin Morris, were generating the lowest yield. For particular reasons, Rover and Jaguar could do better if they were independent of British Leyland. My first intervention at a Board meeting was to comment on the draft Annual Report where the Chairman's encouraging statement highlighted an improvement to a £91 million profit since the previous year. 'This was not due to company performance,' I said, 'but to the weakness of sterling.'

To discover more I arranged a few visits to Longbridge, Cowley and Leyland putting on, as it were, a 'McKinsey hat'. They were revealing.

Basically, the company mindset was wrong. Not one of those I met gave a thought to the competition. Plant leaders' training was not directed to help raise productivity or improve reliability. Many at senior management level did not have the authority to take decisions. When I raised issues concerning customers, suppliers, employers or competitors, the discussion invariably turned to the intransigent strikers, or to government inflexibility, or to the ineffectual NEB. I did learn, however, that Mercedes was eating into the truck market, Renault cutting into the Allegro, Ford Fiesta into the Mini and Ford Cortina into the Marina. Chrysler and Fiat were beginning to make inroads too.

In an attempt to set out my views, I tried to relate the potential impact of measures that might be taken, against their ease of implementation, and the time required to take effect, hoping I could recommend some priorities. I was hampered by the unbelievable lack of information. Not even costs and profit margins for each product range were available. When I told the Chairman that we needed this information to take decisions, all he could say was that he agreed and that Ian MacGregor had written to him from Amax in Connecticut precisely to the same effect. We checked and the relevant data was just not being kept.

After meeting one of the shop stewards at Longbridge, who was quite articulate, I asked whether I could be excused lunch with the management and have a beer and sandwich with him. We went off to the stewards' canteen. His union had asked for a 47% increase in pay without indicating any prospect of improved output. I asked him, 'What would you do if you were a member of our Board, controlled by the Government, and Dennis Healey as Chancellor would not under any circumstances allow pay increases beyond single figures?'

He replied, 'Refuse to accept it. What about Lucas?' he added. 'Those on strike there only returned to work when, in spite of the Chancellor, they were finally given twice the original offer, plus a lump sum – all in direct contravention of so-called Government policy.'

One of the things I continued to press for, for several months, was a ranking of models and plants, in terms of their importance and profitability, to see where resources might best be used. When I suggested we could slim down in Liverpool, where the Triumph was being made, and Bathgate for trucks and buses, I was immediately told that the Government would not allow the closure of these plants or any major lay-offs in these key constituencies before an impending general election.

I admired the courage and the perseverance of our industrial relations director Pat Lowry. Since 1970 he had been trying to cope with the consequences of company mergers. These had brought into the fold more than seventy plants, each with different union representation, payment systems, wage bargaining units, and facilities to strike. During my first full year Red Robbo, the most militant of all the shop stewards, called 500 strikes. Just fifty delivery drivers on strike at Grunwick succeeded in bringing all production to a halt. Ian McGregor, at the end of a Board Meeting, said to me, 'In America I would have called out armed police in force. The courts would have backed me to avoid disruption on this scale. They are their own worst enemy. Only higher productivity warrants higher wages. Only thriving companies can offer better employment prospects.'

McGregor saw Dennis Greenhill and called him over, saying, 'You must have the best intelligence to identify the troublemakers.' 'We know who they are,' Dennis replied. For my part, I began to think of the long-term consequences of mass unemployment. The image came back to me of the marching hunger strikers I saw as a child in the Twenties.

Richard Dobson remained level-headed and outwardly cool throughout, but he had to spend much of his time trying to appease the tough, no-nonsense Chief Executive, Alex Park. He in turn spent even more of his time trying to calm down the fire-eating Managing Director of the Cars Division, Derek Whittaker. Dobson had always maintained that he had run British American Tobacco smoothly. It was a company much bigger than British Leyland, but he could just not get to grips with what he called the 'emotional intensity' of British Leyland and was inclined to alternate between elation and depression.

One pervasive issue was that of training and management development. Surely I could help here. I prepared a short paper with recommendations. In just two years labour turnover, new hirings and transfers would call for the replacement of about half the company's entire labour force. The plan in 1977 was to increase employment by up to 15,000, necessarily introducing much 'green' or 'itinerant' labour, and for a while at least, lowering levels of productivity. The key responsibility for shop floor performance rested on supervisors whose expertise and attitudes were critical. Yet many of them had only recently been operators or craftsmen themselves and they had been given just one to four days of training, much of it covering non-performance topics such as relevant legislation.

The cost of training represented less than 1% of the payroll. No attempt had been made to judge how cost-effective further training might be. The benefits of course could not always be quantified – for example, more attractive working conditions or job enrichment in an industry calling for monotonous assembly line work or a sense of security – but I did find one example within the company where some calculation had been attempted, in the old Pressed Steel factory. As a result of a ten-week training course given to 250 operators on each line, double the number of car bodies was manufactured. It was agreed that something approaching this level of success should be attainable in many types of operation. The amount of off-standard work could also be reduced by about 25%.

On one visit, I had seen dozens of new Princess cars on the assembly line shipped back from the USA under guarantee, all because of corrosion in one corner of the windscreen. The paint gun had apparently been set at the wrong angle to cover the corner. The warranty costs were high. For a

Jaguar they were £1,000 per car, for the best Japanese cars only £2, and 94% of the new Rovers (SDI) were unfit for sale. Des Pitcher, Managing Director of Trucks and Buses, had inherited an even more costly warranty liability in his huge Division.

My paper had been approved, but then there was reluctance to release individuals for training courses. At Cowley supervisors were in such demand they were actually being withdrawn from training in mid-course. Those who qualified were liable to be promoted, transferred and lost to those who recommended them. So nominations for training were held back.

One day I thought I had come up with something really useful, a revised plan for the company's foundries. Imports from Mexico, Spain and Thailand were now so costly, it was very well worth our while developing production at home. Aluminium castings were being produced by Birmid Industries so Richard Dobson and I met their Chairman, Robin Leigh Pemberton, to discuss our proposed foundry strategy. Having all agreed what was best we sent our proposal off to the National Enterprise Board (NEB). In due course we received a response: 'You should also evaluate all other possible options and re-submit your proposal.' No thought of the trade balance, the competition, the urgency, but second guessing our management judgement.

Press coverage in 1976/7 was such that in April, we gave a lunch for City editors to brief them on the Board's policy and intended actions and give them the opportunity of asking questions. More than two dozen journalists joined us in the Abraham Lincoln Room at the Savoy, including Peter Sissons, industrial editor of ITN, Patrick Hutber, City Editor of *The Sunday Telegraph*, and Richard Lambert, editor of the LEX column in *The Financial Times*. I was particularly impressed with the relevance of the questions that Lambert raised and I am not at all surprised to see what a successful career he has had since then.

Towards the end of May, I woke to see the front page headlines of *The Daily Mail*. Apparently we were operating a worldwide slush fund!

Documents in the newspaper's possession showed that over £11 million had been paid out abroad 'as bribes' over and above legitimate commissions. One of our internal auditors, Graham Barton, had reported a 'special billing ledger' and had sent it together with supporting documents to David English, the editor. The potential damage was enormous. We issued a statement that we knew of no illegal payments. Alex Park, the Chief Executive, later received a letter from the editor apologising for what was admitted to be the publication of a forged letter. After a few weeks he was able to write to Lord Ryder at the NEB, that after a very thorough investigation three items might still be considered doubtful, amounting in total to £127,000. The only known recipient was apparently a captain in the Pakistani army, then in prison, and there was the gift of a new Land Rover to King Hussein! However the damage had been done. The reputation for operating a slush fund could not easily be dismissed.

Sir Richard Dobson always took the moral high ground and he reacted as might have been expected. Throughout his career he had enjoyed the friendship and loyalty of all those he employed in China and the developing world, and he always referred to them as 'wogs.' 'If I didn't, they would believe I was cross with them,' he insisted. But then he made a huge mistake which cost him his job. At a private lunch his speech was secretly taped and sent to Tariq Ali, Editor of the *Socialist Challenge*, who published extracts. There was an immediate outcry. Dobson's appointment had been made directly by Harold Wilson, but it was Eric Varley who demanded and received Dobson's resignation.

The Press and public opinion were polarised. Some described the resignation as a triumph for cant and hypocrisy, 'wog' being a word that might have been used light-heartedly years earlier, but had gradually come to be considered racist. Is a man to be barred from public life for being slightly behind the times in his slang? I suppose the answer today is 'yes'. Dobson was due to fly to Canada to attend a meeting at Exxon, as an overseas Board member. He telephoned Exxon's chairman before arriving: 'Perhaps, now that you have seen the newspapers you won't wish me to remain on your Board either?' 'Come over anyway. We'll begin the meeting without you,' the chairman replied. 'I'll raise the question and we'll let you know the outcome.' Dobson had been sitting in the outer office for just one minute before the chairman came out to escort him back where the entire Board stood to receive him with an impressive demonstration of hand-clapping.

In the dying days of the Callaghan administration in 1978, Leslie Murphy succeeded as Chairman of the NEB and in December chose Michael Edwardes of Chloride as the new Executive Chairman. It was known he would be tough with the Unions, but he immediately fired all the part-time Board members too, deserted Leyland House, the corporate HQ, took an office over a car showroom in Piccadilly and appointed 'three staff I can trust', all from Chloride. He had done well in raising their profitability, but union problems did not arise there.

I was surprised when he called me to come and see him. He said, 'I have had a note from Dobson that I would do well to retain you. I would like you to join us as a consultant.' I said, 'I couldn't make much difference as a non-executive Board member. I am sorry, but as a consultant surely I would have less chance still?' 'I must make a complete sweep of the Board,' he added. I wished him well and we went our separate ways.

Edwardes had picked up the worst hand of cards possible; wages could not be paid for a while and there was near anarchy. Dysfunction and strikes in the previous ten months had resulted in the loss of a quarter of a million vehicles and there was no realistic recovery plan. Managers were demoralised, working as though in a goldfish bowl with politicians, the Press and public peering in and commenting on their every move. Leyland's ageing models, declining market share, highly publicised industrial disputes and chaotic individual bargaining arrangements with seventeen unions operating in fifty factories left the company with an image that was badly damaged worldwide.

The lessons I had learned were typical of much of British industry, but more acute. The outlook was insular rather than global. There was complacency in the face of competitors' new models. Both management and labour, with outmoded industrial relations, neglected and tolerated low productivity. There was over-dependence on financial help from outside irrespective of performance and no real collaboration with the government. Company chairmen continued to be appointed from among 'the good and the great', with politics as the main criterion, in stark contrast to its competitors abroad.

Thanks to the efforts of Michael Edwardes and a Conservative administration prepared to back him, performance improved as he 'read out the riot act' during industrial disputes. Yet he did not succeed in returning the company to profit. In 1981 it sustained a net loss of over $500 million and, by the time he left, it was clearly in the second division of world car manufacturers in terms of output. It was however still alive and a major exporter. He wooed successive governments for fresh injections of public money. Sir Keith Joseph contributed a billion dollars of government funds that year and taxpayers had to fork out a further billion a little later, ironically whilst they were also importing cars from Japan, France and Germany.

Edwardes had sought collaborative arrangements with Renault, General Motors and Chrysler, all of which came to nothing, but he was able to collaborate with Honda in the production of the Triumph Acclaim: 60% British, 40% Japanese.

The company's subsequent history was no less turbulent. For a while I followed its sad history. In 1984 Jaguar and Daimler were floated off, being bought by Ford in 1989, and then the Rover Group in 1995 was bought by BMW. When Peter Mandelson, as Trade and Industry Secretary, visited Rover's Longbridge car works in 1998 he was shocked to see a rambling and ramshackle industrial sprawl straddling motorways and railway lines, much of the work now being carried out in buildings little more than prefabs. The 10,000 workers at Longbridge and the tens of thousands in the surrounding Birmingham area, who for a century had worked in these factories, woke up to the news that BMW had had enough and wanted to sell Rover. They had bought it because they wanted to build a volume European carmaker, really believing that German working practices and engineering knowhow could turn around the ailing British flagship and that a £3 billion investment plan would see successful new models emerge. It was a monumental miscalculation.

I paid one last visit to Warwickshire where I saw a huge hangar packed with gleaming British models – Wolseys, Standards, Triumphs and Raleighs – all unwanted. The ghost of Red Robbo, the Communist shop steward, who came to symbolise the dire state of labour relations at the Longbridge plant, lived on.

British National Oil Corporation

If I had done nothing to help British Leyland, surely a modern industry, such as the rapid development of North Sea oil and gas, would give me much more scope? In 1975, Sir Frank Kearton had told me that after Royal Assent of a Bill, giving the Government sweeping new powers of control, he would probably become the corporation's first Chairman, to be appointed by Tony Benn under whom I'd served in the Ministry of Technology. 'Would you be interested in joining me?' he asked. 'Sadly, my present commitment to McKinsey will not permit it,' I had to tell him.

Four years later I was asked again, when I received a formal invitation to join the BNOC Board from David Howell, the Energy Secretary in Margaret Thatcher's new administration. I was now free to do so. I was particularly delighted that Frank Kearton, though he had now lost his job there, wrote to me 'on joining the most exciting enterprise in Britain today, with many first-class people'. My new office was in the grandeur of Stornaway House, alongside St James's Palace.

The change in Government had brought about changes in attitude, as well as policies to reduce state involvement. It was planned to introduce private capital into the public-owned oil and gas exploration and production enterprises. Sir Ronald Utiger, already a member of the corporation, was appointed Chairman for eight months until he had to return to British Aluminium. I found the entire Board, though holding diverse political opinions, unanimous in wanting a credible national oil company, opposed to any company split into a trading company and an upstream exploration and production company, as envisaged by the Government. To compete with the world's oil majors for talent, we believed fragmentation and limited career opportunities would put us at a disadvantage.

Alongside me at the Board room table was Douglas Allen (later Lord Croham), a former head of the civil service who was in no doubt that, if split, the sum of the parts would be far less effective than the whole. Clive Jenkins and Gavin Laird, the two trade union Board members, were opposed to the split for 'political, philosophical and emotional reasons', as they put it. I commented on how other major oil companies had benefitted from an integrated management team, in terms of competence and effectiveness and proposed a compromise, providing for wider share ownership, like certain other private sector oil companies. Our Managing Director, Alistair Morton, commented that Kearton had suggested something similar – what they called 'the Gallic alternative'.

Sir Dennis Rooke, who had done so much to develop the gas industry and was strongly independent, reminded the Board of its statutory duty. 'We cannot be overridden by Government, only by Parliament.' Morton went on to speak eloquently on the subject of 'the national interest', spelling out the financial advantages and the benefits, in terms of oil diplomacy and in developing the UK Continental shelf. 'These would be lost,' he said, 'if control passed to the private sector. In any event, equity sales should be spread widely.'

Clive Jenkins and Gavin Laird were adamant that we should sell nothing more than revenue interest bonds. I said, 'political objectives will no doubt prevail, so our organisational aim should be to minimise any harm to management effectiveness in the process.' The Board collectively favoured a transfer of assets into a controlled subsidiary, whilst retaining the integrated management.

The Government wanted to provide the maximum security for our oil supplies with widespread ownership of the upstream operations only. They appointed Sir Philip Shelbourne of Rothschild's to the Board and to take over the Chair to do this. He made his views clear from the outset. 'The disadvantages in management terms resulting from a split would be more than offset by the financial benefits nationally, when the industry comes out of the Public Sector Borrowing Requirement to reduce our deficit.'

Alistair Morton was furious. No friend of Shelbourne's in any event, he said, 'The Prime Minister should realise he can't put together the management of major industrial corporations in the way he chooses party political leaders.' He stood up and marched out, never to return.

After many meetings and the passing of the Bill, the company was indeed split. Sadly, our agenda almost from the outset was not concerned with the successful management of the industry, but how private sector capital could be introduced without the loss of security of supplies. We carried or rejected numerous resolutions and counter-resolutions with variable majorities. But the only one carried unanimously was to urge the Secretary of State to reconsider the entire policy of splitting the unified business.

In the House of Commons, there was much debate on how we could preserve the 'Britishness' of the company and retain control of North Sea oil, no matter who owned the majority of the shares. Following the Queen's speech, from the Gallery I heard Nigel Lawson's remarks on the perennial socialist confusion between the nation and the State: 'The MCC is not owned by the State, but it is nothing if it is not British,' he said. He would ensure effective safeguards. My understanding was that the Treaty of Rome actually made it impossible to control foreign shareholders, so any restrictions would have to apply to all shareholders alike. The Stock Exchange rules just did not allow companies to restrict the free trading of shares. Somehow these rules seemed to have been waived in the case of Cable and Wireless.

Brit Oil was formed and all its share capital was transferred to the Secretary of State and a nominee, for no consideration. Fifty-one percent of the profits of all upstream activities would now be sold to the public. An optimistic tender price was arranged, in consultation with Warburg's. But partly because Sheikh Yamani had just forecast a fall in oil prices, the shares were undersubscribed and underwriters were left holding nearly three quarters of them. From the Opposition front bench Tony Benn said that a future Labour government would re-acquire them, without any compensation.

I did not feel I had been entirely pulling my weight, but my two-year appointment to the Board was renewed in 1982 by Nigel Lawson, the new Energy Secretary. This would be for one further year only as the Government intended to privatise the upstream exploration and production activities, abolish the National Oil Account and remove Brit Oil from the public sector. He said he had to avoid any possible conflicts of interest and so required the resignation of Board members. After the split I continued to serve under Lord Croham, who took over the Chair of a now emasculated BNOC.

We then all took part in the opening of the Nigg platform by Princess Alexandra and were each presented with a tiny phial containing '2 ccs of Britain's most precious liquid'. I flew back to London wondering whether we were in danger of losing it, and all its benefits to our economy, in the decades ahead.

As for Brit Oil, the 'Golden Share' put it firmly under government control, so that though Philip Shelbourne favoured an acquisition by Atlantic Richfield, he had to go along very reluctantly with its sale to BP. Then he retired to his Queen Anne home in the cloisters of Salisbury Cathedral. He invited Diana and me to visit him there to admire his superb collection of antique furniture and works of art. Edward Heath was his immediate neighbour, but they never spoke to each other.

Departing from BNOC at the end of my three-year stint, my feeling was one of general disappointment. Instead of helping to improve the performance of a crucial industry I found myself necessarily engaged in a political football match. My former McKinsey colleagues would have recognised that BNOC's industrial competence and performance alone did not make it the 'ideal client', given the Government's agenda. To best solve the national problem we would have needed the Government as client too. The Government and business had to work together.

In spite of that, I thoroughly enjoyed aspects of this new experience, not least our visits to Scotland. Because of the heavy unemployment in Glasgow and the much-wanted Scottish political vote we were encouraged to hold our monthly Board meetings there, occasionally in Aberdeen, and one or two excursions to the oil platforms when we landed by helicopter, even in frighteningly high winds. Meetings were normally arranged for Fridays, the most popular day, so that we could find the time to visit a remote whisky distillery. We did this frequently and slowly but surely formed unanimous judgements on their single malts.

Rank Hovis McDougall

The years were going by quickly. I was still hoping to get at least one chance of being a successful innovator and it was eluding me. Not since my timber industry activities in Princes Risborough twenty years earlier had I been in a position to translate research results into a highly profitable business. Now an opportunity came again and it all happened by accident – in the food industry.

In the midst of a small dinner party at home in Denham, I casually chipped into the interesting conversation. 'One day the world would be short of protein.' From across the table Sir Peter Reynolds, Chairman of RHM said, 'I agree. I should tell you that at our Research Centre in Windsor we have cultivated a new raw material for the food processing industry, a fungus-like substance called Mycoprotein. We grow it on chemicals found in corn, wheat, rice, cassava or molasses and, in a process similar to making pastry, produce analogues of chicken, veal and fish. And beef will follow.'

We were all intrigued, some of us doubtful. He went on, 'Because of its fibrous structure, unlike soya, it is indistinguishable from the real thing. We have tested it on hundreds of volunteers and it's now being evaluated by the Ministry of Agriculture and Fisheries.'

I became more enthusiastic about its prospects when he assured me it had no cholesterol, no flavour (which would be added) and its cost was acceptable. I said, 'I would jump at the chance of developing it for the market.' 'Then come and see us in Windsor,' he said.

On arrival I soon recognised the high calibre and keenness of the laboratory staff and confirmed my interest in being associated with it. Reynolds said, 'We plan to form a Partnership with the British Technology Group and the National Enterprise Board to take it forward. Would you chair its Committee? You would have the powers of a Board Chairman.' So I was appointed for three years 'to define policies, see they were adhered to and represent the joint interests of all concerned in its development'.

With a budget of just £50,000, our so called 'Frish-Dytes' partnership was able to demonstrate, within eighteen months, that with a continuous process manufacturing 30,000 tons a year we could provide a product that would cost the same as the food it was replacing, or half the cost of beef. To go further, we recognised that a chemical plant would be beneficial so we formed a joint £1 million company with ICI. The product was branded Quorn – I don't remember who suggested the name. Sales took off healthily, the Press applauded it and it was successful.

On my final departure, Peter Reynolds, in happy mood, asked how they could express their thanks. 'Well, I've already been paid generously, but would you support a local charity?' I ventured. 'The Windsor Festival, where I am a director, would welcome your support.' RHM immediately sponsored a fabulous Viennese Night at Windsor Castle, a *son et lumière* with the London Symphony Orchestra at its very best.

When I wrote to Peter Reynolds, now long since retired, to ask whether it was a real financial success, he wrote, 'The Quorn business was taken over by a private equity company Marlow Foods, then Premium Foods, and is now worth over £170 million.' A modest sum compared with the budgets of British Leyland and BNOC, but highly satisfying at a personal level.

CHAPTER IX

Managing and Governing

With the wider experience I had been able to acquire since my civil service days, I came to realise that without considerable change, the service would soon be unable to provide what the public now needed. When I joined it sixty-seven years ago my colleagues came in the main from well-educated families, who saw their role as servants of the nation, willing to be called upon to administer in the national interest as successive governments came and went. For generations they had aspired to enter public service, and were admired for doing so. Their strength and reputation was the outcome of integrity, honesty, impartiality, and loyalty. As recently as 1996 these four attributes were reiterated in a Command Paper, the two latter being superseded by selflessness, objectivity, accountability, openness, and leadership – all applicable to the spending of public money. Appointments, even of Permanent Secretaries were a matter for the Service itself.

This ethos had now all but vanished. Social change called for changes in public needs and in our policy-making process. We had to be more disciplined, creative and innovative and more open to new ideas and opinion. Accountability was becoming more complex whilst innovation, in the widest sense, with the organisational, staffing and management policies that could make it possible, was being neglected. Management practices, successful in business, were rarely applied to government and the civil service.

Back in 1961, I had attended a ten-day conference on Management and Organisation, arranged by HM Treasury at Peterhouse, Cambridge. We were all civil servants at under-secretary or director level, being invited to consider our own roles in the wider context of public service interests. But all speakers were our Permanent Secretaries or distinguished academics. No industrialists or businessmen participated. A few, brought into public service successfully in the war, had all left long before. By the time I left the service six years later, criticism from outside had grown: 'they are good as administrators only', 'amateurs in outlook and in techniques', 'lacking in creative ideas, isolated, out of touch with the business world, so learning nothing from them'. A story circulating was that when Richard Crossman as Minister of Housing, knowing nothing about building societies, asked his Department about them, he discovered they did not know either, nor had they any contact with them. Ernest Bevin set the tone in another circle with his comment on the disciplined French planning system: 'We don't do things like that in our country; we don't have plans, we work things out practically.' There were many who were easily persuaded there was little we could learn from business or from abroad. Governments brought in political advisers.

The Fulton Committee was set up to look into this. It reported how little change there had been in the service for a century, both for individuals – still a vocation for the brightest, judged by literacy not numeracy – and for the system as a whole. Budgeting designed 'to stop kings spending money on mistresses', the Public Accounts Committee mainly concerned with whether the money spent had been properly authorised, cost-effectiveness unquestioned. Systems which protected the misuse of funds differed from those promoting the best use of funds.

Now that governments had to take responsibility for the direction of the economy, employment, economic growth, the industrial infrastructure – energy, railways, town planning, health and social services – they had to change, be positive and interventionist. But given the culture of the generalist, the lack of skilled managers and contacts with the outside world, it was not easy for the Service. Those trained in the tradition of caution and justification had to adapt their thinking to the issues of profit and loss.

The service required policy makers, managers and presenters. On policy, it perpetuated its traditional role, to give advice and forewarn and forearm ministers, but it also had to devise and operate the machinery necessary to follow through. It needed both generalists and specialists, but the recruitment of specialists also presented problems – e.g. the rules stated that the governor of a prison could not be a leading psychiatrist, because a governorship was reserved as an administrative job.

The changes came along very slowly. In my view, proposals simply to simulate business management practices across the board were not always right. Businesses could often make radical changes of structures and systems because they operated within a framework of limited objectives. For government, the framework could be the whole body politic. And its mores and instincts were different. Whilst the business world had to judge the competition and calculate risks, political judgements at times had to be based on inadequate information and intuition. Notwithstanding these differences, the best approaches had much in common. Both they, and for that matter management consultancies had to formulate objectives and strategies, fulfil projects, collect and analyse data, decide or facilitate implementation and aim to give best value for money.

As I had been brought into the Service, predominantly as a scientist, science and technology were our strong suits and innovation was key to our success, I often considered how we could become better innovators and stronger competitors. This inadequacy had been at the heart of our economic problems for most of the twentieth century. I was sure there were lessons to be learned. There was an old saying: 'Times change and we change with them.' But we hadn't. We should have been saying, 'Times change, be prepared and change with them.' Charles Darwin and others had said something similar, 'It is not the strongest species that survives, but the one that is most responsive to change.'

Initially I assumed there were successive steps in innovation from R&D to manufacturing and services to users. But I came to realise this was not so. A successful outcome usually called for the participation of many interrelated management roles.

At Neddy we had learned of the contribution to the economy to be made by education, vocational skills, capital investment, and tax policy and we made recommendations accordingly. But, in the newly formed Ministry of Technology, we saw what obstacles lay in the way of implementing these recommendations and why most of the promises set out in Harold Wilson's 1964 'White Heat' election manifesto were largely unfulfilled. By the time I left Whitehall, most of us knew that our problems were very deep rooted. Many were problems of management. But we realised too that, as civil servants, we were not well placed to tackle them, if indeed that had been our responsibility.

On moving to serve McKinsey clients, I became sure we needed a wide spectrum of ideas and the orchestration of many talents to be effective innovators. We had to combine technological expertise with the general management of information, assets, risks and people, and establish wider relationships. In a revolutionary change in an industry, such as the move to natural gas, North Sea oil supplies and global transport facilities by container, the boundaries between entire industries could virtually disappear.

It was in this process, I came to see how the issues of innovation and competitiveness embraced economic and political ones. For business, government was the enabler and supporter. It was government's responsibility to improve the infrastructure and deal with fundamental requirements such as healthcare, food and energy supplies and disasters. No less important, business looked to government to provide stability and confidence. Interest and exchange rates, budget cuts and political uncertainties could render business decisions difficult and unreliable. R&D programmes could not suddenly be changed with a change in the tax regime. Upheaval in government machinery, sometimes for party political purposes, could be damaging in other ways. The trade unions could be confrontational to a fault and to such an extent that they failed to recognise that keeping agreements was essential. This would pay for our social services.

In my scientific civil service years, I had participated in some of the debates on science policy and the effects of repeated departmental organisational changes. The upheavals in government machinery at home were more disturbing than anything I had seen elsewhere, in the course of political changes abroad. In 1959 Hailsham became our first Minister of Science. He believed that science was a cultural activity, whose results could not be commanded. It was for scientists through their Research Councils to advise government on the best deployment of resources.

The Opposition took a different view. Hugh Gaitskell, as leader, and his then-deputy Harold Wilson, in preparing for government, gathered around them a distinguished group of advisers. Of its two leading members, J.D. Bernal insisted that scientific progress had to be planned and, if necessary, applied forcefully; Blackett contented himself with tackling particular problems – too few scientists, too little money and poor company management. He advocated contract research on a grand scale. In my view this would be possible in a few situations only.

Wilson, in his famous speech at Scarborough, called for a far-reaching change in attitudes. 'We must mobilise all the resources of science available to us in the new scientific revolution, harness socialism to science, and science to socialism.' When Gaitskell died Wilson, as Leader of the Opposition, put Richard Crossman in charge of policy on science and higher education, creating a Science and Industry Committee with Blackett as his principal adviser.

By 1963 Blackett had brought everyone together for policy discussions, from the most senior Fellows of the Royal Society and the Fabian Society to me, who he had known since Manchester days.

He had visited me in Paris, with his wife Constanza (invariably addressing him as 'Blackett'), where he was favourably impressed by the French planning system and by French calculations of the contribution that science and technology would make to France's economy. Later he came to our laboratory in Princes Risborough and was even more impressed to see that the industrialists we had invited to our Open Days were awarding us research contracts to undertake work on their behalf.

He suggested that, with a change of government, a new Ministry of Production be set up, incorporating Neddy, and also an interventionist Ministry of Industry and Technology, which would deal with major companies in the civil sector just as the Government did in defence. I had just started work at Neddy when he asked for my views. I told him the departmental machinery he proposed was confusing, its effect could be disturbing and, in any event, we had far too few civil servants with the appropriate experience and business understanding for the innovative role they would be given. In defence, because the Government was the customer, the situation was different.

'Do companies tell you why they don't innovate more?' he asked. 'Yes, they tell us that replacing equipment is unprofitable or skilled craftsmen unobtainable; the scientists and engineers they might have recruited are largely committed to defence projects; too many of those employed in the civil sector are unaware of 'customers' needs; trade union practices are highly restrictive; risk capital hard to come by and the returns too long delayed and risky. The list is endless. To me, it seems there is a prevailing laissez-faire attitude, especially in industries that are highly protected against competitive imports, such as textiles.'

In a Neddy Report we had shown that the UK had the highest R&D expenditure of any country in Europe for over a decade, but one of the lowest economic growth rates. There were also wide variations between industrial sectors. Aircraft absorbed up 38% of our R&D spending, but accounted for only 5% of our output and 4% of our exports. On the other hand, little attention had been paid to large, less sophisticated industries, where the benefits of research could be quite disproportionate to their cost.

Sir Burke Trend, the Cabinet Secretary, called me in to expand on what I had reported. 'I would not generalise,' I said, 'but in particular cases additional government support in the civil sector could bring benefits extending beyond the immediate customers, to the community at large and the private rate of return might only be one third of the social rate of return – so the market did not invest as much as was socially desirable.' I gave examples to his Steering Committee. In one well-documented American case, the financial return to DuPont on their R&D on nylon was, in the opinion of the US Government, far exceeded by the contribution it made to their balance of payments – due to the export of nylon yarns and products and reduced imports of wool.

Blackett returned with further questions and slowly revised his plans in consultation with Labour sympathisers. I came into the Athenaeum Club one day and I happened to see Crossman and Blackett chatting together on the drawing-room sofa. They called me over. 'We're sketching out a new Ministerial organisation!' Crossman said, 'How can we best marry a permanent civil service with outside expertise?'

'A most pertinent question,' I replied. 'As with biological organisms, the civil service, given its role and attitude, tended either to assimilate creatures it could live with or eject them if they were indigestible.' And I reminded Blackett of what Lord Woolton had told us both, after the war, over a University Convocation dinner. His particular business experience made him an ideal fit for the position of wartime Minister for Food. Some other businessmen had also been a success as individuals. Wholesale reorganisation, however, was quite another matter.

Just in time for the 1964 election, the idea of a freestanding Ministry of Technology was adopted, Blackett simply telling me, 'As a name, it's more incisive.' By 1970, industry was getting used to this name, but the new Conservative Government under Edward Heath initiated a further wholesale reorganisation. Heath regarded the Ministry as a gimmick, and merged it with the Board of Trade to form the Department of Trade and Industry (DTI). Then it suffered three further changes of leadership in three years. Education and Science became the responsibility of Margaret Thatcher. She was certain that we should concentrate our science funding on universities and research institutes. 'Science is less amenable to political direction than politicians like to think,' she said. 'The transistor was not discovered by the entertainment industry seeking ways of marketing pop music, but by people working on wave mechanics and solid-state physics. Development should be carried out by companies themselves, companies with less tax to pay.' She was adamant.

Trend's Committee eventually recommended that the Research Councils be given responsibility for choosing what they should finance, in effect deciding 'where the national interest lay'. Lord Rothschild, appointed by Heath to head the CPRS (Central Policy Review Staff), the Government think-tank, disagreed. Research Councils could not take political decisions. Both were right in specific cases, in my view. Neither, however, adequately considered the prospects, time and input required from others, for research results to become useful. Whatever the logic, the scheme was strongly opposed by both the Science and Medical Research Councils and a compromise eventually had to be found.

But there were other organisational problems in the way of effective decision-taking and collaboration. The boundaries between the Department of Education and Science (DES) and the Department of Trade and Industry (DTI) and between the DTI and the Ministry of Defence (MOD) were unclear. There was no official route either to build a prototype or to establish whether there was in fact a market. The MOD, for its part, was keen on spin-offs, but did not have the resources; while companies themselves were unsure and slow on the uptake. The Trades Union Congress (TUC), for its part, complained that the Government was discouraging investment. There were no clear ministerial remits and disorganisation inevitably led to a loss of confidence.

Apart from the organisational problems, the performance of British industry well illustrated that we had progressed only where we were innovative, but entrepreneurial too. Bruce Archer of the Royal College of Art made a vivid analogy. 'In industry, as in biology, it takes two parties to bring a viable new system into the world – the innovative or seminal role, and the entrepreneurial or ovular role.'

Where we were all in agreement was that to compete successfully we had to raise our productivity dramatically. US productivity then was 40% higher, and France's and Germany's 20% higher than ours. The latest reasons for our lagging behind, given by our Economic and Social Research Council (ESRC), were almost exactly the same as those given in the first Neddy Report. Higher productivity was the only source of new wealth. This channelled into pay, savings, public services and leisure activities, could bring about a better way of life. The key to its realisation was innovation. This called for effective interaction.

Yet R&D had to compete for resources. Higher income might be achieved for a while simply by advertising more or by acquisition, and innovation could be disruptive. The company chief executive would hear the plea of the research director: 'Give me another two years and I will bring you a winner,' but the marketing director would say, 'That's not what the customer wants, certainly not at that price,' and the finance director, 'I'm worried; we could do better investing in a risk-free long-dated gilt, if we could afford to reduce our gearing.' It was a matter of judgement.

The main responsibility for assessing technologies and selecting projects could lie with government or industry – the former usually, in the case of our infrastructure, on defence or some public works, the latter for most capital goods and all consumer items.

The most prosperous companies tended to be the ones making timely re-evaluations of projects as conditions changed. At McKinsey we had shown the benefit of frequent reappraisal and an ongoing review of the scale of future investment. The early cutting of losses in some projects could reinforce other better prospects. It was valuable to estimate the cost of a delay in a product launch. In one case, the laser printer, with a market growing at 20% per year, prices falling at 12% a year and a life of five years, we showed that whilst a six-month delay would mean a 33% decline in cumulative profits, a 30% cost overrun in product development would mean a decline of only 2% in profit. Now with the speed-up of communication increasing dramatically, estimates had to be made more frequently still.

In the private sector, for some consumer goods, we learned how many ideas of value could come from the customers themselves. In the late Seventies, Procter & Gamble had put their toll-free number on all packaging, receiving over a thousand calls a week – with as many constructive ideas as complaints – and many improvements were made as a result. And, resulting from user inputs too, Marks & Spencer provided machine-washable suits, which would keep their shape (as in Cary Grant's film *Charade*). Since then, the application of nanotechnology has developed so quickly that clothes can now be make to be self-cleaning, anti-microbial, fire-resistant and even protected from fading.

For our largest public sector projects inevitably, not all desirable ones could be supported. Choices had to be made. I had recommended to Trend in 1964 that more systematic techno-economic appraisals be made by government and industry together. This idea was well received but there was no action. When it did come on a formal basis, with government taking the leading role, it was in America, following meetings I had in Washington DC. In Britain it was much later that Neil Kinnock, Jeremy Bray and our Chief Scientific Adviser were advocating a similar approach to appraisals.

I had only gradually come to realise how much companies depended on the assumptions they made sometimes unconsciously about circumstances beyond their own control. Most Boards did not plan for contingencies, such as changes in exchange rates and taxation. One of the questions I was frequently asked by Boards was how should they minimise, diversify or hedge such risks?

I discussed political risk with William Simon after he had served as Secretary of the US Treasury in the Ford Administration from 1974–77 and as Chairman of the US Economic Policy Board. In particular, what difference a change in government policy could make in Britain. By the mid-Seventies our domestic, industrial and economic problems had become really serious; the challenge of the trade unions and low productivity loomed large. The Conservative Party in opposition was beginning to make this a central issue in its bid for power.

My mind was very much on this as a newly appointed Board member of Touche Remnant's Atlas Investment Trust. At my first Annual General Meeting, Sir Peter Hordern, my co-director, introduced me to Denis Thatcher, one of the shareholders. He, over a second glass of champagne, suddenly said to me, 'I want you to meet Margaret, she needs help!' 'In technology?' I asked. 'I'm not a prospective party politician.'

He followed up with a letter: 'Margaret would like to discuss one of her problems with you in the early future. Caroline Stephens will arrange a meeting.'

In her House of Commons office, she asked if I had given party political advice in the past. 'Back in 1965,' I said. 'Sir John Cockcroft (then Master of Churchill College) asked me to prepare a proposal for the Liberal Party's General Assembly debate on research and development, but as a civil servant I had to decline. Then in 1968, Reginald Maudling in the Shadow Cabinet invited me to contribute to the Conservative Party Seminar on Science and Technology, but I had to be in Montreal then. I was able to give a little help to Sir John Eden, on power and technological innovation. I also took part in a Conference chaired by Peter Shore, when the Labour Party was in opposition and had substantial discussions on industrial innovation with Edmund Dell. On these issues the parties' aims and approaches seemed to have just as much in common as they had differences, apart from the specific allocation of funds. It was effective implementation that was needed.'

I found I had been barking up the wrong tree. Margaret Thatcher came straight to the point. 'Our problem is organisation. I will deal with policy. The weakness in organisation that I have discovered in the Central Office – essential to win a general election – is unbelievable; no programmes, no budgets, no priorities, no real management, little cooperation with the Research Department, no liaison with other Party bodies. I'd like you to tell me what we can do about that.'

This was totally unexpected. I said, 'Organisation and policy are not unrelated.' She replied, 'Take these papers. You are free to go through my files.'

On 11th August she wrote to me about getting the structure and strategy right, both of the Party and of Number 10, adding, 'I have already come to the conclusion that I shall have to take most of the major decisions myself.'

Then another message: that we should meet again on 25th August before she was leaving for America. On that day she had squeezed into her diary: 'preparation of speeches for the Party Conference and for a visit to Australia, Sir Dugald Stewart (Yugoslavia – 30 minutes), Mr Maudling (45 minutes), Mr Copisarow (60 minutes), Jilly Cooper, Hairdresser...'

Central Office organisation I found, had been split functionally – finance, research, publications, publicity, community affairs, women's affairs and local government. Following some interviews I realised that action on most fronts would be difficult to coordinate. To prepare for election I recommended a broad four-pronged departmental reorganisation, to encompass them all. The 'key factors for success' to win power were: (i) Formulating policies on critical issues, (ii) ensuring they were reflected in the Party's image, (iii) appealing to the 'undecided' in critical seats and (iv) getting people out to vote. This approach was duly adopted.

She referred to a four page memo I had sent her in manuscript. She produced it from a pocket in her dress, folded in four. 'Pure gold,' she said. 'I can't commit this to the filing system; they probably wouldn't be able to find it anyway!'

She sent me drafts of speeches written for her, which she had freely annotated, not always legibly. The drafts were good, but her changes were revealing. For example, in one by Prof Douglas Hague, for delivery at Central Hall, Finchley, I noticed she had reduced three substantial paragraphs into just one line: 'You cannot strengthen the weak by weakening the strong.' For her speech in Perth, 'The Flourishing Society', ably written by Ronnie Millar, where he had said, 'You can no more choose your school under Mr Callaghan, than you could under Sir Harold Wilson; all that's happened is that where the old shark's mouth was clenched about a pipe, the new shark's mouth stretches in a sunny smile,' Margaret had simply scribbled, 'Delete, too personal'.

She asked, 'How are you getting on with the others – Janet Young, John Moore, Charles Johnston, and Keith Joseph?' I told her. 'Thank you,' she said, 'Your views are for me and for Airey Neave only.'

Her senior colleagues began to send me documents. Michael Heseltine asked for my comments on his paper 'Industrial Policy Recommendations' and Geoffrey Howe sent me a draft of his own, 'Party Strategy, Policy and Organisation', prepared for Peter Thorneycroft, the Chairman. I agreed with both. Howe had written, 'Although leading Conservatives appear to be agreed on aims, the media and party workers have little clear direction and the 1922 Committee should be told, twice a year, what the leaders would like them to do.' I made two initial comments on the organisation's effectiveness: 'First, about 80% of the results appeared to be coming from 20% of the party activity. Secondly, 'The Right Approach' manifesto failed to show how, as a nation, we could improve our competitiveness, when our productivity was declining alarmingly and labour costs escalating, or how far or how fast we could change in the face of serious opposition.'

Ably assisted by my former colleague John Banham, in 1977 I prepared a memo for Thorneycroft: 'Increasing the Contribution of Central Office to Winning the Next Election'. It elaborated on our earlier advice to Margaret. Additions marked 'secret' were contributed by Angus Maude. The Research Department, then led by Chris Patten was, for some reason, left out of the distribution list altogether.

A business forum to which I was invited was convened by Keith Joseph. He told me he had been impressed by the success of Michael Heseltine with industrialists in particular. We met in a 'New Ventures' group at the Centre for Policy Studies in Wilfred Street, SW1. One of our wide-ranging discussions was on 'Removing the Obstacles to Growth'. Over dinner with Howe, Ridley, Biffen and Nott, we were joined by Hoskyns and David Wolfson and two company Chairmen; Kaye of Lansing Bagnall and Mobbs of Slough Estates. I pointed out that I was neither a politician nor an industrialist. They countered, 'but you know what's wrong with British Leyland.' When I told Richard Dobson, our BLMC chairman, that

I was 'assisting the Opposition', all he said was, 'Half our Board members would like to do the same.'

Before our meeting on 25th August, Margaret asked me for a brief, which she could use in meetings in New York with Citibank, Morgan Guaranty and leading US industrialists. Discussing it at her Chelsea home in Flood Street she suddenly said, 'This material will be of wider interest. You'd better come with us.' And so I did – joining her and Denis, Caroline Stephens and Adam Butler, her Parliamentary Private Secretary. It was a new experience for me, meeting in VIP airport lounges and in David Rockefeller's apartment, which he had lent to the Thatchers for their stay.

For another year we revised our recommendations on the future organisation, incorporating contributions from Howe, Joseph, Whitelaw and Heseltine. I challenged uncosted spending commitments and queried the timescale required for results. This Thorneycroft supported. I noticed that, whenever there were differences in view, Geoffrey Howe was so often the bridge, bringing the desired elements together for the Election Manifesto. Also, how adamant Margaret was when the pre-election polls showed that her lead fell from 11% to 5% and the 'wets' urged her to change her line. 'Certainty is total,' she said, 'not a consensus.'

The General Election came in the spring and Margaret became Prime Minister on 4th May. Letters arrived from most of the 'Shadows', all now in the Cabinet and one from Denis, who wrote, 'It has been a long road for four years and it's likely to be a hard road for the next four.' There was a frenzy of activity. I was no longer needed, nor in touch, nor did I expect to be.

In September, however, Margaret invited Diana and me to lunch at Chequers. We found ourselves with the Carringtons, the Menuhins and Lord Blake, the historian. The only 'work-related' topic we touched on was over coffee when Blake turned to me: 'You still see your Civil Service colleagues of the 1960s? What's your view of the Service now?' Margaret had stopped to listen. 'Still a fine instrument if played in the right way,' I said. 'It will respond admirably when party policy is clear, but if not it may seek to 'divide and rule'. Political advisers continue to be regarded with suspicion by the Service, even as adversaries. Some are necessary, but for a new Conservative government I see no problem so long as it works in tandem and keeps firmly in mind the importance of Civil Service morale.'

Before anyone could comment, Peter Carrington said, 'Prime Minister, may I have a few minutes?' 'I'd like a word with Alcon first,' she said and led me out into the garden. 'I don't know whether I thanked you for your help, but I would like to think you can now give us much more of your time.'

I replied, 'I enjoyed my limited involvement very much, but party politics is not my forte. I don't think I would be good at it.' I did not mention Diana's own hope, expressed to me more than once, almost fervently, that I would not go into party politics. She felt, I think, that I was not sufficiently ambitious for political power, that she was not cut out to be the ideal politician's wife and, all too often, 'it all ended in tears'.

Margaret stopped. She made no attempt to persuade me. Instinctively, I thought, she did not disagree. Quietly she said, 'Well, there are other things.' She had noticed I was looking at a small ruby ring on her little finger, with a diamond letter E. 'This goes with the house,' she said. 'It belonged to Queen Elizabeth I. It was taken to Scotland but lost, then they say it was found on a beach and eventually bought by the Farnhams who presented it, with Chequers, to the nation. As the first woman Prime Minister, I suppose I must be the first to wear it.' Yehudi and Diana Menuhin were just coming out of the house to say 'goodbye'. It was time for us to leave too.

Looking back on the eleven years of her administration I had time to reflect on an extraordinary career, from her opportunistic mode of arrival at Downing Street to her departure without ever losing a general election.

One of her faults, though an attractive one, was to trust people too readily, and forgive them for misjudgements – but never for disloyalty. She realised she had misjudged members of her own self-appointed Cabinet, due I think to a developing sense of infallibility which grew the longer she held public office.

However, she was uniquely equipped for her role in so many ways: taking responsibility for a nation in such a desperate state that high-risk, unpopular policies were necessary, adopting an unshakeable set of values and beliefs against which to judge ideas and action, showing brave leadership and clear direction in the face of uncertainty and determined opposition, bringing her innate 'home-keeping skills' to bear on the scale of the national economy, and abroad, attracting the admiration of many world leaders, thereby restoring some of our former national prestige.

If ever I had entered into party politics myself, I think I would have felt comfortable, working with talented people, both in the early postwar recovery administration of Clement Attlee, before the onset of the Cold War, and in Margaret Thatcher's early years – which would have been my preferred choice. The governance of our country, however, came in many forms. I would have enjoyed the intellectual aspects of formulating policies for young entrepreneurs, the disadvantaged and the environment. To be chairman of an influential investigative All-Party Parliamentary Select Committee would have been attractive, but then I would have had to be elected to Parliament. I might not always have 'toed the party line', but I would have aimed to simplify the machinery of government and also orchestrate our many inputs. Though colonial government was so different, I had seen it in action in Hong Kong, particularly in tackling problems of housing, health, education, transport, crime and immigration. Under Sir Murray Maclehose, leading businessmen, professionals, and institutions had cooperated closely with us to great effect.

The careful selection of participants from the business community would always be a key to its success. I had learned how effective the participation of business leaders could be on a number of occasions. Back in 1945, Admiral Sir Arthur John Davies showed me his own copy of the Navy List for 1922, with its blue pencil through entire pages of officers' names. At the time he was Naval Assistant to the Second Sea Lord. He told me how Sir Eric Geddes had been chosen to wield what became known as the Geddes Axe. His experience of the timber and railroad business in America and India and his administrative ability had so impressed Lloyd George, that he brought him directly into the Cabinet. He was so tough in fact that, in aiming to make Germany pay for the war, and he was not alone in this, he famously announced, 'We shall squeeze the German lemon until the pips squeak.' When I told Geddes' son Reay, then Chairman of Dunlop, of the consequences, in the rise of the Nazi regime he replied, 'Well, perhaps we overdid it!'

I learned of another occasion at first hand. In 1939, with the prospect of millions of tons of our food imports being sunk at sea, Sir Frederick Marquis (the future Lord Woolton) was appointed Minister of Food, to oversee its supply and its strict rationing. He had no party affiliations whatsoever, but as Managing Director of Lewis's, knew every aspect of the retail trade, not least the attitude of customers and the importance of effective advertising. Woolton told me, over a Manchester University Convocation dinner, that he was surprised to be called for interview by civil servants and then by Neville Chamberlain, still Prime Minister. They wanted 'to ensure that the authoritative way I would apply my business skills and the way we would work together, would not make me a misfit'.

Woolton was so satisfied personally with his government experience throughout Churchill's time, he not only joined the Conservative Party, but became its Chairman.

Since those days a multitude of businessmen of distinction have been attracted or been persuaded to contribute in particular ways. Beaverbrook, one of the first, was called in by Churchill. Some with a sound track record in relevant situations proving highly effective, others though making valid recommendations, could not see them being implemented and did not remain, others still failed and left, disillusioned. Their appointments or their working relationships could have been the fault of either or both sides. One of them, on leaving unhappily, said to me, 'I assumed that my instructions would be followed. Do you know, when we sought to focus on the central issue of our competitiveness as a nation in the Nineties, eleven Secretaries of State presented separate White Papers to Parliament?' How could we be accountable?

CHAPTER X

Anglo-American Relations

I have always enthused about overseas travel and the prospect of participating in activities abroad. It was with great excitement I ventured, as a wartime sailor, on my first visit to the United States aboard RMS Aquitania in March 1945. Without armament, we depended upon our speed of 23 knots and a nine-day southerly route to evade the U-boats. How different from the one-day return visits I would be making one day by Concorde.

New York, as we saw its thrilling lights in the distance, and berthed after years of black-out at home, appeared surreal. Soon after, when I was able to visit some New England towns I did not feel like a foreigner. They still resembled our cathedral towns of old, like Lichfield and Hereford. I was welcomed warmly at research establishments and had all the security clearances to the government's temporary huts in Constitution Avenue. But relations, I was to discover, had not always been so harmonious.

The Presidency of Franklin Roosevelt, who died during my visit, ended a long period of American isolationism. President Coolidge, opposing a League of Nations in 1923, was saying to Congress 'America must be kept American' and the USA began to distance itself from Europe. Political differences emerged – the Irish question and refusal to adopt the gold standard. Hostility between the State Department and the Foreign Office at times was ill-concealed. Immigration into the USA was restricted, our two armies and navies moved apart. Following the Wall Street Crash and the depression, Roosevelt conspicuously did not attend the London 1933 Summit.

But then came the rise of Nazi Germany, the expansionist aims of Japan and the countdown to war. Still involuntarily isolationist, there were incredibly only three British journalists in Washington in 1939 and the British Embassy staff was never more than twenty. It was 9,000 when I arrived six years later.

Washington was now the lynchpin in our international diplomacy. Americans recognised that Britain was fighting the allied cause alone and, by Lend-Lease, allowed us food and weapons on credit. Very soon the State Department was receiving more calls from the British Embassy than all other embassies together.

The trauma of Pearl Harbour in December 1941 hit America harder, in my view, than 9/11. The Japanese attack, which came out of the blue, was the culmination of nearly a century of competition between the US and Japan for supremacy in the Pacific Ocean. It finally ended America's policy of isolation and neutrality. In the war, collaboration was at its best on the atom bomb project. Britain's nuclear fission achievements gave us the lead, but Germany was likely to follow. To be successful in time, combining resources with the US was essential.

I had kept in touch with Jane Watson, and twelve years after our 1945 meeting she invited me to her 888 Park Avenue apartment and her home in New Canaan, Connecticut, to meet her husband, John Irwin, a Wall Street banker. They gave me a great day trampolining with their two sons in the garden. Jane's brother, who had served in the White House, told me how, when the British and American ministers in Saudi Arabia accused each other of double-dealing over oil concessions, only the personal friendship of Beaverbrook and Harold Ickes healed the breach. I came across other examples of the significance of personal relationships when speaking to American attorneys and bankers. In Hollywood, in an elevator, Bing Crosby introduced himself to me and I found myself chatting with Bob Hope, Douglas Fairbanks and C. Aubrey Smith.

Years later, when we became neighbours in Denham, in Buckinghamshire, John Mills and I swapped yarns about these stars. He did not get to Hollywood until 1947, but his bosom friends were the most glamorous – Spencer Tracy, Humphrey Bogart, Gary Cooper, Jimmy Cagney,

Norma Shearer, Bette Davis and Rex Harrison. John went so far as to bring Rex along as a prospective purchaser of our house in Denham – but 'it was much too big for him!'

John asked me to recount to Rex, an anglophile, what I had told him of one evening on my first visit. In Washington, at a sedate dinner dance, my partner was the seventeen year-old daughter of a 'Daughter of the American Revolution'. In white naval uniform I was considered 'suitable' company for her daughter.

After the dance, as I walked her the few blocks back home, she was showing off a valuable necklace over her pale lemon dress. Some drunks appeared and blocked our way. 'Come on, you in yeller and bring yer feller,' they shouted. She grabbed my arm, we walked steadily on and once safely home she told her father. He poured me a whisky and proceeded to recount his own mother's experience coming to Scotland as a girl in the 1880s. It was intended that American heiresses would marry into the British aristocracy.

'She was invited by the Duke of Buccleuch to stay at Drumlanrig Castle to meet his son. When she couldn't find the way to her bedroom she came down to ask the Duke in his library. 'At the top of the staircase, turn left at the Rembrandt and right at the Leonardo.' The Leonardo clearly did not do the trick. She came back to America to marry my father.'

World-shaking events and disasters had come in rapid succession at the end of the war. Within three days in early August 1945 the atom bombs were dropped on Hiroshima and Nagasaki, and Russia finally chose to enter the war against Japan. Our general election result saw Churchill unceremoniously thrown out of Downing Street whilst Roosevelt, his 'dear and cherished friend', had now been succeeded by Truman. The wartime alliance, for all its arguments and suspicions had been as close a relationship as possible. Within seven days Lend-Lease was stopped abruptly.

The outcome of the war for our two countries, in economic terms, was totally different. The United States was now richer and more prosperous than ever. For the returning GIs opportunities abounded. At home we were utterly exhausted. Our 400,000 dead were more than the USA had, even with four times the population. The Russians had actually suffered fifty-five times heavier losses. The affluence of America made them unpopular. Graffiti everywhere read 'Yankees Go Home'. Giving it a twist, their English girlfriends scribbled 'and take me with you'.

Back at the Admiralty I tried to collect my thoughts on Anglo–American relations. We had become totally dependent on the US for victory, but the world knew that for a whole year we had withstood Hitler alone. I had never heard Churchill's phrase 'the special relationship' in the course of my visit. He used it the following year in his Fulton speech to describe the indispensible wartime alliance. For Roosevelt it applied to all those who fought against Nazi Germany and were given aid. We continued to believe that possessing nuclear weapons would ensure our seat at the top table. We had to wait for this until a new common enemy emerged, the Cold War with the Soviet Union.

Some of our wartime collaboration in intelligence was perpetuated in 1946 in an arrangement from which we all benefitted, as I had discovered on joining the Joint Intelligence Bureau. Our Director, General Sir Kenneth Strong told us, 'I always had direct access to Ike. He listened attentively and acted on my judgement.' But information exchanges were incomplete. Treachery and defections on both sides of the Atlantic prevented this.

During my eight years in defence I paid just three visits to America. With the onset of the Cold War I was at the Europe desk when the Communists seized power in Czechoslovakia and threatened France and Italy. A blockade of Berlin began, NATO was established and Marshall Aid restored. America sought and obtained strategic bases in East Anglia, suitable for atomic attacks on the USSR.

The following year, when Mao Tse Tung proclaimed the Chinese People's Republic, I was moved to the Korean desk. At the start of the campaign the USA, not wishing to be alone, expected us to provide a token ground force. Our own Chiefs of Staff were opposed to this and so was the Foreign Office. They were concerned about Hong Kong and also mindful of the possibility that the Soviet army, with its eighty divisions facing us, was orchestrating the Korean offensive to draw American troops from Europe. But there was a good relationship between Ernest Bevin and Dean Acheson and finally we agreed. It was not easy. When Sir Pierson Dixon came to Paris as Ambassador in 1960, I remember him telling us, 'After our history of deciding and leading, we have to resign ourselves to a role of counsellors and moderators – and then follow the United States.' The Korean War came to a disastrous end. Thereafter, during the Truman, Eisenhower, Johnson, Nixon and Carter administrations I visited America some twenty times.

The warmth of the victorious wartime alliance we had was followed by years of economic decline and our loss of power on the world stage. Churchill had hoped to hide this on becoming Prime Minister again and addressing a Joint Session of Congress. This was the occasion for my third visit. It was at that time that I had the short but memorable conversation with Winston Churchill in Washington, as mentioned earlier.

Churchill had been received enthusiastically, but his mission was hardly successful. The USA followed its own interests, protecting its own competitive position.

The US viewed Britain as still riven by the perpetuation of class distinction, ancestry, accent and etiquette. We saw them as a society divided by money. It seemed natural and a matter of pride that Eisenhower's Cabinet included nine millionaires. Whilst adopting the ideas and values of Jefferson and Madison, Americans lauded the rich for their enterprise, vigour and stability. They were investing heavily in European industry and expected to be admired for job creation. In Europe, however, they were seen as the major competitor, especially in France, following Servan Schreiber's *Le Défi Américain*.

Sympathy with wartime allies also evaporated when a European Defence Community including Britain was vetoed by the French. Then came Nasser's nationalisation of the canal and the Suez crisis in 1956. Eden had approved a disastrous joint attack with the French that led to a run on sterling, a catastrophic loss of British power in the world and any illusions of a continuing special Anglo-American relationship.

Suez, like Panama, was an international waterway. Though Eisenhower was facing a Presidential election and wanted to avoid military action, Gladwyn Jebb, my Ambassador in Paris, was absolutely infuriated that there was no real Anglo-American consultation when it was more necessary than ever. I received a sympathetic message from my US Embassy opposite number. 'I read that 120 of your Conservative MPs have signed a motion accusing the US of gravely endangering the Atlantic Alliance. You know we still need your knowledge and experience of the Third World and through you, an entrée into continental Europe.'

In the following year I had the chance of judging one American's view of Britain at first hand. I was sponsored by the British Information Services in New York to address a few meetings. Socially, I came across nothing but friendliness. My discussions in Pittsburgh, Washington and Philadelphia were constructive. Then I was asked to help out and appear on a TV current affairs programme, WEWS in Cleveland, substituting for a Counsellor who was accompanying the Queen in the course of her visit.

I was interviewed by Dorothy Fuldheim, whose claim to fame was her unique interview of Hitler in 1938. An anti-monarchist, she could not have been more hostile. 'How do you feel in Britain, now you are just the poor relation?' When she went on to ask, 'What is this ineffable quality your Queen is supposed to have?' I could not resist saying, 'Quality is something you wouldn't understand.' I was furious and refused the fee. I went to visit my sister who, with her husband, an academic, was working at the Case Institute nearby. They had invited friends to hear the programme and to meet me over dinner. I was greeted with a cheer. Russ Ackoff, Professor of Operations Research at the Institute, said, 'Excellent! Attack was the only form of defence!'

Our 'special' relations had taken a long dive. They were sweetened, however, by acts of generosity which made possible for example, the creation of Churchill College, Cambridge. They were further restored when Macmillan became Prime Minister. A nuclear warhead agreement was reached with Eisenhower and even though, following the U-2 spy plane fiasco of May 1960, the Big Four Summit in Paris was aborted, a year later John Kennedy, now President, made Polaris missiles available to Britain.

My visits in 1963 and 1964 arose out of new activities in London when I was investigating the relationship between science, innovation, employment and economic growth. It was at the time when Lyndon Johnson was in search of a Great Society and Walter Heller, Chairman of the Council of Economic Advisors, invited me to Washington for two weeks in June 1964 to meet his staff. On arrival I found that meetings had also been arranged with leading businessmen – the Chairman of MIT (James Killian), Senator Hubert Humphrey, and Congress members, to discuss government-business relationships and problems. I discovered that the USA, like Britain, had its own internal arguments. Whilst in Britain HM Treasury did not agree with the National Economic Development Council, in America, the Secretaries of Labour, Commerce and the trade union leader Walter Reuther, ascribing their heavy unemployment to rapid technological change, disagreed with the White House, who maintained it was due to the low level of demand and growth of the unskilled labour force.

I was fortunate to attend, too, the Harvard Association's annual gathering. I will never forget the processional scene from the eldest to the youngest graduate, or the fervour of the voices of four generations of alumni chanting the seventy-eighth Psalm. Nor, on a modest scale, following my talk at the University of Notre Dame, the Reverend Theodore Hesburgh, its President, captivating all, young and old alike, on 'the priceless value of education – the essence of our culture and our lives'.

After Harold Wilson's election as Prime Minister and Johnson's own landslide victory a month later, I was asked to return. I spoke at Harvard,

MIT, Stanford Research Institute and the National Science Foundation, and at Government offices. I thought my opinions were being given greater weight than they were at home. On the morning I was due to leave Washington the telephone rang. 'The President wants to see you.' I was sure it was a leg pull. 'He can't know I exist?' I said. 'We'll pick you up in half an hour, and get you to your plane in time.'

I was shown into the Oval Office. President Johnson came in and greeted me with a strong handshake. I had been told he was all 'cheek and jowl', browbeating and backslapping. He was not at all like that. He asked how I had got on. I raised the issue of the Brain Drain and the intellectual contribution of some of the best qualified people Britain had lost to the USA. He replied, 'The most important intellectual input we have had from you is Keynesianism. It has always helped us to legitimise the role of the Executive in our economy.' And then he added, 'I would like to finish off what Roosevelt began – to alleviate poverty and develop Medicare.

'In any event, thank you for your contribution to our Water Programme, which I have been hearing about. I expect we will act on that.' This was a Five State project I had been consulted on. 'But I gather you are also encouraging us to build a supersonic transport aircraft. Why is that?'

'We are going ahead with Concorde,' I explained, 'Macmillan backed it to help our entry into Europe, but it's beginning to be more time-consuming and costly than it should and, frankly, we need some competition.' He smiled. 'I'm glad to hear you say that, but no. When I was Governor of Texas I received hundreds of complaints about our supersonic tests. The bangs so upset the cattle, I promised that, as President, I wouldn't allow it.'

He stood up. 'Please accept this,' handing me a small 'Lyndon Johnson' medallion. As I was driven to the airport I took a look at it. Even though it was just some base metal, it seemed to me to be a tiny token of a continuing special relationship.

Back in Washington the following year (1965) I had the chance of discussing a problem we both faced: how choices were made in selecting the largest public sector projects. I had recommended to Trend in 1964 more systematic techno-economic appraisals by government and industry together. This idea was well received, but there was no action for years. When it did come, on a formal basis, with government taking the leading role, I discovered how it had emerged in Washington DC.

Congressman Emilio Daddario questioned me on the procedure I had recommended in Whitehall to make such appraisals. It was not until 1972, in the course of another visit, I learned they had finally got a Bill through Congress to establish an Office of Technology Assessment.

I met Daddario again years later, in his Connecticut Avenue apartment in Washington. The door was opened for me by his grandson. In a deep armchair and wearing what might have been pre-war slippers and a cardigan, there, 'forty years on', was Emilio. He reminisced, 'I got the Bill through by quoting Thomas Jefferson in the pre-amble: 'As new discoveries are made, new truths discovered and manners and opinions change with the change of circumstances, institutions must advance also, to keep pace with the times.' Congress agreed – citing Jefferson usually works!' he added.

Daddario was OTA's first Director. 'We began somewhat experimentally,' he said, 'aiming to inject into the legislative policy process some early indications of the beneficial and adverse impacts of a proposal. It was usually a Congressional Committee that asked us to do an analysis, which might take up to two years, as it was for the anti-ballistic missile system and the trans-Alaska pipeline. We reported to a Governing Board comprising six members of the Senate and six of the House.' It continued to carry out its valuable work for over a quarter of a century until it was wound up twenty-five years later, on grounds of cost, by the minority Leader Senator Harry Reed. In Britain it was much later that a more formal, but similar, appraisal arrangement was introduced.

Invitations to return to America arrived at my office in the Ministry of Technology: an Alfred Sloan Foundation offer and the prospect of an Andrew Mellon Fellowship, with encouragement to stay on. They were attractive, but I had already decided I would not become part of the Brain Drain.

We had discussed this issue at a DSIR Directors Conference. Following my meetings with some of the most knowledgeable individuals in America I quoted Robert McNamara's comments at their most pithy. I had told McNamara of one of our highly talented engineers who had been tempted by housing, schools and other family facilities to induce him to move to the United States. He said, 'You know President Kennedy's remark in his Inaugural Address in 1961: 'On the whole, brains, like hearts, go where they are appreciated.''

Well known figures, including Sir Alexander Fleck of ICI and Sir Gordon Sutherland, reporting to the Royal Society considered what could be done to retain these people. Lord Todd appointed me to the Scientific Manpower Committee under the Chairmanship of Sir Willis Jackson. Armed with the results of our investigations I accompanied Lord Hailsham to an OECD Ministerial Meeting on Science Policy in Paris. We agreed that most of the economic growth we all sought would depend upon keeping these people in Europe. Higher productivity and innovation by our scientists, engineers and general managers was critical to our effectiveness.

Yet what I had acquired over the years was such an understanding of America and its people and its values that, when asked, I felt just as comfortable in joining an American multinational company as a British one. This came in 1966 when McKinsey offered me the chance of joining them – free to choose what I did, without moving home if I wished. Had it not been for my repeated visits, wide contacts, easy relationships and presumably a favourable impression, I would not have been invited. And had I not shared so many of their values, I would not have accepted. The prospect of financial rewards alone, for any job, would not have been sufficient inducement. There were always risks, but I couldn't resist the challenge. Thus began a decade of new opportunities.

These continued long after I retired from McKinsey. I had met William 'Bill' Simon, former US Secretary of the Treasury in the Ford Administration, a number of times. In New York he told me of the City's financial disaster in 1975 and his role as an investment banker at the time. The City wanted to borrow from their banks and, 'as a political necessity', wanted Federal and Treasury guarantees of their loans. It was the first time I had heard of Ponzi, the chain letter swindle, a scheme for borrowing on an unprecedented scale on the basis of politicians' promises to repay. 'They have no book-keeping, the accountants are tricksters, politicians promise, borrow and spend as though there is no tomorrow,' he said, 'and they want the taxpayer to subsidise them.'

In Washington, one Sunday morning in 1979, he and I called on Henry Kissinger. 'He will enjoy meeting you.' It was not long before Kissinger was telling me what he thought about Britain. 'When you suffered and were weakened by the war, you didn't waste time looking back on your old global aspirations, you joined us in our own policy debates here; ignoring your views would sometimes have felt like violating Club rules. Despite disagreements, there was real collaboration between our diplomats, military planners and intelligence agencies. And when Edward Heath, a good European, went cool on our relationship I had no difficulty in maintaining direct exchanges with other Ministers and directly with your Cabinet Office. I couldn't have done this with any other country. Now, Margaret is beginning to play the Washington political game skilfully as she has struck up a critically important personal relationship with Reagan.'

Then the telephone rang, his hotline: 'Anatoly, good morning, can't you sleep?...Yes, come right over.' Within ten minutes Anatoly Dobrynin, the Soviet Ambassador, in jovial mood, strode in. He was meeting the President the following morning and wanted Kissinger's opinion on something in advance. So much for US–USSR style diplomacy. Bill and I finished off our champagne and left.

I thought of his remarks later when Margaret Thatcher stopped America from cancelling the Siberian pipeline project and invading Grenada, a member of the Commonwealth, and of the Falkland Islands. When the US Ambassador to the UN, Jean Kirkpatrick, was advocating US support of Argentina, Margaret, strongly backed by Caspar Weinberger, succeeded in obtaining the all-important US missiles and fuel.

It was through William Simon, who arranged for me to stay at the Metropolitan Club, that I was asked to address a Business Conference on 15th and 16th May 1981 attended by Richard Nixon – that is, over six years since he was President. After I had spoken on economic and political risk, the Chairman came over saying he would like me to be seated next to President Nixon at lunch. His questions were mainly about Margaret Thatcher. Then, I thought he might not be forthcoming, but I could reasonably ask him a question, a somewhat provocative one. 'How would you like to be remembered historically?' 'By our ending of the Vietnam war and our successful rapprochement with China,' he replied. 'Its future importance cannot be overestimated.'

'And how about domestic affairs?' I added. 'By what we have done for families, in protecting the environment, and for the Arts,' he replied. He still had not referred to Watergate, so I plucked up courage to do so. He turned directly to me. 'You know, if everyone knew the forthright methods we had to adopt secretly, to be successful with the Chinese, they would have killed it all off. The actions we took at home were no more reprehensible, but we were discovered. We want results. We don't always want to know how they may have been obtained! A President is faced with the oldest of all questions, 'Do the ends justify the means?''

When William Simon, who had also served as Chairman of the US Economic Policy Board, was retained by some multinational companies and central banks to advise them on their own problems, particularly the Banque de France, he asked me to join him in a few meetings. 'Your Bank of England work and contacts in France would be useful.' He was a staunch Republican, with views close to those of Milton Friedman. He believed that interventionist governments, by passing more laws or setting up new regulatory agencies were, more often than not, the problem not the cure. As he put it, 'Private cooperation through the market place' was far more effective than 'the invisible hand of the bureaucrat'.

I learned from him how political risk could have a more far-reaching effect on business performance than the usual insurable risks, or even management error and the relevance of party politics. Boards had to raise their level of understanding of these issues and retain as much flexibility as possible in their plans and actions.

One memory of our time together, incidentally, was when Bill and I were leaving Paris for Riyadh and London, respectively. At Charles de Gaulle airport he said, 'Let's get a pizza at the snack bar; it's the best in France.' Insisting on picking up *l'addition*, he put down a $20 note. 'We don't accept foreign currency,' said the waiter. 'This is the Honourable William Simon,' I piped up, 'You'll see it's his own signature on the bank note.'

Like a shot, the young man said, 'Ah, please sign it again, Sir; I will keep it!'

Looking back, long before my time, it was clear that Anglo-American relations had always ebbed and flowed. I still remembered one remarkable line of Sherlock Holmes: *It's always a joy to meet an American, Mr Moulton, for I am one of those who believe that the folly of a monarch, and the blundering of a minister, in far-gone years, will not prevent our children from being, some day, citizens of the same world-wide country, under a flag which will be a quartering of the Union Jack with the Stars and Stripes.*

Now Britain was the junior partner. Shared values, circumstances and sentiment have often brought us together, but from time to time they have been trumped by our respective national interests.

Trade has always been important. Today the UK and the US have their biggest investments of all in each other. In defence and particularly in the context of terrorism, multinational collaboration is vital. Cyber threats have been added to nuclear proliferation to dominate the security issue. The alleged manufacture of 'weapons of mass destruction' in Iraq and Iran's secret enrichment programme brought Tony Blair into earnest discussions with George W. Bush, reminiscent of the wartime telephone conversations between Churchill and Roosevelt.

With this no doubt in mind Blair took a gift across to the Oval Office – Epstein's bust of Churchill, symbolic of 'his wartime hour'. Then, symptomatic of the ebb rather than flow of our current relationship, President Obama replaced it with a bust of Abraham Lincoln, indicative of a freestanding America. It was not a posture of American isolationism, however. With the ascendency of China and India, closeness to Canada, hopes of closer links with Europe and – with a growing Spanish-speaking population of its own – alignment with South America, it was one of realism. Appraisals and reassessments, national interest more than sentiment, will always determine national priorities, but the power of states shifts. In five centuries Spain, Netherlands, France, Britain and the USA have, in turn been paramount. Now America is the strongest power militarily, and economically is on a plateau, but with limited growth prospects only. Other great powers are emerging rapidly. As American dominance diminishes, it needs to rebalance its foreign policy. Such policy decisions are generally better when taken in conjunction with others. Times change. President Obama wanted Britain to exert more global power, in Libya and Afghanistan for example, not less, as at the time of Suez when President Eisenhower regarded us as acting as neo-imperialists.

America could know more about how others think and feel. We in Britain do not realise how quickly old attitudes must change as the balance of power changes, both between states and by diffusion within them. America should be able to look to us for a better *entrée* into Europe, a clearer understanding of the Commonwealth, and as reliable interpreters of the global scene. Our future strength depends upon this vital relationship. We uphold the same values of freedom and human dignity.

At a personal level, now that Diana and I have an American daughter-in-law, a grandson preferring Marmite and granddaughter peanut butter, the relationship is still quite special. But, at the international level, our relationship rather than being 'special' is still 'essential'.

CHAPTER XI

Out of Office Hours

It was impossible to house hunt in England whilst living in Paris, so in 1960 we decided to rent a tiny cottage in the village of Naphill into which we could all squeeze. It was cold but within easy reach of the Laboratory and a primary school. School proved a bit of a culture shock for Katharine, now five, after her year at l'Ecole Active Bilingue. She was laughed at for wearing leggings with her red Harris Tweed coat with velvet collar, but having a musical ear she quickly adopted the local accent and mixed in well. It was the best part of a year before we could move.

We then took a lease on a small wing of Shardeloes, near Amersham, originally the home of Francis Drake's family — we still have an old engraving of the lake 'where all the ducks are Drakes'. It had been imposingly rebuilt in the 1750s by Robert Adam for the Tyrwhitt-Drakes, their home until 1939, when it became a maternity home. Our wing was the converted coach house. Three of the principal rooms were leased by Elspeth Hoare, who moved there from Aynho, after the death of her first husband Fairfax Cartwright and stayed until her second husband Eustace Hoare died suddenly. Michael Denison and his wife, Dulcie Gray, then moved in.

The Denisons invited us to a birthday party one glorious summer's day. I was seated next to Rebecca West on a sofa, when Frankie Howerd, who'd been staring at me from across the room, came over and said, 'You would make a perfect Sherlock Holmes.' Dulcie had told us, 'A special guest is coming. She will be wearing a hat, but doesn't expect others to do so.' And then the Queen Mother entered, through the open French windows with a flowing dress and happy smile.

Shardeloes was a beautiful spot, not least in the snow. One dreadful winter we were snowed in completely, however, and Diana had to go off with a sledge to bring the milk and the post up the steep, three-quarter-mile drive. There was an ancient ice house dug deep into the grounds. Butters the Gamekeeper, who lived in the lodge at the bottom of the drive, never ventured out without his shotgun and would frighten the children whilst they were picking snowdrops in the woods.

Our two young daughters now went to school at Godstowe in High Wycombe, where the headmistress asked a few parents to join her for lunch on Speech Day. It was there we first met Roald Dahl, his wife Patricia Neal, Enoch and Margaret Powell, and Oliver and Delia Millar, all of whom we continued to see as friends long after our children had grown up. Our neighbours in the village were Ludovic Kennedy and his wife Moira Shearer who I had met in my bachelor days.

Diana and I and the Dahls had all married and returned to England from France and the USA respectively at about the same time. Our children were contemporaries too and when our eldest daughters were seven years old Katharine came home one day saying, 'May I have a shilling for some flowers for Olivia.' We were shocked to discover it was for a wreath. Tragically, she had died from measles and encephalitis. Theo, her baby brother succumbed to another tragedy when, still a baby in his pram, he was severely, almost fatally, brain-damaged, following a road accident in New York.

It was a couple of years later in Christmas week 1964 that Roald and Patricia Neal Dahl (as she signed herself) came to a party at home. And she was soon telling me of the steak dinners she had had with 'Ronnie' Reagan, when they were on a film set in England.

With us too, that night, were a couple about to hit 'the big time': Paul McCartney of Rembrandt, Heswell, Liverpool, as he wrote in our visitors' book, with the attractive Jane Asher. It was Hélène Cordet who had first introduced us at her Saddle Room Club in Hamilton Place.

Paul and Jane returned one day from a country walk and joined us for tea. We found Paul giving our baby, Edward, his bottle. School friends of Katharine, then ten years old, hearing of this clamoured to sit in 'his chair'. Paul told me at the time he was captivated not only by music, but by scenes he wanted to paint. More than thirty years later he published a book of his paintings and sent it to Diana.

With four children now, in 1968, Shardeloes had become a little cramped for us. Because of my new role, also with a McKinsey office in St James's and flying from Heathrow, we were on the look-out for a house closer to London, one with privacy and a secluded garden. We found our 'ideal home'.

Within half an hour of Marylebone Station, Denham Village was a backwater, hidden away by woodland, with a few historic houses and cottages, built over four centuries, one dating back to beyond the Norman Conquest. Fayrestede was recorded in the Doomsday Book as having the value of four cows. Denham Place was originally Tudor. It had been owned by the Vansittarts when he was head of the Foreign Office, and now by his widow. Savay was a fourteenth-century timbered manor house. The White House, partly Georgian, rebuilt on the site of the ancient Rosegullys, was set in seventeen secluded acres. When it came up for sale we couldn't resist. Over two hundred yards of the River Misbourne flowed through the garden which was obscured from the village road by a listed old brick wall.

Soon after we arrived, Denham Place was bought by Harry Saltzman, to be close to the film studios built by Alexander Korda. Almost directly opposite us, in the mainly William and Mary 'Hills House', John and Mary Mills lived, returning in 1976 to the village they loved. They became our great friends. They told us about the studio performances of Marlene Dietrich, Charles Laughton, Laurence Olivier and Vivien Leigh. James Mason took a cottage nearby when filming *Frankenstein: The True Story*. Peter Rogers of the Pinewood Studios chose our house as the ideal location for the production of *Carry on Matron*. He sent us a cheque for £25, as agreed, for the charity we designated. When the first run of the film was examined they wanted a re-take because the faces of three excited children were clearly visible through a bedroom window! It was the perfect family home and there we remained for twenty years.

We continued to see the Mills for the rest of their lives. The yarns he spun could have filled a book. In the film *In Which We Serve* all the Captain's speeches had been written by Dickie Mountbatten. And at his eighty-fifth birthday party in 1999, Johnny wore the precious HMS Kelly tie, badge and crest Mountbatten had presented to him. It was at the same party I was introduced to the fifth generation of the Gieves family, who had provided all the naval uniforms since time immemorial. I was able to tell him a story about Gieves' influence, as told to me by Admiral Sir Arthur John Davies in the war. A Captain, due to retire, received with his bill for £112 a rather peremptory note, instead of the traditional courteous one, demanding immediate payment. He replied: 'Gentlemen, I have always had two ambitions: to become an Admiral and to be able to settle my Gieves bill. I cannot see the second happening before the first.' Two weeks later the Captain was promoted Rear Admiral.

One Sunday after lunch at The White House, Roald Dahl encouraged me to tell him more about my geological mapping in student days. I had traced the underground streams in the limestone of the Yorkshire Dales by pouring some phenolphthalein down pot-holes and following the vivid discoloration emerging downstream. A farmer had tackled me: 'Are you poisoning the water?' I took a sip to show it was perfectly drinkable. Roald immediately became enthusiastic. 'Excellent, I can use that.' In one of his stories (*The Twits*, 1979) I saw he had laced the food to give it an obnoxious colour.

I asked him how he came to write in the first place. 'It was during the war, in Washington, having been wounded flying with the RAF in East Africa, I was sent off to our Embassy as Assistant Air Attaché. A Secretary came into my office saying, 'An author wants to write about your wartime air operations. He has been particularly helpful to us; will you tell him what you can?' In he came, and told me he had been asked to write for *The Saturday Evening Post*, so I recounted one or two of my adventures.'

He went on to write for the *Post* himself and *The Ladies Home Journal* and other magazines also invited his contributions. Their readers were the families of young US airmen, now our allies, who wanted to read of his first-hand experiences.

In 1974, whilst writing *Switch Bitch* he told me he was becoming disenchanted with Knopf, his American publishers. He preferred them to those in literary circles in England, they were his friends and selling millions of his books, but felt he was beginning to be cheated financially. Now they wanted far more books from him.

In 1977, he returned to the same subject. Knopf, with whom he had agreements, was a subsidiary of Random House. They refused to release half the money due. In addition to *James and the Giant Peach* and *Charlie and the Chocolate Factory* all his paperback editions were best sellers. He told them that his income tax and surcharge had escalated, he had hip replacements and other operations to pay for and his prospective inheritance tax liability was monstrous. He wanted them to increase his children's insurance benefits fivefold to £250,000 for each of his daughters, but they would not agree. They would only pay out higher premiums if he guaranteed to give them an irrevocable right to all his works for the rest of his life – or at least his next seven books. There was also a point of American law which was an obstacle.

He was so furious that, bypassing his literary agent, Ann Watkins, he let himself go, on 3rd April 1978 in a letter to a Director, Dick Kimsley, which ended, 'Let's tear up the contract, cancel the insurance and I will find some way of removing my accrued income from your clutches.'

At the time, Roald was under other pressures too, for Pat was away for three months, filming in the USA and the Pyrenees and he was trying to run a house with four children in it and Tessa's baby, Sophie.

By September, Ann Watkins, who agreed he was owed over $750,000 was in New York meeting the Random House directors, but had reached a stalemate. 'They owe me between $750,000 and $1.1 million. There is only one thing for it, Alcon, YOU must go to NY yourself and get it from them.'

I was tempted by the challenge. I felt he had a case and I had a good chance of succeeding. In any event, I wanted to support a friend and so I agreed to go to New York. With Roald's introduction I met the President and General Counsel of Knopf. [photo, page 233]

I was received cordially enough and quickly came to the only two points I planned to make: 'We all have professional backgrounds and I'm sure we share a common interest, an agreed financial settlement, complying with the law on both sides of the Atlantic. I also believe that you and Random House as well as your new owners (RCA) cannot afford to see your reputations suffer through a famous author's allegations of sharp practice.' They listened attentively. I was surprised by their conciliatory attitude. Within an hour they had agreed to pay $750,000 to any account specified by Roald, within two years a further $350,000, and also doubled the entire insurance cover. The cheque was sent a month later.

I returned to my room at the Hotel Pierre quite elated – how easy it had all been. I called a McKinsey colleague in Park Avenue, invited him to dinner and recounted the whole saga. 'I expect they did their homework,' he said. 'They probably looked you up in *Who's Who*, saw you were also a General Commissioner for Income Tax, and decided they would not take the chance that you were not in collusion with our Internal Revenue Service!' The thought had never crossed my mind.

Shortly afterwards, without consulting him, Random House began to borrow on his policies to make premium payments. I thought all had finally been resolved, but Roald sent a letter to me from hospital. 'There's a complication over the further sums due, so put your massive intellect to work. When I come out of here we shall have to open up a bottle of something to celebrate. If this sort of thing goes on,' he announced, 'I will leave Knopf.' [photo, page 233]

The two-way correspondence became more acrimonious, accusatory and downright rude, until he received a letter dated 5th March 1981, from Knopf's President, which concluded, 'Your threat to leave Knopf leaves us far from intimidated... Business reasons are not strong enough to make us put up with your manner to us any longer... You've managed to make the entire experience of publishing you unappealing for all of us.'

Within six months he went on to publish through Michael Joseph, both *Tales of the Unexpected* and *My Uncle Oswald*. I recommended he arranged for a further $500,000 of death benefits for $50,000 which, at the age of sixty-three, given his state of health, he regarded as a very good bet.

I found it strange that a writer who was so talented and successful seemed to have something of an inferiority complex. At a small dinner party a year or so before he died the conversation turned to whether it was better to emerge from university with a Double First or a Double Blue. Christopher Chataway insisted it was a Double First. Not having been to university Roald showed his irritation. Minutes later he walked out of the dining room. When he didn't return I went to investigate. I was shocked to find him on the drawing room floor writhing in pain. As soon as he saw me he tried to hide it.

I decided to tackle him on a more serious issue: 'You can be quite rude at times, but why are you so hostile in your remarks about Jews?' He didn't expect it. 'Alcon,' he replied, 'You know me. There are things I should never have said.' I let it go at that. There was one occasion soon after, however, when his behaviour was thoroughly embarrassing. At a garden party at home in Denham, he volunteered to help. 'What can I get you to drink?' he asked one of our guests, a prim and proper lady. 'A soft one, please,' she replied. He almost shouted at her, 'What? Do you have syphilis or something?' I had to tell him off, and he apologised.

Roald could be hot tempered and extremely rude, whilst at other times he was considerate and fun. When Patricia was working abroad he was at home looking after the family. There, he came to understand children of all ages in all their moods, their need for gentleness, their spirit of adventure, how they could rebel – hoping that something nasty would happen to those they hated. Catering for their imagination, he told me just how, for example, *The Giraffe* was written for the youngest, *The Witches* and *Matilda* for the older ones. He was generous to our children too, sending them early personal copies of his books, even from hospital.

In 1986, three years after Roald and Pat's divorce, his tax affairs were being investigated by the Inland Revenue. There had been changes in the tax regulations and the attitude of the House of Lords to tax avoidance had stiffened. He asked me to review a draft reply when they maintained their decision that he was liable to pay more tax because of where his work was done. I was amused by the Revenue's contention that Roald 'waited until he was on the aeroplane and crossing the UK continental shelf before even thinking about his new novel', but I came to the conclusion that he did owe more. A settlement was finally reached.

In 1990 at Roald's funeral at Missenden Church, the whole family gathered. We met Felicity Crosland who had married Roald, after a long friendship, and liked her from the outset. Evidence that the children did so too came in the Service itself.

Among my 'out of office' activities in the world of arts, music had always attracted me. Never a performer, knowing little about music, concerts and opera still brought me great pleasure. I think I was only five or six when taken to see a performance of *The Flying Dutchman*, the Hallé Orchestra being conducted by Hamilton Harty, at the Free Trade Hall in Manchester.

Twenty years later, in 1946 and in uniform, I occasionally went straight from my office in the Admiralty, armed with a sandwich, to enjoy a Royal Albert Hall concert. One evening an elderly gentleman wearing an official badge came up to me. 'I've seen you here before. Tell me, do you buy your own ticket?' I told him I did. 'I'm Superintendant of the Corps of Honorary Stewards. If you were prepared to come fairly regularly, you might like to join us, and not have to pay.' He went on to explain how, since Prince Albert's time, there had been a voluntary Corps, responsible for decorum, showing people to their seats, putting cigarettes out and so on. 'We have a rota, and whenever you attend, you may invite two friends to take seats in our Grand Tier Box.'

I could not resist. Over the next seven years I attended some two hundred concerts. In addition to the world famous orchestras, conductors and soloists – Mstislav Rostropovich, Yehudi Menuhin, David Oistrakh – I enjoyed the Henry Wood Proms, transferred after the Queen's Hall had been demolished in the war, choral concerts, Longfellow's *Hiawatha*, the revels of the Chelsea Arts Ball on New Year's Eve and a succession of wild events, such as Jack Solomon's Boxing Contests and Housewives' League meetings, where we were required to take our turn.

My co-stewards were mainly retired officers, bankers, lawyers and doctors sharing a love of music. Some had been stewards for over twenty years. They reminisced about the vicious scramble for tickets when Fritz Kreisler performed Elgar's violin concerto, which Elgar had dedicated to him and Bruno Walter's personal piano accompaniment, as requested by Kathleen Ferrier and Lotte Lehmann. There were the most popular Sunday concerts too, which starred Dame Clara Butt, Count John McCormack, Galli-Curci, Tetrazzini and Jascha Heifetz. Of the contraltos I heard myself, Kathleen Ferrier was my favourite.

We showed people to their seats. One evening in 1949 the performance had just begun when Ludovic Kennedy hurried in. I was about to stop him but he pointed to an empty seat and sat down next to a ravishingly beautiful girl, who I had already shown to her seat. It was Moira Shearer. They married the following year.

On duty on another occasion the Countess Mountbatten passed me a note. 'Will you take this to Paul Robeson in his dressing room?' This I did. At the end of a wonderful evening, I was leaving the building when I saw a magnificent Rolls Royce and chauffeur. Edwina was there, deep in a back seat, Paul Robeson climbing in to join her. Weeks later we saw each other again, when Sir Malcolm Sargent was conducting. She said, 'We're going to have a drink at Malcolm's apartment next door. Come and meet him.' When I did, I complimented him, not only on the performance, but how superbly his flat had been furnished. He said, 'Well, Edwina sent a few of these items from Broadlands.'

So far as the Albert Hall building was concerned, I had an unexpected opportunity of improving its acoustics. With Imperial College colleagues, mainly by trial and error rather than calculation, we installed an inner roof of fluted aluminium in place of the dusty old valarium. All I had to do was to listen to the reception from place to place and shout back!

It was to be another twenty years before I found myself with a new music role in London. I was most surprised to be asked to join the Board of Trinity College of Music. A club colleague, who was a banker on the College Board, casually mentioned that the College had, for many years, accumulated teaching and examination fees in Ceylon (now Sri Lanka), but exchange control rules prevented them from being transferred. They were sorely needed here. Had I any ideas? I seemed to recall that a McKinsey client in West Germany was developing its activities in Ceylon and was able to tell him that they would be allowed to pay using the local account. They could reimburse the College, with Exchange Control approval, by transfer from Germany. 'Would you come along and explain this at our next meeting?' he asked. In their Board Room in Mandeville Place, the former home of Lily Langtry, I was warmly thanked by the Chairman, Sir Jack Westrup.

That, I thought, was the end of the matter. Before the next Board meeting, however, Myers (Bill) Foggin, the Director, telephoned. My banker friend had just died. 'We would greatly appreciate it if you would come to the next meeting.' There Westrup asked me to fill the vacancy on the Board. I protested I knew nothing about music – to no avail. So began a sixteen-year association with some illustrious musicians. Every member of the Board automatically received the Honorary Fellowship of the College. Diana, Katharine and Rosalind, all with some musical talent (Katharine then studying Music at Oxford) found it highly amusing to see me, 'not knowing a white note from a black', donned in cap and gown, presented with the Fellowship by Yehudi Menuhin, our President, at a degree ceremony at the Wigmore Hall.

Westrup died the following year and of the two other professors, Hutchins and Murray, we elected the latter, who chaired our meetings excellently. Arthur Hutchins, however, had the best collection of anecdotes which he enjoyed telling us even more than we enjoyed listening. He had graduated in Music at Durham University at the same time as Michael Ramsay in Divinity. Both got Firsts. After the degree ceremony, Ramsay had said, 'I expect to see you one day as Professor of Music here.' 'And I expect to see you as a future Archbishop of Canterbury.' 'Absolutely not,' said Ramsay. 'If ever they were to offer it, I swear I'd refuse it.'

Decades later, they met once more at a Garden Party at Buckingham Palace, Hutchins now Professor at Durham, Ramsay the new Archbishop of Canterbury. 'You've broken your promise,' said Hutchins. 'My dear fellow, I had to accept it. If I didn't, do you know who they would have offered it to?'

Hutchins, for his part, gave his popular lectures from sheets of paper which he crumpled and threw under the podium, one by one. The University Clerk was charged with their publication, but horrified to discover all the sheets were blank.

My years with the College were full of pleasure. When Bill Foggin retired, to be succeeded by Meredith Davies, we honoured Bill with a farewell concert at the Royal Festival Hall, so making possible his wish to conduct Britten's *War Requiem*. Very briefly I became Chairman and nominated my successor, before the College finally moved to Greenwich, on the site of the old Royal Naval College.

When it came to sport, Diana and I were usually spectators, although in my case there had been two 'sporting' exceptions. The first was at the age of eleven when my school magazine recorded my 'Spartanesque and exemplary effort in finishing last in the Mile'. The second was my only sports trophy, nearly sixty years later. In a croquet tournament at

Hurlingham, my opponent pushed my ball through the final hoop, to make me the winner of the tournament. I was presented with an engraved wine glass. Otherwise, Diana and I for many years were lucky enough to be invited to see the tennis semi-finals and finals at Wimbledon. This was thanks to a mutual friend of ours and of Pauline Betz, the American winner of the first postwar championship. She received centre court tickets for life, which were far more valuable than the tiny cash prize for women in 1946.

We missed the country. In 1980 we spotted an early nineteenth-century cottage on the Jurassic Coast of West Dorset, which we bought. We had been on the look-out for a peaceful retreat for some time. We discovered it, Meerhay, near Beaminster, in the heart of Hardy country and found there a haven of privacy each August, Christmas time and frequent weekends, for thirty-three years. Our circle of friends and visitors from London and abroad have grown continuously. We improved our garden, laying out a croquet lawn which has seen some cut-throat competitions in the summer months. And every winter, usually on Boxing Day, Diana has organised a five-mile walk, taking in some of the most beautiful scenery. Thirty or forty of us, across all ages and generations, and their dogs take part – excited, exhilarated and a few eventually exhausted. Diana leads, our children ensure that the planned route is followed, and I bring up the rear with stragglers. We return to the cottage, descending on the 'picnic lunch' like a swarm of locusts.

The conversation is always animated, not least because those taking part, from so many different walks of life, have not previously met. Our visitors' book is fascinating. Among our frequent visitors whose conversation I found most stimulating were Edward Pickering, the newspaper editor, John Peyton, formerly in the Cabinet, recounting much about Harold Macmillan, Robert Armstrong, Cabinet Secretary, and Robin Day, whose weekend cottage was nearby in Morcombelake. Robin was regarded as the innovator of a form of broadcast journalism which changed the character of British politics. What he revealed to me, however, was how he had failed miserably to achieve either of his two dearest ambitions.

He wanted to become a Member of Parliament, if not, a distinguished lawyer. But he achieved neither, nor Director General of the BBC for which he was considered. He denigrated himself as a consequence.

He told me that at the age of five he'd run away from school and after military service and, studying law at Oxford, became President of the Union. Being a little boisterous, he then took part in their debating tour in the United States. He was brilliant as a news presenter, making his name interviewing Nasser in Cairo just after Suez, and winning all the BBC and Independent Television Awards. His style was tough and relentless, but always courteous and fair. He told me, 'When I asked President Truman, 'do you regret having authorised the dropping of the atomic bomb?' he replied thoughtfully. When I attempted searching questions on Margaret Thatcher, however, I could not move her. I asked her, 'Can I get this question in, Prime Minister, because we're having an interview which depends upon my asking some questions? Do you intend to sack certain Ministers?' She replied, 'You're going further than I wish to go.' So I said, 'Well naturally, that's part of my job.' To which she said, 'Yes indeed, and it's part of my job to stop you!"

'You must write this up in your memoirs,' I said. 'I am writing something, possibly entitled 'Grand Inquisitor', but I doubt it will sell well.' 'It will be a best-seller,' I added, encouragingly – 'at least 50,000 copies.' 'Never.' He took on my bet. No sooner than 52,000 copies had been sold, he sent us a case of very decent champagne.

As he and I and his dog sat down together one afternoon, on a cliff top near Golden Cap to admire the view he recounted a talk he'd given as a former patient, to a group of surgical cardiologists in Scotland. He explained he was now in the Departure Lounge of Life, having been treated by two doctors, one of whom committed suicide, the other breaking his neck sleep-walking. He described two post-operative experiences: first on a train journey on the Bournemouth to Winchester line when the passenger seated opposite suddenly said, 'Am I right in thinking we have had the same operation?' It was General Sir Richard Worsley. Passengers, peering in from the corridor, saw two apparently respectable gentlemen in a first-class compartment rolling up their trousers and pointing admiringly at each other's bare legs.

'Then, after a successful multiple bypass operation a lady of my acquaintance happened to be resting her head on my chest, I forget why,' he said. 'I think we were discussing either the public sector borrowing requirement or unilateral nuclear disarmament. 'Anyway,' she suddenly said, 'You're clicking, go and see your doctor.' So I did, to be told, 'You have a disunited mobile sternum, you'd better be opened up and renewed."

It was not long before Robin died, that I had congratulated him on his achievements as 'counsel for the public' and asked him, 'What has been your greatest?' He replied, 'After I had stopped smoking completely, declining a luxurious Havana cigar.'

Among the most original and entertaining people whose friendship we enjoyed were Fernando and Violetta Saverese. He came from a large Neapolitan family, 'originally further north,' he would say, 'until the Roman brigands forced us out'. She was the Russian prima ballerina, Violetta Prokhorova (later Elvin) from the Bolshoi who defected to England around 1952. Her divorce thwarted his judicial career, so after they married they settled in Vico Equense, where they ran an enchanting small hotel by the sea. That is where we first met them after an introduction by a mutual friend.

Fernando was an extraordinary Anglophile. His and Violetta's only child was educated at Harrow. He dressed in British tweeds and was a member of the Reform Club. Despite his quite appalling accent he was more well-read than most English gentlemen and was a quite exceptional letter writer. The only year in which they did not visit us was in 2001. They received an official warning not to come because of 'your mad cow disease, foot and mouth disease and because 60% of your eggs are infected with salmonella'. But then a post-script from Fernando: 'I've tracked this down to a Dutch Ministry of Agriculture report – no doubt trying to protect their own exports to Italy.'

Violetta had danced at Covent Garden with Margot Fonteyn and Moira Shearer, but had lost touch with Moira after retiring to Italy. It gave us great pleasure to reunite them over dinner in London, and their friendship continued until Moira's death.

We eventually moved to London in December 1986. It changed our lives considerably. The children were now in their twenties, becoming independent; we were no longer obliged to maintain a big house with a large garden and we were therefore able both to entertain and to travel more; as we did to Peru, Alaska, India, China, the Middle East, South Africa and Brazil.

There is nothing we enjoy more than having a dozen or so friends to dinner at home. Most of my friends were scientists, diplomats, politicians, businessmen and civil servants; whereas Diana's were art historians, judges and colleagues from a number of charities. Dinner was always lively, Diana's Meerhay mulberry ice cream always a winner and the decibels rose as the wine diminished.

Her passion for art and opera rubbed off on me very many years ago and though we love going to Covent Garden and Glyndebourne for the major productions, Stanley Hall, the Tudor home in Essex of Christopher Stewart Smith, for a wonderful annual event, and such diverse places as Drottningholm and Riga, it is in discovering the lesser known Italian opera houses like Macerata and enjoying that country's festivals, which gives us the greatest pleasure. The opera house in Parma is an absolute gem and the musical standard amazingly high.

Of our two most memorable trips to Italy the first was to Busseto in 2001, to celebrate the centenary of the death of Italy's most famous son, Giuseppe Verdi. We stayed in a splendid small hotel run by Marco, the son of the famous Italian tenor Carlo Bergonzi and enjoyed a morning concert outside the farmhouse at Roncole, where Verdi was born.

The other visit was to the Puccini Festival in Torre del Lago. Fortunately we had been able to find local accommodation, a small room two floors above the restaurant 'Butterfly' near the open air stage. During the performance, a huge piece of scenery collapsed into the orchestra pit, injuring a cellist. I succeeded in summoning an ambulance, but the ensuing union arguments between the orchestra, the maestro and the cast as to whether and when the performance could be resumed, went on for more than two hours. They finally agreed to resume the performance which ended at three o'clock the following morning. Fortunately, unlike all the visitors from afar, all we had to do was to cross the square and negotiate a steep staircase, before collapsing into bed.

The Athenaeum

The potpourri of characters I have written about so far, have been professional colleagues, family, friends and neighbours. No less interesting and diverse have been members of London clubs I joined. Initially, a club simply offered me a convenient base within reach of my office in the heart of London. But that was to change. I never expected that in time I would owe so much to the Athenaeum in particular, for my general education, widening interests, developing understanding, and influencing my thinking, as well as long-lasting friendships which I treasure to this day.

At the end of the war, my naval friends encouraged me to join them at 'The Junior' (the Junior United Service Club). The facilities were excellent, but the club was not particularly well managed and in the face of competition did not survive. A few of us were then admitted to 'The Senior' – built for the heroes of Trafalgar and Waterloo, whose portraits cover the walls. I was told that the Duke of Wellington, on being shown the superb landscape of Waterloo at the top of the staircase, simply remarked, 'Not enough smoke'. The number of serving officers declined in the postwar years and though The Senior merged with the Royal Aero Club, it too gave up the struggle, becoming a further serious casualty in the slimming down of London's club land.

In 1961 my Civil Service boss said to me, 'Look, you're no longer a sailor, you should join another club – my club, the Athenaeum.' I took the opportunity of comparing it with one or two others. At the Travellers, guided by a retired diplomat, after quite a few pink gins he told me, 'In that corner they're swapping tales of their adventures in the Hindu Kush and plotting the downfall of governments.'

At Boodles, I was introduced to someone who Ian Fleming had written about in *Moonraker*, still dressed like 'M' in a 'dark grey suit, white stiff collar and dark blue bow tie with white spots, loosely tied'. My guide at Brooks told me that members had been the owners of sixty-seven Derby winners. I did not know anyone at the Garrick to show me round, but I did at the Reform, a Liberal MP, who recounted the details of how Jules Verne's Phineas Fogg set out around the world in eighty days.

But when Sir Patrick Reilly, my Minister in Paris, later Ambassador there, joined forces with Bertie Blount, then a member of the Athenaeum Committee, and advised me, 'You can judge a man by his tastes and usually his character too by the club he joins – the Athenaeum is the one for you.'

I felt immensely privileged. Those eligible for membership 'had to have published some substantial literary or professional work, or a paper in *The Philosophical Transactions*, or be bishops, judges or Members of Parliament – none of whom can perform their high duty without a competent knowledge of literature.' How could I resist? And that became 'my club' for half a century – so far!

For a variety of reasons, I joined others too: the MCC for many years because I enjoyed watching cricket at Lords; Whites for eleven years, from which I resigned after my proposer and seconder had died and I was rarely able to get there; and the more intimate Beefsteak, which I still frequent when I can. I thoroughly enjoy hearing the exploits of convivial members gathered around a single table there for a traditional lunch – invariably served by 'Charles'. Nor is there any shortage of gossip.

Lord Boothby had been forced to resign from government because of a wartime scandal and his subsequent love life seemed to have run the full social gamut from the heterosexual, with the Devonshires at Chatsworth, to the homosexual, at the Blind Beggar pub in the East End of London.

I had met Victor Cavendish-Bentinck (the Duke of Portland) in Paris, but it was at the Beefsteak he told us that he blamed the war on a Romanian couple whose noisy lovemaking, in a hotel room adjacent to the Marquis of Curzon, kept Curzon awake all night before the crucial decision was taken over the future of the Ruhr.

Kenneth Clark (later Lord Clark of Saltwood) told some of us more than once of his time in Florence with Bernard Berenson, before he was Director of the National Gallery. He presented the superb television series *Civilisation*, but he could also be supercilious. We heard his address at a memorial service: 'Looking around this congregation, one cannot help wondering about the ways of providence in taking away one so universally loved and leaving behind so many who could less usefully be spared.'

And then there was Rex Harrison – Henry Higgins in *My Fair Lady*. He was celebrated for that, but his favourite story was about the behaviour of an irritating customs official at Rome airport. 'Take your hat off when you talk to me, you pompous baboon,' said Rex. The Italians, hearing of this, maintained this was an insult to the officer, the President of the Republic and the flag. 'I had to apologise to the entire nation,' he said. 'Nonetheless they went on to make me a *Commendatore* of the Italian Order of Merit.'

My first recollection of the Athenaeum was a day in February 1963. I hurried into the club, slightly late for a meeting over afternoon tea, rushed upstairs and the Hall Porter called out, 'Excuse me, sir, are you a member of this club?' 'Yes, a new one,' I said. 'My apologies, sir, I have never before seen one of our members running up the staircase!'

We were joined for tea by Sir Alan Burns who was soon telling us of his life and responsibilities in 1905 on Colonial Service in the Leeward Islands.

By the mid-Seventies, with less overseas travel, my club visits became more frequent and 'being seen around', like many others, was asked to join the General Committee. I was intrigued to see how members from quite different disciplines and walks of life could together contribute to the club's welfare. In operational terms, they looked to the secretary and staff. In terms of top management and of policy they were usually unanimous. Occasionally I did sense rival traditionalist and modernist viewpoints. These became apparent among the membership much later, notably in resolving the burning issue of women members.

By the Eighties, the Secretary told me that a few opening speakers at club dinners were asking if I would introduce them. This I did and enjoyed. I encouraged them to be slightly indiscreet if they could. Sir Robin Butler, on retirement as Secretary of the Cabinet, came to speak on *Yes Minister* and obliged by revealing his quick thinking. The occasion was in 1982, in his office at No 10, when he discovered his trousers were torn. He sent them out for express repair. He was seated behind his desk trouser-less when the Attorney General came in. Robin couldn't stand so he gesticulated wildly, pointing to the ceiling and mouthing, 'the office is bugged, we can't speak now.' And Michael Havers, with appreciative gestures, crept out.

When Roy Jenkins (Lord Jenkins of Hillhead), after being President of the European Union, came to speak on 'Europe Unfrozen' I revealed that in his student days at Oxford he had collided with the Socialist party and founded a Democrat Socialist party. It survived for just one year and remained forgotten. That was forty years before the SDP was founded. Over dinner, incidentally, he extolled our claret and proceeded to compare it with the Mouton-Rothschild he had been served by the family at Waddesden. On that occasion he spotted the heraldic shield on a fire screen and asked his Rothschild host, 'Is that your family motto?' 'Yes. It means 'service' and, by God, we get it!'

Dr Mary (now Lady) Archer, a member of Lloyd's Council and a colleague on our Tercentenary Foundation, was another speaker. In introducing her I said she had lived up to the hopes of her parents. They had sent her to Cheltenham Ladies' College, where the school motto was 'may she grow in heavenly light' and she went on to be an authority on solar energy. She was Chairman of Cambridge University Hospitals and also of Lloyd's Hardship Committee, which considered claims and made financial provision for many distressed Names. One or two of my Athenaeum Club colleagues who had been hard hit themselves wanted her to speak so they had an opportunity to question her. She readily agreed. On the night, I saw her husband, Jeffrey, hovering at the Coffee Room entrance. He told me he wanted to hear Mary speak. As he was not a member, I had to tell him he couldn't join us, but could listen in from another room.

On the spur of the moment, I added, 'I don't suppose you can tell me anything about Mary for my introduction, which would surprise her?' 'Yes,' he said. 'When she was six years old, her headmistress told her, 'You don't burst into tears, Mary, just because you came second!'' She was surprised anyone knew. With a typically gracious compliment, she told them: 'The erudition of Alcon's questions to Fellowship candidates is matched only by the occasionally deceptive courtesy with which he puts them.'

At the end of an excellent evening, I accompanied her to her car in St James' Square and remarked on Jeffrey being so different from her. I plucked up courage to go on to ask, rather cheekily, 'Why did you marry him?' It was in a private conversation that she told me.

Another planned speaker was Prebendary Chad Varah, founder of the Samaritans, and a Companion of Honour. His life and sermons were unconventional and he believed in reincarnation. But in agreeing to speak on 'What happens when we die', he insisted that I should be the one to introduce him.

Diana and I were leaving for America just as he was taken ill. The Secretary said he was expected to be back from hospital in good time to give his talk. But when we returned, that very morning, he was still in hospital. Too late to cancel, I was asked to speak on that subject in his place. I hadn't the slightest idea what I could say. Then, by a stroke of good fortune, as we were entering the Coffee Room I overheard a guest say, 'I had an extraordinary experience once. I thought I was going to drown...' That was my moment of inspiration. After a very short introduction I asked, 'Have any of you here thought that you were suddenly about to die?' Four hands went up, so I invited them to recount their own stories. An animated debate followed and we ran out of time. Chad Varah heard about that episode and thereafter tried to recruit me to all his other good causes.

Time and again I was to discover the remarkable knowledge and intellectual calibre of some of our members. Making my way to a lunch table one day, Enoch Powell waved me over. He had been both a Professor of Greek and a war time Brigadier whilst still in his twenties, before becoming a controversial MP and minister. He was lunching with another MP, Peter Tapsell, later Father of the House. 'Tell me,' Powell said suddenly, 'why were there no breathing holes in English helmets between 1200 and 1225?'

'I have no idea,' I replied. 'I've been staying with Peter in the country,' he continued, 'and we saw the murals in the village church; quite definitely the barrel helmets of their armour had no breathing holes.'

As I had recently become a liveryman of the ancient Armourers & Brasiers, I promised to ask the Master of the Royal Armouries, an expert, when next dining in the Livery Hall. 'There must have been breathing holes,' he said. 'No doubt the murals were badly preserved.' I passed this reply to Enoch Powell, who quickly sent me extracts of erudite publications and a Kirkstead Abbey photograph to pass back. Eventually I received a call from Guy Wilson, Keeper of Armour: 'Following Mr Powell's casual observations, we will have to revise our opinion completely.'

Members of the club had, by then, attracted more Nobel Prizes for their work than any other institution in the world. When I accompanied the

Swedish Ambassador Leif Leifland to show him the Nobel Book I could not resist saying, 'Before we elect a candidate to the club we make sure he has won the Nobel Prize.' He immediately replied, 'And before we select a Prize winner, we always check that he is a member of the Athenaeum.'

Other members with whom I had fascinating conversations and learned much included Isaiah Berlin, who came to England from Latvia and Petrograd. A great philosopher, becoming President of the British Academy and receiving the Order of Merit, he held us spellbound. At great speed he would hold forth on some aspect of the history of ideas. He pronounced 'recapitulation' as though it was all one syllable. Once, when he was happily talking on at great speed I had to interrupt him. 'Sorry, I must go, I'm meeting Diana at the Royal Opera House, we're off to see *Boris Godunov*.' 'Ah yes,' he replied, 'I heard Chaliapin sing that role at the Mariinsky Theatre, in the winter of 1916.'

Then there was David Hunt, a predecessor as Chairman, once Private Secretary to Attlee and to Churchill, a diplomat and author of the 'Winds of Change' speech, famously delivered by Harold Macmillan. With a formidable memory, he became Mastermind of Masterminds, ascribing it to his military training when he was Field Marshal Alexander's Chief of Intelligence. When Alex wanted him in Europe he was spotted bathing near Carthage. The High Command was furious: 'Why on earth are you there?' 'For inspiration; it was here that Hannibal received advice from his own intelligence officer, then known as his Soothsayer. His name was Bogus.' When I gave the Address at St Margaret's, Westminster on the occasion of his Thanksgiving Service in November 1998, I retold this story.

And in a memorable conversation with Yehudi Menuhin, just before he died, I asked him what the club meant to him. 'It's a place for privacy, personal service and space; civilised, courteous, respectful and friendly, with a time for talk and a time for silence, a place that honours learning, but is not over-awed by it.'

In 1989, the General Committee elected me Chairman. It came as a surprise and, given the long line of distinguished predecessors, for me a signal honour. The committee members and staff were so capable, I was sure the club would continue to thrive without any onerous involvement on my part. I asked whether there were any disagreeable things I had to do. 'Yes,' they said, 'in the absence of unanimity decide whether a troublesome member should be called upon to resign.'

I looked up the precedents and there were quite a few. It had happened to Bertrand Russell, the philosopher. Following on his anti-conscription campaign in World War I, he marched from the Club and lay prostrate on the church floor. A policeman started beating him with a truncheon. The congregation called out, 'Stop! He's a famous philosopher.' The policeman beat harder. 'Stop! He's the brother of an Earl.' 'I'm very sorry, sir,' said the policeman. Russell had to resign in 1916, but was re-elected in the 1950s and made good use of the club. He gave us these memorable epigrams:

> *I would never die for my beliefs because I might be wrong*
> *War does not determine who is right − only who is left*
> *The place of the father in a modern suburban family is a very small one,*
> *particularly if he plays golf*

Throughout my stint as Chairman I was so ably supported by Brian Gilmore, my Deputy, that I could not fail. In due course Brian became Chairman and my co-Trustee too. As a highly knowledgeable classicist, I turned to him for guidance: 'What exactly is a Prebendary?' I asked. 'It is from the Latin,' he said: 'Praebo (I donate) and Benda (an alcoholic evening) and it means Chad will pay for the drinks!'

One of my pleasant duties as Chairman was to welcome Ambassadors accredited to the Court of St James. We enjoyed entertaining and being entertained by Baron Herman von Richthoven, grandson of the famous Red Baron, the World War I German flying ace, and also Boris Pankin. He had been an influential Soviet newspaper editor who advanced the cause of Glasnost and Perestroika. Gorbachev appointed him Foreign Minister, following Molotov and Gromyko. He told me, 'Politics is NOT something I enjoy. After a hundred days in the job I chose to come to London. Here I had to haul down the Embassy's Hammer & Sickle and say goodbye to all those of my staff who were Armenians, Byelorussians and Ukrainians – they were now foreigners, returning to their own countries.'

Chairmen could be re-elected to serve for three years, as I was. On just two occasions I had to recommend to the Committee whether a member who had misbehaved should be required to go. In both cases, my advice was that they should simply 'make themselves scarce for a while'. This was accepted. One continuing *cause célèbre* was that of women membership. Under our rules women never had been inadmissible; members just did not put their names forward. Ten years earlier, when Margaret Thatcher became our first female Prime Minister, we had a dilemma, for all Prime Ministers were invited. I told the Committee that though she was an honorary member of the Carlton Club she probably did not wish to accept another. As a result I was asked by the club to sound her out and, by Margaret, to graciously decline.

Over the years, however, attitudes changed and after three referendums, finally by a large majority, women could become full members. Many did so, to the enhancement of the club. The few members who threatened to resign over this issue changed their minds.

My final social event as Chairman was the centenary celebration of the Club Ballot Day in 1892. It was famous for the fierce canvassing of 1,600 candidates – some on the waiting list for seventeen years – and for the *Illustrated London News'* fine portrait of the occasion, which they presented to the club. Happily, when we invited their current editor to join us, we discovered we could celebrate together. It was also their 150th anniversary.

Over the following few years, whilst no less busy otherwise, I had a further approach. Donald Coggan, formerly Archbishop of Canterbury, now a Trustee of the club, said to me, 'I propose to retire as Trustee and propose you as my successor.' 'You can't retire,' I replied, 'You have lots of active years ahead of you.' 'No, it's time I went, but I won't be idle. In any event, I spell retirement with a letter 'Y', like a tyre going in for a re-tread. I intend to write a substantial work on the Psalms.' 'Surely there are plenty of books on the Psalms?' 'Not like the one I have in mind, with all the source material I have. Do you know, ordinands now only have to study a little Latin and Greek? I had to master Hebrew and Aramaic too. Incidentally the occasional quotes you made from the Old Testament, in introducing speakers did not go unrecognised.' Needless to say he completed his two-volume work in four years.

I went on to put in almost twelve years as his successor until I retired in 2008. Two of the most memorable social events were our 175th anniversary in 1999 and the centenary dinner of the *Entente Cordiale* in 2004.

On our 150th anniversary in 1974, Prince Philip as Honorary Life Member had spoken. Twenty-five years later, when asked again, he replied, 'You don't want me to get my notes from the file and repeat it – you'd better do it!' And so he sent a message, proposing a Toast to the Athenaeum 'as the bastion of intelligent and civilised life'. It was left to me to respond. The club decided to publish my remarks and allow me to include them in these memoirs. [see Appendix, page 399]

In its preparation I was greatly helped by contributions from individual members. One I did not use, but well worth recounting came from the Lord Habgood (Archbishop of York). He quoted a story from Bell's life of Randall Davidson. When Davidson's appointment to Canterbury was announced in 1903, Canon Scott Holland of St Paul's wrote an article pointing out the dangers of his attachment to the Athenaeum:

> '*There dwell the sirens who are apt to beguile and bewitch him. They have ceased to be mermaids with harps and have adopted the disguise of elderly and excellent gentlemen of reputation, who lead you aside into corners and, in impressive whispers, inform you of what you will not do and what the intelligent British public will not stand. The Bishop has a*

deep veneration for the judgment and the wisdom of important laity of this type. Yet the Athenaeum is not the shrine of infallibility. Its elderly common sense has no prophetic 'afflatus'.'

Davidson was undeterred, and the Club responded handsomely by giving a special dinner for him, chaired by the Prime Minister...

For nearly two centuries now, the club has perpetuated its original polymath culture, maintained standards of dress and behaviour and safeguarded the all-important balance between tradition and modernisation. And in keeping with the times, the election of women as members, some now serving on club committees, has proved to be a conspicuous success.

For me it has been an honour and a pleasure to have been Chairman of the Athenaeum for the maximum three years and Trustee for a further twelve whilst the club has flourished. Appointed under the old rules before the retirement age was sensibly changed to seventy-eight, I could only leave by resigning when I was eighty-eight, thereby making way for much-needed new blood.

CHAPTER XII

Jobs Offered, Accepted, Declined

By the end of the Seventies the publicity my activities had attracted resulted in a rapid succession of invitations to add to them.

I had certainly been engaged in a wide variety of endeavours and developed contacts in many walks of life. I was surprised however by the number of approaches I received from unexpected quarters – quite 'out of the blue' – to join public and private institutions, regulatory bodies and educational, scientific, engineering and financial concerns.

In each case I weighed up the pros and cons. Would they be compatible with each other and with family life? One or two I did not accept, but in one at least, which I would have accepted, the formal invitation did not materialise, as I will explain.

Taken together, for the following twenty years I was fully occupied with an exceptionally interesting portfolio of at least ten of them.

The Press Council

Without knowing who proposed me, I was invited in 1975 by the Appointments Commission, chaired by Lord Redcliffe-Maud, to become a Lay Member of The Press Council. Founded twenty-two years earlier, to adjudicate on complaints made against the Press and build up a code of conduct, in accordance with the highest professional standards, it was certainly needed. I was in my last year in McKinsey; it was an appointment initially for three years, not demanding much time, so, with approval, I readily accepted.

Notwithstanding the development of television, politicians continued to believe in the power of the Press to determine the content of the political agenda. Newspapers, having established close economic and editorial links with television companies, felt reasonably secure. But then came the economic slump which made them vulnerable, and this was exacerbated by the industrial relations problems arising from new print technology. Criticism followed from Parliament and from government.

Politicians wanted an acceptable public image, government wanted to test public reactions to their policies and not see fundamental issues trivialised; most were opposed to the private lives of public figures being pursued beyond the bounds of decency. Tension centred around the duty of the Press to expose and criticise and was heightened by resentment against invasion of privacy and lax editorial standards. A Royal Commission was set up to look into the economics, management and ownership issues involved, and the responsibilities of the Council. I arrived soon after, when Sir Hartley Shawcross was Chairman.

My fellow Lay members came from all walks of life: a Bishop, the Rt Rev Bill Westwood, a comprehensive school headmistress, Dame Mary Green, and Dame Jean Rivett-Drake, formerly Director of the Women's Royal Army Corps. Sir Edward Pickering was the most experienced Press representative together with Sir Denis Hamilton of *The Times* and Charles Wintour of the *Express*. Admiral Sir John Treacher joined us a little later. When I asked him what his interest was he said, 'As I was running the Playboy Club in Park Lane in retirement, it seemed a good idea to join too, a council with a Bishop as a member.'

From the outset I wondered, given our make-up, how effective we could be. The Appointments Commission chairman was certainly non-partisan, but the Council comprised editors, representatives of proprietors and trade unions too. Collectively we were called upon to censure the Press when they themselves were footing the bill for adjudications and regulations they often disliked – out of the proceeds, as they put it 'of giving the public what it would buy'.

At our meetings, we tackled a selection of the hundreds of complaints a year. In cross-examining journalists and editors, the most flagrant breaches of acceptable standards concerned chequebook journalism and questions of privacy. We aimed to get compliance with our code. Very often we did, with published corrections and apologies. My early impression was of growing numbers of complaints being made against inexperienced journalists, but some adjudications were being neglected by experienced editors and, in a competitive industry, new temptations for sensationalism were arising.

How could our success be measured? Did an increase in the number of complaints signify a deterioration of Press conduct, or a higher regard by the public of the work of the Council? Did fewer complaints mean a more influential and effective Council, less to complain about, or a loss of confidence in the value of our work? We came to the conclusion that publicising our activities was the main cause of more complaints addressed to us.

My appointment was renewed twice, enabling me to serve for seven and a half years as Sir Patrick (later Lord Neill of Bladen) succeeded to the Chairmanship, followed by Sir Zelman Cowen (formerly Governor General of Australia). Despite occasional disagreements with the National Union of Journalists, our procedure was speeded up, we became more decisive and came to be regarded as far better than our broadcasting counterpart. In fact, we became a model for arrangements in some other countries too. We aimed to adjudicate between rival interests. Three Prime Ministers had commented adversely on the consequences of untimely Press publication, jeopardising government achievements, whilst there was a wider public concern that something that should have been known was being swept under the carpet. Our adjudications indicated where the line should be drawn – e.g., the exercise of freedom of conscience to stop publication, when the *Camden Journal* operators refused to print a National Front advertisement, a stoppage of *The Times* when the print unions criticised remarks of David Astor, and sabotage in stopping newspapers altogether, thereby making a direct attack on the freedom of the Press.

In cases of invasion of privacy, we distinguished between a responsible interest in public figures – the case of Maureen Colquhoun MP, who would be facing the electorate – and prurient curiosity in the wholly private life of her partner and her harassed children. We even aimed to show in our adjudications how a balance should be struck between the need to reflect contemporary morals and manners, and actually trying to influence them. Above all was the balance between ethics and commercialism. We came forward with a Declaration of Principle, in the important matter of chequebook journalism. This was made after the Moors murder trial, where the chief prosecution witness had a contract to receive payment from the Press. It was highly effective and adhered to for some years.

What concerned most of us, however, was our lack of adequate power. We were being labelled as 'toothless,' or a 'paper tiger'. Royal Commissions and Parliaments had always decided it was better not to interfere by statutory control, but we certainly needed to make our adjudications more feared and effective action taken. A few of us recommended that we refer the most serious cases to an independent tribunal. This was not accepted by the powerful National Union of Journalists. We pressed them, but by 1980 they withdrew their support of the Council altogether. Some new arrangement was necessary. I discussed the options with others, most of all with Sir Edward Pickering. He and I shared the same view. Urbane and unflappable as Deputy Chairman and Press member, he was the pioneer in establishing the Press Complaints Commission which followed. No-one did more than he to counter any challenge to Press freedom, yet he insisted on the highest professional standards from his journalists whilst being invariably loyal to them when they were attacked by their newspaper proprietors.

I had become the longest serving Council member when I retired in 1982. A year later over lunch, Zelman Cowen invited me to 'reflect on my earlier views with hindsight'. This I particularly appreciated as he himself was totally opposed to any form of government control. 'The only authority,' he had said, 'was that of persuasion'. He was inundated with paper at the time so my reply was fairly brief.

What we were aiming to achieve, I wrote, *might be out of reach. In the USA freedom of speech was written into the Constitution. In South Africa and totalitarian states there was full statutory control. That was by far too high a price for us to pay. What we should look for was a more demanding system of accountability for journalists, editors and proprietors, both for what was published and the methods used to acquire the information. There would always be lapses in professional standards, morality and misjudgements, but transparency would help restore public trust. And as years went by new information technologies, competition, management methods, and cultural changes would emerge, so from time to time the measures to be taken would have to be reviewed and revised. Difficult cases, such as those balancing public interest with the right to privacy could often be considered by senior judges and their judgements guide the code of practice for the profession. In my view our successors, as regulators, should all be individuals independent of government, but with much greater powers to control and penalise. Only if this should fail, should some element of statutory control be contemplated. On rare occasions this could be necessary, but it should be a last resort given the risk of losing our precious Press freedom.* I lodged my note with Kenneth Morgan, the Director.

We continued to see the Pickerings, our neighbours in Dorset, for many years thereafter. With his wife Rosemary, 'Pick' regularly joined our family and friends on Boxing Day coastal walks. He would tell me of his own experiences as a radar instructor in the war. 'When my other 'talents' were discovered', he said, 'I was quickly sent off to draft communiqués for General Eisenhower, to encapsulate the very different inputs from the British and American service chiefs.'

On his eightieth birthday, Rupert Murdoch threw a party for him at Stationers' Hall. Pick told us that Sir Keith Murdoch, Rupert's father in Australia, originally telephoned Lord Beaverbrook asking for Pickering to give Rupert his first job on coming down from Oxford. When Rupert proposed the birthday toast he said, 'Only Pick could have survived as

Editor under three tyrants; the proprietors of the *Mirror*, the *Mail* and the *Express*, before joining *The Times*.' To which Pick replied, 'I really owe my survival to a small book of Chinese proverbs I was given as a boy. One said, 'When you find yourself caught in a cage with a tiger, you quickly learn in which direction to stroke its fur.''

Pick's memorial service was my last link with former Press Council colleagues. Then in the post one day a letter arrived. It was from A&C Black, publishers: 'We regret to inform you that in the forthcoming issue of *Who's Who* we have made an error, now too late to correct. Instead of Lay Member of the Press Council you appear as Lady Member...'

The Zoo

Nothing could have been in greater contrast to that than the short stint I served on the Council of the Zoological Society. In the 1940s and '50s I had been a Fellow of the Geological Society and the Royal Meteorological Society and the Institutes of Physics and Electrical Engineers. I knew nothing about animals.

John and Mary Peyton, our West Dorset neighbours in the village of Merriott, frequently joined us on our country walks in the Eighties. John and I had once served together in the Ministry of Defence, forty years earlier, but did not meet for he was a Parliamentary Secretary and I a junior civil servant. He went on to be a member of the Cabinet in the Heath administration, declined an invitation to join Margaret Thatcher's, accepted a peerage and among other appointments became Treasurer of the Zoological Society of London.

In 1989 he told me that Lord Zuckerman, who had done so much for the Zoo, suggested he could do worse than recruit me to join its Council. Zuckerman had not only had a profound influence in the Cabinet Office, but his name had been synonymous with the fortunes of the Zoological Society ever since the 1930s after writing *The Social Life of Monkeys and*

Apes. We had met in Paris at a NATO conference in the 1950s. All I remember of our conversation, however, were stories about his friends – the Gershwins, William Walton and Ben Nicholson. I said to John, 'My only qualification for the Zoo is that I did once win a school essay prize entitled *Whipsnade!*' I joined its Council as one of 'the good and the great'.

The Council had responsibility for over thirty-six acres of Regents Park, which were attracting up to three million visitors a year, but running into financial trouble.

Two years earlier the Department of the Environment, the Zoo's sponsors, had announced a once and for all capital contribution of £10 million. Now in the recession, the income and number of visitors had fallen, maintenance was being discontinued alarmingly, and local residents were objecting to the Council's future plans. Though inadequate, the Council had been obliged to accept the Government funds. When Peyton was told by Chris Patten, then Minister, 'but you agreed to accept it,' he replied, 'I have never been in the position of a drowning man, but I would never say, when offered a lifebelt, even a thin one, 'No, take it away, I would like a bigger one.''

When the Council met, we agreed with others that the Zoo operators would have to concentrate on conservation, education and research and economise in exhibiting a large collection of animals. In any event there was a growing public reaction against keeping animals caged in an urban environment, which it had done since 1928. We made the point that London was the only national zoo not receiving regular public funding. The Royal Botanical Gardens and Natural History Museum were supported by other government departments. In my view the Zoo should now operate on a lower cost base and be selective in its plans. It was time for a review by consultants. Four contenders were considered. McKinsey's were brought in, with the agreement of the Department of the Environment, and undertook the study without charge. We prepared a proposal for the Government.

A year later Lord Peyton told us, to his dismay, that the Government had finally refused to recognise they had any sponsorship or supportive role whatsoever. Ministers, rejecting a review of a select committee, maintained that the Society was just a private sector operation so, by disposing of our assets, we could have sufficient funds to reduce the size of the Zoo, remove the animals and pay off the staff.

This was announced the very next day, *The Times* stated, 'This marks an end to a three-month poker game between the Zoo and the Government over funding, with the Government having in effect, called the Zoo's bluff.' The Council maintained that the Zoo had to be kept open for a further year. Peyton, considering that the Government just did not believe what he said to be true, resigned forthwith.

On 13th July when I opened the newspapers I read the front page report 'Fifth Member Quits' – naming me. Robert Armstrong, Alastair McAlpine of West Green, Clinton-Davies, the former European Commissioner and Walton – all Peers. Our younger son Edward contacted the newspaper to complain that I was actually the third to resign, not the fifth, but having only a second class stamp available, my letter arrived last!

The saga continued long after we all departed. In the meantime I had been made Fellow of the Society. My one happy memory, however, was of a fascinating conversation with a scientific member of the Zoo's staff, an authority on bird navigation. He told me of a flock of shearwaters taken from their nests on the Welsh coast to unknown territory on the NE coast of the USA and released. Within a few days, they had found their way home. Their maps and compasses comprised optics, acoustics, magnetism and celestial mechanics. The wonders of nature never cease to amaze me.

Lloyd's of London

When we moved to Denham Village, many of our neighbours appeared to be 'Names' at Lloyd's. Income tax rates were at an all time high, but could be reduced dramatically, in return for an apparently acceptable risk. They encouraged me to join them. I checked out its suitability as best I could with Freshfields. Lloyd's had invited Lord Cromer with Sir Alexander Johnson and Sir Alex Cairncross to propose how they should operate to expand their capacity.

I came before a Rota Committee to be 'vetted'. They hinted at their exclusivity, alluded to their patriotism and, quoting from the Cromer Report, I would be 'playing a part in adding to Britain's invisible exports and Lloyd's' good name overseas'. I joined in 1968.

My association turned out to be a bittersweet experience. For nearly three centuries Lloyd's had been a self-regulated private marketplace for insurance. My forty years there resulted in a substantial financial loss for me, but hardship and tragedy for others, and eleven suicides. Then almost by accident, my chance came to contribute to a humanitarian initiative, which extended over the final twenty years.

Financial returns were good at first. When problems in regulation began to arise journalists were critical. Sir Henry Fisher, a former judge was called in to investigate and recommended safeguards. To restore confidence under a new (1982) Lloyd's Act, the committee of Lloyd's would be supervised henceforth by a Council and an independent Chief Executive. Eight places on the Council were to be filled by external Names elected by ballot. Gordon Richardson, by now the Bank of England Governor, suggested I stood. Even though I was unknown in insurance circles, out of eighty-three candidates I attracted four thousand votes and, surprisingly, came second in the poll.

At our first Council meeting, joined by the nine leading underwriters and brokers, Sir Peter Green, the Chairman, welcomed us to the luxury of Leeds Castle. But I was disturbed by what I was hearing. Key statistics I'd asked for were not kept; two Department of Trade investigations into our largest insurance brokers were underway and we were locked in litigation with one of our very own Council members, Ian Posgate. As we were going into dinner I was told that Sir Peter Green himself, a director and shareholder of a Cayman Island company, to which Names' funds were transferred, was receiving benefits not available to them. I tackled him over a glass of brandy about this, but he assured me and two colleagues standing alongside 'that was nothing improper'.

A greater concern was to follow. When we asked to see a full version of the Cromer report and of the Committee's subsequent actions we were told we couldn't. In the interests of Names, Cromer had stipulated that certain all-important changes be made by the committee. It was very much later that I succeeded in being shown the records, deposited in the Guildhall Library. With disbelief I read the Committee's Minutes. At its seven meetings, under Henry Mance, in January and February 1970, the Committee had decided: 'It was dangerous to compile statistics and underwriters' loss records for publication; they would not abolish guarantee policies, nor agree on the responsibilities of underwriting agents.' The trouble this would lead to was momentous.

Peter Miller succeeded Sir Peter Green as Chairman a year later and presented him with the coveted Gold medal, as 'one of the greatest leaders of Lloyd's we have ever seen'. Almost immediately Green was summoned to face Lord Wilberforce's Disciplinary Committee. He was found guilty of repeated discreditable conduct from 1978–82, censured and fined £20,000. I asked what other skeletons there were in the cupboard, but firmly told I was unduly concerned.

My seven external colleagues and I, all unpaid, were kept busy on Council committees. I realised, when chairing Rota Committees myself, that candidates did not know what questions to ask, could not judge the risks they took in accepting unlimited liability, or the costs and benefits of 'stop-loss' policies. The few Americans I interviewed better understood what they were letting themselves in for. I said to a prospective Name in the presence of his agent, 'You realise you are liable to your last pair of cufflinks?' I could tell he had been forewarned. We were exaggerating to shake his resolve to be admitted to this exclusive club. Many of those admitted had assets largely tied up in a single property, but did not have the liquidity needed to meet losses. Some employees in the market who sought stop-loss policies to limit their own risks were told of penalties for disloyalty, 'for not having total confidence in their directors'. Attempts to get disclosure of relevant information were frequently thwarted.

By October 1983 when Robin Leigh Pemberton succeeded as Governor, many of us began to lose heavily. He was invited to lunch by the Council. He asked for my personal comments on developments, so I wrote to him. In essence, there was a tradition of entrepreneurial initiative and speculative risk-taking, but action was urgently needed to establish a framework for fuller disclosure of information, for discipline, and to suspend malefactors. I had an uneasy feeling that the growing reinsurance market was taking on risks they did not fully understand and reinsuring them with other reinsurers who knew and understood even less of what they risked.

On 22nd November, the Governor invited me to the Bank to discuss this. Ian Hay Davison, our Chief Executive, had been recruited by Gordon Richardson and charged with the task of 'cleaning up Lloyd's'. Davison gave a pledge to 'pick out every rotten apple in the barrel'. He called for more transparency: 'If you let in the sun, the mists will fade away.' He was right, but could also be insensitive. He said, 'I was able to catch the crooks, but was let down by the authorities who would not act on the evidence.'

My Council colleague Sir Kenneth Berrill's comment was, 'Ian has butchery skills, but lacks cookery skills.' Peter Miller himself refused absolutely to accept Davison's advice or even position of independence. 'I am Prime Minister, Davison is head of the Civil Service.' It did not work. Davison suddenly read out his letter of resignation to an astonished Council and walked out.

By 1986, I was a member of eight committees, a record apparently, including Finance, External Relations, Investment, Claims and Recoveries, Suspension (dealing with eight cases of expulsion) and Chairman of two others. It meant a briefcase full of papers most days. I was asked to go to America for a few days, because the acquisition of a US firm, Toplis and Harding, would facilitate Lloyd's' valuable insurance business in the dollar area, and my McKinsey experience would be valuable. As I had no office at Lloyd's, the rules required me to pay for my own ticket and accommodation and claim reimbursement. This I did – only to be taxed at 60% on the expenses because I was travelling 'from home to work' and not 'from work to work'.

When my time was up after four years, though the oldest, I was asked to continue on the Council for a further term of four years, if re-elected. I did so because the all important data collection and analysis promised was still lacking, losses were compounding with a concentration of disasters and under-reserving and downright fraud was rife.

As Chairman of the Training Committee, I went out on a limb and recommended that prospective underwriters and some agents should be required to pass some professional examination. This was unheard of. Typically, a young man sat alongside an underwriter for ten years, kept the records and his nose clean until he was finally allowed to write a little routine business. In another ten years he would blossom into a fully qualified underwriter, becoming 'a world expert', for example in the shipping of cocoa beans from Apapa to Liverpool. All this time, he had sat in the same Box, meeting the same brokers, talking about the same type of business. All of this was within the provisions of the 1870 Lloyd's Act of Parliament.

The immediate internal reaction to an examination was quite hostile. The chairman of the Insurers Brokers Committee said to me, 'The life blood of the London market over three hundred years has been its entrepreneurial skill. It would be a tragedy if we prevented someone participating merely because he was not good at passing exams. High standards can be better achieved by on the job training, careful supervision and pride in the market place.' Attitudes took time to change, but I persisted and within two years an examination, in close collaboration with the Chartered Insurance Institute system was agreed – active underwriters being excused, at least for the time being.

Davison had been succeeded in March 1986 by Alan Lord. He had held a wide range of senior Whitehall appointments, and went on to the Court of the Bank of England. His was a safe pair of hands. However, operational costs were escalating dramatically. In the early 1970s they were just 4% of premium income, now they were almost 14%. The Government was under pressure to bring Lloyd's within the Financial Services Bill. The Neill Enquiry was set up to revise our Regulatory arrangements. I gave evidence and, in spite of my criticism, was re-elected to the Council. Patrick Neill remarked, 'It must have been a case of 'better the devil you know''! I had, incidentally, stated that many Names were recruited by over-persuasion. Neill looked into it and confirmed that in 1985, 179 Names had been sponsored by individuals who received commission from Underwriting Agents for their successful efforts. The personal wealth of many was totally inadequate to meet possible losses.

Lloyd's Tercentenary Foundation

My opportunity of making a long-term contribution arose from a paper I had presented to the Council in 1985. Lloyd's would be 300 years old in three years' time. I was asked to propose how we should celebrate.

I could not discover when exactly Edward Lloyd had opened his coffee house. The first reference appeared in an advertisement in the *London Gazette* for 18th February 1689 (ascribed to 1688 as that year began in March), but records covering the previous two years were missing. My Committee proposed an arbitrary date, which fitted in to the Lloyd's timetable of events. Our aims would be both philanthropic and social. We sounded out all at Lloyd's, inviting ideas and received many. The Non-Marine Association wanted scholarships for entrants into the insurance industry. Motor Underwriters simply wanted to advertise for more Lloyd's policy holders, which would not have been a charitable purpose. Aviation suggested financing youth unemployment and inner-city projects; others wanted a new Lloyd's yacht, to replace the Lutine. Le Boeuf, the US Company, sought international research on environmental hazards.

As Lloyd's was such a famous City institution, Peter Miller was keen on having a great London firework display, accompanied by the music of Jean Michel Jarre. Then we were told the cost would be $4 million: many members of the Council were keen to sponsor a new operatic production at the Royal Opera House for their 1988 programme – to remain in its repertoire for eight years. Their first choice of opera was *Carmen*. But when I proposed this to Robin Hambro, Covent Garden's Development Director, she said *Carmen* had already been reserved by the London Taxi Drivers' Association!

Our main endeavour, therefore, was to establish a Foundation, a charitable trust in perpetuity for the advancement of research for the public benefit – medical, scientific, engineering, environmental or business-related. The Council was quite clear; the research was to be undertaken for its own sake and not for the benefit of the insurance industry. I was delighted. This was almost a replica of the programme of grants which I had helped to initiate forty years earlier for the Humanitarian Trust of the Hebrew University of Jerusalem. I was appointed to be the first Chairman, stepping down to Deputy when Sir Peter Miller eventually stood down as Chairman of the Council. We invited and received the active participation of Sir Edwin Nixon, Dame Mary Donaldson, Kingman Brewster of Yale and Oxford, Sir Brian Flowers of Imperial College and the Nuffield Foundation and, later, Mary Archer. The Lloyd's Central Fund contributed £1 million and our assets climbed to £4 million, thanks to donations and investment gains.

We went on to award over a hundred one- and two-year Fellowships, all to quite outstanding postdoctoral candidates in the UK. There was much competition. The research projects ranged from malaria vaccines, diabetes, cancer genes, lung inflammation and leukaemia, to safety in passenger transport, stresses in aerofoil structures and even theoretical aspects of UK public expenditure and export strategy. In time these Fellows came to be leaders of highly successful teams, building on their own original ideas and achievements.

My fellow Trustees' interrogation of candidates was formidable in their own specialist fields. Nor was there any shortage of anecdotes to go with them. Brian Flowers regaled us with one experience as Rector of Imperial College when he was approached by the Foreign Office. President Ceauşescu of Romania and his wife were about to make a state visit to Britain, coinciding with a degree ceremony when their son, studying at Imperial, was due to graduate. Mme Ccauşcscu informed the Palace that she wanted to receive an Honorary Degree herself on the same occasion. Flowers replied that it was the University not the College that conferred degrees, but in any event, their son had failed in his exams and would not be there! The Foreign Office, duly embarrassed, conveyed this to the Palace. Flowers then received a formal invitation to spend the weekend at Windsor Castle, as guests of the Queen and Prince Philip – so as to explain this to the Ceauşescus themselves!

Over the years, research costs were growing faster than our capacity to fund them. There was, too, an easing of the Charity Commissioners' rules which allowed funding in projects of value to the insurance industry as a whole, e.g. the nature and incidence of risk. This was attractive to the Trustees as well as the Lloyd's community and in 2008 we made our first major grant for this purpose. By then, after twenty years, it was long past my time to stand down. I was eighty-eight. I retired. There was a farewell lunch, an honorary Fellowship of Lloyd's, a present and only then was I asked to continue for another two years. This I did, in a little more leisurely fashion.

English Speaking Union

Throughout my Press Council years I was also a member of the English Speaking Union of the Commonwealth. A well established non-political charity with 70,000 members for the promotion of mutual understanding, in the English speaking world, it was beginning to attract those in other countries. With Prince Philip as the proactive President, Sir Patrick Dean, formerly our Ambassador in Washington, as Chairman, I was appointed Deputy Chairman of Governors, with duties less onerous than the title suggested. We organised conferences on political and economic issues, management, careers, and education which attracted enthusiastic audiences.

Anne Armstrong, the US Ambassador in London, was an especially valuable ally. Given the American participation, with a different perspective and greater resources, an event we held in the Café Royal in Regent Street, was so well attended that we overflowed the Dubarry, Dauphin and Emperor Napoleon Suites we had booked. The theme was 'Present Politics and Future Investment' – at the time potentially controversial. I set the tone in my formal introduction by quoting Oliver Wendel Holmes: 'It is not where we stand that counts, but the direction in which we are going.'

The Opening Speakers were Milton Friedman and Sir Keith Joseph on the politics of monetary policy, then two trade union leaders, Joe Gormley and Frank Chapple, on changing attitudes towards work, education and lifestyles, followed by company chairmen, who were already showing their concern for our slow-down in innovation. Tom King, Minister of State, spoke about environment issues and over lunch Margaret Thatcher, four months after becoming Prime Minister, on the attitudes of politicians to state and free enterprise. Already certain of her ground she glanced at her notes only once.

1980–81 was a time of high unemployment, not least for those about to leave school and university. I proposed and led a programme to assist them in discovering where their interests and suitability really lay. It happened to come at a time when ESU membership was ageing so attracting the young could help to reverse the trend. I had done something like this before, in 1978 for the annual Eton College Careers Convention, a two-day event attended by all senior boys and their parents, where captains of industry and leaders of the professions were the invited speakers. Later, they were joined by panels of younger people to speak too. School leavers could thereby learn of the experiences of the new recruits, those in mid-career and those who had reached the top, and question them. The discussions were invaluable in giving them an idea of the needs, the risks and rewards and 'the likely flavour of their lives', to make a better informed choice as to their further education and occupation. The convention was repeated for three years.

My proposal was accepted by the Governors and strengthened greatly when Dame Molly Green, a retired headmistress, joined me as Co-Deputy Chairman, extending the audience to include many young people from comprehensive schools. We went on to revise the ESU Graduate Programme to select, from about two hundred applications a year, those to be placed at leading American universities.

We followed up on a novel proposal to concoct a form of English suitable for professional communication between non-English and native English speakers. Initially to assist air traffic controllers, further ideas developed. Dr Peter Nancarrow who, with a grant from Shell International, was already engaged on a Chinese language project in geological texts – 'Techspeak' – set to work compiling suitable computer programmes for translation. At a conference in Cambridge Prince Philip, who took the chair, was keen to see something useful materialise from this. We brought together leading linguists, educationalists, engineers, the BBC and the British Council. Professor (later Lord) Quirk was among those who pointed out the alarming rate at which the language of communication was changing, but in any event, as an authority on symbolic logic, he raised serious doubts about achieving useful results. He proved to be right.

The Maxwell Effect – and Goldman Sachs

There was no shortage of invitations coming my way to discuss other openings. Sir Alex Jarrett, Chairman of Reed International, called me.

Would I be prepared to join the Board of a new company, Mirror Group Holdings, which Warburg's and Lazards were preparing for sale? It would publish *The Daily Mirror*, *Sporting Life* and three Sunday newspapers. In order to complete the Prospectus and get a Stock Exchange listing, an early decision was needed. Clive Thornton of Reuters and Abbey National would be Chairman.

Thornton telephoned with a dinner invitation to meet 'his new Board'. Pudding had just been served when he was called to the phone. Robert Maxwell had just bought the company for £90 million and would take over Thornton's desk in the morning! We were no longer required. I still have a copy of the uncirculated *Daily Mirror*, compiled that night, with my name on the Company Prospectus.

In fact, Maxwell barged into the building in the middle of the night to set up a Board meeting of his own. It went on, apparently, for twelve hours and, at some stage, he obtained from the others the authority of sole signatory.

A couple of days later he telephoned me: 'Come along for chat. I have a proposition you'll like.' If he had in mind asking me to join his Board I would not have accepted – and I think he knew it. And I wanted to avoid being bribed or bullied, so I made my excuses.

I had first heard of him early in the 1950s when I was in the Ministry of Defence. Having founded the Pergamon Press he was distributing translations of valuable wartime German reports to British and US intelligence agencies. I could well imagine his 'marketing' did not stop there but, though suspicions may have been raised, he was far from being a controversial character then. Czech by birth, his entire family having perished at Auschwitz, by the age of twenty-one as a soldier he had received the Military Cross personally from General Montgomery. By 1964, he had published 600 books and seventy journals, become MP for Buckingham and Chairman of the Labour Party's Science and Industry Committee. He was so bounding in confidence he believed he could emulate the Press achievements of Beaverbook and Northcliffe.

His first setback came in 1968 when he lost out to Rupert Murdoch in a bid for *The News of the World* and then for *The Times*. In 1971 he ran into deep trouble. The Board of Trade was so concerned about Pergamon Press it commissioned a report on his business affairs from Sir Ronald Leach, Head of Peat Marwick. He pronounced that Maxwell could not be relied upon to exercise proper stewardship of a publicly quoted company. But Maxwell survived.

'Cap'n Bob', as he was called, had a gargantuan appetite. At work he surrounded himself with 'yes men', plying them with caviar and champagne, and firing them without ceremony. He flaunted his wealth. Almost incredibly he succeeded in recruiting three former Attorney Generals and banks, notably NatWest, continued to lend him money even when they were suspicious. But at times he could be generous, so when I was seeking support in 1983 for the Prince of Wales' charities, he was one of a dozen chairmen who responded. Others sent cheques; Maxwell offered 'something more valuable'. 'You may have the full-time services of my son Ian,' he said, 'I will continue to pay him for a year or two.'

Then he invited me to tea at Headington Hall, his ostentatious home in Oxford, where Elizabeth, his wife, joined us. She was called out to meet a visitor. On her return she said, 'Bob, it is the wife of someone you have just fired who came to see me. She's in tears, pregnant, looks terribly ill. Do give him his job back.' Out he went, back in seconds saying, 'He's starting again tomorrow.'

I had recruited John Pervin, formerly with Unilever, as Managing Director of Youth Business Initiative and together we decided, after interviewing Ian Maxwell, to take him on as a YBI Coordinator. Ian told us, incidentally, he had been fired by his father over the most trivial matter. He began with us well enough, but then complained that his father was also giving him an impossible amount to do. 'Would you speak to him?' This I did. 'You've broken your promise,' I said. 'At Ian's age, I was working ten times as hard as him,' Maxwell replied. Our arrangement came to an end in June 1984.

There was another occasion involving Maxwell in 1991 when I was asked by Sir John Grenside to appeal for funds for Talking Newspapers for the Blind. He knew my father had been blind, and I was joined by five of the 'good and the great' – Runcie, Pilkington, Devonshire, Wagner, and de Ferranti – each knowing at first hand blindness in their own families. Our son Edward, also registered blind, volunteered to prepare a comprehensive plan, which impressed all five. We made an encouraging start and built four new recording studios.

I discovered it was Maxwell who had helped initiate this charity, so he was one of those I wrote to, seeking further support for expansion. An immediate reply came from Anna Reece of Maxwell Communications, but nothing more from him. In November, sensationally, he disappeared from his yacht. What did surprise me was the succession of laudatory remarks that immediately followed his presumed death, from Callaghan, Kinnock, Ashdown and Douglas Hurd. When Foreign Secretary, Hurd had said, 'the world will be poorer for his absence'. These sentiments quickly faded away when his activities were revealed.

Early the following year (1992), I was approached by Goldman Sachs International in London. Gene Fife, Chairman and Managing Director, told me that competition for the services they wanted to offer was severe. Had I any views on how they might develop in Europe? I made the point that their strengths as a US investment bank were their able young technocrats and a considerable transaction capability; their disadvantages, they were not yet close enough to the 'establishment' to be brought into confidential discussions, nor did they know enough about the substantive problems facing potential clients. He introduced me to his colleagues, John Thornton, Evans and Sharp, invited me to prepare a preliminary note, and in May we had a further discussion on that. He said that Hans Friderichs, a German member of their International Advisory Board, had spoken warmly of me. Would I go to New York to meet Robert Rubin, head of the firm?

It was a pleasant surprise to be received in his New York office by someone so quiet and thoughtful, not at all the powerful investment banker I had envisaged. 'I'm sorry I'm not free to be your host. May I introduce my two senior colleagues – Roy Zuckerberg and Steve Freidman?' Over a working lunch they told me that Rubin, a Democrat, would soon be leaving to become Clinton's Secretary of the Treasury and I revealed I had been working with William Simon, his Republican predecessor. On returning to London I was told by Fife, 'They have no objection to your joining us in Europe!'

Without as yet any contractual arrangement, over the following four months I worked on an outline strategy for moving ahead, Gene Fife occasionally making a specific request. 'What are the investment opportunities for real estate in Europe? Could we generate 25–30% return over a five-year period? I would appreciate your input.'

I responded quickly with a proposal and occasionally discussed these issues with his partners over lunch. Then quite suddenly he wrote to me:

> *Recently there have been several developments in regard to the Firm's use of consultants and advisors. This year we have had to make some difficult decisions regarding budgets for our next fiscal year. I regret to say we cannot continue our current arrangement, which will be terminated as of the end of April 1993. I want to thank you for your wise counsel … I value our relationship greatly.*

As the fee I had been receiving had been quite modest, I found this development strange. I wanted to know what had happened. No-one said a word. Then John Thornton gave me a clue. Over lunch with the partners I had casually referred to Robert Maxwell. I was asked how I knew him and innocently recounted my experience. I did not think more of it at the time, but I was listened to in utter silence.

It was months later I found out that Maxwell's name, to Goldman Sachs, was apparently a red rag to a bull. One of their senior partners had been jailed for insider dealings in 1988 and, in 1991, another partner, Eric Sheinberg, who was also Maxwell's broker, helped him divert his employee's pension funds to his private companies. Together they aimed to keep up the price of Maxwell's shares which were collateral for a bank loan, Sheinberg trading the shares in his own account. Eventually Goldman had to pay out $250 million to aggrieved Maxwell pensioners. No wonder, they dared not risk being associated with anyone who had, as I had, a history of contacts with him.

Back to Business

The closest I came to the investment world was in venture capital. Even during my McKinsey years many new high technology businesses were being created in the USA, young entrepreneurs being attracted to the prospect of setting up rewarding venture funds. In Europe, recognising that the risks were high and rewards, if successful, highly taxed, would-be entrepreneurs were slow to take the plunge. Our culture was different too. Attitudes were inhibiting: if it didn't work out it served you right!

One who did so, however, was Ronald Cohen. As a young immigrant from Egypt, Duke of Edinburgh's Gold Award holder and Oxford graduate, he joined McKinsey from the Harvard Business School. After a couple of years in London he sounded me out on whether he should take the plunge. I told him he was doing well where he was, but I recognised his entrepreneurial aspirations and felt he had, in any event, more or less decided to make a move. So I wished him well.

After a shaky start during the economic downturn, in collaboration with a Harvard colleague, he tackled one transaction after another. It was in 1981, four years after I had retired from McKinsey that he asked for my help, by when he had joined forces with Alan Patricof Associates in the USA. Under Margaret Thatcher's administration, tax rates became low enough to be a real incentive for risk takers. In the UK I agreed to be Chairman of their first venture capital fund which attracted £10 million and then their second, of £40 million. We went round together making presentations to the directors of pension funds, insurance and utility companies and local authorities and I also introduced a reputable broker. Alan Patricof and Maurice Tchénio, in Paris, also a McKinsey alumnus, joined us, the company initially being designated Alan Patricof Associates (APA).

The small team recruited had a sound grasp of economic and commercial issues, displayed competitive and entrepreneurial abilities, and could generally judge people and their management capabilities. Spotting opportunities, recognising risks, learning from mistakes, our investment decisions in due course turned out to be more often right than wrong and so the company expanded rapidly. I presided over our Board meetings, about eighty of them in all, held in the tax havens of Bermuda and Monte Carlo. After ten years, they expected me to continue indefinitely. After nearly fourteen years, I announced it was definitely time I retired. The business had already evolved from venture capital, my main interest, to private equity with little early-stage financing – more in under-managed firms with a prospect of quicker returns. Re-designated APAX Partners, by the time I left it had some $7 billion under management and since then far more.

Those good enough to stay the course became rich. We had had substantial discussions on what 'carried interest' we could fairly charge on the capital gains we made. Excessive bonuses were not to become a common matter for concern until later, with financial disasters, when performance did not warrant it. When asked for my views I emphasised the fair sharing of both risk and return with all subscribers. Everyone warmed to my account of the huge amount of prize money paid out to our Royal Navy captains, officers and other ranks following a victorious engagement. 'But don't forget,' I added, 'on the downside they paid with their lives.'

My business links continued alongside other activities. As Special Adviser to Ernst & Young I found myself having to warn and to demonstrate how conflicts of interest could arise between consulting and auditing practices. Standards were slipping, it was necessary to clarify the duties of a professional firm. And even after my eightieth birthday, I was called out to chair for three years the international Board of a Belgian information technology company, ARINSO International. That ended with a highly successful merger, achieved by Jos Sluys, the astute Chief Executive.

In parallel with this I much enjoyed participating in a wide range of unrelated activities. For ten years, as a Governor of Benenden School, where our daughters were educated before going on to Oxford, my central interest was in counselling and in facilitating a greater awareness and interest among school-leavers of job opportunities, and how to prepare for those they were interested in. Occasional lectures, outside speakers and external visits brought worthwhile results and new interest arose in science and business. On two occasions, we selected new Headmistresses. Once, having decided but not revealed who we intended to appoint, we invited senior staff members to join our shortlist of candidates at a reception and give us, in confidence, their own preference. It was the same individual who proved to be a conspicuous success. When it was time for me to leave I strongly recommended I should be succeeded by someone of a younger generation and recommended a former Benenden girl then studying law. Although not gifted academically, she so distinguished herself in due course, she became a member of the House of Lords.

In 1992, surprisingly, I was back in the world of engineering again. Now, as Patron, I was not allowed to retire for a further twenty one years. I had been approached by Lord Gladwyn. Long after retiring from his diplomatic career he became UK patron of 'The French Civils', as they called themselves, the *Conseil National des Ingénieurs et Scientifiques de France*. He told me I would be his ideal successor, 'Far better qualified than me. The only reason they asked me,' he added, 'was because Cynthia (his wife) was the granddaughter of Brunel. In Paris, that carried immense prestige.' Duly flattered and presented with a role that was not at all onerous, I accepted with pleasure. I have taken part since then in maintaining, professionally and socially, the historic connection begun in World War I between British and French engineers and scientists. At each Annual General meeting, there is a change of presidency, when the Patron is warmly thanked, no matter how little he has done. I have in fact welcomed a succession of distinguished engineers to our gatherings and made many speeches, whilst Diana has led tours of our members at the V&A, the Royal Courts of Justice, and institutions she knows so well.

At times, as a diversion, I dipped into our long history from the Middle Ages to the *Entente Cordiale*, Concorde and the construction of the Channel Tunnel. Incredibly, that was first proposed 200 years earlier, but within a year we were at war and the prospect of war in 1914 held it back again. When the possibility of joining the Common market arose in the Sixties, it was agreed that a rail tunnel would be a good investment.

My patronage must have been among the least demanding of honorary non-executive positions. Enjoyable and most interesting as it was, I was sure a younger person could make a more valuable contribution. Twice I proposed to step down. Only when I insisted the job needed someone thirty years younger than me, now ninety-three, the Council took it seriously and I was allowed to go. My successor Robert Mair, former Master of Jesus College, Cambridge, far better technically qualified than me and exactly thirty years younger, and his wife were a delight to meet and make a great team. I was not exaggerating when I forecast that my successor would do a better job than me.

IN
RETROSPECT

CHAPTER XIII

From Moss Side to Eden and Beyond

Eden Project

The most worthwhile opportunity, well worth waiting for, did not come my way until 1995. I had always been concerned about protecting the global environment. Three years earlier at the UN Conference in Rio de Janeiro, the stark problem to be solved had attracted worldwide publicity. The problem, according to one wit, was not the apple on the tree, but the pair under the tree!

In Biblical times, the Garden of Eden had been a paradise. Our few ancestors cultivated the soil and cut down trees for fuel for their own use, but the impact was minimal. Scars soon healed and we lived in some sort of harmony with nature. With the onset of industrialisation and the application of science and engineering to farming and manufacturing, in the pursuit of 'progress', we sought to dominate the environment. Even during my lifetime, the world's population had trebled, resources exploited and depleted. It was necessary to control pollution and protect habitats, species and landscapes.

Without plants, there would be no human life. We depended on them for air, food, fuel, clothes and medicines. Fortunately there was a growing realisation that we now had to sustain them and, as stewards for future generations, shift from exploitation to conservation. But whilst we thought globally, we also had to act locally.

It seemed to be Britain's ideal response to the UN's Agenda 21, so I was delighted to be invited to take a leading part in the creation of the Eden Project in Cornwall.

Tim Smit and Jonathan Ball had the great idea of constructing huge, spectacular plant houses – biomes – in the virtually abandoned china clay pits at Goonvean near St Austell. There they would display exotic plants, whole populations of them, and explain how they were being used.

Tim Smit, who had studied archaeology, had spent ten years in rock music and opera, but was best known for his discovery and development of the Lost Gardens of Heligan. Something of a maverick, teeming with ideas, his enthusiasm and public relations were outstanding. Jonathan Ball had an architectural practice in Bude; as Senior Coxswain of the Cornish Lifeboat Service he was admired throughout Cornwall and his wide range of contacts was invaluable. But the media concentrated on Smit.

As a celebration of the forthcoming Millennium, the Millennium Commission was offering up to £50 million to support each project it selected. Smit and Ball recruited a project team to develop their idea and apply for adequate funding, mainly from the Commission. The idea was warmly received, but the project was considered far too expensive and too risky a use of public funds.

The original draft application of 22nd February 1995, submitted by Smit, based on the estimated capital cost, was for £240,920,000. Even though this was revised to £150 m (on flat lands), it was turned down firmly by the Millennium Commission. There were no ideas as to how such money could be raised or how adequate income could be generated to repay debt. We were fascinated to discover later that Smit had told everyone that the Commission had actually approved it! He did this to maintain morale – and succeeded.

To take this forward the Commission stipulated that if responsible Trustees they approved of were appointed, and they were accountable for a less costly proposal, they would consider it. Four of us, initially, were chosen: Sir Richard Carew Pole, who had already given distinguished public service especially in Cornwall; Sir Ralph Riley, of the Agriculture and Food Research Council, who had discovered the gene to transfer disease resistance from wild to cultivated wheat; Sir Alan Donald, formerly

Ambassador to China, with a keen personal interest in ecology, and myself. I was thrilled when they immediately asked me to become Chairman. In this single project many of my hopes might be realised. First, our role as trustees with a duty to sustain our environment for others, secondly a project in which so many of my earlier disciplines were relevant, thirdly to be involved at the very outset, when strategic inputs were critical, and fourthly allowing me to orchestrate the performance of a talented group of individuals and teams, as I had learned to do at McKinsey. With luck too, we could develop the economy of Cornwall. I accepted happily, even though it involved more travel than I would have wished. Ian Hay Davison joined us for a while, and later Guy Whalley, a solicitor who I invited as a highly valued partner of Freshfields. Smit and Ball, the co-founders, now joint Principals, reported to us.

The site was mainly in the ownership of The Falmouth Estate and English China Clay Ltd, where the Chairman was my former co-director and friend, Sir Henry (later Lord) Chilver. The 116 acre site might have been purpose built for its new role. The floor stood at sea-level, which would keep heat loss to a minimum and, in effect, it was a south-facing valley, with the back wall often bathed in sunlight.

The clay pit had been virtually worked out. The kaolin content was neutral, which meant that, with the addition of organic material, the project could create its own soil on site. Its location on the western approaches gave it clean air and good ultraviolet penetration. Never did I expect my early education in geology and meteorology in the Navy and subsequently in engineering to come in useful again. It was exciting. We bought the option on the site, set up management teams, and prepared to apply for funds.

The Trustees considered that the maximum realistic figure that would be acceptable was between £74 and £80 million and that that would be feasible. We therefore submitted the proposal in December 1996, the Millennium Commission accepted it in March 1997 and agreed, in due course, to pay half of it. For the remainder, a concerted effort was then begun, not least with the European Regional Development Fund, with whom we shared an objective of creating many new jobs in an area of high unemployment.

Before agreeing to join as a Trustee, I had visited our prospective architect Nick Grimshaw's office. The architecture of our biomes would be stunning. What impressed me was the way he had collaborated with engineers and designers, in the great tradition of those who created the Georgian and Victorian glasshouses – Decimus Burton and Richard Turner at Kew, and Joseph Paxton and Charles Fox for the Crystal Palace in 1851. They had influenced the construction of our railway stations, first in the age of Brunel and Cubitt, and in our own time, the new Waterloo International Terminal (at a cost of £130 m). I had learned much about this also from civil engineers, as Patron since 1992 of CNISE.

We interviewed all the construction companies that made proposals. The three finalists were Tarmac, Costain Hochtief and the McAlpine joint venture and we finally agreed unanimously on McAlpine's.

All worked well together. We decided that the displays would trace the entire history of plants and human life in different climates: a) the original plant life in the wilderness – untouched by man, b) primitive cultivation where hunter gatherers foraged for local plants or crops, shelter and medicine, and c) modern cultivation and processing, from spices to timber, that entered into world trade and supermarkets and, frequently, leading to irresponsible exploitation, decay and decline.

Following the General Election of May 1997 Chris Smith, Minister for Culture & Environment, became responsible for the Millennium Commission. A great hive of activity followed so that we could complete the project as planned for its opening in 2000. We had to agree the business plan, the management structure, the activities of the constructors and contractors, develop the nursery for plant propagation, landscape and design and raise further funds.

By 1998 all the infrastructural work was complete and a year later the biomes and Visitor Centre too. It represented over one thousand man years of construction work. To translate the Eden proposal into reality required the orchestration of many talented players – scientists, technologists, surveyors, designers, architects and engineers, lawyers, accountants, publicists and financiers – all determined to succeed. It involved balancing different specific objectives, sometimes conflicting. This called for particular management skills. I saw it as rather like staging an opera in harmonising a group of totally committed individual performers. There was just one tricky episode, I now remember, to avert a row. A senior colleague had come to me most upset that in a Press statement credit for his own idea had been taken by another. I told him, 'There's no limit to what a man can do, or where he can go, if he doesn't mind who gets the credit.' It wasn't an original thought: it was a plaque I remembered seeing over the Coca Cola Chairman's desk. I saw to it that the thanks of Mike O'Connor, CEO of the Millennium Commission, were directed to him.

In 1998 considerable matching investment was still needed to attract tourists and developers and to cater for the educational and research facilities offered. So in February, when we were three quarters of the way to our target (including £10 million from the European Regional Development Fund and £12 million from commerce, local government and loans) I made a personal appeal for the remaining funds. At a well chosen gathering at the Athenaeum I quoted Samuel Butler: 'The three most important things a man has are his private parts, his money and his religious convictions. We are only interested in your money.' This achieved the desired effect. By October 1998, we had received over 95% of our target.

We invited the Minister to the ceremony of 'turning the first sod' and laying the foundation stone. It was raining heavily. In the midst of a deluge, ankle-deep in water, he picked up the spade and was perched dangerously over the huge crater. This image suddenly reminded me of a remark once made to Boris Yeltsin when visiting President Kravchuk of Ukraine: 'Yesterday Mr President, we stood at the edge of an abyss. Today we are taking a great leap forward.' The photographers brilliantly caught

Chris Smith teetering over the edge, looking terrified. Later he told us that Tony Blair had singled out Eden, when he spoke at the Commonwealth Prime Ministers' Conference, as the environmental project the UK should be most proud of.

The management required was demanding. For two years, at the request of the other Trustees, I interrupted my Ernst & Young activities to spend more time visiting Cornwall so I could chair Eden Projects Limited, the operating company. In total, I had participated in 200 meetings in Cornwall and London. I was overdoing it. I was then told I would have to undergo surgery and take it easy for a while. I didn't mention this to my colleagues immediately, but in any event, I felt it was time for me to go. So, in January 2000, after a five-year stint, I said goodbye. We had completed our project within budget and just in time. [photo, page 238]

Of my able co-Trustees, all unfailingly supportive, Richard Carew Pole proved to be the star – he invariably encouraged me to do just what I wanted! And he remained longest as a Trustee. Sir Ronnie Hampel, a former Chairman of ICI, who now lived near the site, was my most able successor.

On my first visit thereafter, Diana and I asked the Laidlaws to join us as guests. As a former Chairman of BP International, Christopher Laidlaw knew all about major projects. He was thrilled by a single incident. A small schoolboy emerged with a bar of chocolate. 'What did you learn in there?' he asked the boy. 'If we don't look after the cocoa plant, we won't get our bar of chocolate', came the reply.

The Eden Project continued to flourish, Tim Smit becoming Chief Executive and Eddie George, the next Chairman of Trustees. He told me he enjoyed the rainforest every bit as much as being Governor of the Bank of England.

For my part it had all been the greatest privilege, to have presided over its foundation and opening and to see the difference it had made – for the economy of Cornwall, in educating the public, and in meeting the ideals of the first Earth Summit.

Over the past decade only one of the objectives universally adopted at the Kyoto Conference in 1997 has been seriously debated, that is climate change. The prospect of global warming due to carbon emissions leading, some authorities maintain, inevitably to disastrous flooding, drought, coastal erosion and mass migration have all been the subject of scientific and public argument.

There is no consensus that human activity is the major cause. Politically, scope for remedial action is limited by resources and Britain's response, or the USA's shale oil strategy, have not been emulated by the European Union or even entertained in China or India. Estimates of the risks, the magnitude, time-scale and cost of damage are widely divergent. Different nations put different values on prosperity and life. The collection and analysis of more global data, extending over a long period is a pre-requisite for reducing uncertainty. It would be wise for all those who can to allocate resources for this at least. The information would prove to be of great value.

The Millennium year coincided with the start of my tenth decade. I thought nothing could surprise me now. But I was wrong. I had mentioned to an American friend long before that my favourite mode of travel was by sea. I had 'caught the bug' ironically in war, when my sea-going time was short and dangerous moments few – I told him I was actually paid for the privilege and would love to go to sea again.

The invitation came from Silver Seas, a Florida based cruise lines company operating five luxury ships worldwide. Would I join them as Guest Lecturer on an eighteen-day cruise around South and West Africa and the mid-Atlantic islands? I was thrilled to be asked, but I revealed my age. They dismissed it and said I could speak on any topics I chose. I gave five talks about personal experiences, global events, and personalities I had known, to fellow passengers from all over the world and so many different walks of life. When I was introduced as The Guest Lecturer it was described as my first career! Our travelling companions included like-minded professional people and a few became our friends. It was a great experience, but with just one misfortune. Diana said, 'Remember there are Germans aboard; don't embarrass them with your wartime stories.' So from our balcony armchairs, I was going through my carefully prepared notes when a sudden gust of wind carried them off into the Gulf of Guinea. Diana knew how much I depended on them. At the end of the cruise I was told that according to the appraisals received my best talk was the one without notes!

And then six months later, I was asked to join them again, this time on a cruise from the Caribbean to the Amazon and Brazil. Again we accepted. They asked if I would deliver two extra lectures. I said I would add one and if they wished to invite Diana, she might give one too – which she did. And by all accounts hers was 'the best of the lot'.

In Retrospect

For many years in my youth little seemed to change. Gradually, however, I noticed long-term changes under way and in looking back, over the best part of a century some were profound.

In science, the speed of change was slow at first. Only in my undergraduate days did it begin to be taken out of its ivory tower and put to use. I remember Sir Edward Appleton showing me the draft of his first Reith Lecture 'Science for its own Sake', a component of natural philosophy. For long there had been barriers to certain types of investigations. Just as the position of the earth at the centre of the universe could not at one time be questioned, even now the mysteries of life could not be investigated in the laboratory. The questions began to be asked 'Are we allowed to do this? Is it within the rules?'

The prospect of World War II partly freed us of such constraints. The questions now became 'Can we change the rules? Can we change the boundaries or position of the goal posts in the course of the game itself?

The moment I graduated I and fellow scientists were directed to where they could be useful – in my case RDF, later known as radar. This, together with the atom bomb, would largely determine the outcome of the war. In both cases, arising out of fundamental scientific principles the means were found to develop and deploy them, with profound consequences. Thereafter, the scale of resources allocated to research and development were significantly increased. The time span required for results to be reflected in social policy and political action also shortened. Scientists in closer collaboration with others, now catering for the new opportunities, changed their agenda. Wisdom, once retrospective and then contemporary, gradually became anticipatory.

In parallel with the evolution of science and technology the art and science of management began to advance initially in America, to help solve business problems. I remember seeing the T-model Ford developed with the aid of new management tools. Later the Harvard Business School led the way in their own curriculum on competition and consumer choice, illustrating it with the respective decisions of Robert McNamara of Ford and Alfred Sloan of General Motors, as to how they went about using physical, human and financial resources more efficiently.

Here in Britain we were slow on the uptake. The Chairman of our University Grants Committee, the highly regarded Sir Hugh Beaver, reported, 'The University view is that management has not the intellectual content to justify it as a subject for a degree course.' And so the launch of our own business schools was long delayed. We have lived through the birth and death of many industries since then. Some have moved to other continents, others now under foreign ownership and better management have survived and even prospered in Britain. We could have done much better.

In time the service industries, the public sector with their agencies and other institutions all adopted improved management methods with notable benefits. With the emergence of information technology, the internet and the speed of access to it the most far-reaching changes to people's lives are being made. The compression of time and space may prove to be one of the most remarkable changes in human history. I am proud to have been able to play even a tiny part in this.

The explosive growth of science, technology and progressive management has not been matched unfortunately by the development of man and human institutions. This disparity has contributed to cultural and social problems such as unemployment, loneliness and delinquency. Loyalty, patriotism, courtesy and mutual respect are now less common. This is an issue for governments, businesses and institutions as well as individuals. Democratic governments approve or turn a blind eye to arms sales to dictators and secret trials to dispense justice. In a global trading context there is no consensus on the use of slush funds or financiers shifting risks they recognise to less well informed clients. In a business ethics conference I remember the debate 'Can you charge the earth and still go to heaven?' We have strayed from our ethical and moral tradition and social justice is harder to realise. Sermons no longer prevail over the clamour of a more materialistic and fanatical world. Admittedly this has been offset sporadically by an end to capital punishment and flogging, for example, and conspicuously in some countries by social welfare systems whereby health and education are no longer a privilege for the few.

On at least four occasions between 1954 and 1966 my appointments and promotions, as a scientific civil servant, were largely dictated by a need to derive greater economic and social benefit from the resources government allocated to them. As Scientific Counsellor serving abroad I was asked what developments in Europe were of the greatest interest to British institutions. As Director of the Forest Products Research Laboratory, selecting appropriate research projects and developing them was the key to generating the best returns for government and industry. At Neddy we tried to calculate the contribution of R&D to economic growth and propose the allocation of resources between the alternative claims on them. In the new MinTech, following the Harold Wilson 'White Heat' general election, we sought to translate our agreed recommendations into the means of raising productivity and economic growth. These extended from investment in education and more qualified scientists and engineers to a wide range of related management issues. For long, however, they met with little success.

Well before taking the considerable step of moving on from the service altogether I was thinking of how, as a nation, we might best harness our scientific, technological and entrepreneurial skills to speed up innovation to benefit our economy and bring prosperity. I was in no doubt that government, business and academia acting in concert could make our performance more effective and our nation more competitive.

My decade with McKinsey certainly improved my analytical skills, problem-solving approach and versatility and allowed me to build up relationships. It was to be another forty years before I set out my considered thoughts. Now I imagined the process of innovation to be like the flow of a river from the initial ideas with tributaries which replenish it, rapids which quicken it, shoals which impede it, dams which obstruct it and lock gates which control it. Based on this I entitled my Churchill Archives Lecture in 2005 'The Springs of Innovation, the Floodgates of Prosperity'.

Additionally we had to move far from the traditional civil service approach to achieve much of this. It called for attitudinal, as well as institutional, change. Civil servants of my generation at the end of the war were instinctive patriots who saw themselves as servants of the nation, largely independent of the government and willing to be called upon by government in the national interest. Substantial change began twenty years later when I was about to leave, and Fulton reported on the real need. Since then the change and resulting tensions have been more far-reaching, transforming the service into something closer to a political class.

Criticism abounds. There is mutual distrust. Civil servants ask for more time to think of the consequences of government intentions. Ministers maintain that officials are thwarting progress and making government look directionless and incompetent. Special advisers believe that they are best in providing ideas and selling them to the public. The Parliamentary Public Accounts and Select Committees identify wasteful and inefficient practices. As a result the service feels undervalued and is not respected in the way it used to be.

Part of this change has been due to the inevitable change in tasks imposed on the service, requiring managerial and some commercial experience for which civil servants were not recruited. The need is for political judgement and expertise to come together.

In part it is due to the economies that must be made, reducing civil service numbers with its effect on careers, remuneration and pensions. As the original meritocracy is under threat, mass exodus of 'non-political' Permanent Secretaries is now underway. Some highly qualified individuals are moving overseas. Our future administration is likely to model itself on others, where more of those engaged in politics are not elected and senior staff and ministers have short-term appointments rather than careers. Mistrust sadly has extended more widely to the public at large. Judges and nurses are among those professions and vocations which are still largely trusted, but as events have unfolded more politicians, bankers and journalists are being regarded as dishonest, unreliable or incompetent.

Trust is all-important. It can certainly be misplaced. I witnessed this in the financial activities of Lloyd's of London in the Seventies, in the use of intelligence reports and of expert scientific advice. What was not recognised at first was that the curiosity and analysis involved in scientific research was called for in intelligence work too, and both, in drawing conclusions were faced with uncertainties.

In defence, intelligence aimed to optimise decision-taking by informing users of opportunities, explanations of possible outcomes and perhaps how objectives could be achieved. The information was generally incomplete and often unreliable, but our analyses and tentative judgements were always called for, even if not acted on. Assessments by those who subsequently formulated policy, at times unconsciously reflected their own hopes and fears. So in conveying our assessments we had to be cautious, stick to the evidence, and use guarded language. The decision makers on the other hand, in our case the Chiefs of Staff, had to take into account wider considerations. At a political level this included the attitude of the media and the electorate.

In my own appraisals in the Joint Intelligence Bureau, I tried to guess how my reports might be used, but was rarely sufficiently in the picture to know. Overridden by other factors, our conclusions could be misleading.

The degree of risk always looms large. Absence of evidence is not evidence of absence. Whilst improving the odds that objectives could be achieved, we had to explain that a low risk was not 'no risk'. Public perception was always critical. After my time, the mindset in the early 1990s, leading to the belief in the USA that Saddam Hussein had weapons of mass destruction was shown to be wrong and lessons were learned.

On the domestic scene the same applied. In the recent Italian earthquakes disaster, six leading seismologists issued a warning, but the courts decided its wording was not sufficiently alarming. It was a criminal offence and they were sent to jail. Their defence, that the likelihood of disaster and the warning they gave were precisely the same as on earlier occurrences of the same severity, did not prevail. The population, growing accustomed to such warnings, were inclined to ignore them, 'crying wolf again'.

More widely, in public policy formulation, much more timely open debate is needed for a better understanding of the pros and cons and uncertainties associated with legislation and action. It has been provided for in some scientific and medical issues, the legal framework on embryos and stem cells, for example, has been admired. But governments have to contend with conflicting advice affecting the risks taken in dealing with such issues as global warming, flooding, drug use and terrorism. Well informed and earlier open debate entertaining political economic and ethical considerations has become critical.

Now approaching advanced middle age and following my ninety-fourth birthday, one of my delights is being steeped in a warm bath, alleviating any aches and pains, and in letting my mind wander. Not simply revisiting old times and recognising how fortunate I have been, but in realising how very different things would have been, but for time and place.

I have witnessed key events spanning most of the twentieth century. Had my parents remained in Russia and I had been born there, no doubt I would have been one of twenty million soldiers lost in its Patriotic War. Had my father, a budding scientist, chosen to study at a pre-eminent German university, and we were all there, we would all have perished once Hitler came to power.

What if I had been born in England at another time? In the mid seventeenth century, when Jews were admitted by Cromwell, at best I would have been a moneylender. By the early eighteenth century, if I had been here then, in the elegant London of Canaletto and Handel, I may have had to hide my religion – as Catholics had to do in Elizabeth I's time. In the nineteenth century, throughout the Victorian era, more professions and vocations were increasingly open to Jews, though I wouldn't have been able to join the establishment. But early in the twentieth century, as immigrants to Manchester, my parents were welcomed, survived and flourished. England allowed us to live less fraught and hectic lives, than in so many other countries.

From the outset my life has been a totally unplanned journey. I had no map, but have been guided perhaps by a compass and a memory. At its essence I consider the four factors that contributed most to my life and work were my upbringing and education, my being British, being Jewish and my marriage.

My parents put everything they could into ensuring that their children would have a better life than they had. My mother as homemaker created a happy family life, which made us feel secure and confident. My father, with a record of scholarship, prematurely blind, deprived of a livelihood, displayed good humour and exemplary courage in adversity. He was a source of great encouragement. He left us in no doubt, however, that we would have to make our own way in life and that our education would go far to determine what we could achieve.

We came to live in Moss Side, within walking distance of the university. As I remember it throughout the Twenties it was a peaceful leafy suburb; we lived just a few yards from the gates of Alexandra Park. Our neighbours were our friends and we felt secure. At school too, the impressions I had were of stability, taking for granted that things would never change. At my infants' school we were proudly shown a map of the world, mostly covered in pink, marking the Empire over which we ruled. The Rector arrived to lead us in *All Things Bright and Beautiful* and heartily we sang 'The rich man in his castle the poor man at his gate; God made them high and lowly, and ordered their estate'. And when the long line of hunger marchers went by it left us believing that poverty was divinely instituted.

By the end of the Thirties, just as I was beginning my daily walk to university, air raids began and the scene changed. Bomb craters everywhere and casualties were devastating. But nothing prepared me for the change I would see years later. These came first on a visit with the Prince of Wales and then in 1993 at a 'Mancunian of the Year' ceremony. On the bombed-out sites, tenements had been constructed which attracted notorious drug runners. The walk ways were rat-runs; children on bikes delivering heroin and crack, terrorising the neighbourhood. On the Alexandra Park housing estate two rival gangs, the *Goochies* on the west with red bandannas and the *Doddies* to the east were armed with Sten guns and AK-47 assault rifles, no doubt smuggled into the country following the Gulf War.

I distinctly remember my first lesson about life coming from a school production of *As You Like It*, taking Shakespeare's 'seven ages of man' quite literally. Then, in my Hebrew class I was introduced to something a little more comprehensive – the Biblical version – set out some two thousand years before Shakespeare. At first, life is learnt from parents and teachers, by guidance and example, then developing relationships, gaining a better understanding and more responsibility, setting one's own standards of behaviour, learning to judge and be judged, providing a livelihood to support a family. At full capacity, taking on wider responsibilities, the welfare of the needy and less fortunate, applying one's knowledge, understanding and experience to counsel the young, and finally, with a broader perspective still, if granted, the wisdom, insight and reputation to set a good example.

At the time, I thought these were successive milestones. But then I discovered that life was not quite like that. They did, however, bring things into context and indicate a way of measuring one's development and performance. This was a significant realisation, which brings to mind *Through the Door in Which I Went* (Omar Khayyam).

My school performance was relatively undistinguished, but it qualified me to study Geology at Manchester University with highly qualified lecturers. We were now at war, so no question of careers arose on graduation. It did leave me, however, with a wish for further education whenever the opportunity arose. Working in London after the war I was able to continue my early research part-time at Imperial College and eventually in 1960 obtain my doctorate at the Sorbonne. And much later still, when as Academic By-Fellow at Churchill College, Cambridge, presented a Paper based on my experience of translating science, technology and management into the means of benefitting the young and future generations.

Throughout this time my thoughts were developing on how the young might best be prepared for careers in a changing world, how engineers could become better qualified to take on managerial responsibility and how girls could be attracted and better equipped to take on employment opportunities that were not previously open to them. Vision and longer term objectives were needed. Today's schoolchildren will not be my age until the last quarter of this century. There will be no linear careers given the speed of change. Technology's 'half life' is now five to seven years. One cannot be academically qualified for a career. More intelligence, initiative, leadership and enterprise will be needed and new skills increasingly acquired. Yet youth is anticipatory. I would not wish to see any brake applied to their vision, idealism, challenge and enterprise – those dynamic qualities which give us most hope for a better future.

All four of our children were well educated giving them choices and the opportunity to pursue their dreams and ambitions and succeed in their chosen fields. Their choices were all quite different: for Katharine, music, the arts and media; Rosalind, finance and opportunities for the poorest in the world; Richard, publishing and services in the USA; and Edward, medical charities and antiquarian hobbies.

Though both my parents were foreigners and my father came to England only at university entrance age, the atmosphere at home was so completely English that never for a moment did I think I was anything but British. Throughout the Twenties and Thirties our national loyalties were progressively reinforced as my father's critically important contribution to the war effort became recognised.

Britishness nowadays may not provide the same uniformity. The ethnic origins of immigrants to Britain have multiplied. Cultures have become more globalised. National identity has been fragmented and there are fewer homogenous communities. Immigration may become a matter of public controversy as 'patriotism' is now questioned, or even ignored. In my time, however, every appointment I was given made me keener to serve my country, to which I owed so much – the Navy, the Civil and Foreign Service, the Duke of Edinburgh's Award Scheme and Prince's Trust, the Press Council, other public bodies, Chairman and Trustee of the Athenaeum, and so on until, in the end, I was being introduced as a member of the establishment.

Throughout this time Britain has been transformed from Empire to a Welfare State. The world's population has multiplied and women in the main have emerged from oppression. At the same time I have also witnessed war and the aftermath of the Holocaust – haunted by the mountain of tiny shoes at Auschwitz taken from the toddlers being thrown in to the gas chambers and incinerators. We survived, virtually alone for a while. The filling of bomb craters and food rationing long continued, but then we slowly recovered. Now terrorism is rife, it is a source of pride to have lived in a country that, with diminishing resources and not always well governed, has weathered these storms and acted with integrity under a Queen who has provided personal stability and a constitutional platform inspiring confidence.

What will remain with me all my life is one of my earliest recollections. As a child, I had little sense of time, until the Sabbath candles appeared at home, radiating their warmth and I knew another week had gone by. High Days and Holy Days and Passover coming once a year seemed far apart, but everything then revolved around them.

I continue to conduct the Passover Seder Service to this day and still recount how, for countless generations Jews had been victims, living in fear, and worse. Without power, statehood, political organisation or even choice of occupation, through learning, faith and hope many had survived. Now liberated, some across the world assimilated, but more held on to their traditional religious beliefs and practices.

Today there is a resurgence of orthodoxy. World Jewry is now more numerous than it was forty years ago, thanks in part to the demographic explosion among the orthodox. For me, this is a cause for hope. So too is the development in parallel of some Reform synagogues, such as those in England led by the late Hugo Gryn, a Holocaust survivor, and Julia Neuberger who brilliantly attracts the keen participation of all, the very youngest and the oldest, to our faith.

At family gatherings we occasionally discuss the central themes of Judaism, touching on ideas that have changed and evolved, written at different times, handed down through the generations, reflecting diverse social, geographical and intellectual backgrounds. I remember we argued about a caption I saw at the gates of Churchill College, Cambridge: 'If only youth had the knowledge; if only age had the strength'. Then the issue became how can our beliefs be translated into action?

I have always regarded my Jewishness as integral to being British. I remember, in the war, the same sentiment being the theme of a sermon by the Chaplain to the Jewish Forces: as British Jews fighting for the Allied cause our loyalties were undivided.

On two other issues I have met conflicting views – as a scientist and on Israel. My own scientific and religious views have never been in conflict and it is well documented that scientists throughout history have held similar views. Observation, analysis, and interpretation or explanation are the essence of science and rabbis have never argued against logic, but the Hebrew Bible after very briefly describing how the universe came into being goes on, in great depth, to address quite different questions. Why was it created? Why are we and all forms of life here? The answers call for syntheses with the guidance of the prophets and commentators on God's purpose. In an increasingly secular environment there is disagreement, but my scientific colleagues share my view more widely than not. I would like to have contributed to a revised commentary on the Hebrew Bible with inputs from my generation of thinkers and doers.

My attitude to Israel now, at a time of great concern, has always been dominated not by political considerations in general, but by the vital issue of security and most of all by religious ones and the significance of Jerusalem in particular. My attachment at the outset was formed by my parents' experience in Russia, their continued support of the Zionist cause, once they were in England, and then the Holocaust. Today Israel, out of all the UN member states, is the only one whose people have lived in the same land, spoken the same language and professed the same religion as did their ancestors 3,000 years ago. Almost half the world's Jewry now lives there. I favour the sharing of the land and economic opportunities with others – those who espouse peace and tolerance. So far as Jerusalem is concerned, apart from the exhortations of the Prophets and the Psalms it is central to so many of our traditional prayers – 'In Jerusalem I will comfort you', 'May the voice of joy and gladness soon be heard in the streets of Jerusalem' and, in concluding the Passover Seder in earnest hope, we still say, 'Next year in Jerusalem'.

The fourth factor influencing my life has been my marriage. It was said that Diana and I had nothing in common apart from our four children. What was not said is that we shared the same values and aspirations and, with different backgrounds, education and talents, teamed up to cope with all aspects of our family life, from the daily minutiae to the major events. This has been the key to a marriage continuing happily when fewer and fewer couples now celebrate their diamond wedding anniversaries, as we have. I continue to send her a bouquet of red roses every birthday. Their number equal to her age until she was fifty-nine, when the well intentioned florist sent sixty, which did not go down too well! Since then her bouquets have no longer been age-related.

Talented in so many ways as homemaker, wife and mother, bringing cohesion to the family, renowned for her hospitality, bringing together those in different walks of life often to meet for the first time, once our own children were being educated, finding time to add to her own qualifications with an honours degree and to take on responsible roles in the arts and access to justice, notably as Trustee of the Victoria & Albert Museum, Founder and Chairman for ten years and Life President of the Personal Support Unit, based at the Royal Courts of Justice, spreading rapidly across the country, to help thousands of litigants in person a year. Most of all, however, she has gone far out of her way to help others who did not know where their help came from. The combined burden of these duties calls for extraordinary organisation skills.

So far as our marriage is concerned, constancy has been its hallmark. Of course, we have had our occasional rows, but I just cannot remember what they were about! Just like the sundial engraved 'I only record the sunny hours'. Except for just one occasion, on a summer's night in Denham in the course of an argument Diana threw my underwear out of the bedroom window and I couldn't find them. Our window cleaner found them dangling on a climbing rose and, though suspicious, brought them back to Diana, who said dismissively, 'Oh, the wind must have blown them out of the window'!

Among my correspondence I have found a letter received in 1998 from a leading member of the British Academy of Graphologists who, on seeing my handwriting wrote, 'He appears self-confident and there is a good balance between needs which motivate him and their fulfilment, but his needs are mostly short of his abilities.' Whether or not her analysis was right, my own motivation has simply been to be a good influence. It is not for me to judge whether I have been successful. I do not think I have ever been particularly ambitious, not at least in the usual sense – ambitious to do, or to be, or to know. I have been thanked in so many ways on numerous occasions for services rendered. My own abiding sense is one of gratitude, grateful to those, including unsung heroes, to whom it is due. To Gladys Besso, who inspired me as a child in Hebrew classes, so that I wanted to know more. To my father, who by personal example convinced me that early setbacks and disappointments were not an indictment, but an opportunity to adapt and to grow, reassuring that, with perseverance, effort trumped talent. To Harry Hoff, who took the trouble to discover what I might do best to serve my country at war. To Fred Hoyle, as well as my father, who stimulated me with the sense of wonder, attracting me to science. To Edward Appleton, John Cockcroft and Patrick Blackett, all Nobel prizewinners, who gave me confidence at an early age in sending me as a representative to the USA and later to help develop a better government/industry interface. To Marvin Bower, who took the risk of recruiting me as the first non-American senior partner of McKinsey, which gave me the opportunity to learn so much. To Murray Maclehose in Hong Kong, for letting me loose to change the organisation of a colonial administration and seeing it maintained to this day. To Margaret Thatcher, even though I declined her offer, for her invitation to join her administration and to all those who invited me into 'the establishment' with offers I did accept.

I am grateful to the Athenaeum Club for new interests, over five decades, for much of my later education, for long-time friendships and, on my ninetieth birthday, the honour of a wonderful party. So many 'old friends', not least the late Mary Soames, Lady of the Garter, coming along. In replying to the Toast, and recognising that I should be making no more speeches after this, I referred to Shakespeare's 'seven ages of man' speech. And now in my own 'second childishness' perhaps I could tell a childish anecdote. Charles Darwin had been a member of the Athenaeum in mid-Victorian times. An elderly clergyman told me that his predecessor in the diocese invited Darwin to his home, hopefully for a non-controversial discussion at a family gathering. His two young nephews rushed into the house, full of excitement and showed the great man a creature they held in their hands. 'What's this?' they asked. They had stuck the wings of a bluebottle to the body of a butterfly and artfully attached bits of a daddy-longlegs, a grasshopper and a black beetle. Darwin examined it carefully then solemnly he asked, 'When you caught it, did it hum?' 'Yes, it did,' replied the boys. 'Ah, well then, it's a humbug.'

My special appreciation is due to those who gave me the chance to improve the lives of many of the young, disadvantaged and unemployed, by applying the skills I had gained elsewhere. Without having been given chances myself over the years this would not have been possible: to Jimmy Remnant in the Royal Trusts and Prince Philip and Prince Charles for launching a report and an award, respectively, in my name, and then to the Queen for conferring a knighthood long ago for public service. As time went by there followed the patronage of professional scientific and engineering bodies and as I write, after twenty-one further years with the CNISF, for the medal being struck in my name to be awarded biennially to one whose work in these disciplines should benefit future generations. What I have received outweighs whatever I have contributed.

Above all I am grateful for the good fortune of finding happiness in my family – Diana, our children and our grandchildren. Only time will tell whether all my hopes for our children will be realised. But my entire family has brought untold happiness. Each one of my blessings is a cause for gratitude. Taken together they have spelt great fortune. I feel all this has come from the *Ethics of the Fathers* and the *Duties of the Heart* – honouring parents, valuing human life, sustaining the environment, compassion for the most vulnerable, humility, and loving one's neighbour as oneself. Not seeking distinction for its own sake.

I mentioned this to Sir Herman Bondi when he was about to introduce me as a speaker. 'So what can I say about you? I see you have lots of fellowships, so I can't say you're an unqualified success, but I could say for he's a jolly good fellow.' As we were approaching the lecture theatre I was still wondering what he would actually say. Without any preamble he began, 'We would have been content this evening to have had a less distinguished speaker than Copisarow, but we couldn't find one.'

Appendix

175 YEARS
of
THE ATHENÆUM

**Response to The Anniversary Toast
by
Sir Alcon Copisarow
Trustee**

THE
ATHENÆUM
PALL MALL LONDON

The Athenæum
175th Anniversary Dinner
4th October 1999
A Response to The Toast by Sir Alcon Copisarow

The invitation to respond to The Toast on this evening of celebration is deeply appreciated. It is also undeserved. I would contrast your own generous remarks, Chairman, with my dubious introduction on another occasion, when the Chairman said: "We would have been content this evening to have had a less distinguished speaker - but we couldn't find one."

Though bearing an ancient name, our Club is still quite young as an institution - the last surviving founder member died just as our oldest present member was born. On the other hand, for those of us here it is timely to celebrate, for only one third of us were members on the occasion of our sesquicentenary 25 years ago and only one third of us will be around, I am told, in 2024.

But have we just cause to celebrate? Have we lived up to the hopes of the founders, the successors of the poets and philosophers of ancient Athens, and those who built on their foundations? How should we judge? How should we be judged?

England was so very different in 1824. The scene was set out in the Preface to the Annual Register for that year,

> "No country ever displayed a spectacle of so much industry, wealth, manufacturing and commercial enterprise", it reads, "as England now presents. Nor did any people ever before exert so strong an indirect influence over other states. Her power is not merely that of fleets and armies ... her institutions and the character of her people are doubtless the primary springs of her prosperity and affluence."

1

Chairman, before I consider this question, I would like to acknowledge the wealth of material received from Members and from our Librarian. It has been invaluable. It has also given me food for thought. And speaking of food, I must digress to give special praise for the dinner we have been served, and the delicious wines, in perfect harmony with each course. Never again will it be said of the Athenæum we are "masters of all the arts, crafts and sciences, save that of gastronomy."

Back in 1824, John Wilson Croker convened a preliminary meeting of the Athenæum to-be, in the Royal Society apartments in Somerset House. Sir Humphry Davy, presiding, agreed with the presidents of the Royal Academy and Royal Society of Antiquaries that for membership: "No one shall be eligible except gentlemen who have either published some literary or professional work, or a paper in the Philosophical Transactions, and Bishops and Judges" - to which Davy then added "and members of both Houses, none of whom can perform their high duty without a competent knowledge of literature."

Decimus Burton was just 24 years old when he was commissioned to build these premises. I was reminded of that at a meeting of the General Committee some years ago. A most promising young historian of 26 was up for election, but one Committee member demurred. "Twenty-six? What can the boy know?" I volunteered that by then Burton had already half completed this fine building. And the Chairman added "and by that age Alexander had conquered the world." In 1830, Burton's work done, we moved in here in some style. The inauguration was remarkable, being described as "a fortnight of gay soirées for the ladies from 9 pm to midnight." Organisers of the Summer Ball please note.

More than half the politicians elected were either noblemen or landed gentry and invitations were extended to Whigs and Tories without discrimination, in the hope that the Club would provide an opportunity for rational discourse between them and perhaps soften the political division of the times. Davy tended to attract those Fellows of the Royal Society who were rich, broadly educated and enthusiastic about their hobbies. They came along to discuss and argue - not least the earth scientists with the clergy, who wanted to reconcile what they knew of rock formations and fossils with theological doctrine. Davy himself was an applied scientist, with many brilliant discoveries to his name, but perhaps the greatest of all was his own Man Friday, laboratory assistant, secretary and valet, all in one - Michael Faraday, the first Club Secretary.

Among our original 500 members there were 33 military veterans of the Peninsula Campaign and Waterloo, but of these at least nine were already FRS's, eligible for election on intellectual merit alone. They included celebrities such as the inventor of the Beaufort Scale and intrepid explorers who, in their day, enjoyed a status and glamour comparable to the pop stars of today. Most members, however, were scientists (or philosophers), politicians and those in the arts, medicine, law and the church.

Throughout the reign of Queen Victoria, very many of the leading intellectuals and men of influence in the Empire joined us; our popularity and numbers grew to 1,200. Yet from their books and occasional diaries we read of two regular criticisms. Long established members bemoaned how far standards had fallen - coming into the Morning Room after church on Sunday, for example, and seeing that Knights of the Garter, and of the Bath, no longer wore their Stars. Everyone complained about the interminable length of the candidates' waiting list. But they all applauded Faraday. He was not only bright, he was useful. By removing our dismal oil lamps and installing gas he had succeeded at the same time in preventing further damage to our fine leather-bound books and, outside the premises, illuminating the trade of the prostitutes in Pall Mall, depicted in Rowlandson's memorable cartoons. Michael Faraday went on to recruit as members the best engineers in the land, those who had built our roads, canals, bridges and railways - Telford, the two Rennies, Brunel and then Stephenson. Some of these members were qualified as lawyers too, with interests and ambitions extending well beyond the limits of their vocation. They contributed, by discussion in the Club incidentally, to the drafts of many Parliamentary Bills.

3

402

A little later Sir Joseph Bazalgette was proposed. It was he who constructed the Embankment to take the main drainage of London, with sewers that would no longer pollute the Thames, thereby saving more lives from typhoid and cholera, it was said, than the entire medical profession. Though he was one of the century's greatest engineers, the competition for membership was so intense, that he still had to wait nine years beyond his knighthood, to be elected.

Canvassing for candidates was fierce and no doubt some members joined the Committee to help those they proposed. Charles Dickens and Charles Darwin succeeded in getting elected on the same day, but many candidates of particular merit waited in vain. In 1892 for the April ballot, captured in the Illustrated London News drawing, there were 1,600 candidates on the waiting list, some of whom had been there for 16 or 17 years, but only 50 were elected. One blackball in ten eliminated. One would-be member had 93 blackballs, and not only had another candidate already died, but so had his proposer and seconder. Candidates worried and grew grey or went bald.

It was partly to alleviate this anxiety that membership for the most distinguished was accelerated by introducing Rule II and the total membership increased. Even then Thackeray had recourse to this, having been rejected under Rule III. Thomas Huxley was repeatedly black-balled by the clerics; and Disraeli too, even though his father was a popular member, in his case, because of "his youthful extravagances, malicious wit and strong party sentiments." He was elected, 30 years later, under Rule II.

The atmosphere was convivial, but deeply held convictions led to argument. One particular controversy had long lasting consequences. Before becoming a member, Francis Jeune, had advocated the total transformation of Oxford Colleges from predominantly religious institutions, where two thirds of students took holy orders and some tutors taught all subjects, to specialised secular institutions. He opposed six members of the Club, all Heads of Oxford Colleges and on the Hebdomadal Board, added weight to the changes set out in the Royal Commission of 1852, and left John Wilson, Master of Trinity,

4

403

defiantly but ineffectively proclaiming "Even legislation will not annul the moral force of a College oath." Jeune changed Oxford forever, but when he became a candidate here his opponents took their revenge. He was only elected, when Bishop of Peterborough, four years before he died.

Around the turn of the century, many other changes were gathering pace. We had begun to be a newspaper reading nation, and Kipling was being read as much as Meredith and Hardy. Political power had passed from landlords to capitalists. Keir Hardie, with cloth cap and brass band accompaniment, had taken his seat in the House. From the corner of the Club we could see the queues in the Haymarket for Lady Windermere's Fan and hear the rowdy shouting of Ta-ra-ra-boom-dee-ay all the way from Piccadilly Circus.

The Club was usually at its busiest between 4 and 6 o'clock when the "regulars" included the inveterate whist foursome - Anthony Trollope, George Jessel, Spencer Percival and W.E. Forster. In the South Library you would find the rugged form of Thomas Carlyle, in the opposite corner Roderick Murchison.

Occasionally, the Club quite suddenly emptied, and that was because members had gone to the House of Commons - either to vote, or to the lobbies to hear the results of a Division - for among our members were some 50 Peers and 110 Privy Counsellors.

As for the others, you might find Charles Hallé leaving to conduct at the St. James's Hall, Alma-Tadema taking the chair at a Discourse delivered by George du Maurier and frequently remaining in the Club to dine with Lister, Leighton, Sullivan, Goschen, Baring, Esher, Kelvin or Playfair. Leading the 100 strong church contingent, and 32 bishops, were Benson, Temple and Maclagan. But there was only one banker - John Lubbock, Head of Robarts, Lubbock - and even he was also President of the Linnaean Society and Vice-Chancellor of London University.

5

The new top story at the time was the institution of the Order of Merit. King Edward VII presided over the Dinner, held here when 10 of the first 12 members of the Order were Club members. In the course of that evening Balfour famously declared that in the history of our country there had probably never been gathered in one room such a body of undiluted distinction. A few years ago I had occasion to repeat that story at a Thanksgiving dinner in Washington, with just an element of pride. My host replied "Here we say 'never since Jefferson dined alone in The White House'."

Our links with the Order are now so much weaker, with the very recent loss of Lord Menuhin, Sir Isaiah Berlin and Cardinal Hume.

Since the foundation of the Nobel Prize we have attracted more Awards than any other institution in the world. Some years ago I was showing our new Nobel Book, exhibited at the top of the Staircase, to Leif Leifland the Swedish Ambassador, and could not resist saying "Before we elect a candidate to the Club we make sure he has won the Nobel Prize." He immediately replied "Ah, before we select a Prize winner, we always check that he is a member of the Athenæum."

Over the years the number of anecdotes surrounding our more memorable characters has inevitably grown. Of our lawyers, who have loomed large among our Trustees and Chairmen, Stanhope was spoken of as "the benevolent despot", Lyndhurst was "master of the weapons of sarcasm, epigram and wit". Holland was "not easily moved by argument".

Great play was made of the clergy, particularly by Trollope, or as the subject of Osbert Lancaster's cartoons, as well as London taxi drivers who, spotting the gaiters, renamed the Club Bishopsgate. But the Canon of St Pauls in 1903 went so far as to write an article when Davidson, was appointed to Canterbury, warning him of the dangers of Athenæum membership. He said: "the Archbishop would be beguiled and bewitched by elderly and excellent gentlemen who will

6

tell him what the intelligent British public will not stand; but the Athenæum is not the shrine of infallibility........"

Our military members dwindled rapidly, except for serving engineers and doctors, and the occasional Field Marshal. Alexander of Tunis, as the late Sir David Hunt, his Colonel of Intelligence in North Africa told us, was a highly accomplished artist as well as soldier, and when he left us to become Governor General of Canada he was heard to say he would rather have become President of the Royal Academy.

Our politicians declined in numbers too, but occasionally a Prime Minister, notably Asquith and Baldwin, would escape from official business and enjoy coming in to read quietly in anonymity and security. The Athenæum has always welcomed politicians whatever their party, just as we do members of any religion. In 1924, we elected Ramsay MacDonald when he was quite out of favour in other circles, and even forced to resign, unbelievably, from the Lossiemouth Golf Club. In our own time we have been fortunate to enjoy the company, and sad to lose so recently, two leading parliamentarians, the convivial former Speaker, Viscount Tonypandy and the gifted orator so often attracted to the Club Table, Enoch Powell - both proposed for membership by Sir Patrick Cormack. Happily we still see Lords Callaghan and Jenkins, respectively former Prime Minister and President of the European Union, and Lord Howe here this evening.

A Club does not survive on members alone, nor is it a Club, without a dedicated and loyal staff. We have always been fortunate in those who have served us; they have provided the thread of continuity in our comfort and welfare. Some have devoted their whole working lives to us. Henry Tedder was our Librarian for 46 years and also Secretary for 33. Tom Martin, who looked after newspapers for 45 years, was so trusted that he was called in to adjudicate when Lord Grimthorpe wanted the Library window open and Herbert Spencer wanted it shut. Then there was the famous Major Spaggi, born Aurelio Spacciatrosi, our chef until 1919. He came to London to cook for the ex-Khedive of Egypt, and then for King Edward VII and

George V and the ex-Kaiser, but became a national figure by creating 20 different recipes for bully beef. And we had a Club hairdresser, an entrepreneurial character, who put up a notice which read "Haircut 3d. With the scissors that cut Lord Salisbury's hair - 6d".

Until 1915 our entire staff was male, but when 17 of them were called up, parlour maids took their place and stayed on. In just one period in the 1980's we were obliged to retain outside caterers, but no longer, and throughout all this time we have remained remarkably free from scandals, whether cockroaches in the kitchen or cooking of the books.

Over 175 years our membership, our management, the Club house itself, the Library, and life in the Club have, of course, all been transformed.

Membership has grown towards the present 2000 mark and has broadly retained its original vocational mix. Initially, we were managed rather casually, the first semblance of discipline coming in 1880 when 3 members of the Committee were required to form a quorum - meeting if possible every Tuesday morning. Certain members then regarded the Club so much as their home that they stayed for breakfast, lunch and dinner on Christmas Day. Many lived close by and a further decree became necessary. "No provisions cooked in the Club House may be sent out on any pretext whatsoever." The personal services of a valet were always taken for granted, and, interestingly, the Rule stating that "the charge for a bedroom includes unpacking, laying out clothes for dressing, brushing and repacking" was not changed until 1950.

The decor of our premises slowly changed to reflect changing fashions. Decimus Burton's original design, with its mix of Greek and Roman motifs and quietly painted walls, expressed a certain reserve, a rather distinguished air, as it were, of art and literae humaniores. But after the introduction of electric lighting in 1886, the interior no longer seemed to measure up to the imposing exterior and the Committee considered that a little more opulence would not

8

be out of place.   The artistic coterie of the Club then included Leighton, Millais, Burne-Jones, Poynter and Alma-Tadema, and it was the latter two who gave us the facelift which includes all the coloured marble and tesselated floor of the Hall and Staircase.

By the end of 1950, Victorian décor itself was well out of favour.   It was replaced by something simpler and finally, in 1988, as members wished, the Coffee Room was returned to something closer to Burton's original creation.

Our Library has always been a treasure.   It has grown from the original 4,000 volumes, tenfold by the end of the century, doubling again more slowly to the present 80,000 titles. As a labour of love, Sir Alan Burns counted them all with the aid of a feather duster; he also took the liberty of changing the shelving which had put anaesthetics next to athletics. There has been only one untoward incident recorded in the Library and that was way back in 1833, when the Librarian's clerk absconded with books valued at £200, which a member immediately replaced.

However, it was not only staff that could go wrong.   Among our most distinguished members Lord Palmerston was found guilty of "stealing the club's chef by financial inducement."   And then there was the case of Bertrand Russell which brought the Club quite the wrong sort of publicity.   During his anti-conscription campaign in WW1, he marched from the Club and lay prostrate on a church floor.   A policeman started beating him with a truncheon.   The congregation called out "Stop, he's a famous philosopher."   The policeman beat harder. "Stop, he's the brother of an Earl."   Policeman: "I'm very sorry Sir."   He had to resign in 1916, but 30 years later was invited to return.

After WW1, it was still assumed that club life would remain unchanged - but there was no such assumption after 1945.   There had been financial difficulties in the past, but throughout the 1950's these eliminated some clubs altogether.   We held out, and after some lean years prospered once again, with much of our tradition intact.

9

Some of these activities are never outmoded. I was struck, for example, by the repetition of the very topics chosen for our earliest Club Talk Dinners over 70 years ago:- Need justice be so expensive? Is full Press liberty desirable? Should euthanasia be legalised? Marriage - must we take it seriously? We still debate these same questions.

We enjoy our discussions and even arguments, and the anecdotes that have been recounted along the way. Some stories have been well recorded, like that of Dickens and Thackeray, making up at the foot of the Staircase, after their long quarrel in the Garrick. But we can all add to them, even from our own recollections.

In 1963 I came into the Club to find the Secretaries of the Medical, Agricultural, Scientific and Industrial Research Committees of the Privy Council, all standing in a huddle loudly complaining about the meanness of the Treasury. In walked Sir Edward Playfair, then Third Secretary of the Treasury, responsible for their grant, and like one man they got straight down on their knees and crossed themselves!

I recall two former colonial Governors, Sir Hugh Dow and Sir Alan Burns pressing me to join them in the Light Luncheon room, saying with schoolboy enthusiasm: "It's treacle tart today!"

I remember Sir Ralph Richardson and Sir Alec Guinness picking up the same magazine together from the Drawing Room table, deferentially inviting the other to read it first - until they realised they had a captive audience. They then began to act, first insisting, then imploring that the other took it - until they remembered they were not on the stage and this performance perhaps was not quite in keeping with Club decorum. I remember Patrick Blackett and Richard Crossman, sharing a sofa, sketching out, on a piece of Athenæum stationery, Harold Wilson's first Administration; and Sir Robert Mayer's 100th Birthday concert 20 years ago when he told us how, as a child, he performed for Brahms.

10

409

I asked at the outset, whether we now had just cause to celebrate. If our predecessors could step down from their pictures on the walls and marble busts what, in fact, would they think of us? Much would amaze and even shock them. To judge us in the present context, perhaps they would go straight to the N.W. corner of the Drawing Room and consult the latest edition of the <u>Annual Register</u>. And what would they read? The transformation of our monarchy, the aristocracy and ordinary family life; commonwealth affairs, independence and devolution, NATO and the European Union, human rights and arms control, the end of 156 years of colonial rule in Hong Kong, probes landing on Mars and Jupiter, climate control and the cloning of Dolly the sheep.

They would discover how communication had been unbelievably revolutionised, the written word augmented and in part replaced, by incomprehensible technological achievements, - in which our own members had played a critical part.

They would be gratified to see how well we had cared for the Club, the exterior of Burton's fine building in pristine condition; a new 99 year lease from the Crown Estate Commissioners, use of the garden and a growing art collection that we are proud to catalogue. Intrigued by the casual informality of dress and behaviour, impressed by the larger membership, depressed by the short waiting list for election, reassured to find the original polymath culture perpetuated, the informal dialogue between experts across disciplines flourishing. They would regret the smaller numbers in the church, the arts, literature, and government, and be curious about the replacement of the city merchants and brewers they knew by the information technologists and media exponents among us now.

They would notice more younger members. At a Fathers & Sons Dinner they would be delighted by this bridging of the generations, including the Darwins, Huxleys and Thomsons - and the many threads of continuity needed to maintain traditions. They would see that, for just a few of us the Club is still something of a "résidence secondaire," as essential for life as the leaf is to a caterpillar; that all

11

of us appreciate, in the heart of London's expensive West End, a place for privacy, personal service and space. They would enjoy the present atmosphere - civilised, courteous, respectful and friendly, a time for talk, a time for silence, a time to read, a time for music and a time to listen; a place that honours learning, but is not overawed by it.

All of this was their inheritance to us. Do we ever consider what we in turn might be able to contribute to future generations? We live busy lives, even those of us in so-called retirement. But we also live longer than our predecessors, to enjoy a Third Age. In People of Today there are 870 entries of Club members, a large proportion clearly contributing time, energy and enterprise to some philanthropic endeavour. Could we as a Club not harness more of this?

Whether we are in the academic, government or business world, whether analytical, creative or practical by nature, could we not let it be known we are prepared to help more? In recent years, for example, all the new candidates for election have been proposed and seconded by just 5% of our members. Might we not attract still more of the intellectually eminent? And in support of our Committees, help determine the road we now take -with the prospect of further cause for celebration on the occasion of our bicentenary. Perhaps our response to the Toast this evening, Chairman, might be summed up in a phrase. It was quoted on an official visit to a Government Research Laboratory in the Netherlands, when the Director apologised for receiving me with shirt sleeves still rolled up. "But we have a motto in Delft", he said, "Hats off for yesterday. Coats off for tomorrow."

12

Index

Index

Index

Index

Index